COLONEL EDWARD SAUNDERSON

Colonel Edward Saunderson

LAND AND LOYALTY IN VICTORIAN IRELAND

ALVIN JACKSON

CLARENDON PRESS · OXFORD

1995

Oxford University Press, Walton Street, Oxford OX2 6DP
Oxford New York
Athens Auckland Bangkok Bombay
Calcutta Cape Town Dar es Salaam Delhi
Florence Hong Kong Istanbul Karachi
Kuala Lumpur Madras Madrid Melbourne
Mexico City Nairobi Paris Singapore
Taipei Tokyo Toronto
and associated companies in
Berlin Ibadan

Published in the United States
by Oxford University Press Inc., New York

British Library Cataloguing in Publication Data
Data available

Library of Congress Cataloging in Publication Data
Data applied for
ISBN 0–19–820498–1

1 3 5 7 9 10 8 6 4 2

Typeset by Create Publishing Services

Printed in Great Britain
on acid-free paper by
Bookcraft Ltd., Midsomer Norton, Bath

To the Memory of Thomas Hasson

Acknowledgements

This book has been a long time in the making, and my debts of gratitude have multiplied with the years.

I am grateful to the following individuals and institutions for access to manuscript sources, and for permission to quote from them: the duke of Abercorn; the earl of Balfour; Birmingham University Library; Messrs Carleton, Atkinson, and Sloan; the trustees of the Chatsworth Settlement; the Master, Fellows, and Scholars of Churchill College, Cambridge; Max Egremont; Messrs Falls and Hanna; Kent Record Office; the marquess of Londonderry; the marquess of Salisbury; the duke of Westminster; and Francis Wyndham. I owe a very great debt to John Saunderson, who located and made available much new correspondence relating to his grandfather. His generosity and hospitality are a particular pleasure to record. I tender my apologies to any owner of manuscripts or of copyright whom I have omitted to mention through oversight, or whom I have been unable to locate.

Numerous archives and libraries provided guidance. Once again, I gladly acknowledge the help given by the staff of the Public Record Office of Northern Ireland, where transcripts of the Saunderson papers are at present stored. I cannot fail to mention the friendship and encouragement offered by Trevor Parkhill; equally, I am thankful for the interest and assistance offered by Anthony Malcomson, Deputy Keeper of the Records. Gillian Matthews of the Hove Reference Library was co-operative and generous concerning the Wolseley papers; John Buttimore of Church of Ireland House, Dublin, was kind and welcoming. I am also grateful to the staff of the Imperial War Museum for help with the John French Papers, and to the staff of the Wiltshire Record Office for help with the Walter Long Papers.

Many friends and colleagues have wrestled with Saunderson with scarcely less vigour than I. I am grateful to those who read through versions of my typescript, offering correction and guidance: Paul Bew, A. B. Cooke, Roy Foster, Theo Hoppen, Charles Townshend. My conversations with Richard English and Patrick Maume were helpful and stimulating. I worked on this book while holding lectureships at University College

Dublin, and—later—at the Queen's University, Belfast. My friends at Belfield have borne with equanimity the burden of the Orange Colonel: selection is of course invidious, but I must mention Michael Laffan and James McGuire, who have been consistently patient and fastidious critics of much of my work. David Hempton and Peter Jupp in Belfast offered criticism, friendship, and support, and my debt to them is very great. I remember, too, my friend and tutor, Brian Harrison, who on a summer's day in 1982 dusted down a copy of Reginald Lucas's *Colonel Saunderson MP: A Memoir*, and who simultaneously introduced me to this curious politician and to his first biographer.

A.J.

Contents

Abbreviations

BL	British Library
BNL	*Belfast News Letter*
Breifne	*Breifne: Journal of the Cumann Seanchas Bhreifne*
CC	Churchill College, Cambridge
DMP	Dublin Metropolitan Police
ESP	Edward Saunderson Papers, Public Record Office of Northern Ireland
HH	Hatfield House, Hertfordshire
IHS	*Irish Historical Studies*
ILPU	Irish Loyal and Patriotic Union
IRA	Irish Republican Army
IUA	Irish Unionist Alliance
NLI	National Library of Ireland
PRIA	*Proceedings of the Royal Irish Academy*
PRONI	Public Record Office of Northern Ireland
RIC	Royal Irish Constabulary
TRHS	*Transactions of the Royal Historical Society*
UUC	Ulster Unionist Council
UVF	Ulster Volunteer Force
WRO	Wiltshire Record Office

I

CONTEXTS

1

Introduction

I

He was the founder of modern Unionism when Edward Carson was a penniless barrister. He was the leader of Unionist Ulster when Parnell was uncrowned king of Ireland; he was hailed both by Orange labourers and Tory hostesses as a hero of the struggle against Home Rule.[1] Yet Edward James Saunderson, who for twenty years was the English face of Irish Unionism has been consigned to obscurity, the victim of shifting loyalist priorities and myth-building, and of scholarly disregard. He lurks uneasily at the sidelines of the Ulster Unionists' historical perception, overshadowed by later saints and martyrs. But professional historians have been as dismissive as the party propagandists—and Saunderson, shorn of sectional adulation, has received no compensation in the form of a more critical celebrity.[2]

Perhaps Saunderson's role within the political élite of late Victorian Britain was as slight as is frequently implied (though it is all too easy to dismiss his significance within the arena of high politics). It is more difficult to comprehend his neglect within Ireland, and especially within his own political and denominational tradition. Carson and Craig have each enjoyed an Orange apotheosis, and Carson in particular has been the subject of an intense personality cult.[3] Carson is the yardstick against which subsequent leading Unionists have measured themselves: he is their historical reference point, and the focus of their rhetoric. Yet, as the most fluent exponent of Ulster Unionist 'virtue' and of Liberal or Nationalist 'iniquity' in 1912, Carson fulfilled a political function akin to that of

[1] Some of the contrasts between Saunderson and Parnell are pursued in Alvin Jackson, 'The Rivals of C. S. Parnell', in Donal McCartney (ed.), *Parnell: The Politics of Power* (Dublin, 1991), 72–89.

[2] The only full examination of Saunderson's career to date is Reginald Lucas, *Colonel Saunderson MP: A Memoir* (London, 1908).

[3] Alvin Jackson, 'Unionist Myths, 1912–85', *Past & Present*, 136 (Aug. 1992), 164–85. See also id., *Sir Edward Carson* (Dublin, 1993).

Saunderson in 1886 and 1893, during the debates on the first and second Home Rule Bills. And this similarity of achievement posits a dilemma: if Carson, the opponent of Home Rule in 1912, is consistently resurrected for a contemporary political function, then why has his precursor, Saunderson, encountered virtually complete neglect—and within a tradition which looks to the past for political legitimization? Pursuing the contrast between the political and historiographical fates of the two men would be to court errors of scale and anachronism, yet it is not wholly uninformative. For it seems that the rejection of Edward Saunderson reflects both on the priorities and values of the loyalist movement, and on his own political attainments.

Politically nimble and overtly sensitive to the demands of the Unionist class and denominational alliance, Carson nevertheless distanced himself from some of the grubbier features of northern politics, defining his task more sharply than Saunderson. Sir Edward's 'reign' (to use an expression given currency by George Peel) lasted precisely as long as his involvement with the constitutional struggle—from 1910 to 1921.[4] Thereafter he withdrew from politics, returning only for the purposes of skirmishing (as over the Anglo-Irish Treaty). By contrast, Saunderson long outlived his usefulness, holding onto the chairmanship of the Irish Unionist parliamentary party after the defeat of the second Home Rule Bill—when class tensions within the Unionist alliance, exacerbated by the prospect of reform, forced him to defend his own, landed, interests. By the time Carson died, in 1935, he had maintained the comparatively untainted—because distant—role of guardian and elder statesman of Northern Ireland; when Saunderson died, in 1906, Unionist memories of his leadership in 1886 and 1893 were qualified by the evidence of subsequent political engagements. In a sense, given the sustained nature of the Home Rule threat, and the political effects of the Great War, Carson's task of party leadership was easier than that imposed on Saunderson in the late 1890s. But it is was also true that, where Carson masked considerable private circumspection and even pliability with public intransigence, Saunderson was rather less nimble. And in transferring much of his truculence over Home Rule to the economic and sectarian unrest within Unionism, the Colonel fatally damaged his standing as a consensual leader. In this way he earned expulsion from the Orange Valhalla.

[4] George Peel, *The Reign of Sir Edward Carson* (London, 1914).

II

This book constitutes an effort to re-establish Edward Saunderson within the canon of modern Irish (and British) historiography. It is, at least, the first detailed account of his life to appear since the Edwardian era, and it is the very first work to go beyond the family's papers in seeking to define Saunderson's political achievement. But the book aspires to be more than a political 'life'. Land ownership and Unionism were the twin poles of Edward Saunderson's career, and they represent the two central themes of this study. Saunderson's Unionism was intimately bound up with his status as a landed proprietor, and the Unionist institutions and strategies which he helped to create owed much to the strengths and preoccupations of the landed classes. Equally, the challenges faced by Irish landlords helped to mould Unionism, and the social and economic retreat of the class profoundly affected the structure and direction of the movement. So, this book is—at one level—a political biography of Colonel Edward Saunderson. But it is also a case-study of landed economic decline and political reorientation. Saunderson's career, important in its own terms, serves to illustrate the death throes of the caste to which he belonged.[5]

The architecture of the book requires some explanation. The picture of Saunderson and of his milieu is built up from four themes or sections. The first of these locates Saunderson's political preoccupations in the historical traditions of his family. The second section, an analysis of Saunderson's public life, charts his exploitation of these traditions throughout his early parliamentary career and, finally, his leadership of Unionism. The third section examines the family estates and Saunderson's record as a manager of this patrimony. The fourth section pursues his political legacy into the next generation of the family.

The chapters on land have been grouped together because their subject-matter is simultaneously complementary and difficult. The grouping was created in order to underline the significance of the Cavan acres for the Saundersons, and to help unravel the tortuous processes by which they were divested of this property. The section is positioned following the description of Edward Saunderson's decline and death; for this is the most appropriate point at which to investigate the matters which were central both to Saunderson's public career, and to his political and material legacy. These chapters glance back to the early nineteenth century, and to the

[5] This theme is surprisingly neglected. For an informative and attractive general survey see Mark Bence-Jones, *Twilight of the Ascendancy*, pbk. edn. (London, 1993). See also id., *Burke's Guide to the Country Houses of Ireland* (London, 1978).

landed career of Alexander Saunderson, Edward's father; but the narrative focus also shifts forward, beyond Edward's death in 1906, to the dissolution of the Saunderson empire after 1911.

The study concludes by examining Saunderson's posthumous reputation, and the comprehensive destruction of his legacy by otherwise loyal friends and loving family. After his death Saunderson's friends swiftly located a new and alternative vision of Unionism; after Saunderson's death his sons, accepting and applying his principles, broke his reputation.

2

The Saunderson Family and Gaelic Ireland

In 1902 Edward Saunderson's friend, the polemicist Michael J. F. McCarthy, simultaneously defined and dismissed Cavan as 'a long pear-shaped county lying at the bottom of Ulster'—a county 'which obtrudes itself very little on public notice'.[1] Too Catholic to be a part of Unionist Ulster, Cavan contained too many Protestant farmers and too strong an Orange tradition to be truly a part of the Nationalist heartland. Cavan was where Britishness and Irishness met, and neither tradition was prepared to see the county as thoroughly its own. For late-nineteenth-century Nationalists the true Ireland lay further west, in the Gaeltacht of Connacht, while for Unionists the true Ulster was coming increasingly to mean the terraces of Belfast and of its satellite towns. Cavan, remote Cavan, was merely a bastard child of two cultures, acknowledged by each, but entirely without affection.

County Cavan was the creation of Tudor government in Ireland in so far as it was defined as a distinct territorial unit in 1585. The administrative bond between Cavan and the province of Ulster was formalized at the same time: earlier in the century the economic and political orientation of the region had been southwards, to Connacht, and to Dublin. Yet the work of the Tudor bureaucrats, based as it was primarily on English administrative precedents and ideals, was not wholly arbitrary or alien. The delineation of the county and its inclusion in Ulster reflected an older, Gaelic pattern of conquest and lordship.[2]

Cavan was an administrative alloy, created by the blending of two Gaelic lordships, Tullyhaw and East Breifne, and the territory of two ruling families, the Magaurans and the O'Reillys. The O'Reillys were by far the more important of the two, whether in terms of economic authority or political culture: they were the family whose land Edward Saunderson held, and who were identified by him as the Gaelic archetype. In the

[1] Michael J. F. McCarthy, *Priests and People in Ireland* (Dublin, 1902), 91. Cf. Katharine Simms, 'The O'Reillys and the Kingdom of East Breifne', *Breifne*, 5/19 (1977), 305: 'a hilly no-man's land between three provinces.'

[2] R. A. Butlin, 'Land and People, *c.*1600', in T. W. Moody, F. X. Martin, and F. J. Byrne (eds.), *A New History of Ireland*, iii: *Early Modern Ireland, 1534–1691* (Oxford, 1976), 166.

sixteenth century the family had a close, though not always friendly, relationship with the chief centre of English influence in Ireland, the Pale: they survived by countering the threat posed by the Tudor state with that posed by the O'Neills of Ulster. At the parliament of June 1541, when Henry VIII was proclaimed king of Ireland, the head of the O'Reilly family was in attendance; and in that same year he formally submitted to Henry's Lord Deputy in Ireland, St Leger, surrendering his land in exchange for a regrant under the terms of the English common law.[3] But by the end of the sixteenth century Cavan had been brought more directly under English military and legal authority, and the pre-eminence of the O'Reillys had become correspondingly more precarious. The formal planting of the county after 1609 was merely the culmination of seventy years of effective (though sometimes half-hearted) English bureacratic, military, and economic penetration.

Yet under the influence of the O'Reillys some of the central features of modern Cavan took shape. Cavan town, the family seat, emerged as an administrative, religious, and economic centre in the fifteenth and sixteenth centuries, entering into a decline thereafter. In the 1550s the town, with its O'Reilly castle and Franciscan monastery, was deemed to be a thriving and attractive settlement; but natural disasters (especially fire), English military action, and the growth of the new plantation after 1609 undermined its regional supremacy. The Annals of the Four Masters recorded of Cavan in 1576 that 'there was not so much destroyed in any town among the Irish as has been in that town'; Lord Deputy Chichester, visiting Cavan in 1606, adopted a less lyrical tone, condemning the 'poor towne of Cavan' and observing that 'O'Reilly's Country of Cavan had up to this time been little better than a den of thieves, infesting the two counties of East and West Meath with continual spoils and robberies'.[4]

While Cavan town survived other aspects of the cultural and political legacy of the O'Reillys proved less durable. The family helped to develop the economy of the region, promoting an infrastructure that the Saundersons would later inherit and exploit: markets, trade routes, a cash economy. The private coinage of the family, the 'O'Reilly money' (forged English groats and counter-stamped coins), familiarized the people of the

[3] J. J. O'Reilly, *The History of the Breifne O'Reilly* (New York, 1976), 88; Ciaran Brady, 'The O'Reillys of East Breifne and the Problem of Surrender and Regrant', *Breifne*, 6/23 (1982), 232–63.

[4] O'Reilly, *Breifne O'Reilly*, 91, 106; G. A. Hayes-McCoy, 'Sir John Davies in Cavan in 1606 and 1610', *Breifne*, 1/3 (1960), 183.

region with cash transactions.[5] These coins disappeared from circulation in the sixteenth century, the victim of English legislation, and the local economy was disrupted as result of the civil unrest which characterized Breffny in this and the following century.[6] However, close economic ties with Dublin and Ulster remained vital even in the era of Edward Saunderson, and were one of the last tangible features of the O'Reillys' rule.

The scholarly and literary patronage of the family was remarkable, even by the generous standards of Gaelic lordship. Owen O'Reilly (who died in 1449) codified the laws of his country, the Breffny, providing a formal legal structure which survived until the advent of the English common law in the seventeenth century.[7] More characteristically, the family both patronised and profited from the work of the poets. The political supersession of the family in the late sixteenth and early seventeenth centuries seems to have stimulated this relationship, providing both the material for elegy and the crying need for encomium. The O'Reilly *duanaire*, or poem book, was written between 1596 and 1639 and testifies to the cultural importance of the family, and to its increasingly pathetic endeavours to revive the past.[8] Like the poets of the later Roman empire, those of Cavan sought refuge from external threat through a retreat to the more clearly regulated world of scholarship and the mind. And their encomiums on the O'Reillys have all the pathos and wavering conviction of those celebrating the enfeebled western emperors of the fifth century.

More modern chroniclers naturally emphasized the patriotic traditions of the O'Reilly family. One amateur genealogist, a distinguished veteran of the 1916 rising, succeeded to his own satisfaction in tracing his ancestry to Myles 'The Slasher' O'Reilly, a colonel of the Confederacy, who was killed in 1648; and, from Myles, the family was pursued, generation by generation, as in the Book of Chronicles, back to Adam and the Garden of Eden.[9] One of the sons of Myles, Colonel John, was an ardent Jacobite, and fought both at the Boyne and at Aughrim in 1690 and 1691: John's own son fought on in the war until the siege and Treaty of Limerick in the autumn of 1691. But, these patriotic sacrifices notwithstanding, the political colouring of

[5] Michael Dolley and W. A. Seaby, 'Le Money del Orraylly (O'Reilly's money)', *British Numismatic Journal*, 36 (1967), 114–17.

[6] O'Reilly, *Breifne O'Reilly*, 147–8.

[7] D. B. Quinn and K. W. Nicholls, 'Ireland in 1534', in Moody, Martin, and Byrne (eds.), *New History*, iii. 18–19.

[8] Brian O Cuiv, 'The Irish Language in the Early Modern Period', in Moody, Martin, and Byrne (eds.), *New History*, iii. 522; Michelle O Riordan, *The Gaelic Mind and the Collapse of the Gaelic World* (Cork, 1990), 31–2, 58, 79–80; Seamas P. O Mordha, 'Some Aspects of the Literary Tradition of the Breifne–Fermanagh Area', *Breifne*, 6/2 (1982), 44–5.

[9] M. W. O'Reilly, *The O'Reillys of Templebridge, Kildare* (Dublin, 1940), 12–18.

the family was not an unsullied green, at least so far as its allegiance in the sixteenth century is concerned. And, though the equivocation of successive generations at the end of the sixteenth century pained later O'Reilly apologists, this had important implications for both the English government's plantation in southern Ulster and the later political development of the region.

Sir John O'Reilly and Edmund O'Reilly, successive heads of the family, had each been killed in the Earl of Tyrone's rebellion against the English administration in Dublin: both had died in Cavan, at the heart of their territory, Sir John in 1596 and Edmund in 1601.[10] They were killed as rebels, and their lands were automatically forfeit and therefore liable to be allocated elsewhere. The Tyrone rebellion was suppressed in 1603, and by 1605–6 a programme of reconstruction and containment was being outlined by Arthur Chichester. One of the principal institutions of the reconstruction in Ulster was a commission 'for division and bounding of the lords' and gentlemen's livings', and this speedily established that the O'Reilly land was now the property of the crown: 'his Lordship', Sir John Davies said of Chichester in 1606, '... hath cut off three heads of that hydra in the North, M'Mahon, McGuire and O'Reilly; for these three names of chiefry with their Irish duties and exactions shall be utterly abolished.'[11] This judgement assumed greater significance when Tyrone and his confederates, Tirconnell and Maguire, fled from Ireland in September 1607—for the government had now much greater freedom to realize its legal claims. An official survey in 1608 confidently confirmed that Cavan was indeed escheated to the Crown; and the county was therefore incorporated into the detailed scheme of plantation which was being devised for central and western Ulster in 1608 and 1609.[12]

But the political sympathies of the O'Reilly family had been complex, and Cavan emerged therefore as, in some ways, an exceptional component of a plantation characterized by exceptions and evasions. Three heads of the family had died in rebellion. And yet there was a tradition of loyalism among the O'Reillys which, though scarcely a matter of pride for later members of the family, was recognized by the government. The loyalty to Queen Elizabeth of Hugh Conallach O'Reilly (who died in 1583) or Maolmordha O'Reilly—'The Queen's O'Reilly'—who died with Bagenal at the Yellow Ford in 1598—was partly repaid in 1610. In that year six

[10] O'Reilly, *Breifne O'Reilly*, 98, 101.

[11] Hayes-McCoy, 'Sir John Davies', 185.

[12] Aidan Clarke, 'Plantation and the Catholic Question, 1603–23', in Moody, Martin, and Byrne (eds.), *New History*, iii. 194, 197, 201–2.

relatives of these men were granted land, with the chief beneficiaries, Mulmory Og O'Reilly and Mulmory Machugh Connelagh, receiving 3,000 acres and 2,000 acres respectively.[13] These grants, in combination with the servitors' land, the land of the Church, and the land of the Old English proprietors (who all had no obligation to import English or Scots colonists) amounted to well over half of County Cavan.[14] So, even in the original, ambitious scheme of plantation, much of the county was unaffected by intensive English and Scots settlement.

As in the rest of Ulster, the economic position of the Gaelic proprietors in Cavan became increasingly vulnerable in the years before the 1641 rising. And the extensive involvement of Ulster lords in that rising and its aftermath—Archbishop Hugh O'Reilly, an architect of the Confederation of Kilkenny, was a scion of the Breffny clan—meant forfeiture and disaster in the Cromwellian era.[15] Still, more than any of the other plantation counties, Cavan preserved the old order. The most Irish of the planted counties, Cavan, like the Janus-faced gods of Devenish and of the Erne basin, looked two ways: north into what would become the predominantly Unionist Ulster, and south, towards both Connacht, the fountainhead of nineteenth-century Irishness, and the fiercely Nationalist counties of upper Leinster.

Mulmory Og, Mulmory Machugh, and their kinsmen were granted their lands some few years before the arrival in Ireland of a man whose descendants would become a major force in the O'Reilly country and beyond. In 1618 a Scot named Alexander Sanderson became the undertaker of 1,000 acres in Tullylagan, County Tyrone. Sanderson was from Preston in Lothian, and was the son of a wealthy Edinburgh merchant.[16] He inherited his father's business in 1595, married in 1600, and began a family with the birth of Archibald in January 1601 and Robert in October 1602. Robert, baptized in Edinburgh on 12 October 1602, would later found the fortunes of the Sanderson family in the O'Reilly lands of Cavan.

[13] O'Reilly, *Breifne O'Reilly*, 100, 108.

[14] The tactical reasons for this comparative generosity are probed by Aidan Clarke in Moody, Martin, and Byrne, *New History*, iii. 201. See the maps in William Smyth and Kevin Whelan, *Common Ground: Essays on the Historical Geography of Ireland Presented to T. Jones Hughes* (Cork, 1988), 94, 98.

[15] Seamas P. O Mordha, 'Hugh O'Reilly (1581?–1653): A Reforming Primate', *Breifne*, 4/13 (1970), 1–42; id., 'Hugh O'Reilly (1581?–1653): A Reforming Primate (II)', *Briefne*, 4/15 (1972), 345–69.

[16] The Saundersons of Cavan added the letter 'u' to their surname in an attempt, in the mid-eighteenth century, to establish their claim to a dormant peerage. The family were originally called 'Sanderson'. Henry Saunderson, *The Saundersons of Castle Saunderson* (London, 1936), 18 ff.

Alexander's business enterprises failed, and in 1607, burdened by debt, he began the military career which would take him, by a circuitous route, to Ireland. Like Joseph Conrad's duellists, he pursued conflict across Europe: he fought in the Lowlands against the Spanish, probably until the peace of 1609, and then migrated with his sword to Poland, where he fought as a leader of horse and foot under Gustavus Adolphus.[17] It seems that Alexander returned to Scotland in 1617, and mindful both of his commercial ineptitude and military skills, applied for the undertakership of Tullylagan in the O'Neill country of Tyrone.

Alexander established the Sandersons in Ireland, and founded the military tradition of the family—a tradition inherited by his son, Robert, and maintained in the nineteenth century by Edward Saunderson. Robert fought for the parliamentary cause in Ireland, and was rewarded by grants of land in 1654, which were confirmed by the Acts of Settlement and Explanation in 1662 and 1665. Under these measures Robert received over 10,200 acres in County Cavan, and some 900 acres in County Monaghan, thereby establishing himself at the heart of what had been the territory of the O'Reilly family. In 1666 Robert added a further 2,800 acres to his estate, largely the property of a Protestant malignant, Sir William Hill.[18]

With this last acquisition the empire of the Sandersons was largely complete. It provided a power-base for parliamentary politics which survived from the seventeenth through to the twentieth century. It enrolled the Sandersons as a key element in what was perhaps the most significant landed nexus in modern Irish history—the intricate web of landed families which stretched from the Erne basin through to south Down and the interface between Ulster and Leinster. The nature of the Sandersons' wealth, and the history of its acquisition, determined the essential features of the family's politics for almost three hundred years. The intimate involvement of the family with the early history of the Ulster Plantation, and their prominent participation in the Confederate and Jacobite wars, meant that the later Saundersons could claim an almost impeccable loyalist lineage. When Edward Saunderson entered Unionist politics in 1885–6, he could trade from a family tradition of loyalism that was as old as the Plantation. Just as Captain M. W. O'Reilly, who fought with Padraig Pearse, was moved by an undefiled legacy of O'Reilly patriotism, so Saunderson entered politics highly conscious of the traditions of his ancestors. For Captain O'Reilly in 1916 or Colonel Saun-

[17] Joseph Conrad, 'The Duellists', in *A Set of Six* (London, 1908).

[18] Saunderson, *The Saundersons*, 29.

derson in 1886 Irish history was a personal affair, and represented an unusually secure mental cage.[19]

How did the Sanderson, or Saunderson, family interpret the legacy of the O'Reillys? The O'Reillys fought for the Catholic Confederation in the 1640s, and were expropriated under the Cromwellian land settlement, but they remained an active threat to the Sanderson clan until the Williamite victories in 1690 and 1691. Colonel James O'Reilly, a loyal Jacobite, rose to pre-eminence under the patronage of Tyrconnell, and sat as MP for Cavan in the 'patriot' parliament of 1689.[20] His planter rival, Colonel Robert Sanderson, refused to acknowledge the authority of James, and attempted to flee to England: he was one of the 2,400 Protestant refugees attainted by the patriot parliament, towards the end of its life, in the summer of 1689. Colonel O'Reilly's fortunes sank with those of the Jacobite cause, and the Sanderson family was restored to the Cavan estate, and to political authority within the county.

Yet the menace of the O'Reillys remained, albeit in a lurking and diminished form. O'Reillys stayed in Cavan, some as tenants of the Sanderson family, and they stoutly, if discreetly, maintained their title to the Breffny lands.[21] A son of Colonel O'Reilly migrated to Spain, where, as a talented soldier, and as a protégé of Charles III, he rose to the rank of Field Marshal. Alexander O'Reilly's ambition, reportedly, was to lead a Spanish army to Ireland, in order to restore the Gaelic past, and to re-establish the lustre of his people.[22] Even though these plans were merely idle fantasies, the mental recreation and entertainment of a highly pragmatic soldier, it may be assumed that Alexander O'Reilly's progress caused ripples of anxiety within Castle Saunderson. Only when Alexander died, in 1797, at Barcelona, were the Saundersons at last liberated from the military challenge of the Breffny O'Reillys. But the murmured claims of the family remained, and ate into the confidence of the Saundersons until 1921.

For the Saundersons of the nineteenth century, and for Colonel Edward Saunderson in particular, the O'Reillys provided a hint of medieval menace and colour to the well-ordered landscape of their demesne; the O'Reilly memory served the same function as an architectural folly,

[19] An alternative metaphor is offered by A. T. Q. Stewart, *The Narrow Ground: The Roots of Conflict in Ulster*, 2nd edn. (London, 1989), 15.

[20] O'Reilly, *Breifne O'Reilly*, 122–3.

[21] Early nineteenth-century leases granted by the Saunderson family to Hugh Reilly, a substantial Cavan farmer, are preserved in PRONI, Saunderson Estate Papers, D.3480/13/1.

[22] O'Reilly, *Breifne O'Reilly*, 130.

offering a focus of interest, and romantic satisfaction. A tree in the demesne was identified as the gibbet from which the last of the O'Reilly lords was hanged. A fine oil painting, displayed inside Castle Saunderson, allegedly depicted a broken and half-witted O'Reilly clutching the title deeds to his lost lands.[23] In fact this is an improbable interpretation of the subject, but it is significant that Edward Saunderson and his family should have eagerly sustained the myth. For this was the Saundersons' preferred view of the O'Reilly family, a view that was proudly advertised in the castle, and continually conveyed to guests and to visitors. Others chose a different perspective. The land agitators of the late nineteenth century built into their arguments a strong historical dimension, sometimes advocating tenant right on the basis of the historical wrongs experienced by Catholic proprietors. The O'Reilly painting, and the interpretation of its symbolism, embodied Edward Saunderson's response. The O'Reillys were a mentally and physically broken clan; and, like those of Dickens's Miss Flyte, their legal claims were the stuff of madness. If there was a tincture of insecurity in the importance attached to the picture, and to its elucidation, then this was effectively concealed. For Edward Saunderson the O'Reillys fully served their purpose in providing a Gothic thrill to the guests at dinner.

[23] Saunderson, *The Saundersons*, 78.

3

The Saunderson Family and Electoral Politics, 1692–1865

Edward Saunderson was the product of a variety of familial and communal influences, and it would be foolhardy to place too great an emphasis on any one feature. His attitude to Irish Catholicism and to Nationalist aspirations owed much to the historical interrelationship between his own clan and the O'Reillys. The imperfect nature of the Cavan plantation and the lingering, resentful presence of the O'Reillys undoubtedly gave an edge to Saunderson's convictions; but, while he was in many ways indebted to these Gaelic precursors, his conception of politics and of parliamentary responsibility was tailored by other, more immediate influences. Naturally he responded to his personal experiences on the hustings and at Westminster. But he responded, too, to a tradition of parliamentary representation within his own family—a tradition which had its origins in the late seventeenth century, and which is reviewed in what follows.

On 17 July 1865 Saunderson was returned as one of two members for County Cavan. There were no parliamentary boroughs within the county, and therefore no other parliamentary representatives: after the passage of the Act of Union in 1801 Cavan had but two MPs, both of whom were still chosen from among the waning landed interests of the county. In the eighteenth century, however, Ireland had been represented through its own House of Commons in Dublin, and through a large troop, 300 strong, of borough and county members. Of these 300, six members were returned from Cavan, two from the county, and four from the parliamentary boroughs, Belturbet and Cavan town.[1]

Belturbet and Cavan town were close boroughs, of which there were eighty-six in the Irish parliament: the corporation of each town, comprising twelve burgesses in Belturbet, and thirteen in Cavan, returned two members of parliament.[2] These boroughs were, as Viscount Castlereagh commented in February 1799, 'strictly speaking property', and through-

[1] The details of the representation of Cavan may be found in House of Commons, *Accounts and Papers, Session 17 January–16 August 1878*, vol. lxii, pt. II (Members of Parliament), pp. 645, 649, 652, 656, 664, 668, 673, 678, 682, 687.

[2] Edith Mary Johnston, *Great Britain and Ireland 1760–1800: A Study in Political Administration* (*Edinburgh*, 1963), 321.

out the eighteenth century the representation of Belturbet and Cavan town was owned and controlled by proprietors.[3] Around 1715 the Clements and Nesbitt families obtained 'a written compact' which granted them the controlling influence within the borough of Cavan: thereafter, in the disdainful words of a mid-nineteenth-century commentator, they 'used the corporation as their mere puppets'.[4] The Butler family, earls of Lanesborough, were proprietors of Belturbet until the early 1780s, when they sold their interest to the thrusting Armar, first earl of Belmore. Another ambitious ascendancy magnate with interests in Cavan was Arthur Acheson, the second Viscount Gosford: Gosford had been an MP for the borough of Old Leighlin, and acted as a patron of Francis Saunderson, the grandfather of Edward, when Francis first entered the Irish House of Commons in 1788.[5] Lord Gosford was a substantial landowner in County Armagh, and through his protection of Francis a bond between the Saunderson family and Armagh politics was forged. Armagh was therefore a natural retreat for Edward Saunderson when, in 1874, the family interest in his home county was finally extinguished.

County constituencies, as in England, had a generally more extensive electorate than even open parliamentary boroughs; they were accordingly more difficult to control and more highly prized. Possession of a 40*s*. freehold was the minimum franchise qualification in these county constituencies, and between 1727 and 1793 only Protestant freeholders could in fact exercise the right to vote. In the mid-eighteenth century Cavan had a registered electorate of around 1,500 freeholders, but by the end of the century, with the accession of the Catholic vote, this figure was substantially greater. At the general election of 1818 Cavan had around 4,000 voters, the majority of whom were probably now Catholic.[6]

Between 1692 and 1874 the Saunderson family maintained a political interest among these electors of County Cavan. 'Interest' has been defined by Anthony Malcomson as 'influence', or, more specifically, as the combi-

[3] Charles Vane, Marquess of Londonderry, *Memoirs and Correspondence of Viscount Castlereagh, Second Marquess of Londonderry*, 12 vols. (London, 1848–53), ii. 152.

[4] Anon. [Revd. R. McCollum], *Sketches of the Highlands of Cavan and of Shirley Castle, in Farney, Taken During the Irish Famine* (Belfast, 1856), 188; T. S. Smyth, 'Freemen of the Borough of Cavan', *Breifne*, 1/2 (1959), 89.

[5] PRONI, Gosford Papers, D.1606/1/1/195: Francis Saunderson to Lord Gosford, 30 July 1797 (Saunderson refers gushingly to 'your early protection of me'). Samuel Lewis, *A Topographical Dictionary of Ireland*, 2 vols. (London, 1837), i. 203.

[6] Peter Jupp, 'County Cavan', in R. G. Thorne (ed.), *The History of Parliament*, v: *The House of Commons, 1790–1820* (London, 1986), 97.

nation of property and personal influence.[7] At the end of the seventeenth century this interest was weak, and was more thoroughly dependent upon the personal reputation of the then head of the family, Robert Sanderson, than upon property which had been laid waste in the Williamite wars. Robert represented Cavan in the Irish House of Commons between 1692 and 1696, and once again in the parliament of 1713–14.[8] After his death in 1724 the family interest declined under a succession of unsuitable or ill-fated custodians, and reached a nadir with the rakish Alexander Saunderson (who died in 1768): Alexander dissipated the rental income of the Cavan estate, and allowed the parliamentary claims of the family to fall into abeyance.[9] Only at the end of the eighteenth century, under Alexander's son, Francis, was the financial and political potential of the Saunderson interest thoroughly realized—and in ways which would affect the family for a hundred years to come.

Francis was able to restore the family finances after two generations of neglect. The basis of this recovery seems to have lain partly in the general improvement of the agricultural economy in the later eighteenth century, and partly in the particular circumstances of the Saunderson family's leasing policy. Long leases created in the late seventeenth and early eighteenth centuries were expiring during Francis's lifetime, and he was able to profit from renewal fines and improved rental terms.[10] An advantageous marriage between Francis and Anne White, a Glamorgan heiress, may have helped the family fortunes, although Malcomson's strictures on this matter should not be forgotten: 'advantageous marriage was something which was less easy to encompass than historians often assume. Both parties to any marriage settlement were on the make . . .'[11] By the last years of the eighteenth century Castle Saunderson, which had lain in ruins since 1689, was being rebuilt; and Francis was strengthening his political standing by joining the long list of those who had lent money to the Speaker of the Irish House of Commons, John Foster.[12]

This financial recovery facilitated a speedy revival of the Saunderson parliamentary interest. Through much of the eighteenth century the chief

[7] Anthony Malcomson, *John Foster: The Politics of the Anglo-Irish Ascendancy* (Oxford, 1978), 281–2.

[8] Henry Saunderson, *The Saundersons of Castle Saunderson* (London, 1936), 30–7.

[9] Ibid. 41–7.

[10] See the collection of leases in PRONI, Saunderson Estate Papers, D.3480/13/1–2.

[11] Malcomson, *John Foster*, 23; id., *The Pursuit of the Heiress: Aristocratic Marriage in Ireland, 1750–1820* (Belfast, 1982), 48–9.

[12] Saunderson, *The Saundersons*, 50. G. C. Bolton, *The Passing of the Irish Act of Union: A Study in Parliamentary Politics* (Oxford, 1966), 183 n.: John Foster borrowed £1,000 at 6% interest from Francis Saunderson in July 1797.

political influence in County Cavan was that supplied by the Maxwells, earls of Farnham: 'the Farnham family', one later commentator opined, 'is the first in title, rank and influence in the county'.[13] The Saundersons were one of several ambitious secondary interests, among whom the Coote family of Cootehill might also be numbered. In addition to these significant, but subsidiary, influences were numerous minor interests who 'proved capable of coalescing into an effective "independent" force when occasion demanded'.[14] In 1788 Francis Saunderson boldly challenged the Farnham ascendancy by uniting his own freeholder vote with these minor county interests. The Farnham candidate, John James Maxwell, topped the poll in February 1788, but was dramatically unseated after Francis lodged a petition alleging malpractice.[15] Francis's political dexterity was further proved when, at the election of 1797, he was able to construct an alliance with the Maxwells, thereby uniting the two greatest interests in the county. This formidable coalition outlived the Irish parliament, and was deployed at Westminster elections until 1806.[16] Only in the spring of 1806, by which time Francis's antagonist of 1788 had succeeded to the Farnham earldom, was the alliance disrupted: Francis, ill and reluctant to face a ruinous election contest, withdrew from the polls, and his seat fell to a kinsman of Lord Farnham, John Maxwell Barry.[17] Francis was never again returned for parliament, but he lived to see his son, Alexander, reconstitute the Maxwell alliance. In 1826 the Saunderson and Maxwell interests predominated in the Cavan poll, and in 1828 the alliance was formalized by Alexander's marriage to a niece of the fifth Lord Farnham.[18]

This connection was of the utmost significance. It created a powerful political interest which dominated the representation of County Cavan for fifty years; it strengthened the Saunderson family's claims to a Cavan seat, and turned this secondary political force into one of first-rate significance. Because of this connection successive generations of Saundersons could legitimately expect to represent the county. And when the connection failed to deliver the desired result, as it did in the election of 1874, then it

[13] Anon. [McCollum], *Sketches*, 191.

[14] Jupp, 'Cavan', 631.

[15] *The Journals of the House of Commons of the Kingdom of Ireland*, xxv (17 Jan.–18 Apr. 1788), 27–9, 141; *The Parliamentary Register; or, History of the Proceedings and Debates of the House of Commons of Ireland*, viii (Dublin, 1788), 302.

[16] PRONI, Gosford Papers, D.1606/1/1/195: Francis Saunderson to Lord Gosford, 30 July 1797; Jupp, 'Cavan', 631.

[17] Jupp, 'Cavan', 631.

[18] Brian Walker, *Parliamentary Election Results in Ireland, 1801–1922* (Dublin, 1978), 202; Saunderson, *The Saundersons*, 56–60.

appeared that the natural order had been upset. More than any other single event, the defeat of this alliance persuaded the young Edward Saunderson of the existence of new and malign forces in Irish public life.

The Maxwell alliance not only guaranteed the Saunderson family a parliamentary voice, it also determined its tone. By the early nineteenth century the Maxwells were the most evangelical gentry family in a region characterized by pietist enthusiasm.[19] The fifth Lord Farnham, the son of a bishop, turned his estates into a training-ground for a second Reformation, sheltering and encouraging converts, and strengthening the faith of existing evangelical Protestants. He was, in the verdict of W. J. O'Neill Daunt, 'a man in whom sectarian fanaticism spoiled a good patriot', and his combination of political independence and anti-Catholicism, though by no means an original formulation, was both striking in its vehemence, and bold in its impact.[20]

The intellectual origins of Edward Saunderson's Unionism can be located partly in the evangelicalism of the southern Ulster gentry, but also in the politics of the independent interest in the Irish House of Commons. Edward's father and grandfather were country gentlemen of this class, and, like their peers, they were suspicious of government, proud of their Irishness, and convinced in their Protestantism: 'they were separate, unconnected MPs', E. M. Johnston has remarked, 'bound together by their individual loyalty to a common aim, namely the protection of the constitution, the Protestant ascendancy, and the English connection.'[21] Edward Saunderson's Unionism differed little from the modest patriotism of these gentlemen: indeed to a very great extent the Unionism which he defined in the 1880s was merely a modification of several antique political principles, and in particular, the Whiggery and evangelicalism of the eighteenth century. Whiggery and evangelical Protestantism ran deep in the outer counties of Ulster, and at the interface between Ulster and Connacht; and both this area and these convictions would be of the utmost importance in the definition of modern Unionism.

Francis Saunderson represented County Cavan in the Irish House of Commons between 1788 and 1800, and at Westminster between 1801 and 1806. This was a tenure which would aid and influence his grandson, both in terms of the nature of his political support and the shape of his political

[19] David Hempton and Myrtle Hill, *Evangelical Protestantism in Ulster Society, 1740–1890* (London, 1992), 86–91.

[20] Desmond Bowen, *The Protestant Crusade in Ireland, 1800–1870* (Dublin, 1978), 94.

[21] Johnston, *Great Britain and Ireland*, 218.

convictions. Francis founded the alliance with the Maxwell family, and he bequeathed political attitudes which formed the spine of his grandson's Unionism. Like Edward at the beginning of his parliamentary career, and like most of the gentry class, Francis was a largely silent MP, but he said enough in debate to indicate clearly his principles and priorities. Arthur Aspinall has recorded that 'Saunderson was independent of the Castle, and an "old steady friend" of Charles James Fox, as well as "a great friend" of George Ponsonby'.[22] Francis was therefore allied with the Whig leadership in both England and Ireland, and when he entered the Irish House of Commons in 1788 he became one of a hundred or so Whig factionalists. This period—the years between 1788 and 1793—was the short-lived heyday of Irish Whiggery, and the confidence of Francis's first contribution to debate reflects the confidence of his adopted cause. He chose for his début a characteristic Whig concern, official patronage, and he offered a spirited critique of the administration, and of his susceptible colleagues. At the centre of his brief speech was a biblical metaphor, and it is striking that his first parliamentary utterance should have been a Whig complaint cast in revivalist language. The administration, serpent-like, had introduced the Commons to the tree of corruption, whose fruit, 'though pleasant to the taste had been death to the constitution':

> 'Ireland', said Mr Saunderson, 'stands on the page of history as first among the nations who have stood forward to regain their constitutional independence—but she was the first who stained her honour by yielding to her own corruption.'[23]

Many who expressed such convictions were not themselves immune to official seduction. Francis was a convinced proponent of the constitution of 1782, and voted against the Union in 1799 and 1800. But he was allegedly offered the barony of Castleton as the price of his vote, and he certainly toyed with Unionism.[24] Edward Cooke, the under-secretary in the Civil Department of Dublin Castle, thought in January 1800 that both Saunderson and Viscount Maxwell had been won to the Union, and recorded that Saunderson 'talks Union language, and says he must consult his constituents': Cooke had hopes of a Unionist declaration from the

[22] Arthur Aspinall, 'Francis Saunderson', in Thorne (ed.), *The History of Parliament*, v., 96–7. Francis Saunderson's public political career appears to have begun in Nov. 1783, when he represented County Cavan at the National Volunteer Convention: Oliver Snoddy, 'Notes on the Volunteers, Militia, Yeomanry and Orangemen of County Cavan', *Breifne*, 3/2 (1968), 327.

[23] *The Parliamentary Register* (Dublin, 1791), 201.

[24] Saunderson, *The Saundersons*, 52.

freeholders of Cavan.[25] Yet Francis had been for long independent of the Castle, and his mentor, the earl of Farnham, was one of the most prominent anti-Unionists and ultra-Protestants in Ireland. Cavan, Fermanagh, and Monaghan were so thoroughly Orange and anti-Unionist that the Lord Lieutenant, Cornwallis, was deterred from visiting them during his northern tour of October 1799.[26] And, within three weeks of Cooke's enthusiastic account of Francis's conversion, the freeholders of Cavan had petitioned the Irish parliament against the Union proposal.[27] On 5 February 1800 Francis presented a petition from the freeholders of Longford urging that the constitution of 1782 be maintained; and on 6 February Francis voted against the King's message recommending a legislative union with Great Britain.[28]

It is therefore difficult to account for Cooke's optimism. It is possible that the intractable anti-Unionism of the Cavan freeholders took even Francis by surprise, and suddenly and decisively limited his room for manœuvre. It is equally possible that Francis was preparing to bargain with the Castle over the price of his vote, and wanted to demonstrate that his anti-Unionism was of a somewhat superficial and inconsistent quality. Or perhaps he was simply confused by the issues and arguments. In any event, the episode demonstrates the nature of Francis's relationship with the administration—an independent but ambiguous stand which would also characterize his grandson's attitudes. The episode indicates the potency of Francis's alliance with the Maxwells—an alliance which, again, was bequeathed to both his son and his grandson. Finally, in so far as Francis remained an anti-Unionist, the episode demonstrates his conviction that independent Irish institutions best served the Protestant interest. Here, paradoxically, he also provided a basis for his grandson's Unionism, an independent philosophy which was created partly in reaction to British betrayal, and partly out of a desire for political self-sufficiency.

The attitude of Francis and Alexander Saunderson to Catholic political claims was no less ambiguous than their attitude to ministerial dictation. Francis voted for Hobart's Catholic Relief Bill of 1793, while he spoke

[25] William Beresford, *Correspondence of the Right Hon. John Beresford*, 2 vols. (London, 1854), ii. 237. Cooke's predictions were made on the eve of Sir Laurence Parson's anti-Union resolution moved in the Irish House of Commons on 15 Jan. 1800: Bolton, *Act of Union*, 186–7.

[26] Bolton, *Act of Union*, 140.

[27] *The Journals of the House of Commons of the Kingdom of Ireland*, xix (1800), 26.

[28] *A Report of the Debate in the House of Commons of Ireland on Wednesday and Thursday the 5th and 6th of February 1800 on the King's Message recommending a Legislative Union with Great Britain* (Dublin, 1800), 3, 91.

against Henry Grattan's pro-Catholic amendment to the King's Address in 1796.[29] On the latter occasion he justified his stand in terms of the condition of Catholic opinion, although he expressed his qualms in language which might easily have given offence to Catholic voters. Francis, therefore, was a defender of the Protestant interest, but not a Protestant dogmatist: his attitude to the Catholic relief question was essentially pragmatic.

His son, Alexander, took an equally pragmatic line in 1826 and again in 1829, at the time of Catholic emancipation. Although Alexander was later hailed in popular myth and family eulogy as a friend of the Catholic reformers, in reality he acted much more obliquely. On 9 March 1829, in one of only two recorded parliamentary interventions, Alexander announced that he had changed his mind on emancipation for the telling reason that the government had also shifted ground: the government's sanction was clearly a sufficient justification for this reversal of opinion.[30] Alexander demanded only one condition for his support—namely that the 40*s*. freehold franchise, the principal vehicle of the Catholic democracy, be abolished. Like his father, Alexander was a defender of the Protestant interest; like his father, he was far from being an unbending proponent of his faith. He was not opposed in principle to Catholic relief, but he was fearful of its consequences, and fearful of a Catholic ascendancy. Like his son, Edward, he saw the future of the Protestant interest as resting with the Conservatism of a Peel, rather than the Whiggery of a Ponsonby.

Alexander's parliamentary career reflects, therefore, a transitional stage in the politics of the Irish landed gentry. Alexander's five years in the House of Commons coincided with the campaign for Catholic relief, and with a parallel growth in Protestant evangelicalism. Irish Toryism and Irish Whiggery were each in flux, the former exploiting Protestant enthusiasm, and developing at the expense of the latter. The Tories were energized by their single-minded opposition to O'Connell, and by the success of their organizational initiatives of the early 1830s; many Whigs, lacking a popular base, and disoriented by the success of O'Connell, found refuge in Peel's inclusive Conservatism. Alexander Saunderson, like other country gentlemen, was dismayed by the new self-confidence and aggres-

[29] *Report of Debates in the House of Commons of Ireland, Session 1796–7* (Dublin, 1797), 43–4.

[30] *Hansard*, ser. 3, xx. 922 (1829). The other intervention in debate is *Hansard*, ser. 3, xvii. 29 (1827). For a valuable account of Alexander Saunderson's election campaign of 1826, where his ambiguous stand on emancipation aided his victory, see Fergus O'Ferrall, *Catholic Emancipation: Daniel O'Connell and the Birth of Irish Democracy* (Dublin, 1985), 140–1.

sion of Catholic politics; and, like other country gentlemen, he grasped that the political traditions of his family offered an inadequate defence.[31]

Thirty years later Edward Saunderson would trace the same intellectual path. Having lived beyond the British Isles for most of his early life, he was, perhaps, a natural Palmerstonian: the determined Whiggery of Francis, his grandfather, may well have reinforced this youthful adherence. But, just as a combination of Catholic threat and evangelical revival had undermined his father's Whig sympathies, so Edward's convictions underwent a similar sea-change. Inspired by religion, and goaded by Home Rule, Edward Saunderson sought consolation in the party of Protestantism and the Union. The grandfather had been 'an old steady friend' of Charles James Fox; but the grandson devoted his life to the legacy of William Pitt.[32]

[31] K. T. Hoppen, *Elections, Politics, and Society in Ireland, 1832–1885* (Oxford, 1984), 278.
[32] Aspinall, 'Francis Saunderson', 96.

II

THE POLITICAL LIFE

4

Faith and Family, 1837–1879

Edward Saunderson's influence within late Victorian Unionism was immense, and for twenty years at the end of the nineteenth century his achievements, indeed his failings, moulded the nature of his movement. In some respects he was a political anachronism at the very outset of his Unionist career: a landowner in a movement progressively embarrassed by its landed activists, a paternalist when northern constituencies were beginning to demand liberation from their social superiors. He was an eighteenth-century Whig, and was mindful of the legacy of Francis Saunderson, his grandfather. But at a time of political flux, when Irish loyalists were suspicious of British duplicity and Parnellite ascendancy, Saunderson's direct political style proved to be an immense asset. Otherwise unqualified by temperament, and by background, for the normal run of popular politics, Saunderson developed out of crisis. He was a creation of the Home Rule debate. And, as long as he successfully represented the Unionist case, his failings of class and perspective—his essentially antique principles—caused little concern.

He was born on 1 October 1837 at Castle Saunderson—born into an extended web of Anglo-Irish landowners and peers. Unlike a later generation of Unionist leaders, he spent his formative years in France and England. His father, turning away from the Ireland of the Famine, settled at Nice in 1846, and remained there with the family until 1857. This exile had a very great significance for Edward. It equipped him with a sentimental patriotism of exile, and enabled him to lard his early speeches with a romantic Irishness and dismissive references to 'foreign countries where men's thoughts as well as their tongues were not their own'.[1] More immediately, exile disrupted his education.

His schooling was unstructured and haphazard. It concentrated on language in a way which explains his later gift for imagery and word-play: ironically, given the evangelical Protestantism of his family, his tutors were often Jesuit fathers.[2] Nevertheless, the importance of his educational

[1] *Anglo-Celt*, 22 July 1865.

[2] Reginald Lucas, *Colonel Saunderson MP: A Memoir* (London, 1908), 7–8.

career lies perhaps less in the experiences he had than in those he avoided: there was no brash schooling in England, or in Ireland, and there was no university career. Saunderson survived, untainted by the byzantine Toryism of Trinity College Dublin. More important, he escaped the chilling combination of English public school and Oxbridge which had so profound an effect on a range of Irish contemporaries. Saunderson's youthful experience of England was neither wounding nor dispiriting: where the young Charles Stewart Parnell met England in the brutal shape of Mr Whishaw's Academy at Chipping Norton, Saunderson's fate was rather easier.[3] When Alexander Saunderson died in 1857, the family moved from Nice to Torquay, and later to Brighton and the Isle of Wight. In the years of Parnell's exile in the Cotswolds, the 20-year-old Edward Saunderson was circulating among the genteel classes of the English south coast. The political implications of this contrasting experience were immense.

The death of his father seems to have had singularly little impact on the family. Only one of Edward's letters from the time survives, and in this he is exclusively concerned with an £800 annuity, and with his beloved yachts.[4] Alexander Saunderson was an amiable, if ineffectual, figure within the family, neither exercising nor desiring to exercise much influence over his children. His wife, Sarah, however, was an altogether more formidable personality, in the mould of Delia Parnell.[5] Mother and son were devoted to one another, and this bond was strengthened, rather than diminished, as Edward grew into adulthood. When he came of age in 1862, Sarah wrote warmly that he showed her more affection than ever, and that he possessed 'a most amenable and upright nature, and [is] worthy of all my love'.[6] It was to Sarah, and to the Farnham connection, that Edward owed the intensity of his religious faith. But her influence may also have appeared more subtly in the shaping of his personality.

Whatever the source, Saunderson never lost a sensitivity, indeed a timidity, which is at odds with his parliamentary and historical reputation. Saunderson is remembered chiefly through the facile and affectionate account offered by his biographer, Reginald Lucas; but this volume, in so far as it portrays a blustering stage Irishman, obscures the ambiguities of its subject. Significantly, the Saunderson family felt that Lucas's biography

[3] R. F. Foster, *Charles Stewart Parnell: The Man and his Family*, 2nd edn. (Hassocks, 1979), 106–7.

[4] NLI, Vernon Papers, MS 18953/6: Edward Saunderson to John Vernon, 14 Nov. 1857.

[5] Lucas, *Saunderson*, 44; Foster, *Parnell*, 60–4; F. S. L. Lyons, *Charles Stewart Parnell* (London, 1977), 26–7.

[6] NLI, Vernon Papers, MS 18953/6: Sarah Saunderson to John Vernon, n.d. [*c.*1862].

misrepresented and vulgarized the Colonel.[7] The young Saunderson of the biography—the archetypal young buck—contrasts with the other reality conveyed by his correspondence: profound, if occasionally histrionic, religiosity, deep devotion to mother and wife, and an element of doubt and insecurity. The 'markedly eccentric' figure conjured up by Lucas and later scholars is packaged in the hoary stereotype of Irish landlord oddness. When properly understood, Saunderson is an altogether more complicated and demanding phenomenon.[8]

He was a flirt, though sufficiently earnest and responsible to assure the parents of one young woman that 'he had not the slightest thoughts of marrying *anyone*'.[9] This protest notwithstanding, he married in 1865. His bride, Helena, was a daughter of Thomas de Moleyns, Lord Ventry, and a descendant of plain Thomas Mullins who had been ennobled in 1800 as the payment for supporting the Act of Union. Helena had, therefore, elevated, though somewhat brassy, social credentials, and Sarah Saunderson, who naturally took soundings, was well pleased with the match.[10] But Edward, in common with most Irish gentlemen, and contrary to the historical myth, married primarily for love, for he was deeply captivated by Helena's shyness, and by her spirituality. In the early years of their marriage they were firmly united by a shared evangelical faith. When they were separated, with Edward in London, and Helena in Cavan, they arranged to progress through the New Testament, each reading the same chapter on the same day.[11] Edward felt fully confident in reporting to Helena his prayers and the state of his faith. He reported, too, his often futile efforts to win the souls of 'fallen' London contemporaries: 'I went to see Lady Maria, and said a few words to her, but she appears desperately hard, and opposed to the Lord. Poor creature!'[12]

Saunderson's faith flourished within his marriage, but it was ultimately rooted in the Farnham connection, and in the landscape of Fermanagh and

[7] Information from Mr John Saunderson of Newbury, Berks.; Henry Saunderson, *The Saundersons of Castle Saunderson* (London, 1936), 66.

[8] R. F. Foster, *Lord Randolph Churchill: A Political Life* (Oxford, 1981), 247.

[9] NLI, Vernon Papers, MS 18953/6: Sarah Saunderson to John Vernon, n.d. [*c.*1857].

[10] Ibid.: Sarah Saunderson to John Vernon, n.d. [*c.*1865]. She ought to have been pleased: it was well known that Ventry owned 93,629 acres and was worth £17,067 p.a. (John Bateman, *The Great Landowners of Great Britain and Ireland*, 4th edn. (London, 1883)). However, Ventry may have had private difficulties: in 1871 he borrowed £30,000 from the Representative Church Body at 4½% interest. The capital sum was only repaid between Feb. and Aug. 1914 (Church of Ireland House, Dublin, Finance Committee of the Representative Church Body Mortgage Ledgers).

[11] ESP, T.2996/2B/52: Saunderson to Helena, 12 Mar. 1870.

[12] ESP, T.2996/1/21: Saunderson to Helena, 25 June 1872.

Cavan. He was a sincere Christian gentleman, a firm Anglican, whose generally polite evangelicalism was a recognizable feature of many Irish and English landed clans, and a particular aspect of the extensive family network of the Lords Farnham and Annesley.[13] His was neither a gauche nor a parochial faith. In some ways his Christianity facilitated, rather than impeded, his entry into English politics and genteel society: the sensitive and responsive nature of Saunderson's faith bridged the void between the unembarrassed religiosity of Cavan and the more restrained evangelical Christianity of the English gentry. This is worth emphasizing, because some Irish Unionist contemporaries, and numerous later Ulster loyalists, were marginalized in English parliamentary politics because of their pious effusions. William Johnston of Ballykilbeg, the populist Orange MP for South Belfast, willingly incurred parliamentary humiliation in pursuing his simple and emotional evangelical faith: for Johnston the mockery of fellow MPs or of English journalists was a martyrdom as pure as that of any early Christian hero. But Saunderson was less interested in self-abasement than some of his Unionist colleagues, and his faith, though local in origin, was tied to broader experiences, broader perspectives, and greater caution. For this reason he was a much more accessible and therefore much more effective politician than Johnston. For this reason, too, he lacked some of Johnston's messianic charisma.[14]

Yet his was neither a closet Christianity nor a passive faith. He introduced religion into private conversation naturally, and without embarrassment or unctuousness, according to one contemporary.[15] He maintained a small chapel at Castle Saunderson, where he preached frequently and persuasively. He founded and led a burgeoning Sunday school at Belturbet.[16] He was an active lay member of the Church of Ireland, serving on the Kilmore diocesan synod, and achieving prominence between 1871 and 1873 as a firm anti-sacramentarian on the Revision Committee of the General Synod: he was one of an influential group of laymen on this committee who vigorously urged Protestant amendments

[13] David Hempton and Myrtle Hill, *Evangelical Protestantism in Ulster Society, 1740–1890* (London, 1992), 132.

[14] An excellent example of Salisbury's restraint in the face of Johnston's provocation is in PRONI, William Johnston Diaries, D.880/2/47: Salisbury to Johnston, 23 Dec. 1895. The best account of Johnston's career is Aiken McClelland, *William Johnston of Ballykilbeg* (Lurgan, 1990). According to a Belfast satirical periodical, Johnston believed that Saunderson was hypocritical in some of his religious expression: *Nomad's Weekly*, 26 July 1902.

[15] ESP, T.2996/8/1: Delap Memoir, 1907.

[16] ESP, T.2996/7/1: Diary for Jan. 1870.

to the Church of Ireland Prayer Book.[17] In religion as in politics, Saunderson was most strongly motivated when adversity struck his faith: his career as a synodsman effectively developed only after the trials of disestablishment, when (in the words of an obituarist), 'weaker men than he ... broke away from the Church of their fathers'.[18]

Religion strongly affected Saunderson's response to political issues, but, unlike those of William Johnston, his politics were not consistently subordinated to evangelical piety. Saunderson's Protestant Christianity undoubtedly provided some of the fundamental principles of his political creed, but these were frequently overlaid by more obviously secular concerns. As an aspiring politician, the content of Saunderson's religion was sometimes much less important than its form; the theology of the Church of Ireland of less consequence than its structures. The General Synod of the Church helped Saunderson to build up a political connection which would prove to be of value when he came to develop an independent Irish Unionist movement; its debates gave him, a talented but hesitant orator, the opportunity to develop his skills and confidence before a sympathetic audience.

Thirty years after the Prayer Book Revision Committee had ended its tempestuous life, and presented its report, the Church of Ireland Primate, Archbishop Alexander, recalled: 'in our first days of perhaps exuberant liberty after disestablishment, the gift of eloquence—so marked in Grattan's parliament—was renewed. I can certainly say that Edward Saunderson was the most notable of all in that goodly company.'[19] Other evangelical Protestant Unionists, like the gunrunner, F. H. Crawford, obtained their first experience of public speaking within the institutions of the Church of Ireland—in Crawford's case within the Church Mutual Improvement Society.[20] Naturally, the style of speakers like Crawford and Saunderson owed much to this training. Lacking a public school and university education, Saunderson had little acquaintance with the debating societies, and with the classical forms of eloquence which these societies valued: his speaking skills were those of the preacher. Although his oratory lacked the classical allusion and logical rigour of a Balliol man,

[17] Henry E. Patton, *Fifty Years of Disestablishment: A Sketch* (Dublin, 1922), 41, 230–1; R. B. McDowell, *The Church of Ireland: 1869–1969* (London, 1975), 62. Saunderson's contribution may be traced in *General Synod of the Church of Ireland: Revision Committee Report Presented to the General Synod of 1873* (Dublin, 1873).

[18] *BNL*, 25 Oct. 1906, p. 5.

[19] Lucas, *Saunderson*, 316.

[20] PRONI, F. H. Crawford Papers, D.1700/2/17–18: Crawford's 'Record of the Home Rule Movement', p. 21.

like an evangelical preacher, he conveyed a simple message using humour and passion as his rhetorical devices. Of course Saunderson was only one of numerous loyalists who invested their political convictions with the fire of evangelicalism—but as the single most prominent Irish opponent of Home Rule in 1886 and 1893 he may well have had a disproportionate influence over the subsequent development of Unionist rhetoric.

Though his faith was consistent, it was not a static phenomenon, but varied according to circumstances of time and place. The expressions of piety which he committed to his letters home were at a peak of intensity and frequency in the late 1860s and early 1870s, but by the years of his political prominence such expressions had been almost completely excised. Impersonal factors, such as the condition of international evangelicalism, certainly had an influence on Saunderson's religiosity: he was moved by the work of the famous Baptist preacher, Charles Spurgeon, and provided an important eye-witness account of an Islington meeting in 1867.[21] He was impressed, too, by the American revivalist, D. L. Moody, and played a prominent part in arranging Moody's visit to Ireland in 1874: at one meeting, held on 9 November 1874, and attended by 15,000 enthusiasts, Moody honoured Saunderson by inviting him to open the proceedings.[22] But there was a more personal dimension to the intensity of Saunderson's faith. His early fervour is that of the recent convert and the exile. Following the normal pattern of evangelical spiritual development, Saunderson eventually discovered his personal salvation, doing so at around the time of his marriage to Helena: his letters from the late 1860s are therefore fired by this recent, profound change in his religious outlook. But in the first years of his marriage he was also, and paradoxically, intensely lonely. It would be trite to argue that this early religious enthusiasm was solely a by-product of isolation—a by-product of his first exile in London after his election for County Cavan in 1865. Yet his surviving letters clearly suggest such a connection, as they swing from breezy expressions of faith to pleas of intense loneliness, from accounts of his overtures to the spiritually weak to descriptions of his hatred for London.

He rejected Catholicism, though not as vigorously or as offensively as William Johnston. He had an effectively Catholic education. He had a more direct experience of Catholicism, and a wider range of Catholic intimates, than was usual among Irish Unionists. Yet he was a 'convinced and attached member of the Church of Ireland' who believed that this

21 ESP, T.2996/8/1: Delap Memoir, 1907; T.2996/7/1: Diary for 7 Apr. 1867.
22 ESP, T.2996/2/B/136: Saunderson to Helena, 9 Nov. 1874.

Church was 'best fitted to be the witness for the truth all the land over'.[23] He was therefore an opponent of disestablishment in 1869–70, although he was prepared to acknowledge that there were aspects of the Church which were in urgent need of reform. Ulster Protestantism had no moral monopoly for Saunderson, but it came to embody much of what he saw as most desirable in Irish life: law and order, social tranquillity, loyalty to the British monarchy. In the 1880s and 1890s Ulster Protestantism was the chief bulwark against the predatory agitations of the Land League and the Plan of Campaign: in 1884, according to the Saunderson creed, 'Ulster' was the single stumbling-block in the way of revolution and social anarchy.[24] By 1897–8 he had reformulated a similar philosophy in appealing to a different, South African audience: the largely British Uitlanders in the Boer republics were the loyalists of Ireland, a people of pristine virtue, promoting biblical values against the threats and aggression of a brutish majority.[25]

This was essentially the politics of superiority, and its roots lay in the moral exclusivity of Saunderson's evangelicalism. Nevertheless, Saunderson was not a consistent anti-Catholic, any more than his political opponents, inculcated in an exclusivist Catholic tradition, were consistently anti-Protestant. Saunderson often appealed to Catholic Irish people on behalf of Unionism, and he enthusiastically promoted the personal interests of Catholic loyalists.[26] He repudiated the Orange Order at the beginning of his political career, and actively cultivated good relations with the Catholic clergy and laity in his home territory.[27] Yet the political and religious circumstances of the era—the developing sectarian hostility and the accelerating growth of a national and anti-national consciousness—were not the stuff of consensus; and Saunderson's evangelical fundamentalism was, despite his politeness, deeply offensive to many Irish Catholics. His electoral defeat at the hands of a Home Ruler in 1874 signified not merely a personal humiliation, but a further step towards the religious polarization of Ulster: it exposed the thinness of his ecumenical garb. Thereafter, Saunderson's Protestantism and loyalism became more accentuated, culminating, in 1882, with his admission to the Orange Order.

23 *BNL*, 25 Oct. 1906, p. 5.

24 Edward Saunderson, *Two Irelands: Loyalty versus Treason* (London, 1884), 29.

25 Lucas, *Saunderson*, 271–3.

26 Saunderson, *Two Irelands*, 31.

27 *Hansard*, ser. 3, cc. 960 (30 Mar. 1870); Lucas, *Saunderson*, 51–2; ESP, T.2996/2B/68: Saunderson to Helena, 30 Mar. 1870.

Saunderson entered politics as a Whig, under the patronage of Palmerston's Lord Lieutenant, the seventh earl of Carlisle—and it was as an, albeit wayward, supporter of the Liberal front bench that he represented County Cavan between 1865 and 1874.[28] As the head of an influential clan, and as a leading landowner who betrayed a certain political capacity and enthusiasm, Saunderson was returned unopposed, and with little campaigning. The alliance between the Saunderson and Maxwell interest, though now greatly diminished, was still active, and it seems likely that Saunderson was appointed to the representation after discussions with his uncle, the seventh Lord Farnham; certainly he inherited the seat of another uncle, Colonel Maxwell.[29] He was offered no contest when he stood again in 1868. Only in 1874, in the wake of the Ballot Act, was he successfully challenged, and swept, like so many of his class, from the House of Commons.

Saunderson's platform differed little from the Whiggery of his father and grandfather. He traded on his reputation as 'a kindly and indulgent landowner', and on the parliamentary traditions of his family.[30] He advocated a more responsible landlordism, condemning the absentee, and urging that the tenant should be compensated for 'such substantial and permanent improvements as add real value to his holding'.[31] He was 'a friend of civil and religious liberty', but like many such friends in the eighteenth-century Irish parliament, he thought that liberty could only be protected under a Protestant constitution: he was, therefore, a firm advocate of the Church of Ireland establishment.[32] He professed his concern for economic conditions, and in particular for the high levels of emigration which had denuded parts of County Cavan and the rest of Ireland. He airily recommended 'economic development' as a cure for this scourge.[33]

These were, in general, fine sentiments, and Saunderson entered the House of Commons to widespread good will. But he was an ineffective member, sustaining the tradition of silent representation that had characterized his father and grandfather: subsequent apologists were at a loss to identify any achievement in Saunderson's first, nine-year, parliamentary

[28] See K. T. Hoppen, *Elections, Politics, and Society in Ireland, 1832–1885* (Oxford, 1984), 259–60, 263. Lord Carlisle's patronage of Saunderson may be regarded as part of a broader policy—suggested by Palmerston—of encouraging Irish Liberals. Lucas was perhaps wrong to dismiss the possibility of Palmerston's interest in Saunderson (Lucas, *Saunderson*, 26).

[29] Lucas, *Saunderson*, 16–17; *Anglo-Celt*, 8 July 1865.

[30] *Anglo-Celt*, 1 July 1865. [31] Ibid. 8 July 1865.

[32] Ibid. [33] Ibid.

career.[34] His few speeches were often lacking in both style and serious content. His maiden effort, on 17 May 1866, was on the second reading of an ultimately abortive Land Bill: short and opaque, it offered a conventional and patronizing testimony to the loyalty of Irish farmers to the Crown.[35] He was of course offended by the Gladstone government's commitment to disestablishing the Church of Ireland, but he did little justice to his frustration in a slight contribution to the Committee Stage of the Irish Church Bill in April 1869.[36] He supported the Land Act of 1870—a vote from which he would extract considerable capital in later years; but, once again, his effective contribution to debate on the measure was negligible, and was limited to the uneasy mixture of banter and platitudes which would characterize his weakest efforts in defence of the Union.[37]

Some of his most substantial speeches were made during debates on Gladstone's various attempts to restore law and order in Ireland. Saunderson consistently advocated a tough crimes policy, and achieved his earliest and most substantial successes in defending Gladstone's coercive measures. The Peace Preservation (Ireland) Bill of 1870, steered through parliament in the wake of the Land Bill, was constructed to suppress the ribbonism prevalent in the south and west of Ireland at this time.[38] As in his later, Unionist, career, Saunderson was keen to convey to the House the reality of Irish disturbance as viewed from Belturbet. There was always an element of evangelical zeal and revelation in Saunderson's politics, and while this is most obvious in his exposition of the Unionist faith, it is also perceptible in his efforts to give colour to the Liberal defence of the Peace Preservation Bill. He saw the purpose of his speech as being to complement with grim 'facts' the abstractions of the Bill's sponsor, Chichester Fortescue.[39] As he did in his religion, Saunderson avoided abstruse dialectic in his early parliamentary statements. He embraced a genial

[34] Cf. the gloss provided by *BNL*, 22 Oct. 1906, p. 5 ('when he intervened in discussion, he did so in an effective manner') with the greater candour of the *Irish Times*, 22 Oct. 1906, p. 5 ('as a young man he seldom addressed the House').

[35] *Hansard*, ser. 3, clxxxiii. 1108–9 (17 May 1866).

[36] Ibid. cxcv. 1492–3 (23 Apr. 1869).

[37] Ibid. cc. 1315–17 (5 Apr. 1870).

[38] Charles Townshend, *Political Violence in Ireland: Government and Resistance since 1848* (Oxford, 1983), 60–2.

[39] *Hansard*, ser. 3, cc. 341–6 (21 Mar. 1870); ESP, T.2996/2B/57: Saunderson to Helena, 17 Mar. 1870; Lucas, *Saunderson*, 49. Fortescue can hardly have been enamoured of the task of piloting this contentious measure: more recent commentators have referred to the 'unenviable task of carrying the Bill'. See A. B. Cooke and John Vincent, *Lord Carlingford's Journal: Reflections of a Cabinet Minister 1885* (Oxford, 1971), 10.

philistinism, appealing to gut feeling, and he was at his most successful in defining Irish 'realities'.

Despite his later image of hearty *bonhomie*, he was a prickly antagonist. In the debate on the Peace Preservation Bill it was the Solicitor General for Ireland, Dowse, who engaged Saunderson's anger.[40] Speaking on a later coercive measure, the Protection of Life (Ireland) Bill of 1871, his attention shifted to the bishop of Meath, Dr Nulty, who 'from cowardice was afraid openly and manfully to condemn murder!': the hapless Nulty was maligned in a diatribe which foreshadowed Saunderson's later, and more famous, attack on 'the murderous ruffian' and 'excited politician', Father McFadden of Gweedore, County Donegal.[41] This speech, delivered in the context of mounting sectarian tension, was read by Catholic commentators as an unqualified assault on the hierarchy; it inspired a savage counterblast from the main newspaper of Cavan, the *Anglo-Celt*.[42] More violent exchanges were shortly to come, but the episode is significant as the first public indication of a deepening fissure between Saunderson and his principal Catholic supporters.

The personal abuse which occurs in these early parliamentary statements, and with which Saunderson was subsequently identified, sprang partly from a particular conception of his parliamentary function, as a crusading duty to what he saw as the truth and to the repudiation of evil; but it reflected, too, a particular conception of Irish society and politics. For Saunderson, as for many of his Tory and Whig contemporaries, there was a gulf in Irish society, dividing the loyal multitudes from a small and disloyal minority. Geography and religion as yet played no part in Saunderson's exposition of this Manichaean philosophy: the north of Ireland was certainly different, but only in relatively superficial ways (such as the Ulster Custom). Moreover, Saunderson still appealed to the loyal elements of all religions, holding up the plight of an intimidated Catholic tenant during the debate on the Peace Preservation Bill. As late as 1884, in his fullest published defence of this argument, he still looked to the loyal and law-abiding of both Irish religious traditions.[43] Only after the party political polarization of the mid-1880s was Saunderson's rhetoric tailored primarily for Protestant consumption.

[40] ESP, T.2996/2B/58: Saunderson to Helena, 18 Mar. 1870; ESP, T.2996/2B/61: Saunderson to Helena, 22 Mar. 1870; Lucas, *Saunderson*, 50–1.

[41] *Hansard*, ser. 3, ccvi. 1055–7 (19 May 1871). The measure, better known as the Westmeath Act, is discussed in Townshend, *Political Violence*, 63–4. ESP, T.2996/2B/82: Saunderson to Helena, 19 May 1871.

[42] *Anglo-Celt*, 3 June 1871.

[43] *Hansard*, ser. 3, cc. 345 (21 Mar. 1870); Saunderson, *Two Irelands*, 31.

The narrow, Protestant, dimension of Saunderson's subsequent development is certainly discernible in his first parliamentary career. But there is evidence of a broader and more consensual perspective: Saunderson the die-hard Tory and extravagant Orangeman was by no means an inevitable progression from the diffident and paternalistic member for Cavan who was dependent on Catholic votes and a Catholic-dominated local Liberal party. His strong support for the 1870 Land Bill has been noted. He subsequently underlined his commitment to this measure, and more generally to an Irish policy of firm government tempered with material concession—the pragmatic policy of coercion and conciliation which was later seized on by the administrations headed by Lord Salisbury, and glorified as a grand strategy. In fact Saunderson supported the Peace Preservation Bill expressly because it was offered by the government alongside an ameliorative Land Bill.[44]

Thus, Saunderson the proponent of Unionist resistance and Orange might is to be contrasted with the more pacific and emollient figure of the early 1870s. He defended the Party Processions Bill of 1870, and urged that it be enforced even-handedly: yet William Johnston had been imprisoned and 'martyred' in 1867 under an earlier variant of this measure.[45] He condemned the aggressive behaviour of D'Arcy Irvine, a Fermanagh landowner, who, having spread rumours of ribbon outrages, had assembled a defence force of '100 tenants armed with Snider rifles'.[46] In general, Saunderson's attitude towards Protestant excess was still one of repudiation, although he was by no means uniformly unsympathetic. Thus, in commending the Party Processions Bill, he mocked the Orange Order, but he was also careful to defend them from allegations that they had a monopoly on provocative and aggressive display.[47]

Like later moderates within Unionism, Saunderson appears at this time to have been embarrassed by Orangeism; like later moderates he sought to distance himself from the Order, without offering so much offence as to lose contact. Still, it was ironic that Saunderson's chief political opponent at this time, Isaac Butt, should have ditched Orangeism on the road to popular political pre-eminence as a Home Ruler, while Saunderson's own

[44] *Hansard*, ser. 3, cc. 346 (21 Mar. 1870): 'if this coercive measure were the only bill the government intended to bring in for the pacification of Ireland...'

[45] For William Johnston's fate see Henry Patterson, *Class Conflict and Sectarianism: The Protestant Working Class and the Belfast Labour Movement, 1868–1920* (Belfast, 1980), 1–2, and *Hansard*, ser. 3, cc. 960–1 (21 Mar. 1870).

[46] Townshend, *Political Violence*, 182 n. 2; ESP, T.2996/2B/78: Saunderson to Helena, 16 May 1870.

[47] *Hansard*, ser. 3, cc. 960 (21 Mar. 1870).

career as a populist was inextricably bound to Orangeism, and grew only from the political conditions of the 1880s.[48] Saunderson, the member for Cavan, was still the landlord-dynast, untainted by any populist Protestant appeal, and still rising above sectional and partisan considerations in defence of the *status quo*. Responding to political conditions in the wake of the Ballot Act would demand a more abrasive public persona.

Saunderson's personality and lifestyle during these first years in the Commons are again far removed from the myth propagated by Reginald Lucas. The eccentric prankster, aggressively self-confident, appears in his letters as a more hesitant individual, priggishly religious, and earnestly nervous in parliament. He hated London, and not only because he keenly felt the separation from his young wife.[49] He was not without friends—he lived in the London home of his Irish neighbours, the Crichtons, for a while—yet he was displaced and disoriented, cut off from familiar social networks. In this sense of isolation he had, ironically, much more in common with a later generation of Home Rule MPs than with wealthier contemporaries of his own class. Justin McCarthy and T. P. O'Connor's initial horror of London chimes with the experience of the young Saunderson over the first five years of his parliamentary career; Tom Kettle, crossing the Irish Sea, echoed in a more lyrical and pointed form the sentiments embodied in Saunderson's letters to Helena:

> Tonight there will be the million globes of London to look at, gleaming through the fog like monstrous and sinister oranges in some garden of life and death. To-morrow afternoon we shall be in the House of Commons supping full of old calumnies and hatreds.[50]

Little wonder, then, that Irish MPs tended to spend their exile in London in the company of their homesick compatriots; little wonder that, as *Phineas Finn*'s Mr Clarkson observed, the 'Irish gents ... do hang together so close'.[51]

Like many leading Nationalists, Saunderson ultimately penetrated London society. But it was a long and lonely struggle, and invitations only poured in after 1886, when Ireland and Irishmen came, ostensibly, to dominate the British party structure.[52] In these early years, when Ireland

[48] David Thornley, *Isaac Butt and Home Rule* (London, 1964), 15–17; Lucas, *Saunderson*, 27 n. 2.

[49] ESP, T.2996/2B/13: Saunderson to Helena, 29 Mar. 1867; ESP, T.2996/2B/21: Saunderson to Helena, 26 May 1867; ESP, T.2996/2B/24: Saunderson to Helena, n.d.; Lucas, *Saunderson*, 36.

[50] T. M. Kettle, *The Day's Burden: Studies, Literary and Political* (London, 1910), 30.

[51] Anthony Trollope, *Phineas Finn*, pbk. edn. (Oxford, 1982), 194.

[52] Lucas, *Saunderson*, 142.

was of secondary importance, and an obscure Irish Liberal backwoodsman was a dubious social investment, Saunderson moved in a small circle of expatriate and evangelical Ulster landowners. He records only one occasion when, as member for Cavan, he broke out of this genteel ghetto—dining in May 1870 with the Irish Chief Secretary, Fortescue, and exchanging pious observations with Mrs Gladstone.[53] There was one lesser social achievement: his reputation for spirituality won him lunch with the Archbishop of Canterbury in June 1872. But it was an undistinguished record for eight years in the House of Commons.[54]

In part the problem lay with Saunderson's failure to offer any rigorous definition of his political role or his objectives. In an era of heightened partisanship, he was neither a ruthlessly loyal party stalwart nor an effective dissident. He spoke too seldom and dwelt too long on trivial anecdotes to win a reputation or to be taken up by any political hostess. It is probably significant that the principal social achievement of his early career—the Fortescue dinner of May 1870—came in the aftermath of a flurry of activity which represented, in effect, his parliamentary début. It was a damning reflection on Saunderson's first four years in parliament that *The Times* could describe him on this occasion as being 'in the sense of a speaker ... a young man'.[55]

There were sessions—1867, 1867–8, 1872—when Saunderson sat quite silent, making no contribution of any kind to debate. Thus he was scarcely a highly committed parliamentarian, doggedly attending the House; but, while less than industrious, Saunderson's principal failing was nervousness—the fear of having nothing to say, of drying up, or of gabbling, of saying too much. Trollope's *Phineas Finn* was being written during these anxious first years of Saunderson's parliamentary career, and it cleverly conveys the wretchedness of the unpractised speaker: Saunderson may well have read the serialization of the novel in the *St. Paul's Magazine*, for the accounts of his early parliamentary struggles bear a close resemblance to the agonies experienced by Finn.[56] The early letters home, to Helena, depict him half-heartedly attempting to speak, but failing to win the opportunity: it may be assumed that he did not try very hard.[57] Certainly he left the Commons on several occasions, happy that he had not spoken—

[53] ESP, T.2996/2B/78: Saunderson to Helena, 16 May 1870.

[54] ESP, T.2996/2B/111: Saunderson to Helena, 8 June 1872.

[55] Lucas, *Saunderson*, 51.

[56] Trollope, *Phineas Finn*, pp. xii–xiii, 184–5; Victoria Glendinning, *Trollope*, pbk edn. (London, 1993), 384–6.

[57] ESP, T.2996/2B/50: Saunderson to Helena, 9 Mar. 1870; ESP, T.2996/2B/42: Saunderson to Helena, 23 Mar. 1869.

though careful to stress (in the interests of self-esteem) that he had been unable to catch the Speaker's eye.[58] In weaker moments he confided to Helena that he had been afraid ('it takes my pluck away not having you with me').[59] And his anxiety was expressed no less clearly in the nervous platitudes, rambling structure, and, above all, the self-conscious humour of his early speeches. He needed the reassurance of a friendly audience response, and he secured this with laboured metaphors and by appealing to a popular English view of Irish grotesqueness. As a political expedient, his humour was of a more ambiguous value—a fact recognized by Saunderson himself: 'I have a bad habit, and it is this, I cannot avoid making my audience laugh.'[60] Saunderson's audiences often owed their conception of Ireland to Charles Lever, rather than to any more sober narrative; and, by pandering to popular prejudices, he risked sacrificing credibility for popularity. On balance this may not have affected his later political achievement (he probably had too little dialectical skill to achieve more); but it was paradoxical that his success as a Unionist should have been achieved by masquerading as an archetypal Irishman.

His Commons record was not such as to sway the voters of Cavan when he stood for re-election in 1874. He offered little compensation for his silence at Westminster: he made little attempt to cultivate his supporters, offering few speeches or public appearances, and processing local correspondence with no semblance of interest or enthusiasm. In 1865, on first standing, he would have made no public effort at all had he not been advised that a public appearance was desirable in order to ensure victory. As it was, this and later campaigns were nugatory.[61]

Saunderson relied utterly on Catholic support, yet he had been guilty of tactlessness, and later of more unbridled offensiveness, in discussing Catholic institutions and Catholic convictions. His assault on Bishop Nulty of Meath aroused the anger of his supporters, but it did not in itself create any irrevocable break. This came rather in April 1873, when he publicly condemned the doctrine of the Real Presence, and aggravated the

[58] ESP, T.2996/2B/30: Saunderson to Helena, 14 Mar. 1868; ESP, T.2996/2B/33: Saunderson to Helena, 17 Mar. 1868.

[59] ESP, T.2996/2B/29: Saunderson to Helena, 12 Mar. 1868.

[60] ESP, T.2996/2B/68: Saunderson to Helena, 30 Mar. 1870. See also the reflective comment of the second earl of Selborne: 'Saunderson was leader of the Ulstermen; Carson was not then in the House. The style of the two men was totally different. Saunderson never could refrain from joking, even when he felt most deeply; Carson's style was and is almost gloomy, but he was much the biggest man of the two' (Bodleian Library, Oxford, Selborne Papers, MS Eng. Hist. 191: 'Some Memories and Some Reflections in My Old Age' (1932–3)).

[61] Lucas, *Saunderson*, 17.

insult by reserving his views for the General Synod of the Church of Ireland:

was it possible that in the nineteenth century they were to believe that a priest could turn a piece of bread into the body of Christ, and could say to those who knelt before him, 'Here is your God—eat Him'?[62]

Far from consciously insulting the Catholics of Cavan, Saunderson was seeking to apply these opinions exclusively to his own Church: he was seeking to uphold its reformed character, and to combat what he saw as insidious, ritualistic influences. But, in a context of heightened religious sensitivity, this explanation could not disguise the fact that the member for Cavan had brutally rejected a fundamental article of Catholic belief. And this heresy undoubtedly helped to provoke a realignment of the Catholic clergy of Cavan behind the cause of Home Rule, and away from Liberalism.

Yet Saunderson's defeat in 1874 was as much a party as a personal failure. Irish Liberalism had been decimated. From a total of sixty-six seats captured in 1868, only ten were salvaged from the rout of 1874. The principal agency of this collapse, as well as the principal beneficiary, was Isaac Butt's Home Rule League, which, from unpromising beginnings as the Home Government Association, was now challenging for the support of the Catholic middle classes.[63] The Ballot Act of 1872 had freed electors from the political influence of often Whiggish economic superiors such as Saunderson. Moreover Gladstone's failure to provide a satisfactory Catholic university had alienated the Irish hierarchy and those who looked to the hierarchy for political direction. Thus, released from the bonds of deference, and repelled from Gladstonian Liberalism, many Catholics turned to the alternative proferred by Butt.[64] Following the organizational precedents achieved by O'Connell, Butt laid down the roots of a popular national organization; against this, the flimsy and top-heavy structures of Liberalism (and Toryism) could achieve little. In November 1871 a Home Rule Association was formed in County Cavan, and in September 1872 its first, highly successful, demonstration was held.[65] By 1874 the Associ-

[62] *Anglo-Celt*, 26 Apr. 1873; Lucas, *Saunderson*, 59–60. The episode may have provided the idea for Ian Paisley's address to the Oxford Union in 1966, when he produced and broke a mass wafer before his audience.

[63] Hoppen, *Elections*, 264, 273–5.

[64] Thornley, *Butt*, 178–9; Brian M. Walker, *Ulster Politics: The Formative Years, 1868–86* (Belfast, 1989), 113–16. Hoppen provides an excellent dissection of the structural weaknesses of Irish Liberalism: *Elections*, 258–78; see also ibid. 168–70 for the landlords' retreat to Toryism.

[65] *Anglo-Celt*, 4 Nov. 1871; 21 Sept. 1872.

ation, thanks to Gladstone's mishandling of Catholic concerns and to Saunderson's musings on transubstantiation, was the single most significant electoral force in the county. Despite its recent origins, it had deposed Saunderson and dissolved a 300-year-old regional political interest.

Saunderson had been trained for local ascendancy, and, when the electors of Cavan deprived him of the opportunity for political leadership, he turned to a more reassuring hierarchical environment. The Cavan Militia provided him with amusement in the absence of parliamentary preoccupations; more important, it provided the electorally marketable kudos of a military title. It was as Major Saunderson that he entered the political cauldron of the mid-1880s; it is as Colonel Saunderson that he has entered the textbooks of Irish history. If London had been daunting, and the Commons demanding and unfriendly, then the mock battles, rifle competitions, and drill imposed by the Cavan Militia were much more alluring. His letters from London had conveyed fear and a sense of isolation; the letters from Saunderson's militia exercises reveal a more relaxed and confident individual.[66] He was consolidating old family ties and, incidentally, an important local political network. In a sense he had withdrawn from the disturbing and incomprehensible arena of Cavan politics into a hermetic world of loyalty and discipline; but he was also preparing effectively for a political reorientation.

His transition from Whiggery to a mutant Toryism has much to do with his militia career. He was spending more time with Tory landowners like the Crichtons and Maxwells: the Tory whip, Viscount Crichton, was a near neighbour and occasional host; Somerset ('Sommy') Maxwell was a cousin and a fellow officer of the Militia.[67] But the militia had a more immediate political impact. It provided Saunderson with a certain military expertise, and it provided him, too, with a military vocabulary which would be provocatively and extensively employed. Lastly, it offered a new self-image: the diffident Saunderson of the 1870s re-emerges in Irish politics as a self-consciously martial figure, staring defiantly into the camera lens, posing stiffly on horseback.

He was also an accomplished yachtsman, building and sailing boats throughout his life; and Lough Erne offered an alternative haven in the years of exile. His first yacht had been built at Torquay, where he and his

[66] ESP, T.2996/2B/148: Saunderson to Helena, 21 June 1879; ESP, T.2996/2B/149: Saunderson to Helena, 24 June 1879. Saunderson joined the Cavan Militia in 1862, was promoted Major in 1875, and further promoted (as Lieutenant-Colonel) in June 1886. He retired as a full Colonel in 1893 (Lucas, *Saunderson*, 62 n.).

[67] ESP, T.2996/2B/152: Saunderson to Helena, 1 July 1879; ESP, T.2996/2B/154: Saunderson to Helena, 23 July 1879. Lucas, *Saunderson*, 62.

mother had lived after the death of his father.[68] But yachting was also a favourite pastime of the gentry whose estates bordered on the Fermanagh lakeland, and when the family moved back to Belturbet from England, Saunderson was given full scope for his passion. After 1865 there was an annual regatta on Lough Erne; but there were also lesser, weekly events and informal 'buckles' between rival crews ('as fiercely contested as if we were sailing for the Americas Cup').[69] One close friend recalled that Saunderson was 'far from sorry' at his Cavan defeat, for it brought him back to the easy, boat-obsessed, society of the lakeland.[70] He was a committed, perhaps over-zealous sportsman; he was conscientiously sportsmanlike in defeat, though he regarded those who flexed the rules—even in wholly insignificant contests—with little humour.[71] Above all, he exulted in victory, describing in redundant detail (Helena was quite uninterested) his successes and near-misses.

If his pleasure in boats was ingenuous, at times boyish, it also possessed a more serious dimension. As did the militia, Irish yachting provided Saunderson with a propertied social network, and ultimately with an important political audience. Yachting took Saunderson to Cowes, and to the Royal Yacht Squadron; and there, in the late 1880s and 1890s, his skill and enthusiasm won him an entrée to a world far removed from the county society of Fermanagh and Cavan. His passion was shared by political leaders and by British and European royalty; and it was at Cowes that Saunderson met both the Prince of Wales, and Kaiser Wilhelm II.[72] Boats were their initial point of contact—but, as Saunderson's letters show, conversation moved inevitably on to British and Irish politics. Boats, therefore, provided Saunderson with unique opportunities for expounding his political faith.

As yet this faith was not bound to any rigorous party loyalty. Given the insubstantial structure of Liberalism in Ireland, Saunderson's main contact with organized party opinion and the leadership had been in England: Westminster, in a very clear sense, had buttressed his sense of political identity. After his election defeat, he drifted from Irish Liberalism, and Irish Liberalism in turn had drifted from Whiggery and political reality. Party developments were temporarily outpacing Saunderson's personal evolution, just as they would at a later stage in his career. Thus, he had

68 Lucas, *Saunderson*, 11.

69 ESP, T.2996/8/1: Delap Memoir, 1907.

70 Ibid.

71 ESP, T.2996/2B/140: Saunderson to Helena, 24 May 1876; ESP, T.2996/1/193: Saunderson to Helena, 19 Aug. 1877.

72 See below, pp. 133–5.

been guilty of anti-Catholic allusions within a party increasingly dependent on its Catholic support; he was a landlord within a party increasingly impatient of landed authority; he was a committed Anglican when the party's (half-hearted) Protestant support was essentially Presbyterian.

Though Ulster Liberalism enjoyed a brief, land-oriented renaissance in 1880, throughout Ireland a familiar party polarity was emerging—that of Conservative and Home Ruler. The years of opposition between 1874 and 1880 had deprived Irish Liberalism of essential government patronage, and with the Tory and Home Rule monopoly over constitutional principle and sectional appeal, the party had little to offer to a Whig landowner. Thus political pragmatism and personal faith led Saunderson to shed his Gladstonian façade; but it was only in 1882 that he constructed a new identity to take its place.

5

Loyalism and Class Diplomacy, 1879–1884

It seems that Saunderson deliberately cut himself off from politics between 1874 and 1882. In part this was because he had been thrust out of Liberalism, but there were other, more personal and emotional, factors at play. He had hated his exile at Westminster, and though he had almost overcome his fears of addressing the Commons, he still felt isolated in London. After the Cavan débâcle he pursued a frenetic but aimless career, building a barrier of boats and militia romps between himself and the failing agrarian economy. There are few political references in his letters to Helena of the period: while one would not expect much evidence of local party activity amongst this intimate correspondence, there ought, on the basis of his later career, to be more political allusions among his incoming letters. And yet there are scarcely any. Saunderson's political activity in these years seldom rose above relaxed conversations with Sommy Maxwell and Lord Crichton; his only speeches were delivered to evangelical assemblies. While the rains brought crop failure and impoverishment to his poorer tenants, Saunderson sailed his yachts to escape these disturbing realities, and sublimated his anger in fighting the imaginary enemies of the Cavan Militia.

The unpleasant fact of crop failure in 1879 had, however, revolutionary implications, and Saunderson's isolation proved impossible to sustain. Within Ulster, tenant unrest had smouldered since the Land Act of 1870, and particularly because there was no legally defined, and therefore defensible, conception of the Ulster Custom.[1] Landlords were making inroads into customary rights, provoking farmer disquiet, and—after the disastrous 1879 season—raising the prospect of radical political convulsions. Counties Cavan and Fermanagh—Saunderson's homeland—were among those most severely affected by flooding and crop failure. Crippling hardship and poverty were located in both counties, but especially among the smallholders of Cavan, with the consequence that rent arrears were

[1] R. W. Kirkpatrick, 'The Origins and Development of the Land War in Mid-Ulster', in F. S. L. Lyons and R. Hawkins (eds.), *Varieties of Tension: Ireland under the Union: Essays in Honour of T. W. Moody* (Oxford, 1980), 203–4.

mounting during the period 1879–80.[2] Saunderson was philosophical about the likelihood of little or no income from rents: 'we must refrain from buying any unnecessary article', he instructed Helena, 'as the prospects are very bad in this country.'[3] Some months later, in September 1879, he reduced the rents on his estate by 25 per cent.[4] Wealthier friends and neighbours, like Lord Erne in Fermanagh, were able to react more constructively to the distress of the smallholders: Erne, who had three times Saunderson's rental income, was responsible for organizing a major drainage scheme. But the tractability of many landlords ceased when, after two better seasons in 1880 and 1881, tenants still failed to pay. And the immediate and explosive consequence was a growth in the number of evictions.[5]

Yet, though there was a direct link between the non-payment of rent and eviction, it seems likely that landlord aggression had also a political rationale, and that eviction was used as a pre-emptive sanction against Land League sympathizers.[6] In the context of both rural distress and a venerable tradition of farmer agitation, the Land League had put down roots in Ulster shortly after its foundation in July 1879. One of its first branches was in County Fermanagh, close to the Saunderson estate where, despite condemnation by the hierarchy of the Order, Orangemen joined in considerable numbers.[7] In fact, the League attracted Protestant farmers throughout Ulster, although many clung to the independent tradition of tenant agitation which had its origins before 1879.[8] Nevertheless, the indirect significance of the League was immense, both in inflating the currency of reform rhetoric, and in inspiring a readjustment within northern party politics. The electoral choice for northern farmers no longer lay between landed Whiggery and landed Toryism, but rather between Toryism and a revitalized Liberalism, working in an informal association with the League. So long as northern Leaguers remained ambiguous about their constitutional objectives, and so long as they

[2] Kirkpatrick, 'Land War', 212–13, 216. On the origins of the Land War see W. E. Vaughan, *Landlords and Tenants in Mid-Victorian Ireland* (Oxford, 1994), 208–16.

[3] ESP, T.2996/2B/153: Saunderson to Helena, 2 July 1879; Kirkpatrick, 'Land War', 217.

[4] *Freeman's Journal*, 17 Sept. 1879. I am grateful to Dr Patrick Maume for this reference. See Francis Thompson, 'Land and Politics in Ulster, 1868–1886', Ph.D. thesis (Queen's University, Belfast, 1982), fos. 483–4 for evidence of other rebates.

[5] Kirkpatrick, 'Land War', 221. See the table in Thompson, 'Land and Politics', fo. 492.

[6] Kirkpatrick, 'Land War', 223.

[7] Ibid. 226.

[8] Ibid.

distanced themselves from violence, the conditions existed for a reform-based fissure within Protestant politics.[9] These criteria were fulfilled until at least 1882–3.

By the autumn of 1880 the Orange Order and Tory party were preparing a joint response to the tacit alliance between Liberalism and the League; but in so far as this response was constructed around a traditional sectarian, anti-repeal, programme it fell flat.[10] In November 1880 the Grand Orange Lodge of Ireland had sanctioned a campaign of counter-demonstrations arranged to coincide with Land League meetings. These attracted insignificant support, the League meetings being held with relative ease and success: one Orange counter-demonstration, at Derrygonnelly in December 1880, attracted only a similar number of Protestants to its much larger and religiously mixed League rival.[11] More significant than tired Protestant appeals, and their well-worn medium, was the tentative adoption by some Orange leaders of reform rhetoric.[12] In the long term these hesitant gestures towards flexibility among landed Tories would develop into a vehicle for a cross-class alliance, based on concession for Protestant by Protestant, for Unionist by Unionist. But, in the absence of any recognizable external threat, this Orange reformism was for the moment inadequate: Ulster Liberalism held an increasing sway over Ulster farmers.

Several of Saunderson's class, especially within the 'frontier' counties, either joined the Order at this time, or revived their membership, assuming a higher profile within the movement. Viscount Castlereagh and Lord Hill-Trevor were frightened recruits; and Saunderson's near neighbours—Captain E. M. Archdale (Grand Secretary of the Fermanagh Orangemen), Somerset Maxwell, and Viscount Crichton—all emerged as leaders of the Orange response in 1880.[13] Viewed from Crom Castle, or Rossmore Park, the threat suggested by the League was vivid and immediate: Captain Boycott, after all, was the agent of Lord Erne, and it was Somerset Maxwell who led the Orangemen of Cavan and Monaghan,

[9] Paul Bew and Frank Wright, 'The Agrarian Opposition in Ulster Politics, 1848–1887', in Samuel Clarke and James S. Donnelly (eds.), *Irish Peasants: Violence and Political Disturbance in Ireland, 1790–1914* (Manchester, 1983), 221–2.

[10] Thompson, 'Land and Politics', fos. 469–96.

[11] Bew and Wright, 'Agrarian Opposition', 214, 218–19, 222; Kirkpatrick, 'Land War', 230; Thompson, 'Land and Politics', fos. 475–6, 479–81.

[12] Thompson, 'Land and Politics', fos. 481–3.

[13] Bew and Wright, 'Agrarian Opposition', 214 n. 83; Aiken McClelland, 'Orangeism in County Monaghan', *Clogher Record*, 9/3 (1978), 397.

united as the Boycott Relief Expedition, to Lough Mask.[14] Yet Saunderson himself remained cut off from the frenzy of his neighbours, taking no part in this first, abortive expedition against the League. He was still not a member of the Orange Order, and he still sought to preserve the fragments of an anachronistic rural idyll.

It was only in 1882 that Saunderson achieved his Orange Damascus. While this epiphany might have been predicted from the earlier convulsions within his own class, his political comeback also coincided with a more popular agitation in Ulster against the League. Many farmers were temporarily satisfied with the new Land Act, passed by Gladstone's government in August 1881. Lynn Doyle's Cousin William was probably typical:

[he] did not love landlords and had been a great tenant right man in his own day. But on the question of Home Rule he was what in Ulster would be called 'sound'. He admired Gladstone, but thought his reforms should have stopped at the land acts.[15]

Apart from Cousin William, others had been shocked by the growth in crime over 1881–2, which had culminated in the Phoenix Park murders. Subsequent events—the decline in political ambiguity which accompanied the new National League, the repercussions of Tim Healy's Monaghan campaign of 1883—consolidated these trends, making possible the reconstruction of a Protestant class alliance.[16] But it was in the aftermath of Phoenix Park that Edward Saunderson put on an Orange sash, formally repudiating his Liberalism. It was as a reaction to this threat of anarchy, and not to the earlier and generally pacific land agitation, that he rationalized his transformation on 12 July 1882.

He appeared at the sanctuary of Orangeism, Ballykilbeg, County Down, offering (in tones reminiscent of an evangelical testament, or conversion experience) his reasons for joining the Order. Aside from the divine sanction which the principles of the Order self-evidently enjoyed, it was an obvious—indeed the only obvious—social cement:

The very foundations of society were shaken, and about to crumble in the dust, and

[14] F. S. L. Lyons, *Charles Stewart Parnell* (London, 1977), 138. *BNL*, 29 June 1886, p. 8: Saunderson resurrected Maxwell's record during the North Belfast nomination contest of June–July 1886.

[15] Lynn Doyle, *An Ulster Childhood* (Dublin, 1921), 44. See also Bew and Wright, 'Agrarian Opposition', 220; J. Magee, 'The Monaghan Election of 1883 and the "Invasion of Ulster"', *Clogher Record*, 8/2 (1974), *passim*.

[16] Bew and Wright, 'Agrarian Opposition', 221; Kirkpatrick, 'Land War', 232–3.

he [Saunderson] said to himself was there any organisation capable of dealing with this condition of anarchy and rebellion? There was only one answer...[17]

Yet, this apocalyptic rhetoric notwithstanding, Saunderson's critique of the Land League was carefully formulated. It was not because of its work for tenant farmers, but because of its 'disloyal' ambitions and 'unfair' methods, that he opposed the League: Saunderson never convincingly squared his hazy commitment to the farmers within any detailed programme of action.[18] Yet he took pains to point out that 'if the Land League was an open, fair society'—the precise definition of 'fair' again eluded him—no matter how radical its claims for the farmers might be, he would offer no objection.[19] Having made obeisance to farmer demands, he hurried on to the crux of his address: a proposal to turn the Orange Order into 'a disciplined body' in order to resist 'rebellion and treason' in the shape of Home Rule and Captain Moonlight.

It was the first of many calls to arms by the major of militia, and—in its express purpose—it was as ineffectual as its successors. Yet the Ballykilbeg speech was a considerable personal achievement: in the midst of much patronizing and threadbare bluster, Saunderson offered a marketable package of businesslike aggression, a nominal reformism, and a highly charged Unionism. In the short term it brought him local celebrity, pushing him into the rather aimless flap of Orange administration; it brought him, too, an anonymous threatening letter, which Helena, who was also targeted by its threats, opened by mistake.[20] From a broader perspective, however, the Ballykilbeg speech was an important step within the trend towards an anti-Nationalist class consensus—and all the more important because it had been delivered by a landlord and sometime Gladstonian.

Saunderson made little obvious effort to exploit this temporary celebrity: over the following fourteen months he delivered only two major speeches, both, significantly, to Orange meetings.[21] But his interest in parliament was renewed, and his ambitions were fired in 1883 when, from the Visitor's Gallery in the Commons, he observed the limited and incoherent performances of the Ulster Tories.[22] He made the acquaint-

[17] *BNL*, 14 July 1882, p. 6.

[18] Ibid.

[19] Ibid.

[20] ESP, T.2996/2B/185: Saunderson to Helena, 20 July 1882; Reginald Lucas, *Colonel Saunderson MP: A Memoir* (London, 1908), 68–9.

[21] ESP, T.2996/1/50: Saunderson to Helena, 12 Oct. 1882; T.2996/1/52: Saunderson to Helena, 13 Mar. 1883.

[22] *Portadown News*, 2 Dec. 1905.

ance of the eccentric Lord Rossmore, and, by May 1883, the two landlords were discussing Orange strategy at luncheon parties.[23] It was as a lieutenant to Rossmore during the latter's brief political celebrity that Saunderson developed the policy which he had outlined at Ballykilbeg. And when Rossmore entered the Orange martyrology—having been dismissed from the magistracy because of a rabble-rousing speech at Rosslea, County Monaghan—disciples like Saunderson enjoyed a lesser, but still useful, reverence.

Throughout the autumn of 1883 Healy and the National League attempted to build on their electoral success at Monaghan through a series of public meetings held in mid-Ulster and in the southern counties of the Province. The Orange reaction took the form of noisy counter-demonstrations, echoing the tactic of 1880. It is not altogether clear whether this was a centrally formulated and directed initiative: in any event, from modest beginnings at Aughnacloy on 26 September 1883, when only 800 Orangemen attended, the reaction swiftly grew in strength and precision, culminating in the Rosslea meeting of 16 October.[24] After Rosslea a high standard of organization and unity was sustained, and a small band of influential newcomers emerged, who co-ordinated the movement from the extremity of Orange opinion. Among these was Edward Saunderson.

These Orange protests shared a common rationale. They were designed to demonstrate, particularly for a British and parliamentary audience, that Ireland had not fallen uniformly under the sway of the League: Ulster, as Saunderson later wrote, had to be shown to be 'the stumbling block in the way of the revolutionary leaders'.[25] Thus the meetings were crude demarcations of territorial supremacy, and in so far as they were successful they heightened perceptions of a political frontier. The meetings may also have been used as a bait to tempt the government into proclaiming both any League demonstration, and its Orange counterpart. Related to this was the Orangemen's gut desire to deny their opponents a hearing, whether through government proclamation or intimidation. Though there was surprisingly little violence as a direct result of the rival meetings, the potential was always there, and was occasionally realized. But violence may not have been necessary: it seems clear that Orange organization, especially after the political martyrdom of Rossmore, outstripped that of its oppo-

23 ESP, T.2996/2B/196: Saunderson to Helena, 29 May 1883.

24 Magee, 'Monaghan Election', 158 ff; J. W. Taylor, *The Rossmore Incident: An Account of the Nationalist and Counter-Nationalist Meetings held in Ulster in the Autumn of 1883* (Dublin, 1884).

25 Edward Saunderson, *Two Irelands: Loyalty versus Treason* (Dublin, 1884), 29.

sition—with the effect that large Orange demonstrations, recruited from a wide area, overawed the relatively small and local gatherings sponsored by the National League.[26]

Saunderson sought to justify this confrontational approach (potentially offensive to British observers) by arguing that British standards of political practice would only work within a British patriotic and constitutional consensus.[27] But in contrasting the pristine loyalty of Ulster with 'the uniform crime and disaffection' of the League and of the southern provinces, Saunderson was effectively (and prematurely) writing off the strength and value of southern Toryism: and he delved further into fantasy and inconsistency by predicting that Ulster would soon be the fulcrum of a national loyalism.[28] He did not, therefore, accept the partitionist implications of his own logic, and of the Orangemen's action. In reality the Orange campaign of 1883, and indeed Saunderson's rhetoric, contributed, not to a renaissance of loyalism throughout Ireland, but to its specific identification with north-east Ulster.

The Rosslea meeting was an important turning-point in the agitation, since it provided the Orangemen with a noble martyr in the paunchily unheroic frame of the fifth Lord Rossmore. A League meeting had been called for Rosslea on 16 October, when a crowd of 3,000 gathered.[29] The much larger Orange counter-demonstration comprised men from both Fermanagh and Cavan: many travelled by special train to Clones, and marched in their lodges—forming a procession two miles long—to the village of Rosslea.[30] Unfortunately Saunderson has left no account of the demonstration, even though he played an important and emollient role, and shared the command of the Fermanagh Orangemen with William Archdale.[31] At the request of a sub-inspector of the Royal Irish Constabulary, Saunderson and Archdale adjusted the route of their march to avoid confrontation with the League meeting; but Rossmore, at the head of the Monaghan contingent, refused to follow the new route, marching with his followers provocatively close to the rival gathering.[32] A large police and military force under the command of a resident magistrate, Captain McTiernan, kept order, and despite Rossmore's potentially disastrous

26 Ibid. 28. Saunderson held the view that the League meetings 'did not come within the ordinary category of political manifestation'. Kirkpatrick, 'Land War', 233–4.

27 Saunderson, *Two Irelands*, 28–9.

28 Ibid. 30–1; *BNL*, 17 Oct. 1883, p. 8.

29 Taylor, *Rossmore Incident*, 14.

30 *BNL*, 17 Oct. 1883, p. 8.

31 Ibid.

32 Magee, 'Monaghan Election', 162; *BNL*, 17 Oct. 1883, p. 8.

defiance, there was little violence apart from sporadic stone-throwing, and few injured (two journalists were assaulted by an Orange mob). The main meetings also passed off without serious incident.[33]

It was a triumph for the Orange conception of a Protestant class alliance. The Rosslea meeting was led by the landlord-dynasts of southern Ulster, and Saunderson's friends and relatives were well represented among the platform party. Moreover, the meeting received the blessing of official Toryism in the form of the Fermanagh MPs, Lord Crichton (who chaired) and William Archdale.[34] The speeches varied in quality and acerbity, but a prevailing theme was the unity of Ulster Protestants in the face of an allegedly sectarian and aggressive nationalism. Allusions were constantly made to the magnanimity of the Ulster propertied élite—to a paternalism especially constructed for Protestant consumption. Even Rossmore, in an awesomely violent and offensive address (the people at the League meetings were 'rebels', 'scavengers', and 'scum') introduced a note of friendly condescension in urging the Orangemen to disperse peacefully ('he hoped that they would all do him the favour of keeping quiet that day and going home by the other road').[35] Rossmore's equally blunt Orange brother, Captain Barton, recalled the halcyon days of the Williamite wars when a few landed families were the rallying point of Protestant resistance in Fermanagh: men looked naturally for leadership to the Crichtons, and to their class, against the 'socialistic set of rebels', whether in 1689 or in 1883.[36] It was in fact Lord Crichton, followed later by Edward Saunderson, who argued most forcefully for a pan-Protestant class alliance, and stressed that the National League's campaign constituted not merely a threat to landlord status but to all Protestant property: 'It was now "the land for the people", and for what people? Not for those present before him, but for the descendants of those who, they asserted, were dispossessed by their ancestors ...'[37] Here was an appeal to primal northern fears of expropriation, and it was trumped by an assurance that Protestants could always reconcile their own economic quarrels. Indeed the whole force of the Crichton argument was directed towards establishing the need for arbitration between different classes of Protestant.

Saunderson took up Crichton's war-cry, emphasizing that in the wilder Nationalist rhetoric they all—Protestant landowners *and* farmers—were

[33] Magee, 'Monaghan Election', 163.
[34] *BNL*, 17 Oct. 1883, p. 8; Taylor, *Rossmore Incident*, 13–14.
[35] *BNL*, 17 Oct. 1883, p. 8.
[36] Ibid. [37] Ibid.

the English garrison, liable to attack and expulsion.[38] On the other hand he clearly felt that he did not have to offer the same concessions to tenant farmer feeling as he had been compelled to make in July 1882: the sectarian hackles of the farmers had been independently raised, and any appeal to Protestant solidarity did not require the same compromise of economic interest. Indeed Saunderson's tone was essentially pacific: he made some conventional allusions to defence of faith and the constitution, but uttered nothing to equal the belligerence of his Ballykilbeg speech. He had accepted the redirection of the Orange march, and he had underlined (with more hope than accuracy) that 'they did not come here to interfere with the enjoyment of any legal right on the part of their fellow countrymen'.[39] Yet he was clearly more committed to the peaceful termination of the demonstration than Rossmore (to judge, at any rate, by the rabble-rousing venom of the latter's address). In fact it seems that Saunderson, confronted perhaps for the first time with the reality of popular Protestant feeling, and the potential for political violence, was shocked and therefore consciously pacific. The interests of northern landowners, after all, were no more consistent with popular Protestant anarchy than with the violence associated with the League.

Rossmore's conduct at Rosslea earned him dismissal from the bench. As recompense, indeed to his own subsequent and intense embarrassment, he was venerated as an Orange martyr, as a victim of Nationalist spleen, and trimming Gladstonianism. But, more important, the government's action provided the sequence of counter-demonstrations with greater impetus and greater credibility within official Toryism than had been achieved hitherto. Saunderson remained at the heart of the campaign, speaking at a reception for Rossmore on 7 December; and he followed Rossmore's lead in calling his own counter-demonstration for Cootehill, County Cavan, on 1 January 1884.[40] In the event this, with its National League counterpart, was proclaimed by the Lord Lieutenant. Rossmore's unexceptional punishment had generated a greater Protestant backlash than had been foreseen, and the threats of violence between rival meetings were now often too great to be countenanced. Moreover, a broader range of the Protestant establishment, previously nervous if tacitly sympathetic, had joined the Rossmore bandwagon. Thus, at the Monaghan reception for the rebel peer the speakers included not only swashbuckling veterans like Saunderson and Maxwell, but also staider newcomers like the archdeacon of Clogher,

[38] Ibid. [39] Ibid.
[40] Ibid., 8 Dec. 1883, p. 7.

and Saunderson's future parliamentary rival, John Monroe.[41] Indeed, to a perceptible extent, Saunderson (and even Rossmore himself) were overshadowed by their own political creation—and at a banquet given by the Constitutional Club of Dublin for Rossmore in January 1884 Saunderson was not thought worthy of inclusion among the principal speakers.[42] Given that these included metropolitan Tories of the calibre of Edward Gibson and David Plunket, this was not perhaps so very great a snub; and, in the event, Saunderson was called on (by popular acclamation) to address the gathering. He was not, however, reported in the Belfast press. But the episode was a useful reminder that, whatever his fame within the Orange hierarchy, Saunderson remained for many Tories no more than an obscure and suspect convert from Liberalism. Wider celebrity would depend on a more sustained and tangible demonstration of loyalist conviction.

The Rossmore affair generated a minor rash of partisan literature—from Tim Healy's *Loyalty Plus Murder* through to J. W. Taylor's deceptively unassuming *The Rossmore Incident*.[43] (Healy was unashamedly partial; Wallace Taylor, in sifting through the facts of the Orange campaign, was evidently more coy, and was reluctant to publicize his dual role as Secretary to the Monaghan Orangemen and companion to Rossmore on the Rosslea march). These pamphlets were exploited by the leading spokesmen of both parties, Tory and Parnellite, to fuel a controversy which centred on the government's handling of the Orange counter-demonstrations and of Rossmore: this raged well into 1884, reaching a parliamentary climax on 8 February. On that occasion Parnell moved an amendment to the Loyal Address ostensibly in order to bemoan the conduct of the Irish government; but the main focus of his icy and effective speech was the excesses and pretensions of the landlord-inspired campaign against the League.[44] The basis for his address was probably Healy's pamphlet, just as the material for Lord Crichton's able reply was probably culled from Taylor's research. In the war to establish the facts and justice of the case, different reports and interpretations of the Orange and League speakers' actions were offered; and, for his part, Parnell returned to the

[41] *BNL*, 8 Dec. 1883, p. 7.

[42] ESP, T.2996/2B/207: Saunderson to Helena, 30 Jan. 1884. Saunderson suggested to his wife that there had been no reporters present. In fact, the gathering *was* reported, although Saunderson's contribution did not as yet merit attention.

[43] T. M. Healy, *Loyalty Plus Murder* (Dublin, 1883); J. Wallace Taylor, *The Rossmore Incident: An Account of the Nationalist and Counter-Nationalist Meetings held in Ulster in the Autumn of 1883* (Dublin, 1884).

[44] *Hansard*, ser. 3, cclxxxiv. 321–39 (8 Feb. 1884).

details of the Rosslea meeting, singling out Saunderson for particular attention and obloquy.

Thus Saunderson, whose immediate political interests lay in self-advertisement, was gradually drawn into the grubby and protracted aftermath of the autumn campaign. He presented his own contribution to the pamphlet fusillade in *Two Irelands: Loyalty versus Treason*, published in the spring of 1884. Regarded as a personal testament, this is of frustratingly little value, and some of its more significant insights into Saunderson's political pique have already been mentioned in earlier contexts.[45] Nevertheless, judged within its immediate genre, *Two Irelands* sheds some light on Saunderson's ambitions and limitations, if not on the more elusive articles of his faith. It was published when the leaders of the Orange campaign, except Rossmore, were beginning to lose their fame. Furthermore, it was an answer to the developing Parnellite criticism, which had been directed towards Orange leaders like Saunderson, and their allegedly provocative rhetoric. There was clearly a need for one of the more prominent organizers of the campaign to offer an apologia for his own and his colleagues' actions, and Saunderson had also an immediate, personal need for the publicity which such a task offered. Moreover there was little opposition to his claims. Taciturn and choleric squires such as Rossmore or Sommy Maxwell were wholly unfitted for the task of constructing an effective Orange response, while the more able Crichton had parliamentary duties to fulfil (including the daunting assignment of replying to Parnell's brilliant indictment on 8 February).[46] Thus personal interest and broader political expediency forced the task on to Saunderson.

Since much of Saunderson's later career involved tailoring an Ulster Unionist case for British consumption, *Two Irelands* is of particular interest as an early example of his response to this challenge. *Two Irelands* was not primarily an Orange apology for a northern Protestant readership; it was rather a contribution to a propaganda duel conducted largely in England and with British political implications. Lord Randolph Churchill, for example, had wholeheartedly supported Rossmore, using the affair as a bludgeon against the Government, and against more vacillating Tories like Stafford Northcote.[47] Though Saunderson had infused sectarian overtones into speeches in Ulster, he was more even-handed—self-consciously so—in *Two Irelands*: the Orange campaign, he stressed, was 'against

[45] See above, pp. 50–1.

[46] *Hansard*, ser. 3, cclxxxiv. 339 (8 Feb. 1884).

[47] R. F. Foster, *Lord Randolph Churchill: A Political Life* (Oxford, 1981), 138–9; R. E. Quinault, 'Lord Randolph Churchill and Home Rule', *IHS*, 21/84 (Sept. 1979), 393–4.

revolution ... not against Roman Catholicism'—indeed it 'enlisted the sympathy of all law-abiding Roman Catholics in Ireland'.[48] Loyalism, he argued, should ideally be free from creed and party affiliation: indeed, his own most significant political achievement might be interpreted as an effort to realize this benign, if fantastic, ambition. He was conscious that British opinion might be shocked by what had been evidently a loyalist campaign to deny political rights to the National League, and he sought at length to repudiate this charge.[49] He was conscious, too, that his co-author, Edward Caulfield Houston, had referred offensively to the humble social origins of various leading Parnellites, and in an afterthought to his own text he attempted to clarify these allusions by arguing (characteristically) that the Parnellites had used their knowledge of the people in order to dupe them.[50] He was reverting to the paternalistic themes of his Rosslea address, but he was now clothing these in the more general language appropriate to a liberal British audience, and without special reference to the susceptibilities of the Ulster farmers.

If *Two Irelands* was constructed for Britain, then it need not be assumed that it was a disingenuous creation, retailing moderation for political effect. *Two Irelands* says as much, or as little, about Saunderson's convictions as his most belligerent Orange address. He was always capable of careful and circumspect language, though thundering loyalist declarations were much more popular and more easy to deliver: his public generally sought from him an articulation of loyalist basics, rather than any rigorous dialectic, or telling ambiguity. Saunderson's great political strength at this time was that he responded to the challenge of his audience; the tragedy of his career was that they asked so little from him.

If the pamphlet reveals Saunderson at his most nimble, then the history of its construction offers an insight into some of his more personal qualms and limitations. The weakest section of the text—the first 18 pages—was written, not by Saunderson, but by the priggish Edward Caulfield Houston (later to win disgrace through his association with the forger, Pigott).[51] Saunderson's own contribution was less than six pages of text, together with his work on the large section of quotations and extracts which constituted the third part of the pamphlet. But, even with this last, he relied heavily on predecessors, and particularly on the pamphlet, *The Truth about the League*, compiled by the young H. O. Arnold-Forster: the

48 Saunderson, *Two Irelands*, 31.
49 Ibid. 28–9.
50 Ibid. 32–3.
51 Ibid., preface (p. 3).

third edition of this had appeared a little earlier, in 1883.[52] In addition, Saunderson had the advice of the distinguished historian, Richard Bagwell, and the services of two research assistants. Yet, despite this formidable support-team, the pace of production was not particularly swift: Saunderson had mooted the idea of a pamphlet as early as February 1884, was in the middle of writing (and the depths of despair) throughout April, and only finally achieved publication in July.[53] The fact was that he was a reluctant and limited author, whether in maintaining a personal journal, or in approaching the more awesome task of a first publication. He wrote jaunty and interesting letters to Helena, but he trembled before addressing a wider audience, and indeed posterity. His private letters are by no means models of their type, but they are relaxed, pleasant, and frank. In writing what he assumed would be less ephemeral literature he became stilted and prissy. The for him unique literary challenge posed by *Two Irelands* focused Saunderson's self-doubts; and in the end he evaded the problem by thrusting much of the responsibility on to Houston.

Whatever the division of authorial labour, *Two Irelands* contributed decisively to Saunderson's fame as an Orange apologist; but, even by mid-1884, this identity located him firmly at the periphery of Irish politics. He had unequivocally repudiated Liberalism, yet his association with erratic extremists like Rossmore meant that his relationship with Irish Toryism was, to say the least, ambiguous. Had it not been for Rossmore's dismissal and martyrdom—the elevation of the ridiculous into a matter of broader Tory honour—Saunderson would have remained at the fringe of practical politics. As it was, events played into his hands, and he became the herald of a more acerbic, Protestant political tone, rather than a militant and eccentric embarrassment. Irish Toryism developed to meet Saunderson's ideal, while he reaped popular and party acclaim.

In 1883, though an Orangeman, he had distanced himself from official Toryism: while close friends like Crichton and Maxwell were active partisans, Saunderson possessed no clear party identity. Indeed, some of his public statements argued strongly against the traditional factions. Though less forceful than some proponents of this line (the Revd Jago at Rosslea, for example), he was beginning to advocate the creation not only

[52] H. O. Arnold-Forster, *The Truth about the League, Its Leaders and Its Teaching*, 3rd edn. (Dublin, 1883); ESP, T.2996/2B/214: Saunderson to Helena, 29 Feb. 1884.

[53] ESP, T. 2996/2B/211: Saunderson to Helena, 21 Feb. 1884; ESP, T.2996/2B/220: Saunderson to Helena, 23 Apr. 1884; ESP, T.2996/2B/221: Saunderson to Helena, 23 Apr. 1884.

of a cross-class, but also a cross-party loyalism.[54] It was perhaps because of these heresies that Saunderson played no part in the reception of Stafford Northcote, the Tory leader, in October 1883—while loyal party men, who had been just as militant, occupied a more prominent role.[55] Clearly Saunderson's achievements were as yet too slight to make him worth courting; and, for his part, Saunderson had no more than dallied with Conservatism.

When Irish Tories rallied around Rossmore and his lieutenants, Saunderson became an object of greater interest, and it was then, evidently, that he was inducted into the party. But his new faith was still implied rather than substantive—he was an anti-Gladstonian, rather than a zealous supporter of the Conservative front bench. In October 1884 he made an early public appearence at a wholly Conservative demonstration, when he was invited to speak by the Dublin City and County Conservative Workingmen's Club: this endorsement by Tory democracy is highly suggestive. But though he had been asked to second a motion applauding the action of Tory peers, Saunderson chose instead to dwell on the iniquities of Liberal foreign policy in the aftermath of Khartoum.[56] He was still cautious, therefore, but he was gradually constructing an alliance within the most influential sections of Irish Toryism. At the Dublin demonstration he met two important and senior figures within the party, David Plunket and Edward Gibson: Saunderson's speech had been sandwiched between their respective efforts, his Orange sniping complementing their prosy wit. And he consolidated a growing reputation in Tory Dublin by addressing an audience at Trinity College. This apparently 'made a great impression upon the public mind'—at any rate William Moore, who would succeed Saunderson in the representation of North Armagh, could recall the meeting almost twenty-three years later.[57] Saunderson's Orange colleagues in the Dublin-based Grand Lodge of Ireland responded to the wider political acceptability of their protégé by electing him Deputy Master of the movement.[58]

[54] *BNL*, 17 Oct. 1883 p. 8. The Revd Mr Jago called on his audience 'to drop altogether the considerations of whether some of them incline more or less to the English parties of Conservatism and Liberalism, but to the one solid party of themselves—the Irish Protestant Party'.

[55] A. B. Cooke, 'A Conservative Party Leader in Ulster: Sir Stafford Northcote's Diary of a Visit to the Province, October 1883', *PRIA* 75c/4 (Sept. 1975), 61–84.

[56] *BNL*, 21 Oct. 1884, p. 8; ESP, T.2996/2B/251: Saunderson to Helena, 20 Oct. 1884; Lucas, *Saunderson*, 76–7.

[57] ESP, T.2996/2B/254: Saunderson to Helena, 11 Nov. 1884. ESP, T.2996/6/3: William Moore to Reginald Lucas, 25 Nov. [1907].

[58] ESP, T.2996/2B/255: Saunderson to Helena, 4 Dec. 1884.

Thus, by the end of 1884, Saunderson had begun to establish his usefulness with the different elements of Irish Conservatism—Dublin, Ulster, and Orange—yet he had also retained a measure of freedom from any potentially damaging party constraint. He had influence over extremists; yet he had shown that he could be subtle, and that he was capable of persuasive and emollient language. These qualities, allied with his unflagging ubiquity, would shortly propel Saunderson to the forefront of loyalist politics.

6

The Evolution of Organized Unionism, 1884–1885

Saunderson's militancy, and his suspicions of official Toryism, were vindicated by the actions of the British party leaders over the complex of measures known loosely as the third Reform Act. For all the alarmist rhetoric of the 'frontier' Orangemen in 1882–3, the electoral security of northern Toryism, indeed of northern Protestantism, was guaranteed by franchise qualifications, and by the preponderance of small boroughs with parliamentary representation. Most of those who held the vote in the counties did so under the £12 rated occupier franchise of 1850; the Irish Representation of the People Act of 1868 had also created a borough franchise, limited principally to occupiers of property with a rateable valuation of over £4.[1] This had the effect of giving Protestants a voting strength disproportionate to their numbers. Moreover, most of the Ulster boroughs which returned a member of parliament—there were ten in all—returned Tories: only one, Dungannon, elected a Liberal at the general election of 1880. Thus, when the Gladstone government set out in 1884 both to broaden the franchise, and to redistribute the seats from the small boroughs, the threat posed by Parnellite agitation became more acute. In 1880–3 Tory fears had hinged on the possibility of Protestant farmers being recruited to the League; after 1884–5 their anguish was caused by the reality of Catholic electoral strength.

For in the discussions on reform which had been conducted by Gladstone, Salisbury and the increasingly ineffectual Stafford Northcote, Irish Tory claims had been discreetly pigeon-holed. The inter-party consensus which emerged from these discussions contained no special provision for the preservation of Irish Toryism, whether through fancy franchises, or through an especially favourable scheme of redistribution.[2] The reforms of 1884–5 were, ironically, an achievement for a rigorous, integrationist, Unionism: a uniform householder and lodger franchise was created for the

[1] Brian Walker, *Parliamentary Election Results in Ireland, 1801–1922* (Dublin, 1978), pp. xii–xiii; id., 'The Irish Electorate, 1868–1915', *IHS*, 18/71 (Mar. 1973), 359–406.

[2] Andrew Jones, *The Politics of Reform, 1884* (Cambridge, 1972), 72.

entire United Kingdom, while the Redistribution of Seats Act of 1885 disfranchised small boroughs throughout Britain and Ireland (twenty-two Irish boroughs lost their representation). But the fact that Ireland enjoyed similar treatment to Britain did little to mollify Irish Tories—for all the evidence suggested that they had been abandoned, not only by Gladstone, but also by their own leaders. Fears of Nationalist aggression were now compounded by the spectacle of ministerial treachery, aided and abetted by the leaders of the British Conservative party. And this new emotional chemistry meant that northern Protestantism became more receptive to Saunderson's brand of wary and independent loyalism.

In fact British treachery was less comprehensive than Saunderson and other Irish Tories believed. It is much more likely that the particular claims of the Irish party were relegated because its members were ostensibly the clients and supporters of Northcote, rather than of his rival Salisbury. It was thus unfortunate from the Irish loyalist perspective that Salisbury had grasped the initiative in the reform discussions (playing, in Gladstone's phrase, the commanding 'mother hen' to Northcote's 'chick').[3] Moreover, even setting aside the politics of the Tory leadership contest, it is clear that both Salisbury and Northcote believed (or, at any rate, wanted others to believe) that the interests of Irish Toryism hinged largely on the composition of the Boundary Commission. Both leaders quietly sounded out their respective Irish lieutenants concerning the acceptability of those nominated to serve on this body, Northcote writing to Crichton on 17 December 1884, while Salisbury approached Lord Arthur Hill on the same day.[4]

The immediate response to these concerned enquiries was encouraging: Hill forwarded to Salisbury a letter from the key local apparatchik, E. S. Finnegan, which indicated satisfaction at the nature of the commission.[5] But an evidently sympathetic commission did not guarantee an overtly sympathetic scheme of redistribution, and when the Boundary Commission reports began to appear in early 1885, Irish Tories saw the prospect of electoral annihilation.[6] The security offered by their British leaders had been shown to be utterly inadequate; and, in the absence of any freely offered aid, Irish Tories turned both to a strategy of lobbying and

[3] Alvin Jackson, *The Ulster Party: Irish Unionists in the House of Commons, 1884–1911* (Oxford, 1989), 27.

[4] PRONI, Erne Papers, D.1939/21/10/10: Northcote to Crichton, 17 Dec. 1884. HH, Salisbury Papers: E. S. Finnegan to Lord Arthur Hill, 23 Dec. 1884.

[5] HH, Salisbury Papers: Finnegan to Hill, 23 Dec. 1884.

[6] Jackson, *Ulster Party*, 27.

political pressure, and to the cultivation of their independence from British control.

Saunderson was at the forefront of both elements within the loyalist campaign. His Trinity College speech of 11 November 1884 had made public his suspicions of the British party's intentions and, once the Boundary Commission reports had given force to this distrust, he was hailed as a leader of the Irish reaction. At a meeting of the political committee of the Ulster Constitutional Club held in Belfast on 14 January 1885, Saunderson was elected (in his absence) to a small parliamentary directorate: this included several MPs, and was charged with the task of preparing amendments to the reform bills for presentation to the House of Commons.[7] It was the particular responsibility of this directorate to attempt to revise the Redistribution of Seats Bill along lines more favourable to Irish Tories. Its objectives were indicated and endorsed at the 14 January meeting—but in practice it was delegated with much wider powers. Even in the theory of its function, sketched out by E. S. Finnegan, the directorate had rights of co-option, and it could construct amendments which needed only to be 'based upon' the proposals sanctioned in Belfast.[8]

Grandiose plans were laid for the future of the new ginger group. That these came to nothing, however, reflected no restoration of confidence within Irish Toryism. On the contrary, what was conceived as a genteel if independent propaganda committee became, through the incitement of Saunderson, a vehicle for the anger of the Irish party. The climax of the campaign was to be a set-piece interview with Northcote at St James's Place, London, on 18 February 1885, when it was hoped that some commitment to the Irish case might be extracted. Saunderson was commissioned to wind up the loyalist statement at this confrontation, and he fulfilled this task 'with a vengeance'.[9] He was now looked upon as a useful and persuasive speaker, and the invitation to corner Northcote was, as he wrote to Helena, 'complimentary to my renown as a windbag'.[10] This renown was somewhat consolidated by the success of his onslaught; for the hapless Northcote, tied to broader Tory interests, could only respond with friendly banalities. 'The deputation was delighted', Saunderson observed smugly, 'but I don't think Sir Stafford was.'[11]

[7] *Irish Times*, 15 Jan. 1885, p. 5.

[8] Ibid.

[9] ESP, T.2996/2B/259: Saunderson to Helena, 21 Feb. 1885; Reginald Lucas, *Colonel Saunderson MP: A Memoir* (London, 1908), 80.

[10] ESP, T.2996/2B/256: Saunderson to Helena, 17 Feb. 1885.

[11] ESP, T.2996/2B/259: Saunderson to Helena, 21 Feb. 1885.

Yet, though Saunderson and his colleagues were gratified by Northcote's discomfiture, they gained nothing substantial from the interview. Saunderson himself, while gloating quietly over his triumph, was aware of the more disturbing reality—'that Salisbury and Co. have thrown us over'.[12] Northcote, who had blundered into the Orange political arena in October 1883, offering a wide variety of commitments and encouragement, had been the Ulster Tories' only source of redress.[13] When he politely vacillated on 18 February, they felt acutely pained and deceived; and they were once again thrown on to their resources.

From Saunderson's personal perspective, however, the St James's Place débâcle had been far from valueless, for he had had the opportunity to impress his colleagues by a virtuoso Orange rodomontade—and he was able to exploit their disappointment by winning approval for a long-held ambition. On 20 February, the passions aroused by the confrontation having died down, a cooler loyalist parliamentary committee met to form 'an independent constitutional party in the House of Commons, entirely free to act for the good of Irish loyalty, unfettered by party ties'.[14] This was conceived, in the first place, as a purely parliamentary initiative: hence it was two senior Tory members of parliament, Sir Thomas Bateson and the Marquis of Hamilton, who moved and seconded the proposal to found the new 'party'.[15] But, in reality, Saunderson contributed significantly to the success of the idea; and he was clearly overjoyed that the independent loyalism which he had so consistently advocated was now closer to realization.

The new parliamentary party was, in practice, a failure. But its symbolic significance—as a precedent for future loyalist action—was immense. A group of the most influential Irish Tories had voted to break permanently with their British leadership, and to speak and vote according to the narrow interests of loyalism. There were other important aspects of this departure. Though the southern, Dublin-oriented interest was still well represented within the Irish Tory contingent at Westminster, the call to independence had originated among the Ulster elements, and particularly with the MPs and senior party men from the 'frontier' counties (Saunderson, Crichton, and Maxwell). Whatever the catholicity of its definition, parliamentary independence had a peculiarly Ulster flavour; and the initiative of 20

[12] ESP, T.2996/2B/257: Saunderson to Helena, 18 Feb. 1885.

[13] A. B. Cooke, 'A Conservative Party Leader in Ulster: Sir Stafford Northcote's Diary of a Visit to the Province, October 1883', *PRIA* 75c/4 (Sept. 1975), 64.

[14] ESP, T.2996/2B/259: Saunderson to Helena, 21 Feb. 1885.

[15] Jackson, *Ulster Party*, 31.

February reflected and encouraged the increasing marginalization of southern Toryism and of its Dublin spokesmen, Plunket and Gibson. This of course merely anticipated the electoral fate of the southern party in December 1885. But it was an early demonstration of what would become one of the fundamentals of loyalist party structure—that threats accompanied by organization and popularization implied a narrowly Ulster-based movement.

Equally significant were the implications of this parliamentary rebellion for the Tory relationship with Irish Liberalism. The unfolding of Salisbury's and Northcote's painfully vague plans for Tory survival in Ireland had led traditional organs of the party—like the *Belfast News Letter* and the *Irish Times*—to take up the cry for a loyalist *Bund*.[16] Discarding party tags and abandoning aggressive class interests had long been Saunderson's hobby-horse, and the vision of the new party embodied his political aims and evasions. Tentative discussions had already taken place between Liberals and Tories concerning joint action against the Parnellite threat: these dated back to at least 1884. But, for the moment, they came to nothing, since the Liberals, arguing from an apparent position of comparative electoral strength, were suspicious of Tory sincerity.[17] The initiative of 20 February, involving (as it did) local Tory repudiation of the British party, began the process of allaying these fears; and certainly the Tory rebels were acutely aware of the usefulness—and the susceptibilities—of northern Liberals.[18]

Though this strike at parliamentary freedom collapsed into disorganized sniping at the Tory front bench, relations between the Irish and British parties improved only slightly through 1885. The Redistribution Bill retained its unsatisfactory shape; and Salisbury's first administration, formed in June 1885, was dependent on Parnellite good will for its immediate survival. Salisbury was by no means unfriendly: seven Irish Tories were built into the government, and a parcel of peerages, baronetcies, and Privy Counsellorships was distributed to other influential MPs and party elders. But he could not offer any more broadly satisfactory measure, and meanwhile Randolph Churchill, despite his Rossmore credentials, was playing the Irish party field, and generating intense suspicion

16 See e.g. *Irish Times*, 12 Feb. 1885, p. 4: 'There is no one who read the recent able speeches of Major Saunderson and Lord Waterford who will not admit whatever have been his political attachments that the Irish minority has at present grave grounds for complaint.'

17 Jackson, *Ulster Party*, 29.

18 Ibid.

in Belfast.[19] Thus, as yet, there was no foundation for a reconciliation, and the work of constructing a popular Irish loyalist movement continued apace.

Irish Toryism was seriously divided in its attitude towards the new government, but Saunderson swiftly emerged as one of those most thoroughly suspicious and critical of its intentions. He had discreetly indicated his opinions as early as the autumn of 1884, and, as has already been made clear, he had been one of the prime movers behind the first, abortive parliamentary grouping of loyalism in February 1885. But, in the short term, personal considerations dictated a certain restraint: Saunderson, the emigrant from Whiggery, was hardly a credible leader for an all-out campaign directed against the Tory front bench. Even much later, in the autumn of 1885, when he publicly challenged the leadership in the form of the Irish Solicitor-General, his former political faith, and his suspiciously recent Orangeism, were flung in his face.[20] But by that time the swell of anglophobia, which Saunderson himself had helped to direct, meant that loyalty to the front bench was no longer a prerequisite for a full-blooded Irish Tory.

Through the summer of 1885 he was active in promoting the political organizations which, in aggregate, constituted the new, independent loyalism. He was present at the inauguration of the Loyal Irish Union on 8 August, and was responsible for proposing one of the motions; more important, from the point of a view of a weakening Tory commitment, he was an early sponsor of the non-sectarian and cross-party Irish Loyal and Patriotic Union.[21] He was sympathetic to William Johnston's populist challenge to the Tory establishment in South Belfast, and he mounted his own challenge in North Armagh by threatening to run against the official Tory candidate for the seat, John Monroe.[22]

As a hero of the campaign against the League, and as a trenchant and successful speaker, Saunderson had singled himself out as a likely focus for Orange affections. Because of trimming statements on the land question,

[19] For the relationship between Irish Unionists and the new government see: R. E. Quinault, 'Lord Randolph Churchill and Home Rule', *IHS* 21/84 (Sept. 1979), 394–5; R. F. Foster, 'To the Northern Counties Station: Lord Randolph Churchill and the Prelude to the Orange Card', in F. S. L. Lyons and R. A. J. Hawkins (eds.), *Ireland under the Union: Varieties of Tension: Essays in Honour of T. W. Moody* (Oxford, 1980), 265–8. A revised version of this last essay appears in R. F. Foster, *Paddy and Mr Punch: Connections in Irish and English History* (London, 1993), 237–61.

[20] See below, pp. 66–70.

[21] *Irish Times*, 10 Aug. 1885, p. 5; ESP, T.2996/2B/281: Saunderson to Helena, 18 Dec. 1885.

[22] PRONI, William Johnston Diaries, D.880/2/37: 5 Nov. 1885; 11 Nov. 1885.

and because of his general independence and militancy, he was viewed with less favour by the string-pullers and functionaries of Ulster Toryism. Sectarianism had long been an element of the Ulster political situation, and was tolerated, and ultimately exploited, by the Tory establishment. But the combination of Orange militancy and agrarian liberalism which characterized Saunderson's platform was a more recent development. Born in the outer counties of Ulster during the League campaign, this blurring of class frightened propertied Tories while providing Saunderson with electoral acclaim. And, in the medium term, it foreshadowed the rhetoric of Ulster Unionism.

Saunderson's appeal to Protestant feeling was directly attuned to the difficult political realities of Ulster in the wake of the League and the franchise reforms—and he was hailed by the Orangemen of several constituencies as a desirable parliamentary candidate. In both mid-Antrim and North Armagh he was seized on by Orange factions as a useful candidate. In both constituencies, however, the Tory hierarchy reacted more coolly. John Young of Galgorm, one of the leading patrons of the Antrim seat, spearheaded the official opposition to any maverick candidature; and though Saunderson was invited to address two meetings of the Antrim Orangemen on 13 July, enthusiasm was not such as to justify any challenge to the Tory nominee.[23] Mid-Antrim had little of the loyalist fervour and class consensus so conspicuous in more polarized constituencies; and with the Tory, R. T. O'Neill, attracting respect both as a recent, if nominal, convert to Orangeism, and more particularly as a leading landowner of the area, Saunderson's candidature swiftly withered. He reported to Helena on 31 July that representatives of the mid-Antrim and North Armagh Orangemen had competed that day for his favour; but there seems little doubt that he was effectively propelled from the former constituency through lack of support. On the other hand, there is also little doubt that Saunderson had consciously attempted to overthrow an inefficient Tory élite. Though Young, writing in the 1930s, would blandly suggest that the challenger 'did not know the position' in mid-Antrim, Saunderson's correspondence with Helena suggests the reverse; and in fact he maintained a hostility towards O'Neill for many months after his ignominious withdrawal.[24].

North Armagh initially offered little more hope of success. Saunderson's official rival was John Monroe, appointed by Salisbury as Solici-

[23] *BNL*, 20 July 1885, p. 8; ESP, T.2996/2B/273: Saunderson to Helena, 14 Aug. 1885.

[24] ESP, T.2996/2B/270: Saunderson to Helena, 31 July 1885. See also PRONI, W. R. Young Papers, D.3027/7/9: 'Recollections of 75 Years in Ulster' (1931), fo. 133.

tor-General for Ireland, and one of the most successful QCs of the period. His political marketability was further enhanced both by his family roots in North Armagh (he was born near Lurgan in 1829, the son of a tenant farmer) and by his valiant, if futile, campaign against T. M. Healy in County Monaghan in 1883. Monroe was ruthlessly promoted by an influential Tory functionary, J. B. Atkinson, and was duly nominated as the party's candidate at a number of meetings held in July 1885.[25] But, behind this façade of local strength, lay a more complex reality. Though Monroe had patched together a consensus of support between different Tory associations in the constituency, intense local rivalries meant that this consensus was never translated into a secure electoral base.[26] Nor, in the most self-consciously Orange of constituencies—Loughgall was traditionally regarded as the birthplace of the movement—had Monroe either joined the Order, or been blessed by the local Orange hierarchy. Moreover, he was tied by professional and administrative commitments. His work kept him out of the constituency during crucial periods of the campaign. And, even when he could attend, he had to juggle both official and electoral priorities—for the Solicitor-Generalship provided not only prestige, but also restrictions on what he could offer the voters of North Armagh.[27]

Saunderson, on the other hand, was free from all party and professional commitments. He was both an Orangeman (albeit of recent extraction) and had, on 6 July, been adopted by the County Grand Lodge of Armagh.[28] He clearly did not command unanimous Orange approval: there were regional variations in his support, the Orangemen of Portadown uniting more clearly behind him than those of Lurgan. There were social variations in his support, Orange artisans and craftsmen responding much more enthusiastically to his candidature than the farmers: his sponsor among the Orangemen of North Armagh was an evangelical coach-builder, W. J. Locke. But his strength lay in commanding the support of the chief Orange body of the county; and its disciplinary influence, allied with Saunderson's

[25] The best modern account of the contest is by Frank Thompson. 'The Armagh Elections of 1885–6', in *Seanchas Ardmhacha: Journal of the Armagh Diocesan Historical Society*, 7 (1977), 364–8. See also T. M. Healy, *Letters and Leaders of My Day*, 2 vols. (London, n.d. [1928]), i. 225–6.

[26] Thompson, 'Armagh Elections', 364.

[27] PRONI, Carleton, Atkinson, and Sloan Papers, D.1252/42/3. The correspondence between Monroe and his agent suggests that the former was seeking, at times, to conduct his campaign by proxy.

[28] Revd Thomas Ellis, *The Actions of the Grand Orange Lodge of the County of Armagh (and the reasons thereof) on the 6th of July 1885* (Armagh, 1885).

own political background and skilful handling of the campaign, allowed him to seize the advantage.[29]

Whenever he faced a political challenge—whether in 1882–3 or in 1885—he adopted a populist approach, while his conservatism developed with political security. Throughout the difficult campaign against Monroe, Saunderson presented himself as the radical landowner, the early convert to tenurial reform. His support for the Act of 1870 was repeatedly publicized, a hoary testimony to his paternalist credentials. He cultivated the moribund class of handloom weavers, missing few opportunities to acknowledge the justice of their claims, and the pathos of their condition. He met and mollified weaver deputations; and his electoral address fulfilled earlier promises by referring prominently to the need for government encouragement through interventionist and ameliorative legislation.[30] By contrast, Monroe was portrayed (often by snide allusion) as the archetypal bourgeois: even if he claimed humble origins, he now fraternized only with the well-to-do, and adopted inappropriate airs and graces. In fabricating a radical image for himself, Saunderson created, too, a popular perception of an unsympathetic and brassy opponent.[31] This was all the more persuasive for being repeated so frequently: Saunderson pursued his campaign with a ruthless efficiency, while the mousy and genteel Monroe fussed about his career, and was condemned in his absence.

Saunderson's alternative line of attack lay with the attitude of the Tory government. He was genuinely concerned by its ambiguities: he was intensely distrustful of Randolph Churchill, and angered by the references of John Gorst, the choleric Solicitor-General for England, to 'the reactionary Ulster members'.[32] But, whatever Saunderson's private feelings, it was personally advantageous to highlight the iniquities of an administration to which his opponent belonged. Monroe's office might, given a popular Tory regime, have counted decisively in his favour—but, with a more suspect administration, he was condemned by association. At the very least Monroe could only prove to be an ineffective MP because of the

[29] Thompson, 'Armagh Elections', 365–6.

[30] ESP, T.2996/2B/275: Saunderson to Helena, 18 Aug. 1885.

[31] See e.g. Saunderson's speech of 4 Sept. 1885, reported in *BNL*, 5 Sept. 1885, p. 8 ('He thought if Mr Monroe were there that night he would not believe as apparently he did that only the rif-raf and bobtail of the division supported him [Saunderson]. He did not know what Mr Monroe's test of respectability was . . .').

[32] *BNL*, 30 July 1885, p. 8; ibid., 18 Aug. 1885, p. 8; ESP, T.2996/2B/275: Saunderson to Helena, 18 Aug. 1885.

division of his loyalties between government and constituency. On 30 July Saunderson referred testily to Gorst's repudiation of the Ulster Tories; at Clonmacate and Loughgall, on 17 and 18 August respectively, his criticisms of the government became much more vigorous.[33] He vilified its refusal to enact coercion, its unwillingness to countenance the tough crimes policy associated with the earlier Liberal Lord Lieutenant, Lord Spencer. It was a tool of the Parnellite party, and its dithering was of a piece with its earlier sell-out on parliamentary reform.

His later campaign speeches were more circumspect. This may have been because, with the likelihood of selection and electoral victory, Saunderson's priorities had shifted: from undermining Monroe, he now had to come to terms with the prospect of negotiating with the vile Tory administration. But there were also immediate local worries. The turning-point of the campaign came on 2 September, at a meeting in Lurgan, where—though his criticism continued—Saunderson mellowed perceptibly, and indeed was thrown briefly on to the defensive.[34] For his earlier diatribes had given rise to doubts about his own political credentials, and in the course of his address he had to cope with the suggestion that his abuse of the Tory leadership was merely the gall of a Whig renegade. His next meeting was at Portadown two days later, on 4 September, and he found it expedient to shift from unmitigated criticism to qualified approval of the government—and particularly to commending the integrity of Lord Salisbury, and the high principles of Toryism in the abstract.[35] He did not wholly abandon criticism, yet it had been unsettling to discover that his Whig ancestry remained a cause for Tory suspicion. When he was safely returned for North Armagh, and when Protestant neuroses were heightened by the election of eighty-five Parnellites, he was able to revert successfully to this line of attack. Thus, in condemning the government so bitterly, he had again anticipated the development of loyalist popular feeling; but, in forcing the political pace, he came close to discrediting himself with northern Tories.

In the event, by obscuring his trimming and shifting with the coat of loyalist intransigence, Saunderson overcame his opponent. But the result had been in doubt until a comparatively late stage. Indeed Saunderson, despite otherwise ferocious campaigning, only ventured into Monroe's heartland—Lurgan—on 2 September. Even then he was given an un-

[33] *BNL*, 19 Aug. 1885, p. 8.
[34] Ibid. 3 Sept. 1885, p. 8; ESP, T.2996/2B/276: Saunderson to Helena, 3 Sept. 1885.
[35] *BNL*, 5 Sept. 1885, p. 8.

comfortable reception, though his good humour and an intrinsic element of farce resolved the tension: at the height of the disturbance between the Monroe and Saunderson factions the No. 48 Conservative Flute Band valiantly sought to counter the tumult through a noisy rendition of 'See the Conquering Hero Comes'.[36] By 11 and 12 September the *Belfast News Letter* was reporting that a bevy of local Orange lodges had declared for Saunderson.[37] Two weeks later, on 26 September, Monroe was desperately trying to recapture his flagging Orange support. But, by that time, the widespread expressions of approval for Saunderson, combined with his own revised rhetoric on the government, meant that the Tory managers were at last tempted to intervene.[38] Monroe was demonstrably the weaker candidate, and the Tory party could not afford either to risk the seat, or to threaten a breach with the Orange Order, by maintaining its support for the Solicitor-General. When Lord Arthur Hill wrote to Monroe on 26 September advising him to retire to the mid-Armagh constituency, Saunderson's triumph was practically assured.[39] By the beginning of October Monroe had resigned himself to defeat; on 8 October he confirmed his withdrawal to Atkinson.[40]

For Saunderson it was an immense achievement. At a basic, practical level he was now reasonably assured of a parliamentary platform for his opinions. He had a distinguished Liberal opponent, Thomas Shillington, when the election was held on 30 November—but the real campaign was much less frenetic than the preliminary contest, and Saunderson won with a majority of 1,819 in a poll of a little over 6,500.[41] Of no less significance was the fact that the tournament with Monroe had attracted considerable popular attention, and had provided Saunderson with unprecedented publicity. Formerly his public statements had been briefly paraphrased (major speeches often being rendered down to a few sentences): now he was reported fully in the provincial press. The *Belfast News Letter*, generally orthodox in its Toryism, preserved a strict editorial neutrality during the contest between Saunderson and Monroe, providing verbatim

36 *BNL*, 3 Sept. 1885, p. 6. ESP, T.2996/2B/276: Saunderson to Helena, 3 Sept. 1885.

37 *BNL*, 11 Sept. 1885, p. 6; ibid., 12 Sept. 1885, p. 8.

38 PRONI, Carleton, Atkinson, and Sloan Papers, D.1252/42/3/39: Monroe to Atkinson, 26 Sept. 1885.

39 Ibid., D.1252/42/3/40: Lord Arthur Hill to Monroe, 26 Sept. 1885.

40 Ibid., D.1252/42/3/44: Monroe to Atkinson, 8 Oct. 1885. The correspondence was, in part, published: *BNL*, 12 Oct. 1885, p. 4 (editorial comment) and p. 7 (text). See also PRONI, Carleton, Atkinson, and Sloan Papers, D.1252/42/3/43: Monroe to Atkinson, 3 Oct. 1885.

41 Walker, *Parliamentary Election Results*, 327.

reports of both candidates' speeches. Indeed, the journal hailed Saunderson's triumph with satisfaction, commenting on his speaking ability.[42]

His speeches had been attracting significant editorial attention, even in the influential *Irish Times*, as early as January 1885: but his campaign with Monroe was a turning-point in his relationship with the Irish press. The obscure lieutenant of Rossmore had proved that he was capable of an effective and sustained modern election campaign, and he had proved that he could command the support of the Orange democracy. However suspicious many propertied Tories may have been of his reforming rhetoric, it was becoming clear that Saunderson was articulating the future forms and ideals of loyalism in Ireland.

The form of loyalism was to be a largely Protestant class alliance; the ideal, as sketched by Saunderson, embraced an alliance between both class and religion. To these ends, at least in the early and mid-1880s, he was prepared to compromise both the immediate interests of the landlord class, and the imperatives of his faith. He believed in the rightness of the Church of Ireland, but his perception of the demands of the political situation led him to appeal to Catholics as possible recruits within a loyalist alliance. Speaking at the inaugural meetings of the anti-boycotting associations in Cavan and Monaghan in October 1885, he asked for Catholic members—but his conception of a non-sectarian loyalism had of course long predated these appeals.[43] If, as a last resort, he pandered to Protestant exclusivism, then this was a political expedient, made easy and strategically desirable by the condition of Ulster at the time of the National League. But it was ironic that Saunderson, whose ideal was a cross-sectarian loyalism, should have been one of the chief architects of the primarily Protestant movement which survives today.

Beside the ambiguities of his stand on the religious question, Saunderson's belief in an independent loyalism was more sharply defined. In the Orange campaign of 1882–3 he had fought for an anti-League alliance between farmer and landlord, and between farm labourer and landlord; in 1885–6 he worked to develop the independent political structures which would rest on this electoral alliance. His role in the formation of the Loyal

[42] The satirical Belfast journal, *Nomad's Weekly*, reviewing these events twenty years later, suggested that the published reports of Saunderson's speeches had been falsified. The veteran journalist Steven Heron ('H.S.') wrote that 'the Colonel had only one set speech, which he had committed to heart and rattled off like a phonograph'. Heron, as a *BNL* reporter, was covering the by-election, and was compelled to draft more eloquent and wide-ranging 'speeches' in order to enliven his copy: these he attributed to Saunderson. *Nomad's Weekly*, 5 Nov. 1904.

[43] *BNL*, 9 Oct. 1885, p. 8; ibid., 13 Oct. 1885, p. 7; ibid., 27 Oct. 1885, p. 5.

Irish Union and the Irish Loyal and Patriotic Union has already been noted. But his greatest personal achievement in this field was to promote the emergence of an independent Irish Unionist party in parliament. Within three weeks of his election for North Armagh he was campaigning for the formation of a loyalist party in the House of Lords. At a meeting of the Irish Loyal and Patriotic Union held on 18 December 1885 the proposal for a separate Lords party was received warmly: moreover, Saunderson felt confident that he could carry the leadership claims of his friend and neighbour, Viscount Crichton, now the fifth earl of Erne (he wrote to Helena, high-handedly dismissing the Duke of Abercorn's suitability).[44] Two days earlier Saunderson's political associate, William Johnston, had drafted a resolution for the Grand Orange Lodge of Ireland, calling for the creation of 'an Ulster Party'—and this was approved under Lord Erne's chairmanship and patronage.[45] But the parliamentary Ulster party, if and when it emerged, could only realistically be a Commons body; and Saunderson, who privately hankered after its leadership, had to approach this new organizational task much more obliquely, satisfying a dual commitment to principle and to self.

Privately, and prematurely, he cast himself in the role of spokesman for the Ulster members. But he evidently grasped that the formal recognition of his claims would require greater evidence both of his own indispensability, and of his disdain for advancement. The success of his ambition, indeed of the whole enterprise, depended, too, on the sustained ambivalence of the weak Tory government. If, after the election of December 1885, and after Gladstone's commitment to revision of the Union, the Tory cabinet had immediately come forward with a clear Unionist policy, then the whole campaign for independent action would have been deprived of purpose. Only Randolph Churchill, with his privileged insight into northern politics through Gerald FitzGibbon and the Tories of Howth, grasped the dangers and potential of developments within Ulster: it took more serious loyalist threats and pressure to win the unequivocal allegiance of the rest of the cabinet. And, in the event, the delay between the original initiatives for independence and this evidence of government sympathy was too great to defuse loyalist suspicion.

[44] ESP, T.2996/2B/281: Saunderson to Helena, 17 Dec. 1885.
[45] PRONI, William Johnston Diaries, D.880/2/37: 16 Dec. 1885.

7

Redefining the Bond with British Toryism, 1885–1886

I

In the political vacuum created by the Tory government's vacillation over Ireland, Saunderson promoted the concept of an independent Commons grouping; in the political tumult created by the triumph of Home Rule at the polls, he promoted a much more vigorous loyalism. At the end of December 1885, and in early January 1886, he delivered a series of speeches in Dublin and Ulster in which he warned of the Irish and parliamentary consequences of any Tory alliance with Parnellism. He threatened an Irish Conservative revolt, and alluded heavily to the possibility of military resistance.

In personal terms this initiative had an immediate and satisfactory result for, after a peculiarly belligerent address in his home territory of Belturbet on 28 December, Saunderson won a significant editorial appreciation in the *Irish Times*.[1] The inescapable domination of Parnellism allowed the southern loyalist readers of the *Times* to abandon their party allegiance more readily than in the north, where Home Rule was still only one, albeit worrying, element of a complex party political scene. Saunderson's ideals, which had perturbed some northerners even during his contest with Monroe, were therefore more immediately attractive to Dublin Toryism, and on 30 December he was hailed by its leading organ as an appropriate leader for the new loyalism.

The *Irish Times* editorial was specifically addressed towards a visitor to Dublin, Lord Randolph Churchill.[2] Loyalist perceptions of his influence, combined with his unsympathetic reputation, rendered Churchill an obvious target for pressure. Indeed, by planting himself at Howth, in the home

[1] *Irish Times*, 30 Dec. 1885, p. 2. For the rest of Saunderson's campaign, and its significance, see Alvin Jackson, *The Ulster Party: Irish Unionists in the House of Commons, 1884–1911* (Oxford, 1989), 44–5.

[2] *Irish Times*, 30 Dec. 1885, p. 2: 'these statements [Saunderson's speech] which need no exposition or enforcement may perhaps be commended to the notice of LORD RANDOLPH CHURCHILL.'

of Lord Justice FitzGibbon, Churchill may have been consciously inviting an assault from the various representatives of northern opinion.[3] At any rate, Hugh Holmes, the Attorney-General for Ireland, and a fellow Ulsterman, brought Saunderson to meet the maverick cabinet minister; and it seems that Churchill traded gossip concerning Gladstone's manœuvring and the intentions of the government for an account, provided by Saunderson, of the extent of loyalist grievance. The sources for the interview are irritatingly scanty, but there is reason to believe that Churchill was emollient, offering personal pledges, and possibly indicating the good will of the government. According to Holmes, the 'rough outline of the campaign in Ulster' was drawn up, and this in itself suggests that a rapport between the two men was established.[4]

But the reality of their relationship was more complex. Saunderson had distrusted Churchill since the Maamtrasna debate in June 1885 and, while he was flattered by the minister's apparent confidences and gossip, he never lost his original wariness. For his part, Churchill may have assumed that Saunderson possessed a greater political pre-eminence at this stage than was the case. When Churchill was in Dublin the Conservative press was full of flattering references to the Belturbet speech and to its author, and when he returned to England, his mail contained further allusions to the Ulster leader's 'cleverness'.[5] In any case, whatever Saunderson's reputation, he represented a useful lever on Orangeism at an appropriate political juncture.

Saunderson was no less opportunistic. Himself a pawn in the shifting politics of the Tory leadership, he deployed Churchill within his own, equally complex, strategy. Churchill had effectively courted him as the spokesman for northern loyalism, and this was a gratifying (if premature) recognition of his ascendancy. In agreeing, provisionally, to an Ulster visit (he confirmed his decision on 27 January 1886), Churchill provided Saunderson with some semblance of influence at the highest rank of the party leadership.[6] And, throughout January, he retailed government gossip to his Irish client. Again, these tokens of recognition and confidence

[3] R. F. Foster, *Lord Randolph Churchill: A Political Life* (Oxford, 1981), 247.

[4] A. B. Cooke and John Vincent, 'Select Documents XXVII: Ireland and Party Politics, 1885–7: An Unpublished Conservative Memoir (1)', *IHS*, 16/62 (Sept. 1969), 167.

[5] CC, Randolph Churchill Papers, RCHL/1/11/1235: Lord George Hamilton to Churchill, 2 Jan. 1886. Alluded to in Roy Foster, 'To the Northern Counties Station: Lord Randolph Churchill and the Prelude to the Orange Card', in F. S. L. Lyons and R. A. J. Hawkins (eds.), *Ireland under the Union: Varieties of Tension: Essays in Honour of T. W. Moody* (Oxford, 1980), 272–3, and id., *Churchill*, 253.

[6] ESP, T.2996/1/69: Saunderson to Helena, 27 Jan. 1886.

could be used by Saunderson as evidence of his growing political stature.[7]

Thus, Saunderson's interest in Churchill was intimately linked with his own ambitions; but this also meant that the apparent rapport established in Dublin was not immediately reflected in the Irishman's public statements. Saunderson's short-term political advantage lay in a combination of political crisis and British recognition—but he had only received this last in the form of bland assurances of official good will. These assurances he had to reject (in the interests of loyalist independence), although he simultaneously welcomed all communication with the government since this bolstered his credibility. His contact with Churchill was a useful personal asset, while the latter's soothing tones were of a more doubtful value. Thus Saunderson did not—indeed he could not—abandon his role in the vanguard of loyalist resistance. And, despite this flirtation with Churchill, Saunderson's speeches at Lurgan (6 January 1886), Dublin (8 January), and Cavan (11 January) reiterated his earlier anti-government rhetoric.[8]

Saunderson was now at the forefront of loyalist politics, but as yet he had achieved no substantial recognition of his leadership. After parliament met, on 12 January, he threw himself into the task of organizing an independent loyalist party in the House of Commons. Since Irish Tory MPs would have a unique responsibility in helping to defeat any future Home Rule Bill, their leader—the chairman of their putative party—would exercise considerable influence within parliamentary and Irish politics. It is clear that, while believing sincerely in the desirability of loyalist independence, Saunderson wanted personal control over the determination of its nature and forms. He distrusted the influence of the English leadership, and feared that by surrendering initiative to Anglicized loyalists like Lord Arthur Hill or the Duke of Abercorn, he would be sacrificing effective independence. This is why he promoted the claims of his friend, Lord Erne, to the leadership of the loyalist party in the Lords, and why he sought for himself the leadership of the evolving Commons party.

He faced two main difficulties in achieving these ends. First, he was not the only contender for leadership. Yet, at the same time, he could not advance his own claims directly and obtrusively, since there remained the risk of provoking a reaction. Secondly, his was not the only initiative for independent action. Thus Saunderson had the dual task of fighting both

[7] For Churchill's volubility see e.g. ESP, T.2996/1/62: Saunderson to Helena, n.d. [17 Jan. 1886].

[8] Jackson, *Ulster Party*, 44–5.

for himself and for his own conception of the party. Moreover, he had to fight off all his rivals without irretrievably alienating them. That he was ultimately successful in establishing his claim was a tribute to his tactical agility, but his plans for wholehearted independence were, at least in the short term, hopelessly compromised. By January 1886 Saunderson had clearly emerged as leader: it remained to be seen what he was leader of.

He pursued his loyalist programme with zeal, translating the hazy discussions over Christmas and the New Year into organizational reality by the end of January. He spent 13 January in negotiation with other representatives of Tory Ulster, and it was soon clear that there was (a by no means unqualified) approval for the organization of a distinct grouping.[9] Doubts seem to have emerged from those who feared the consequences of even this modest rejection of Tory discipline. But there were also some MPs who may have feared a surrender of initiative to one who, whatever the actual ambiguities of his thought, had come to prominence through the extremities of the Orange Order. These potential waverers were led by R. U. Penrose-Fitzgerald and Edward King-Harman, working through Lord Claud Hamilton, and the climax of their bid to outflank Saunderson came in the Carlton Club, on 19 January.[10] Saunderson sketched out an uncompromising, independent stand: he was polite about Salisbury, by no means irremediably rude about the cabinet, but wholly unwavering in his conception of complete parliamentary independence. His opponents wanted a more qualified autonomy, and probably also hoped for freedom from Saunderson's control. The vehicle for their plans was a party which contained not only Ulster Tories but also any English member who might sympathize with their case.[11]

In the event this bid to dilute Saunderson's Orange orthodoxy came to nothing—for the Carlton meeting of 19 January seems to have brought no agreement for future action. Saunderson had actively campaigned against the moderates' initiative—and it was he who benefited most from its collapse. Yet he had been careful to urge his policies, and not himself—with the result that after the Carlton débâcle he was able to establish both his own leadership and a form of unity within the new party. The original, tentative assembly of the Ulster Tories had been on 14 January: Saunderson, with ostentatious self-denial, moved William Johnston to the chair

[9] ESP, T.2996/1/59: Saunderson to Helena, n.d. [13 Jan. 1886]; Reginald Lucas, *Colonel Saunderson MP: A Memoir* (London, 1908), 92.

[10] ESP, T.2996/1/61: Saunderson to Helena, 15 Jan. 1886; E.S.P., T.2996/1/63: Saunderson to Helena, 17 Jan. 1886; Lucas, *Saunderson*, 92–3.

[11] Lucas, *Saunderson*, 92–3.

'in order to show', as he remarked to Helena, somewhat disingenuously, 'that I had no personal motive in the matter'.[12] In fact the nomination of Johnston, like a similar scheme to nominate Lord Arthur Hill, was probably a feint. Johnston was both a close political associate of Saunderson, and yet—whatever his abilities—totally out of place in the House of Commons: he was quite unsuited for the leadership Saunderson slyly pushed on to him. Saunderson's idea to move Arthur Hill into the chair of the Ulster party was no less tactical.[13] Hill, as a party whip, could scarcely assume the leadership of a dissident element within Toryism, for such a course would have cut him off irretrievably from the party leadership. On the other hand, declining the leadership would have damaged Hill in the eyes of those Ulster members whom he normally sought to influence. Either course of action would have weakened Hill's standing within British and Irish politics, and this could have only been to Saunderson's benefit. In fact, it seems probable that Hill stayed away from the meeting of 14 January, effectively forcing on Saunderson the alternative option of playing Johnston.

Johnston's reign was predictably short-lived. The second meeting of the parliamentary Ulster party was held on 20 January, and Johnston stood down, proposing that Saunderson should take his place.[14] The chairmanship of the embryonic party at this time may have been held in weekly rotation—so that Johnston possibly considered that he was merely repaying a courtesy extended originally by his friend. But, as Saunderson had immodestly foreseen, permanent authority within the party would 'belong by unquestioned right to the best and the wisest'—and he seems to have assumed that this defined his own claim on the chair.[15] He declined any permanent right of leadership; but, once elected, he displayed rather less self-denial, and held on to office until his death in 1906. Towards the end he was neither the 'best' nor the 'wisest', judged by any standard, and others, younger and more able, came to challenge his authority. But in January 1886, on the basis of his work in Ireland, Edward Saunderson seemed an appropriate leader for northern loyalism. And it was widely expected that the ruthlessness and energy which he had hitherto displayed would readily translate into parliamentary influence.

[12] ESP, T.2996/1/59: Saunderson to Helena, n.d. [13 Jan. 1886]; PRONI, William Johnston Diaries, D.880/2/38: 14 Jan. 1886. Lucas, *Saunderson*, 92.

[13] Lucas, *Saunderson*, 92.

[14] PRONI, WIlliam Johnston Diaries, D.880/2/38: 20 Jan. 1886.

[15] ESP, T.2996/1/59: Saunderson to Helena, n.d. [13 Jan. 1886]; Lucas, *Saunderson*, 92.

II

Contrary to his historical reputation, Saunderson did indeed achieve a form of parliamentary influence, although this was less secure than that of, say, John Redmond or Tim Healy. Both these men appear to have been more able than Saunderson: both were prepared to debate the technicalities of legislation, and both were conspicuously successful as parliamentary orators.[16] Redmond and Healy could each be unsparing in their preparation of speeches, and in their deployment of legal acumen. Neither of them was free from public political vices: Healy, in particular, created enemies through his elaborate ironies, and through the sectarian lapses into which he was tempted by his ardent faith. Saunderson also came to play a sectarian political role, but his parliamentary virtues and abilities were of a different order to those of the Nationalists. In later years he became lazy: he shunned the labour of poring over a Bill—labour which allowed his opponents and some of those within his own party (like Carson) to contribute more tellingly to debate. Sir Richard Temple spotted this aversion to detail: 'when it comes to labouring in the trough of the sea of the Committee Stage, then he [Saunderson] is no longer able to take an oar, and is almost like an Othello whose occupation is gone.'[17] His appeal was certainly not to the intellect, for his speeches were firmly grounded in emotion. Yet, though he could be sometimes superficial, he was far from ineffective, for what he was presenting to the House was essentially the material of a skilled platform speaker; and what was applauded among the electors of Ireland and, later, of England, was equally appreciated by many backbenchers. This success, combined with his undoubted influence over Irish loyalism, lent him an impact at ministerial level which his failings could not undermine.

His first and greatest ministerial conquest was Lord Randolph; and, through Churchill and his acolyte, Sir Michael Hicks-Beach, Saunderson received an insight into the ways of the Conservative leadership. Churchill, imitated now by Hicks-Beach, continued to flatter him with confidences, so that Saunderson began to feel that he had at last attained rank

[16] Like Saunderson's, Parnell's political début and early parliamentary efforts were, of course, very weak: R. Barry O'Brien, *The Life of Charles Stewart Parnell*, 2 vols. (London, 1898), i. 74.

[17] Edward Marjoribanks and Ian Colvin, *The Life of Lord Carson*, 3 vols. (London, 1932–6), i. 160. Sir Richard Temple, *Letters and Character Sketches from the House of Commons: Home Rule and other Matters in 1886–7* (London, 1912), 161.

within the battalions of senior politicians.[18] If he formally disclaimed any idea that he had been won over ('I don't feel in the least elated, but take it as it comes'), the tone of his letters belied his apparent equanimity: he was indeed elated by celebrity, and was confident about his influence over ministers.[19] In reality Saunderson's political significance lay somewhere between this self-assessment and the equally facile dismissal of his pretensions by some subsequent commentators. He was too lightweight to be recruited permanently to the inner sanctum of decision-making, yet he was dangerously capable of making difficulties for the Conservative party, as the Monroe episode clearly proved. He was received, therefore, with ambivalence: he was treated cautiously, and he was patronized, but he was also occasionally allowed an influence over policy.

The crisis precipitated by the Hawarden Kite of December 1885—by the publication of Gladstone's likely acceptance of Home Rule—undoubtedly enhanced Saunderson's value for British Conservatives, just as loyalism as a whole came to exercise more influence within Britain. In a sense Saunderson came to fill the vacuum in the party's Irish policy created by the failure of more consensual figures (such as Lord Carnarvon). And, in addition to his effective speechifying, there was the blunt reality that Saunderson had influence over perhaps twenty-six votes in the House of Commons, allied to a larger lobby in the House of Lords. Indeed there is some circumstantial evidence to suggest that Churchill and Hicks-Beach perceived Saunderson's value largely in terms of his influence over the other Irish loyalist representatives. On 26 January 1886 they begged him to use his party to avoid a premature division on the Royal Address: Saunderson refused. More broadly, Saunderson was a useful, because relatively accessible, intermediary with Orange opinion: other Orange MPs, like William Johnston, or local leaders, like R. R. Kane, were decidedly more alien and alarming (as early as 1880 Churchill had 'feared Kane').[20]

In January 1886 Saunderson benefited from his ministerial links through having a privileged audience for his coercionist demands, while possessing, in Churchill, a useful debating ally. On 21 January he had to be defended from Tim Healy, who had carefully dissected and refuted a blustering attack: Churchill intervened to rescue his associate, praising his

[18] ESP, T.2996/1/62: Saunderson to Helena, n.d. [17 Jan. 1886]; ESP, T.2996/1/66: Saunderson to Helena, 23 Jan. 1886.

[19] ESP, T.2996/1/62: Saunderson to Helena, n.d. [17 Jan. 1886]; ESP, T.2996/1/66: Saunderson to Helena, 23 Jan. 1886.

[20] ESP, T.2996/1/68: Saunderson to Helena, 26 Jan. 1886; Lucas, *Saunderson*, 96; R. F. Foster, *Paddy and Mr Punch: Connections in Irish and English History* (London, 1993), 249–50.

'fire' and 'true eloquence'.[21] Churchill's greatest display of sympathy came on 27 January. Sidling up to Saunderson at the Carlton, he gave a firmer and more generous commitment to speak in Ulster than had been offered at Howth: 'Churchill came to us today', Saunderson reported drily to Helena, 'and placed himself at my disposal for a meeting in Ulster whenever I thought it necessary to hold one.'[22]

Saunderson was thus one of the prime movers behind Randolph Churchill's famous visit to Belfast on 22 February 1886: at any rate he served as the medium of communication between Churchill and the Orange hierarchy in Ulster. He was a little captivated by Churchill: indeed it may well have been that Churchill genuinely liked Saunderson, for the former was characterized as much by his mercurial affections as by his ambition.[23] Yet Saunderson ultimately maintained his distance, even when Churchill was courting Irish loyalism most intensely in January and February 1886. He could sketch an affectionate portrait of Churchill dozing in the Carlton; but, whenever he ventured a personal judgement, it was at best non-committal, and more often frankly distrustful. He shared the platform with Churchill at the Ulster Hall, Belfast, on 22 February, yet he played a curiously minor role in the proceedings. He had the task of seconding a subsidiary resolution, and delivered a short address, sandwiched in the agenda between a comparatively insignificant clergyman (Robert Hannay, Vicar of Belfast) and the ill-fated member for East Belfast, Edward De Cobain.[24] Perhaps this obscure position was a calculated snub perpetrated by the leaders of Belfast Toryism. If so, it was a maladroit display of pique, which might easily have rebounded on its perpetrators. It seems more likely that Saunderson had his own reasons for seeking to bury himself in the proceedings.

He was Churchill's Ulster ally—and, with the latter's co-operation, could easily have turned the Belfast visit into a triumph for himself, as the prospective leader of Irish Unionism, no less than for the prospective leader of British Toryism. He chose not to, and this self-denial reflected the personal distrust and strategic caution evident in his letters home. He had criticized Churchill since his own campaign against Monroe in the previous autumn, and he bluntly expressed his distrust to Churchill's face when the latter visited Howth at the end of December 1885. Churchill's overtures during January may have begun to heal this breach, but they

21 *Hansard*, ser. 3, ccciii. 173 (21 Jan. 1886).
22 ESP, T.2996/1/69: Saunderson to Helena, 27 Jan. 1886.
23 Lucas, *Saunderson*, 95.
24 *BNL*, 23 Feb. 1886, p. 7.

were certainly not sufficient to win any unqualified expression of loyalty, either in public or in private, from the suspicious Irishman. In fact, Saunderson's attitude sprang from a mixture of personal and political considerations. As has been argued, he could not allow the political separation between Irish loyalism and British Toryism to be undermined: it was what he had fought for, and his fame and pre-eminence rested on the achievement of independence. Moreover, his criticism of the Tory leadership had been given credibility by the sustained ambivalence of the latter—so that his own success, ironically, was bound up with British treachery. Saunderson gladly accepted expressions of sympathy from those of relatively pristine loyalist virtue, like Salisbury; but that Randolph Churchill should begin to make direct appeals to mass opinion in Ulster must have been extremely worrying. If loyalism was to be a credible force within British politics, then it could not simultaneously be a tool of Churchill's ambition.

Yet Churchill had been the first to acknowledge Saunderson's leadership, and he had been the first to offer to come to loyalist Ireland. Saunderson could scarcely rebut these overtures, but he certainly did seek to isolate himself from any subsequent and potentially damaging developments. Moreover, Saunderson was wary at a purely personal level: where Churchill's patronage might have flattered a younger, more ambitious, and more malleable figure, Saunderson's personality was of a different and grittier texture. He saw himself as the leader of a 'fourth' parliamentary party, and he referred pompously to the political stature which he presumed this title granted him.[25] Though his speeches were sometimes weak in content, he was hailed by the partisan press in both London and Ireland. If there was an element of conventionality and politeness in the congratulations offered by fellow MPs, they nevertheless convinced Saunderson, who reported back to Helena each of his parliamentary triumphs.[26] Saunderson was defensive and proud about his position: he would not be patronized by Churchill (Churchill could be mildly condescending towards his putative ally); and he would not be the tool, at any rate consciously, of British political expedient. 'I don't intend acting as a

[25] ESP, T.2996/1/65: Saunderson to Helena, 22 Jan. 1886 ('it was thought best that I should answer him as the leader of the Party'); ESP, T.2996/1/66: Saunderson to Helena, 23 Jan. 1886 (where he gives Hicks-Beach short shrift); ESP, T.2996/1/69: Saunderson to Helena, 27 Jan. 1886 ('as virtual leader of the party I am tied by the leg').

[26] ESP, T.2996/1/65: Saunderson to Helena, 22 Jan. 1886 ('I was much congratulated and think I have secured the ear of the House'); ESP, T.2996/1/67: Saunderson to Helena, 23 Jan. 1886 ('I am still receiving congratulations from both sides of the House').

political catspaw to any man', he had once said to Helena, and he conveyed this recalcitrance to Churchill with grim directness.[27]

The subsequent development of their relationship merely confirmed its original lack of substance. Neither Saunderson nor any other Irish Unionist pursued Churchill 'indefatigably', though Saunderson's tone was perceptibly frostier than that of Churchill's other Irish loyalist correspondents.[28] Where Rossmore and the Revd R. R. Kane were conventionally obsequious or laudatory, Saunderson, like Lord Deramore, addressed Churchill on terms of presumed equality.[29] Saunderson's pretensions have already been noted: Deramore claimed seniority within the party because of his long service—he had entered the Commons under Peel in 1844, and had served as a whip during the 'Who? Who?' ministry of 1852. Saunderson was not prepared to offer substantial concessions to Churchill—whether before or after the Belfast visit—and accordingly he demanded little from him. When he ran an independent loyalist for the North Belfast constituency in June 1886, Saunderson did indeed submit his case to Churchill, and bowed to the latter's advice (and to political reality) by withdrawing his nominee, Somerset Maxwell.[30] His only other petition to Churchill came in August, when he urged the new Chancellor of the Exchequer to help defuse the tensions within riot-torn Belfast:

> I know and all Ulster knows the deep interest you feel in the interests [sic] of Irish loyalists in general and Belfast in particular, so we trust you will do all you can to assist a state of things which is sowing seeds of hatred in the minds of a section of the people it will take years of exertion to eradicate.[31]

The denouement of their brief relationship came in September 1886, when Churchill, sensitive to all parliamentary nuances, attempted to chain Saunderson to his own shifting recognition of advantage: his treatment of Saunderson clearly suggested opportunism and exploitation. On 2 September Churchill advised Saunderson to broach the alleged connection between Parnell and Fenian conspiracy in an amendment to the Loyal Address. Saunderson accepted this advice, approaching the task with anxiety, as he confessed to Helena shortly before his performance: 'I wish

27 ESP, T.2996/2B/273: Saunderson to Helena, 14 Aug. 1885.

28 Foster, *Churchill*, 257.

29 CC, Randolph Churchill Papers, RCHL 1/14/1648: Deramore to Churchill, 9 Aug. 1886; RCHL 1/13/1572: Kane to Churchill, 23 July 1886; RCHL 1/12/1396: Kane to Churchill, 27 Feb. 1886; RCHL 1/12/1393: Rossmore to Churchill, 25 Feb. 1886.

30 CC, Randolph Churchill Papers, RCHL 1/13/1549: Saunderson to Churchill, 25 June 1886; ESP, T.2996/3/19: Saunderson to Churchill, 28 June 1886 (copy).

31 CC, Randolph Churchill Papers, RCHL 1/14/1653: Saunderson to Churchill, 10 Aug. 1886.

you were here. In an hour's time I shall be engaged in making what will undoubtedly [be] the most desperate speech which I have ever attempted.'[32] Immediately after this was written, Churchill, influenced by his perception of Parnell's tone, asked Saunderson to abandon his plan to speak. In expecting Saunderson to follow his own volte-face, Churchill was threatening to humiliate his Ulster colleague. And the affront was compounded when, his advice being declined, Churchill exploded in rage (thereby anticipating a similarly brutish, though more notorious, outburst before Hicks-Beach).[33] Relations were superficially healed when 'Randolph made it up' on 21 September, but there seem to have been no subsequent dealings of any significance between the two men.[34] When Churchill left the Exchequer and the government on 22 December 1886, Saunderson sent a polite but ultimately non-committal letter, thanking him for his work for Irish loyalism while reserving judgement on the merits of his precipitate resignation.[35]

By the end of January 1887 the relationship between patron and client had materially altered. With criticism of his resignation mounting, Churchill had to keep open as many opportunities as possible, and this implied a fuller *rapprochement* with Saunderson. On 26 January the Irishman found Churchill 'sweet to a degree'; at the latter's special request Saunderson handed over his Commons seat, choosing himself to sit immediately behind the ex-Chancellor.[36] On 4 February, shortly before his trip to North Africa (which took many less intimate contemporaries by surprise), Churchill offered Saunderson 'a tender farewell'.[37] But Saunderson had no need of an ex-minister, who was increasingly isolated, and for whom he had never felt any unqualified affection. There were now other, more propitious, openings for the advancement of loyalism, and gradually and inexorably the two men fell out of contact. The letters to Helena contain a description of one chance meeting on the train from Cowes in August 1887; but thereafter they offer only silence—even at Churchill's premature death in January 1895.[38]

At the end their relationship had been deprived of purpose. Saunderson had foreseen this, but he had wholly miscalculated the circumstances of the

[32] ESP, T.2996/1/104: Saunderson to Helena, 2 Sept. 1886.
[33] ESP, T.2996/1/105: Saunderson to Helena, 4 Sept. 1886.
[34] ESP, T.2996/1/115: Saunderson to Helena, 21 Sept. 1886.
[35] ESP, T.2996/3/20: Saunderson to Churchill, 12 Jan. 1887 (copy).
[36] ESP, T.2996/1/119: Saunderson to Helena, 26 Jan. 1887.
[37] Foster, *Churchill*, 329; ESP, T.2996/1/124: Saunderson to Helena, 4 Feb. 1887.
[38] ESP, T.2996/1/138: Saunderson to Helena, 8 Aug. 1887. Saunderson's valedictory assessment was 'He [Churchill] is certainly a "rum un".'

disruption. Where he had imagined that conflicting ministerial and loyalist commitments would lose Churchill to cabinet solidarity, the reverse was true. Saunderson's ambiguous conception of loyalist independence demanded that his Ulster party should be in contact with the Tory front bench, while stopping short of integration or intimacy. Churchill the loyal minister, or Churchill the rebel escapee, embodied too decisive an attitude towards the party for Saunderson's local purposes. As Tory rule strengthened, there was less to be gained from claiming independence, since the bargaining position of the Ulster party was proportionately weaker. But this was certainly not the case in 1886, and Saunderson was suspicious of Churchill's good will, seeing him as an unhelpful ministerial influence. In the event Saunderson was right to be wary of Churchill's patronage, but for quite the wrong reasons.

The crystallization of Tory policy after 1886 along the lines of loyalist orthodoxy (support for coercion, unqualified Unionism, the glorification of Ulster) meant that Saunderson had an alternative ministerial audience beyond that represented by Churchill and his cronies. On 19 January 1886 he helped to introduce a loyalist deputation waiting on Salisbury, and petitioning his support for coercion.[39] This was judged to have gone well, and it is probable that Saunderson expressed his relative satisfaction to Churchill who, in turn, conveyed it to the Prime Minister: 'the Ulster MPs etc', Churchill reported, 'left you greatly impressed by your words.'[40] Salisbury had been venerated by Ulster Tories from the time of their disillusionment with Northcote; and even Saunderson, who had been one of the most determined critics of Salisbury's first government, generally excluded him from his otherwise expansive vituperation. Though there was little, if any, direct contact between the Tory leader and Saunderson through the remainder of 1886, Salisbury consolidated his hold on Orange affections by a series of uncompromising commitments to Ulster Unionist militancy. In the early years of his second government Unionism was comparatively weak, threatened by personal and factional defections. Saunderson as a guardian of loyalist piety was well worth cultivating, where, against a more secure party background, he might have been dismissed with alacrity.

Saunderson and his nominal leader met several times in the early months of 1887: and it seems clear that he enjoyed relatively unrestricted access to the mythically reclusive Salisbury at this time. W. R. Young, an

[39] *BNL*, 20 Jan. 1886, p. 5; ESP, T.2996/1/64: Saunderson to Helena, 19 Jan. 1886.

[40] CC, Randolph Churchill Papers, RCHL A/11/1307B: Churchill to Salisbury, 20 Jan. 1886 (printed copy).

acquaintance of Saunderson, and a leading force behind the Ulster Loyalist Union, recorded that:

[Saunderson's] trenchant attacks on the Nationalists and piquant denunciations of Gladstone's policy brought him under Lord Salisbury's notice. His advice was eagerly sought by Lord Salisbury on all questions of Irish administration...[41]

He saw the Prime Minister almost whenever he wanted, and he felt free to correspond on a wide range of concerns—from problems of policy through to the financial plight of friends like Rossmore. Twenty-seven letters from Saunderson to Salisbury survive, the overwhelming majority written between 1887 and 1895. This distribution, confirmed by references within his own papers, suggests that Saunderson's influence over the Prime Minister may have declined as Unionism gained in strength.[42] But then his own position within Irish Unionism was also beginning to decline from its peak in the late 1880s and early 1890s. In any case, Salisbury, paternal and emollient, retained the affections of Saunderson until both had slipped from political pre-eminence.

Other, more ephemeral, ministerial relationships developed through 1886. Saunderson's early dalliance with Dublin Toryism had brought him into contact with the unctuous Edward Gibson, who had sprung into national politics with the help of a firm electoral base in Trinity, and with the patronage of Disraeli and Northcote.[43] This contact was strengthened once Saunderson was returned to the House of Commons. Gibson, elevated to the peerage as Lord Ashbourne, was Lord Chancellor of Ireland in Salisbury's first government and, as an Irish Tory and a cabinet minister, he was a natural object of loyalist attention. Saunderson had at least one 'long talk' with Ashbourne in January 1886, lobbying him in favour of coercion; but, while the minister was slickly avuncular, he offered much less by way of commitment than Randolph Churchill.[44] Their next re-

[41] PRONI, W. R. Young Papers, D.3027/7/8–11: MS of 'Recollections of Seventy-Five Years in Ulster' (Nov. 1931), fo. 138. See also e.g. ESP, T.2996/1/130: Saunderson to Helena, 13 Feb. 1887 (where he decides to see Salisbury); ESP, T.2996/1/135: Saunderson to Helena, 18 Feb. 1887 (when the interview is granted); ESP, T.2996/1/136: Saunderson to Helena, 19 Feb. 1887 (the day of the interview). See also HH, Salisbury Papers, E/Saunderson/4: Saunderson to Salisbury, 6 Mar. 1887.

[42] The Saunderson letters are classified at Hatfield as: Salisbury Papers, E/Saunderson/1–27; Salisbury Papers, E/Saunderson/6: Saunderson to Salisbury, 31 Aug. 1887. A cache of letters from Salisbury to Saunderson, some of which were used in Lucas's biography of 1908, have recently come to light at Newbury, in the home of Saunderson's grandson. See also Temple, *Letters and Character Sketches*, 160

[43] A. B. Cooke and A. P. W. Malcomson, *The Ashbourne Papers, 1869–1913: A Calendar of the Papers of Edward Gibson, First Lord Ashbourne* (Belfast, 1974), pp. xii–xiv.

[44] ESP, T.2996/1/62: Saunderson to Helena, n.d. [17 Jan. 1886].

corded meeting was during the Easter recess of 1886. At a time when, it would seem, other ministers and front-benchers had suspended all political activity, Ashbourne arranged a dinner-party for Lord Halsbury, the ex-Lord Chancellor, Sir Michael Hicks-Beach, and Saunderson, held in his retreat at Boulogne, the Château de la Cocherie.[45] As usual, Saunderson offers scanty information concerning this intriguing gathering—but the conversation must have returned to the parliamentary opportunities and strategies presented and suggested by the forthcoming Home Rule Bill. At any rate, the Boulogne dinner-party is a good illustration of an important, and developing, social dimension to Saunderson's political achievement. If Ulster Unionism was being glorified in Tory rhetoric after January 1886, then the Ulster Unionist leaders enjoyed a reflected celebrity; and Ashbourne was only one of a growing number of hosts who waited upon the witty and gallant member for North Armagh.

Ashbourne, like Randolph Churchill, was partly a product of the period of Tory opposition between 1880 and 1885. In terms of national prominence he had fatally impaired his opportunities for advancement by taking on the Irish Lord Chancellorship in June 1885 (even though his position remained comparatively strong as a useful bulwark against Lord Randolph).[46] Hugh Holmes noted that Ashbourne was gradually retiring from matters of broad concern into the petty details of office—and by the end of the century the Lord Chancellor had become a byword for genial jobbery and nepotism.[47] At any rate, Saunderson, like many Unionist contemporaries, came to dislike him—and, as Ashbourne was steadily marginalized within cabinet politics, so Saunderson's political connection with him strained and broke. At the beginning of 1886 he had been worth cultivating as a lever on cabinet opinion, but by early 1887 Saunderson had established closer contact with Salisbury, and Ashbourne was accordingly ditched. In February 1887 the loyalist leader denounced Ashbourne before a meeting of the Commons parliamentary party as insufficiently partisan. The dinner guest of April 1886 was now opining that 'if Ashbourne be discredited, we may succeed in doing something'.[48]

[45] ESP, T.2996/1/75: Saunderson to Helena, 26 Apr. 1886. *Pace* A.B. Cooke and John Vincent, *The Governing Passion: Cabinet Government and Party Politics in Britain, 1885–6* (Brighton, 1974), 408–9.

[46] Cooke and Malcomson, *The Ashbourne Papers*, p. xv.

[47] Cooke and Vincent, 'An Unpublished Conservative Memoir', 168; Cooke and Malcomson, *The Ashbourne Papers*, p. xviii.

[48] ESP, T.2996/1/137: Saunderson to Helena, 21 Feb. 1887.

III

Establishing links with individual ministers was only part of a larger scheme of proselytism. Through 1886 and 1887 Saunderson established the broad outlines of his future political activity, veering away from the goals and the emphases of his earlier work. He now possessed a platform at Westminster, where formerly his political activity had had a purely local foundation. And, in the early years of the constitutional debate, he fully exploited his parliamentary opportunities, delivering substantial speeches in defence of the Union. A favourite early technique was the compilation of a series of quotations from the wilder statements of the Nationalist MPs. These would be strung together into an aggressive denunciation of the Parnellite record, whenever the opportunity arose (such as during debate on the first reading of the Home Rule Bill): as Sir Richard Temple observed, 'he is evidently always fortified with a stock of pointed extracts from their [Parnellite] speeches, from which he draws his shafts like arrows from a quiver'.[49] Quotations from Gladstone's speeches were similarly favoured by Saunderson, both in the House of Commons, and in Ireland. Carlo Pellegrini's *Vanity Fair* caricature of Saunderson dates from February 1887, and portrays the Orangeman in a characteristically truculent pose: in his right hand he clutches a scrap of paper—his list of Parnellite quotations, ready for impromptu delivery.[50]

Favourite quotations were repeated time and again before widely divergent audiences, and this reflected a more general congruity between Saunderson's British and Irish statements, and between his parliamentary and constituency speeches. Parnellite MPs had commitments to an agonizingly wide political constituency—from staid Westminster through the inner city of Dublin to the suburbs of Boston—and this produced (as Saunderson never ceased to point out) considerable variations in tone and commitment. Within the context of the House of Commons, at any rate before Gladstone's declaration of support, Nationalist interest lay in presenting a passionate but reasoned statement of their faith. But, so long as a Home Rule Bill threatened, Saunderson and many of his colleagues perceived a quite different political need. This was obliquely voiced by Saunderson during Randolph Churchill's Ulster Hall meeting in February 1886:

He found that when speaking to a mixed audience of Conservatives, Liberals and

[49] *Hansard*, ser. 3, ccciv. 1381 (12 Apr. 1886); Temple, *Letters and Character Sketches*, 161.
[50] *Vanity Fair*, 26 Feb. 1887.

radicals, there was nothing moved them so much in favour of the Irish Loyalists as to be told that the Ulstermen were ready to fight in the maintenance of the Union, and he intended to announce that at every meeting he would attend in the future, and to repeat it again and again both inside and outside the House of Commons.[51]

Saunderson and his Unionist colleagues may genuinely have believed that Home Rule would promote civil war—and have felt an obligation to warn the House of Commons; but the distinction between statesmanlike foreboding and fatuous belligerence (or, indeed, criminal incitement) was often barely perceptible. And the political reality was that the interests of loyalism lay in exploiting this ambiguity, both in the Commons and in Ireland. In Protestant Ireland loyalists maintained their command by articulating and directing the anger of their supporters, while in the House of Commons their gloomy forecasts could also serve as threats. Indeed, it might further be suggested that the importance of sustaining this ambiguity far outweighed the political desirability of actual violence—and that the interests of the loyalist leaders lay in implying a threat, rather than in realizing it. Real violence suggested too many local and national dangers to be politically useful.

Saunderson's interest in the possibilities of northern anarchy was thus highly constricted and highly tactical. He had been in or near the vanguard of Orange resistance since the Rosslea incident, and he had often alluded to the prospect of future military action. But he shrank from the blood-curdling threats of Rossmore and Johnston: where Johnston's threats were wild and immediate, Saunderson's violence was a vague and future phenomenon, qualified by pleas for immediate restraint. At Rosslea he had acted to avoid confrontation, where Rossmore had blithely risked a riot; and in 1886 he was similarly ambiguous. On 29 January, at Chester, it was the British people who, according to Saunderson, 'could finally settle this [Home Rule] question'—and not Ulster loyalist violence. At Lord Randolph Churchill's Belfast meeting he was a little more forthcoming, but still impenetrably vague: 'By that demonstration they meant to show Lord R. Churchill they were prepared to come forward and follow the example set down by their fathers and the deeds which they commemorated every year.'[52] The allusion to 1690, and to Orange resistance, was unmistakable—but the force of the statement lay in its emphasis on the need for determination and show. It was the threat of violence—not, significantly, the reality—which had to be conveyed to a British audience. And he shuffled further from an outright commitment by prefacing his already

[51] *BNL*, 23 Feb. 1886, p. 7.
[52] Ibid.; *Irish Times*, 30 Jan. 1886, p. 6 (Chester).

qualified comments with a deprecation of bloodshed: 'He did not wish to enter into any untoward conflict. Enough blood had been shed in Ireland, and enough sorrow and misery caused, and they did not mean to add further to the sorrow which already existed...'[53]

In May 1886, speaking during the second reading of the Government of Ireland Bill, Saunderson clung to his ambiguities, rejecting a rising 'in arms' against any Home Rule executive—while pledging Ulster's refusal to acknowledge such a regime.[54] How in practice this refusal would be registered was not explained. However, even when Ulster belligerence was at its most intense—immediately before the rejection of the Home Rule Bill—Saunderson remained comparatively reserved. He was not at the public forefront of loyalist provocation: William Johnston still claimed this distinction, through calls to arms at Dungannon, the Maze, and Belfast in April and May 1886.[55] Saunderson condoned this talk of resistance, while probably sharing the belief of other senior Orangemen that Johnston had spoken out of turn (Johnston recorded that at a Grand Orange Committee meeting 'some objection was taken to my Dungannon speech').[56] Saunderson would not risk a public dispute on the main issue; but he did distance himself from the reality of violence by admitting that the preparations for resistance were less well advanced than had been reported in the press.[57] On 17 June 1886, after the defeat of the Home Rule Bill, Saunderson chaired what Johnston called an 'Ulster Armament Committee meeting'; but it is not clear whether this was anything other than a talking-shop, or whether its ominous title reflected Johnston's fantasies more than the immediate threat of bloodshed.[58] Either way the 'Ulster Armament Committee' seems to have achieved nothing beyond the sublimation of Orange anger.

Threats of violence were useful to loyalism—but the reality of violence was not necessarily high among Saunderson's own priorities at this time. In rhetorical terms Saunderson had aimed principally at denigrating Parnell and his associates; in terms of broader strategy, he aimed to carry the loyalist campaign into England. Hitherto his public political activity had been based solely in Ireland; but, now that he had been confirmed as

[53] *BNL*, 23 Feb. 1886, p. 7.

[54] *Hansard*, ser. 3, cccv. 1771 (21 May 1886).

[55] D. C. Savage, 'The Origins of the Ulster Unionist Party, 1885–6', *IHS*, 12/47 (Mar. 1961), 202; James Loughlin, *Gladstone, Home Rule and the Ulster Question, 1882–1893* (Dublin, 1986), 168–70.

[56] PRONI, William Johnston Diaries, D.880/2/38: 11 May 1886.

[57] *Irish Times*, 3 June 1886. Jackson, *Ulster Party*, 124–5; Loughlin, *Gladstone*, 170.

[58] PRONI, William Johnston Diaries, D.880/2/38: 17 June 1886.

the leading Irish Unionist, the limited *rapprochement* between Toryism and Ulster loyalists presented a more fertile political opening. Once Salisbury had tied Toryism to coercion, and had begun to glorify 'Ulster' (as he did at the Crystal Palace on 3 March 1886), it was inevitable that English electoral opportunities and duties would be thrust upon the more accessible loyalist leaders. As an able and (on the whole) a good-humoured speaker, Saunderson found himself closely involved with the English presentation of the Ulster Unionist case; and this, in turn, meant a withdrawal from local politics. Between 1882 and 1885 he had been intimately involved with each stage of loyalist development; thereafter his grasp on the minutiae of loyalist politics slackened. He was flattered by the applause of a parliamentary audience and by British celebrity, and the plainer and more compromising obligations of local leadership became progressively uncongenial.

The battle for the Union meant, in the short term, the electoral defeat of Gladstonian Liberalism, and Saunderson devoted himself to this, and to the concomitant task of encouraging Liberal Unionism through the early months of 1886. He was a prime mover behind several significant demonstrations of cross-party Unionism, and he spoke at a series of meetings in important British cities. Working with the Irish Loyal and Patriotic Union, he helped to promote an important Unionist gathering at Chester on 29 January 1886, at which Tories, Whigs, and Radicals joined in condemning Home Rule. He had liaised with the ex-Gladstonian Duke of Westminster in order to 'find out how far the Whigs will go with us': the result had been a firm and united Unionist platform, and a meeting which was deemed 'a great success'.[59] Saunderson continued to cultivate Whig opinion through the spring and summer of 1886, organizing a second display of Unionist solidarity at the Haymarket Theatre, London, on 14 April.[60] There were lesser demonstrations: in the interval between Chester and Lord Randolph's visit to Belfast, Saunderson spoke at both Sheffield and Edinburgh.[61] And this was achieved, moreover, while maintaining a parliamentary presence and ministerial contacts.

Yet, though he was effectively fighting a Tory electoral battle, Saunderson still cast himself in the role of rebel. Indeed, part of his success in promoting bipartisan demonstrations lay in the fact that he avoided any

[59] ESP, T.2996/1/69: Saunderson to Helena, 27 Jan. 1886; ESP, T.2996/1/71: Saunderson to Helena, 30 Jan. 1886. Details of the meeting may be found in the *Irish Times*, 30 Jan. 1886, p. 6.

[60] Lucas, *Saunderson*, 377. Details of the meeting may be found in Cooke and Vincent, *The Governing Passion*, 405–6.

[61] ESP, T.2996/1/71: Saunderson to Helena, 30 Jan. 1886.

offensively and rigorously Tory statement of belief. His own Whig ancestry remained important, as Lord Randolph Churchill astutely recognized: 'Although on good & solid grounds you have adhered to the Tories, I feel sure that all your sound Liberal principles influence you as strongly as ever . . .'[62] On public platforms Saunderson contented himself with exposing Parnellite iniquity, describing (with an occasionally insensitive humour) the plight of victims of agrarian violence and intimidation. Yet, if he avoided a blunt confession of his Tory allegiance, then he also began to modify his former convictions in several respects. When he was concentrating his efforts on building a loyalist alliance in Ireland, he had rarely attempted to defend the landlord interest, or to emphasize his own plight as an Irish landowner. By the spring of 1886 he was identifying his economic sympathies with less reticence, and shedding the earlier references to tenant claims. In this, as ever, he was responding to the character of his audience, which was now largely British and parliamentary: formerly he had been appealing exclusively to a more sensitive and reform-conscious Ulster constituency. Pragmatism, then, must partly explain Saunderson's reversion from a populist stand in 1882–3 to the more genteel landlordism of 1886.

IV

His challenge to the Ulster Tory establishment had lost an economic dimension, therefore, but it remained none the less a challenge. While his energies had been harnessed to a cause beneficial to Conservatism—the Union—Saunderson was still highly intolerant of party discipline: the truculence and impatience which had helped to generate an independent Irish Unionist movement made him baulk at the normal factional ties and allegiances. Though Irish Toryism had a longstanding and effective freedom from British control, this (in Saunderson's eyes) was imperilled by weak or jobbing individuals who, for one reason or another, would collapse under British pressure. He had campaigned against John Monroe because Monroe's position as Irish Solicitor-General had allegedly impaired his effectiveness as a loyalist representative; and, in June 1886, he mounted a challenge to the aged and amiable member for North Belfast, William Ewart, because the latter's evident inefficiency made him a pawn of the Tory leadership.

62 Lucas, *Saunderson*, 120.

Saunderson's campaign against Ewart should be seen as an exhibition of his fundamental convictions concerning the purpose of loyalism; but at a more basic level it was also a test of strength. Saunderson had been widely hailed as a leader of Irish loyalism, and the North Belfast election offered an opportunity to gauge whether these acclamations were more than the conventional response of the party faithful to a new, able spokesman. Moreover, the success of Saunderson's candidate, Somerset Maxwell, would have been both a snub to the Belfast Tory leadership and a valuable (because immovably loyal) addition to the Irish Unionist parliamentary party. Its symbolic significance would have been immense: the victory of a new, brusque, and articulate loyalism over a more sullen and frigid orthodoxy; a victory for righteous, provincial loyalism over the unprincipled string-pullers of Belfast.

Outright victory, however, proved beyond his reach—and this was because Saunderson, captivated for six months by parliamentary politics, had blinded himself to local realities. It was a failing which would recur throughout Saunderson's later career, and which was rooted in an unrealistic conception both of his own indispensability and of the importance of narrowly high-political achievement—judged from the Irish perspective. In June 1886 the local reality was that Belfast Toryism had too many props to be casually defied. The chief Tory organ, the *Belfast News Letter*, was owned by Sir James Henderson, a long-time friend of the sitting member for North Belfast, and the paper came down unequivocally in Ewart's favour. Saunderson and Maxwell were characterized as two blundering intruders who had offered an insulting challenge to a venerable and effective representative of Belfast: it was hinted that this provincial impudence would rebound on its perpetrators: 'in one important County Division [an unmistakable reference to North Armagh] there is sure to be a change in the representation should further opposition be given in North Belfast.'[63] Saunderson, who had been hailed by the Tory press of Dublin and Belfast, was now deemed to be 'comparatively unknown' in the latter city. His Liberal ancestry was resurrected as a taunt, although it was also claimed that Saunderson's actions would imperil the Liberal commitment to the Unionist alliance.[64]

Thus, in the condemnations of Saunderson there was a certain lapse in consistency, and this in turn reflected the fear which his impromptu challenge had inspired among the Tory managers. So vital was the need to rebuff Saunderson that, working through Lord Arthur Hill, the Belfast

[63] *BNL*, 29 June 1886, p. 5. This issue also carried Maxwell's election manifesto (p. 4).
[64] Ibid., 30 June 1886, p. 4.

Tories extracted a letter from Salisbury which endorsed Ewart's candidature.[65] Saunderson counter-attacked by soliciting a note of approval from Lord Randolph Churchill; but Churchill would not risk a breach with the Prime Minister over the pretensions of his Irish client—and he, too, urged moderation on Saunderson.[66] Bereft of influential allies, either in Ireland or in the House of Commons, Saunderson advised Maxwell to surrender the contest; and Maxwell accordingly announced his withdrawal on 30 June.[67] The relief of the *News Letter* was palpable. From ranting abuse on 30 June, before the publication of Maxwell's decision, the paper swiftly graduated to loyal affection for Saunderson by 1 July.[68] The blame for the maverick candidature was, in time-honoured Tory custom, laid at the feet of anonymous advisers, who had temporarily misled an otherwise impeccable Ulster leader.[69]

The rebuff administered in North Belfast may have served to shatter several illusions which Saunderson cherished. First, while he was the Irish Unionist leader, this command did not imply any autocratic ascendancy over local politics. He was popular, but, as the *News Letter* icily pointed out, he was not thereby immune to shifts in electoral opinion; and he was not so popular that he could push Maxwell into North Belfast in defiance of Belfast Toryism and its front-bench patrons.[70] This knowledge may have led to a certain disenchantment with his local political role and responsibilities. Secondly, the mobilization of traditional Tory elements behind Ewart demonstrated that the paternalist flexibility within the Unionist alliance which had accompanied the Home Rule debate was rather less evident in its aftermath. Saunderson had been tolerated, even admired, at a time of acute anxiety for northern loyalists—and he had ridden roughshod over official party susceptibilities, most prominently in the Monroe campaign. By July 1886 he found himself the parliamentary leader of Irish Unionism—in spite of his earlier defiance. But he found, too, that his energies and abilities had not freed him from extreme suspicion among certain influential northern Tories. There were thus

65 ESP, T.2996/1/81: Saunderson to Helena, 25 June 1886. Salisbury was not amused, blaming the subsequent Conservative failure in West Belfast on Saunderson: W. C. Lubenow, *Parliamentary Politics and the Home Rule Crisis: The British House of Commons in 1886* (Oxford, 1988), 309.

66 CC, Randolph Churchill Papers, RCHL 1/13/1549: Saunderson to Churchill, 25 June 1886; ESP, T.2996/3/19: Churchill to Saunderson, 28 June 1886; Lucas, *Saunderson*, 104–5.

67 *BNL*, 1 July 1886, p. 3 (notice dated 30 June); ESP, T.2996/1/84: Saunderson to Helena, 30 June 1886.

68 *BNL*, 1 July 1886, p. 4.

69 Ibid.

70 Ibid. ('even Colonel Saunderson might lose popularity').

considerable problems in sustaining a local political ascendancy; and, after July 1886, Saunderson largely abandoned the effort in order to concentrate on a British and parliamentary audience.

8

Diplomacy and Political Evangelism, 1886–1893

I

There were numerous pressures which contrived to shunt Saunderson out of Ireland after 1886. Since Irish politics had undergone a rapid polarization between 1884 and 1886, there was comparatively little to be gained by campaigning at home, beyond the consolidation of existing party sympathies. Saunderson had been one of the architects of a cross-class loyalist alliance; and, given the relative success of this endeavour by the summer of 1886, his talents as a political evangelist and proselytizer were temporarily redundant. The defeat of the Home Rule Bill in June 1886, followed by the electoral defeat of Gladstone in July, demonstrated that the Ulster Unionist guarantee lay within the British parliament and, above all, within the House of Commons. For Saunderson, as indeed for many of his Irish Unionist contemporaries, it became clear that the constitutional front line no longer lay in the divided counties of Ulster, but rather in the marginal constituencies of Great Britain.

The allure of England operated at a more fundamental, personal level. Saunderson had heartily detested the House of Commons during his period as member for Cavan: a taciturn representative from an obscure constituency, he had made little impact on either front bench, departing from the Commons as anonymously as he had entered it. But as member for North Armagh, and as chairman of the Irish Unionist parliamentary party, Saunderson now occupied a rather more important role, and he was finding himself the object of attention and blandishment. He was older, and less intimidated by London society (more especially because he was now courted by some of the brightest social stars within metropolitan Toryism).[1] Above all, in 1886 he had a cause to argue, whereas his earlier parliamentary career had been distinguished by an egregious lack of commitment. He was now the principal Ulster Unionist spokesman—and this role provided a prominent parliamentary position, and a broader and more popular political reputation. In short, Saunderson could now feel at

[1] Reginald Lucas, *Colonel Saunderson MP: A Memoir* (London, 1908), 142–3.

home at Westminster; and the prospect of a convivial meal and a cigar, followed by a bantering speech to the Commons, evidently began to exercise a greater appeal than the dank and more brutal forum provided by County Armagh.[2]

II

If Saunderson's greatest achievement between 1886 and 1895 lay in his Unionist campaigning, then this was essentially an English achievement. Within the House of Commons, Saunderson played an important role in opposing Parnell and the Nationalist members. Indeed, in many sessions his chief contribution to debate lay in responding to the Parnellite amendments to the Motion for a Loyal Address. These amendments fell along similar lines, all generally relating to Home Rule, or to lesser grievances perceived by the majority community in Ireland. At any rate, Saunderson's response varied little in form from year to year. Armed with references and quotations (almost certainly supplied by the Irish Loyal and Patriotic Union) he aimed to portray the Nationalist members—the prospective governors of Ireland under a Home Rule parliament—in the worst possible light. Discrediting his opponents was Saunderson's chief aim, and to this end he sometimes sacrificed both equanimity and relevance: he was often cautioned by the Speaker for wandering off the subject under debate and on to more familiar rodomontades. He was choleric and provocative: many illustrations of this time portray him with an angry expression and extravagant declamatory gestures of hands and arms.[3] But, if he was sincerely impassioned, then he may also have consciously desired to goad his opponents into a compromising and damaging response. And when the parties of Ireland were most bitterly divided—under Arthur Balfour's Chief Secretaryship—the Nationalists frequently reacted as Saunderson would have wished.

[2] Saunderson seems to have been fond of Italian food, and of cigars. The former passion probably developed in his childhood, which was partly spent near Nice in (at that time) Savoy. See e.g. ESP, T.2996/1/127: Saunderson to Helena, 8 Feb. 1887: 'I have found a first rate Italian restaurant.' On his enthusiasm for cigars see PRONI, Hugh de Fellenberg Montgomery Papers, T.1089/272: Saunderson to Montgomery, 8 Sept. 1895.

[3] See e.g. the portrait by H. Harris Brown reproduced as a frontispiece to the Lucas volume and in Henry Patton, *Fifty Years of Disestablishment: A Sketch* (Dublin, 1922), 230. See also the sketch by Begg in Lucas, *Saunderson*, 276. Even the *Vanity Fair* caricature depicts Saunderson in truculent mood (28 Feb. 1887).

Saunderson's accusations frequently involved attempting to link the members of the Irish party, either individually or collectively, with illegality. Thus, in a phrase which he hoped would become famous, Saunderson described Parnell as having his hand on 'the throttle-valve of crime'.[4] He drew attention to allegedly inflammatory speeches by the Irish members, coupling his quotations with statistics of violence, which, he claimed, represented the direct consequence of his opponents' oratory: for their part, the Irish members were prepared to make similar accusations against Saunderson (in 1883–4, 1886, and 1893). His own language was certainly violent, though he only occasionally transgressed the formal bounds of parliamentary propriety. He was becoming better acquainted with the eccentricities of the Manual of Procedure, and could gauge with increasing precision what he could get away with, and what would provoke the intervention of the Speaker. Even when he was asked to withdraw a phrase, he could contrive to win some advantage. In February 1893, speaking on the Address, he referred to the controversial parish priest of Gweedore, County Donegal, as 'this murderous ruffian'.[5] Asked to amend his language (not in fact by the Speaker, but by Balfour and Gladstone), Saunderson substituted 'excited politician' for the offending reference. He thereby gained a laugh, scored a point off his opponents, and ensured that the slur, even though now swathed in good humour, would remain in their minds.

Saunderson's Unionism was therefore frequently expressed in negative and antagonistic terms, and it was only comparatively late in his career that he began to develop a wider dimension to his political faith, and to curb his early stridency of tone. Before the mid-1890s—certainly before 1890—Saunderson was febrile and acerbic, driven by despair, both at his perception of the condition of Ireland, and by the suspicion that he was fighting for a doomed cause. It was rumoured in the late 1880s that he had resigned himself to the inevitability of Home Rule, and indeed some of his speeches during the debate on the second Home Rule Bill seem to confirm this suggestion.[6] His belligerence was therefore that of the 'last ditcher'; and he sustained an at times self-defeating defiance—even when moderation might have offered political advantages, as after the Parnellite split of 1891.

He was selectively pained by violence, and disturbed by the long lists of

[4] ESP, T.2996/1/100: Saunderson to Helena, 25 Aug. 1886; *Hansard*, ser. 3, cccviii. 524 (25 Aug. 1886); Lucas, *Saunderson*, 110–11.

[5] *Hansard*, ser. 4, viii. 256 (2 Feb. 1893). Lucas, *Saunderson*, 190.

[6] PRONI, Montgomery Papers, D.627/428/50: Richard Bagwell to Montgomery, 12 Aug. 1888. See also *Hansard*, ser. 4, xii. 486 (20 Apr. 1893).

crime which he proffered to the House. But the turmoil of the land war also had a more direct and personal impact: at the beginning of the Plan of Campaign in 1886–7, when unrest in Ireland was beginning to escalate, William Johnston found that his leader's London home (in Deanery Street, off Park Lane) had been placed under police guard.[7] Gradually and unsurprisingly, Saunderson began to cast his faith in apocalyptic terms: 'the war between us', he told John Dillon in July 1890, 'is war to the death.'[8] This was a rare admission, evidently inspired by a genuine, uncontrollable rage (as opposed to the ritual anger which he more frequently deployed). Cautioned by the Speaker, Saunderson explained his violent language in a passage which revealed the intensity of feeling which underlay such criticisms:

> I regret, Sir, if my warmth has betrayed me beyond the rules of debate. It is not easy for hon. Members who do not understand the condition of affairs in Ireland, and who do not know what boycotting means, to realise the misery that has been brought about by the action of the League, but it makes my blood boil to think that these things should be supported by a great Party in the State . . . It would be a great satisfaction if some of the most eloquent of Ireland's sons would forget this policy, which must end in nothing, and join with me, as I am ready to join with any man, in promoting the good of the country.[9]

Before the defeat of the second Home Rule Bill, the polarity between Saunderson and his Irish opponents was perceived by him as virtually absolute. They were the 'heathen' of his correspondence with Helena—a malign force, susceptible only to brute strength, whether in terms of rhetoric or of coercive legislation.

Indeed, Saunderson's own bitter stand had a physical and pugilistic dimension which confirms that his relationship with parliamentary Nationalism could be decidedly cool. In March 1893, when T. W. Russell moved an adjournment, and after a characteristic accusation of incitement, Saunderson was challenged by Willie Redmond to repeat his imputations outside the House. Reginald Lucas, in keeping with the tone of much of his biography, describes the ensuing fracas in terms of farce and of the ridiculous; but at least one press report suggested that the two men nearly

[7] PRONI, William Johnston Diaries, D.880/2/39: 28 Apr. 1887. Saunderson was a friend of Major Gosselin, the (in Christopher Andrew's description) 'provincial spy-master' who was in charge of police intelligence on Irish crimes: East Sussex Record Office, Wolseley Papers: Saunderson to Wolseley, 11 May 1890. See also Christopher Andrew, *Her Majesty's Secret Service: The Making of the British Intelligence Community*, pbk. edn. (New York, 1987), 18.

[8] *Hansard*, ser. 3, cccxlvi. 1017 (7 July 1890).

[9] Ibid.

came to blows, and were only prevented from doing so by the intervention of fellow MPs—and (possibly) by the presence of a police officer.[10] The potential for violence accelerated into reality on 27 July 1893: on the completion of the Committee Stage of the Home Rule Bill, a fight developed in the Commons in which Saunderson and several of the Irish members were involved. Descriptions of the 'scene' entered a host of parliamentary memoirs, many observers or participants dismissing it as being little more than a temporary aberration, caused by the peculiar parliamentary circumstances.[11] Saunderson suggested that relations between himself and the Nationalist members would quickly be healed. Indeed Reginald Lucas reports that Saunderson had gone to T. P. O'Connor, saying that 'he was indebted to him for ten minutes of the best fun he had ever had'.[12] But this is an ambiguous anecdote, for it contains not only a suggestion of rough good humour, but also an accusation of responsibility—that O'Connor had started the fight. It seems more probable that the 'scene' of July 1893 should be regarded in the context of years of bitterness. The sad reality was that, before 1893, even basic civility between Saunderson and the Irish party was unusual; and, despite his belief in the 'typical' Irish ability to reject bad feeling, Saunderson's own quarrel with Parnellism proved to be too deeply felt to permit the growth of any worthwhile relationship.

Nevertheless, within this spectrum of distrust, there were perceptible gradations. Saunderson never softened his attitude towards Parnell during the latter's lifetime. His references were uniformly antagonistic—and it is probable that he regarded Parnell as, in effect, a traitor to class and to creed.[13] Dillon and O'Brien were similarly objects of Saunderson's ire. Conversely, even when Saunderson was at his most belligerent, he preserved a grudging respect for Michael Davitt—for his directness of purpose, and for his courage. This limited tolerance is first perceptible in

[10] Lucas, *Saunderson*, 193; *Hansard*, ser. 4, ix. 840 (2 Mar. 1893); ESP, T.2996/12/5: scrapbook containing, *inter alia*, Redmond's challenge. See also *BNL*, 7 Mar. 1893, p. 5 (London letter).

[11] Lucas, *Saunderson*, 199–202; *Hansard*, ser. 4, xv. 732 (27 July 1892). Other observers were thoroughly shocked. Arthur Griffith-Boscawen, writing fourteen years after the event, recalled that it was 'the most disgraceful [scene] I ever witnessed in the House': *Fourteen Years in Parliament* (London, 1907), 33–4.

[12] Lucas, *Saunderson*, 243.

[13] Saunderson's contempt for Parnell expressed itself most clearly in Jan. 1886, when he tried to join forces with Philip Callan. In Dec. 1885 Callan, a lieutenant of Isaac Butt, had been brutally driven from his County Louth constituency by Parnell. See F. H. O'Donnell, *A History of the Irish Parliamentary Party*, 2 vols. (London, 1910), i. 315, 429, 465–6, 495; see also ESP, T.2996/1/61: Saunderson to Helena, 15 Jan. 1886.

the pamphlet *Two Irelands: Loyalty versus Treason*, but it was expressed later, even at the height of the Plan of Campaign. And, up to a point, Davitt reciprocated. After Saunderson's death a Nationalist journalist recalled a conversation with Davitt and others in which the Colonel was referred to as 'a bigot':

'A bigot he may be', Davitt retorted, 'yet I like the man. He can say hard things about an opponent, and he does say them quite fearlessly. In politics he is an open, fearless fighter. He loves his God, and he loves his country—but his country is Ulster.'[14]

After the Parnellite split, John Redmond was also favoured with some comparatively amiable (or, at any rate, comparatively inoffensive) allusions from the loyalist leader. Redmond was tolerated because, as the head of the Parnellites after the schism, Saunderson judged him to be less under clerical sway than either Justin McCarthy or Tim Healy. Redmond can scarcely have welcomed such expressions of approval; and, indeed, if Saunderson had been thoroughly sympathetic, he must have known that statements such as the following, made to the House in 1893, could only have been counter-productive:

I venture to assert that there is only one Gentleman below the Gangway who has the right to say that he speaks in the name of the Nationalist electors in Ireland, and that is the member for Waterford. The Member for Waterford and his eight colleagues profess I understand to come to the House returned to be the representatives of the voters in their constituencies. They can at any rate speak in their name. But, Sir, there is another Party, numbering 71 . . .[15]

Affection such as this had, perhaps, a somewhat shallow foundation. Indeed such statements are possibly better evidence of Saunderson's unrelenting opposition to Home Rule than of any genuine softening of attitude. At any rate they testify to a naïve directness in expressing his sympathies, which was more fully apparent in his heavy-handed mockery of Nationalist division. Mockery, rather than tentative approval for Redmond, was more characteristic of Saunderson's statements after 1891; and thus one is again driven back to the blunt truth that, whatever his wavering, Saunderson heartily disliked his political opponents.

On the other hand there is little unambiguous evidence to suggest that the Nationalist members felt anything other than dislike for Saunderson. There was certainly a development within their attitude over the years—a

[14] Edward Saunderson, *Two Irelands: Loyalty versus Treason* (Dublin, 1884), 26; *Irish Independent*, 22 May 1908.

[15] *Hansard*, ser. 4, viii. 1328 (Feb. 1893).

development linked to Saunderson's own shifting mood ('It is you who have changed', William O'Brien once taunted Saunderson). But it would be quite wrong to suggest, as Lucas did in 1908, that private camaraderie automatically complemented the public antipathy which existed between Saunderson and the Nationalists.[16] In the last decade of his life Saunderson mellowed, and his opponents reciprocated—but there is little evidence of any close personal or professional relationship behind the scenes. Such relationships were certainly possible between members of the Ulster and the Irish parties. William Moore, for example, struck up a quirky and lasting bond with Tim Healy, based on a mutual professional respect—though Healy could still privately refer to his erstwhile chum as an 'operator'.[17] Saunderson and the Nationalists occasionally referred to each other in pacific terms. Thus in 1887, when he denied harbouring any personal rancour for *individual* members of the Irish party, Healy called out 'no more have we for you'. And in 1899 Justin McCarthy could allude affectionately in his *Reminiscences* to his old opponent.[18] But, before the defeat of the second Home Rule Bill, even this superficial banter was rare. A more typical display of their relationship was given when Saunderson interjected a brief remark into a speech delivered by Thomas Sexton in August 1889. Sexton delivered a coruscating rejoinder: 'I trust that the hon. and gallant Gentleman will remember that he is the one member of this House whose interruptions I cannot tolerate.'[19]

Saunderson's Unionism was therefore combative, and within the House of Commons, and particularly among the Nationalists, he won a reputation for pugnacity. However, there was another dimension to his style. Saunderson's humour was acknowledged, even by bitter opponents—indeed there seems to have been a tacit consensus among Nationalist members, originally nonplussed by Saunderson's laboured ironies, to laugh off his efforts. Otherwise this rhetorical cocktail worked quite well, and Saunderson was a popular speaker who could draw debate-stunned MPs back into the chamber. He was certainly a limited speaker in the sense that he only really excelled in presenting a general indictment—and even then only on well-worn subjects such as the iniquities of Home Rule and Home Rulers, and the sufferings of the Irish landowner class. As has been

[16] Ibid. iv. 1606 (23 May 1892); Lucas, *Saunderson*, 133 and n. 1; also 136. James Loughlin, *Gladstone, Home Rule and the Ulster Question, 1882–1893* (Dublin, 1986), 129–30.

[17] Private possession, Nina Patrick Papers: John Caldwell to Nina Patrick, 3 Feb. 1952; private possession, William Moore Papers: T. M. Healy to Moore, 24 July 1929; T. M. Healy, *Letters and Leaders of My Day*, 2 vols. (London, n.d. [1928]), ii. 475.

[18] Lucas, *Saunderson*, 133.

[19] *Hansard*, ser. 3, cccxl. 16 (21 Aug. 1889).

observed, he was weak in offering either detail or dialectic: only rarely would he read up a subject, and later in his career his opponents would accuse him (with some justice) of not studying Bills on which he was prepared to speak.[20] Even within parliament, however, he was a popular and frothy performer; while in the constituencies of England and Scotland his undemanding bluster made him a useful and popular spokesman for Unionism.

III

The period between the first and second Home Rule Bills brought an unprecedented movement of politicians between the two islands. A greater number of cabinet ministers and front-bench Liberals visited Ireland between 1886 and 1893 than in any ensuing period of similar length. Similarly, backbenchers of both parties migrated to Ireland on fact-finding missions or for the purpose of offering encouragement to Irish allies. Saunderson's work in England was therefore only part of a much broader political exchange; and, indeed, several prominent loyalists, including Saunderson and T. W. Russell, led a virtually peripatetic existence while Home Rule was on the *tapis*. Saunderson's proselytizing endeavours appear (from the evidence of his letters) to have peaked in 1888, when he spoke in at least fourteen different locations in Britain, ranging from Edinburgh to Brighton, from Cambridge to Bangor: the number of speeches which he delivered must have been several times this figure.[21] After 1890 his provincial speaking engagements seem to have declined in number, and by contrast he was appearing more frequently in the House of Commons. This decline may be related to several factors: first, the rigorous campaigning was taking its toll on his health. Saunderson's letters to Helena record various, ostensibly minor, ailments endured on the campaign trail—but, taken together with his weak constitution, these may have had an abnormally great and damaging impact. Certainly by 1892–3 the press was reporting that the loyalist leader had suffered from a number of

[20] See e.g. Edward Marjoribanks and Ian Colvin, *The Life of Lord Carson*, 3 vols. (London, 1932–6), i. 160; see p. 78.

[21] See ESP, T.2996/2B/370–414: Saunderson to Helena, correspondence for 1888.

'relapses'.[22] But the decline in the number of provincial venues was also linked to a comparative loss of popular interest in Irish affairs. Arthur Balfour's administration of Ireland (1887–91) had established a measure of rural tranquillity, and the Plan of Campaign had effectively been broken. British public attention was shifting from the Test estates to the more compelling intrigue being played out at the O'Shea villa at Eltham.

In carrying out his campaigns Saunderson often acted under the aegis of independent loyalist organizations like the Irish Loyal and Patriotic Union; but, whatever his claims to autonomy, he was now a loyal servant of British Toryism. The chairman of what Henry Labouchere had dubbed 'the new fourth party' was effectively striving on behalf of a Tory front bench which he had once condemned, and from which he still claimed independence.[23] He liaised with local party organizations through the office of the Tory chief whip, Aretas Akers-Douglas. Equally, whenever a local party luminary desired Saunderson's services as a speaker, the approach might be made through Akers-Douglas. Thus, in April 1890, when Lord Mountedgcumbe, representing the National Union of Conservative Associations in Cornwall, wanted to invite Saunderson to St Austell, it was to the chief whip that he wrote ('Our County Union of Conservative Associations is very anxious to get Colonel Saunderson to come down ... will you kindly ask him about this?').[24] Yet it would be wrong to infer that Saunderson had surrendered his ambition for loyalist distinctiveness: the local and parliamentary structures of loyalist independence remained, and Saunderson continued to belittle English party divisions.[25] At the same time, it must be recognized that the parliamentary independence which had been largely Saunderson's conception and achievement only thrived in the shadow of Tory treachery. And since Arthur Balfour, as Chief Secretary for Ireland, embodied a sufficiently rigorous and partisan spirit for even the most militant loyalist, independence and organization had little purpose, save as a resource for a now beneficent Toryism. Separate Irish organizations like the ILPU or the

[22] *BNL*, 13 July 1892, p. 6 (where Saunderson is too ill to visit his constituents); ibid., 2 Mar. 1892, p. 5 (London letter: where it is reported that Saunderson has had a relapse). Sir Richard Temple, *Letters and Character Sketches from the House of Commons: Home Rule and other Matters in 1886–7* (London, 1912), 161.

[23] *Hansard*, ser. 3, cccxxii. 420 (14 Feb. 1888).

[24] Kent Record Office, Aretas Akers-Douglas Papers, C.387/2: Lord Mountedgcumbe to Akers-Douglas, 6 Apr. 1889; C.481/3: Saunderson to Akers-Douglas, 14 Nov. 1890.

[25] *Hansard*, ser. 3, cccviii. 1101 (2 Sept. 1886): 'personally he had tried to discover the difference between the policy of the Tory party and that of the Liberal party and had always failed ...'. See also Lucas, *Saunderson*, 118–19.

Ulster Defence Union remained, as did Saunderson's parliamentary party, but their forms and purpose had altered.

Outside parliament he was the unflinching partisan, and, within the House of Commons, he upheld an equally loyal front, his parliamentary statements rarely questioning front-bench orthodoxies. Moreover, his flamboyant defiance of Gladstone and Parnell diverted opposition energies and abuse. He was thus both useful and loyal, and yet sufficiently independent to retain a hint of menace for the cabinet. And this combination ensured that he emerged as a figure of first-rate significance within the Salisbury parliament of 1886–92.

He was at first doubtful of Tory resolution in the face of the Plan of Campaign. Against the background of a resurgent National League, boycotting, and the spread of the Plan after its publication in October 1886, Saunderson fretted at the cabinet's inactivity: 'I am in despair with the Government', he confided to Helena, 'they are in a hopeless condition. They are letting everything drift.'[26] Publication of the Queen's Speech and of the government's plans came at the end of January 1887—but proved to be 'a tame affair', offering little to committed coercionists like Saunderson.[27] Yet he kept his head, and while his private opinions were quite well known to senior English Unionists (Hartington, for example, feared an embarrassing attack in the debate on the Address), he did not imperil the apparent solidarity of parliamentary Unionism.[28] Salisbury responded generously to Saunderson's unrest, offering favours over patronage and granting the Ulster leader two interviews (19 February and 7 March) in order to hear his grievances.[29] Salisbury could be less than tactful, but generally succeeded in mollifying the Ulster leader, who judged the February meeting to be 'on the whole ... satisfactory'.[30] Saunderson's nerve was momentarily taxed when, on Sir Michael Hicks-Beach's resignation, an effete nephew of the Prime Minister was apparently jobbed into the Irish Office. But Arthur Balfour belied his reputation, remaining five years in Ireland, and binding Saunderson and Irish loyalism more closely to the English leadership than could have been conceived in 1884. For a

[26] ESP, T.2996/1/118: Saunderson to Helena, 13 Jan. 1887; Lucas, *Saunderson*, 124.

[27] The speech had been leaked to Saunderson's friend and ally, Viscount Crichton (now the fifth earl of Erne): PRONI, Erne Papers, D.1939/21/10/25: Henry Manners to Erne, 21 Jan. 1887. ESP, T.2996/1/119: Saunderson to Helena, 26 Jan. 1887.

[28] ESP, T.2996/1/122: Saunderson to Helena, 31 Jan. 1887; ESP, T.2996/1/123: Saunderson to Helena, 31 Jan. 1887 ('I dined with Chaplin afterwards and met Hartington and others').

[29] See above, p. 85. ESP, T.2996/1/124: Saunderson to Helena, 4 Feb. 1887.

[30] ESP, T.2996/1/136: Saunderson to Helena, 19 Feb. 1887.

time it seemed that the Cecil dynasty, uncle and nephew, constituted the salvation of Unionist Ireland.

Balfour's policy of interactive coercion and conciliation need not be discussed here, but Saunderson's reaction to the policy's component measures is of interest.[31] Balfour's coercive record can be easily dealt with in this context—for Saunderson, to the end of his life, remained a staunch proponent of law and order, and he offered unequivocal approval for the government's efforts to crush the Plan of Campaign. Balfour's policing strategy hinged on the Criminal Law and Procedure (Ireland) Bill, passed on 18 July 1887, and this was stubbornly endorsed by Saunderson both on its third reading, on 7 July, and a year later, on 25 June 1888, when John Morley moved an adjournment motion condemning the Act.[32] During this last debate, he had opined that 'the settlement of this question would never ultimately be reached until they had their heel upon the neck of these people'; and, while this was the crudest expression of Saunderson's convictions, it was clear that Balfour was not going to encounter libertarian scruples on the Irish Unionist benches.[33] Thus, on 21 June 1889, speaking to John Ellis's motion condemning the use of troops in evictions, Saunderson was predictably unrepentant: those landlords on the Test estates who refused the terms offered by the Plan agitators were 'fighting the battle of the law of the land'.[34] Lapsing into jingoism, he flaunted his contempt for the Nationalist members: 'I say that if a landlord has one particle of British pluck about him, he would break stones on the road sooner than give in to hon. Gentlemen opposite.'[35] Nor did he exhibit any greater regard for individual Parnellites when, as part of Balfour's rigorous policy of prosecutions, the member for mid-Cork was imprisoned. Tanner's case was debated in August 1889, and Saunderson gloatingly defended the conviction.[36]

There were all too many opportunities to parade a devotion to law and order. Saunderson was a committed friend of the Royal Irish Constabulary: indeed it was during a Parnellite onslaught against this force that he

[31] The best treatment of Balfour's Chief Secretaryship remains L. P. Curtis, *Coercion and Conciliation in Ireland, 1880–1892: A Study in Constructive Unionism* (Princeton, NJ, 1963). See also Andrew Gailey, *Ireland and the Death of Kindness: The Experience of Constructive Unionism, 1890–1905* (Cork, 1987); Catherine Shannon, *Arthur J Balfour and Ireland, 1874–1922* (Washington, DC, 1988); and Alvin Jackson, *The Ulster Party: Irish Unionists and the House of Commons, 1884–1911* (Oxford, 1989).

[32] *Hansard*, ser. 3, cccxvii. 1125 (7 July 1887); ibid. cccxxvii. 1235 (25 June 1888).

[33] Ibid. cccxxvii. 1240 (25 June 1888).

[34] Ibid. cccxxxvii. 504 (21 June 1889).

[35] Ibid. cccxxxvii. 501–2 (21 June 1889).

[36] Ibid. cccxxxix. 112 (1 Aug. 1889).

had clashed with Sexton so revealingly ('the war between us is war to the death').[37] And he offered a complementary support for the judicial establishment, whenever this was attacked by the opposition (as it was in a supply debate in July 1890).[38] As well as conservative principle there was an element of self-interest in all this: by virtue of his landowning rank, Saunderson was himself a local magistrate—a justice of the peace, and a deputy lieutenant for County Cavan.

This zeal for law and order, allied with his faith in the criminal guilt of the Parnellite leaders, led some contemporaries to suspect that Saunderson had a connection with Richard Pigott, the forger of Parnell's correspondence. Reginald Lucas takes account of this possibility, and is careful to deny it; and indeed Saunderson's surviving papers contain no reference to any contact with Pigott before the Special Commission which investigated the supposed relationship between Parnellism and criminality.[39] Within parliament Saunderson took an interest in the aftermath of Pigott's confession and collapse, maintaining his support for Balfour's crimes policy against the menacing backdrop of Parnellite euphoria. When the report of the Special Commission was debated in March 1890, discussion focused on the forgeries, and on the government's association with *The Times*; but Balfour's record as Irish Secretary was also on trial, with Nationalist members lashing the Tory front bench. On such occasions—a heated atmosphere, a broadly defined subject—Saunderson excelled; and on 6 March he delivered an effective speech lasting an hour and a quarter in which he admitted the damage done by Pigott ('I make them a present of Pigott'), while concentrating on other, allegedly more useful aspects of the report.[40] He unashamedly repeated his old accusations against the Parnellites, maintaining that the report had fully corroborated them:

> I venture to maintain that all the grounds of allegation against that Party, against their methods, their objects, their aims and the goal they seek to attain, has been absolutely proved in the Report.[41]

It was a useful, if tautological, defence of the ministerial record—delivered at a time of looming difficulty, and possible humiliation. He had provided a telling speech, a crucial vote, and even rhetoric for the government

[37] *Hansard*, ser. 3, cccxlvi. 1017 (7 July 1890).

[38] Ibid. cccxlvi. 165 (17 July 1890).

[39] Lucas, *Saunderson*, 152. Lord Riddell of the *News of the World* offers some revealing information concerning *The Times* and E. C. Houston of the Irish Loyal and Patriotic Union: Riddell, *More Pages from My Diary, 1908–14* (London, 1934), 80–1. See also F. S. L. Lyons, *Charles Stewart Parnell* (London, 1977), 368–71.

[40] *Hansard*, ser. 3, cccxlii. 210 (6 Mar. 1890).

[41] Ibid. cccxlii. 227 (6 Mar. 1890).

(Salisbury repeated his old allusions to Parnellism and to the 'throttle-valve of crime').[42] If it was easy for Saunderson to be supportive on law and order, his loyalty to the Tory front bench was no less precious. Thus, when Balfour wrote to one of Saunderson's constituents commenting on the latter's 'invaluable assistance to the Unionist cause', there can have been no reason to doubt his sincerity.[43]

Coercion, therefore, represented an easy test of Saunderson's loyalty. It was rather conciliation—the thread of ameliorative measures which ran through Balfour's tenure—which created doubts and irritation. One of the chief consequences of Balfour's reforms was that Saunderson felt compelled to cast himself in the role of landlords' advocate—and this meant dropping the mask of class conciliation which he had once worn with panache. It was Saunderson's tragedy that he revelled in lost causes, and he paid a high price for his principles: his passionate identification with landlord claims would eventually bring irreparable damage to his leadership of Unionism. In 1883–4 he had been the Orange Parnell, casting off considerations of class in the interests of his particular conception of Ireland's needs.[44] But the success of Unionism in 1886, combined with what were seen as Balfour's predatory designs on the Irish estates, meant that Saunderson's sympathies shifted towards the interests of his own social caste. In climbing into this exclusive last ditch he would jeopardize his claims to popular leadership.

Nevertheless, Saunderson's emergence as a politician of class only involved a sacrifice of his broader party loyalties after the passage of the Land Act of 1896, when Irish landlords in parliament revolted against the government. In the medium term Saunderson generally offered only a muted public criticism of government policy, supporting with varying degrees of enthusiasm each of Balfour's legislative proposals. Yet he contrived to balance this relative moderation with a reputation as a determined landlord partisan, for he fought tenaciously on behalf of his class both behind the scenes and during the Committee Stage of each Land Bill.

[42] Ibid. cccxlii. 1363 (21 Mar. 1890): 'as it has been well expressed, they had their hand upon the throttle-valve of crime'.

[43] BL, Arthur Balfour Papers, Add. MS 49826, fo. 256: Balfour to James Malcolm, 17 Jan. 1888 (copy).

[44] Paul Bew assembles the case for supposing that Parnell's career was one of conservatism 'with a radical tinge': Paul Bew, *C. S. Parnell* (Dublin, 1980), 136–45. Perhaps the congruities between Saunderson's role within loyalism and Parnell's role within constitutional nationalism deserve more attention. For a provisional assessment see Alvin Jackson, 'The Rivals of C. S. Parnell', in Donal McCartney (ed.), *Parnell: The Politics of Power* (Dublin, 1991), 72–89.

Balfour's Land Bill of 1887 was viewed with dismay by a wide range of landed opinion, including not only Saunderson but also Salisbury himself.[45] Originally introduced in July primarily as a sop to Liberal Unionist principle, the Bill had been a limited measure, and in fact it had satisfied none of those to whom it had been addressed. Faced with an uncompromising reception, Balfour withdrew the Bill so that it might be amended in cabinet; but the revised measure which emerged from this reappraisal proved an even greater test of landlord loyalty.[46] Salisbury explained the reasons behind the alterations to the Bill at a party meeting held in the Carlton Club on 19 July. However, the rank-and-file received this apologia coolly, and Saunderson was chief amongst those die-hards who questioned the acceptability of the Prime Minister's arguments.[47] But he was ultimately brought into line by the prospect of a tough response to the National League and to the Plan of Campaign: indeed, when the Plan was proclaimed on 12 August, it was commonly believed that Saunderson's qualms, expressed at the Carlton, lay behind the move. At any rate, this was Randolph Churchill's line, writing to Hartington on 22 August:

> I think I can see the whole position. Lord Salisbury was deeply impressed by Saunderson's speech at the Carlton meeting in which he was told that, if he had held out on the Land Bill, the Liberal Unionists would have knuckled under.[48]

In the event, the Liberal Unionists did 'knuckle under'—but to a series of pro-landlord amendments moved in the House of Lords, which were in turn accepted by the government. Liberal Unionists like the choleric T. W. Russell were irate, but Saunderson, who had been apprised of the government's friendly intentions, was quietly jubilant. He still felt that he could plausibly articulate the mood of the Ulster tenantry—and this body, he claimed, shared his own unequivocal support for the Bill.[49]

Saunderson had had private doubts about the 1887 Land Act, but he offered a more committed support for official efforts to create a peasant proprietorship through state-aided purchase. Balfour sponsored a major Land Purchase Bill in 1888, which made another £5 million available to fund the pioneering Ashbourne Act of 1885.[50] What Saunderson feared

45 Curtis, *Coercion and Conciliation*, 338.

46 Ibid. 340–1.

47 Gathorne Hardy, First Earl of Cranbrook, *A Memoir: With Extracts from his Diary and Correspondence*, 2 vols. (London, 1910), ii. 285.

48 Chatsworth House, Devonshire Papers, 15/340: Churchill to Hartington, 22 Aug. 1887.

49 ESP, T.2996/1/143: Saunderson to Helena, 17 Aug. 1887; *Hansard*, ser. 3, cccxix. 1036 (18 Aug. 1887).

50 Curtis, *Coercion and Conciliation*, 349.

most was the incorporation of an element of compulsion into such a measure—compulsion on landlords to sell up, whether through one 'great, violent and heroic' purchase act, or in a more creeping and limited form applicable only in the first instance to harsh and recalcitrant landowners like Lord Clanricarde.[51] Fortunately for Saunderson's scruples, the government had a crowded parliamentary timetable, and could not risk the ethical and contractual quagmire associated with the debate on compulsion. Once again, therefore, Saunderson was able to fall into line behind Balfour.[52]

The last such measure passed by Balfour as Chief Secretary was the Purchase of Land and Congested Districts (Ireland) Act of 1891; and this aroused rather greater passion among the Ulster landlords, largely because, under its provisions, selling landlords would be reimbursed in stock, and not in cash (landlords suspected—rightly, as it transpired, that the stock would depreciate).[53] Yet here again, Saunderson weighed the interests of his class against broader Unionist needs, and was moved by the latter. The Bill, he calculated grumpily, would diminish the income of landlords 'by one half, and sometimes by one third'; but

> I support it for imperial and for Irish reasons. The first duty of every Irishman is to assist legislation which will benefit his native land, and as I firmly believe that the Bill under discussion will benefit Ireland, I support it. The imperial reason which will mainly induce the House to support the Bill . . . is that by its operation it will build up a class who will array themselves on the side of law and order . . .[54]

The rhetoric—the allusions to duty and to Irishness—was Saunderson's own; but his rationalization of purchase was the intellectual property of Salisbury and Balfour. This last—the conception of a landowning, law-abiding, and West British peasant—proved, at any rate in the short term, an egregious failure. It was ironic, therefore, that the greatest achievement of the Tory propaganda adorning purchase was that it reconciled Saunderson and his like to their own economic supersession.

Fear of compulsory purchase dominated Saunderson's reaction to Balfourian reform in the late 1880s, and this fear engendered a happier attitude to other, less intimidating proposals than might otherwise have been expected. One of his most important surviving comments on the future of conciliation comes in a letter written to Balfour in November 1889; and this suggests that Saunderson and the Ulster landlords believed

[51] *Hansard*, ser. 3, cccxxx. 1733 (20 Nov. 1888).
[52] Ibid. cccxxx. 1725–33 (20 Nov. 1888).
[53] Curtis, *Coercion and Conciliation*, 352–5.
[54] *Hansard*, ser. 3, ccclii. 808 (17 Apr. 1891).

both that a compulsory purchase measure was looming, and that it should at all costs be scuppered.[55] The reasoning was tortuous, but it started from the premiss that, in the aftermath of the English reform of 1888, the democratization of Irish local government was inevitable. With the reform of local government came the threat of compulsory purchase—for a safeguard such as compulsion was deemed essential by many, especially Liberal Unionists, in order to put 'landlords out of the way of open spoilation' by the new county authorities.[56] On these grounds, and on the evidence of some ambiguous comments delivered by George Wyndham at Dover, Saunderson and the landlords calculated that the government would seize on compulsion as a means of clearing the way for local government. Inspired by this, in fact faulty, perception of ministerial logic, Saunderson desperately urged alternative safeguards as an accompaniment to a sweeping measure of local government reform.[57] Clearly the prospect of democratic county councils was a mere irritant when set against the humiliation and ruin threatened by compulsion.

Thus it would be wrong to suggest that landed die-hards like Saunderson offered a blanket disapproval either to the general prospect of Irish local government reform, or to the specific proposal which emerged, finally, in 1892. Saunderson was scarcely enthusiastic in private: he urged in November 1889 his conviction that the majority of Ulster Unionist voters were 'quite indifferent on the matter'.[58] But at the same time, an incongruous mixture of expediency and principle impelled him to support such a reform. The argument of expediency has already been outlined—but local government was also forced upon Saunderson as a matter of Unionist principle. Like many Irish Unionists, Saunderson was both self-consciously Irish, and yet a constitutional integrationist, believing that Irish political and judicial institutions should be tailored to a British paradigm. Once a local government measure had been passed for England, and once the level of disturbance in Ireland was tolerable (Saunderson judged this to be so by 1892), then he was prepared to accept the extension of the reform into Ireland.[59]

This reasoning was presented more fully by Saunderson when, in May 1892, Balfour's Local Government Bill was debated by the Commons. Indeed Saunderson's commitment to the principle of county government,

[55] BL, Arthur Balfour Papers, Add. MS 49845, fo. 156: Saunderson to Balfour, 2 Nov. 1889.

[56] Ibid. [57] Ibid.

[58] Ibid.. Balfour's bill is discussed in Curtis, *Coercion and Conciliation*, 381–7.

[59] *Hansard*, ser. 4, iv. 1609 (23 May 1892).

tentative in 1889, had blossomed as the qualified nature of Balfour's proposal became evident. The fact was that Balfour, innately distrustful of all the Irish, and yet impressed by Saunderson's doubts, had written into his Bill several clauses which were intended to protect the large cess-payer and the Unionist minority at the expense of integrationist principle and Nationalist sensitivity. These clauses enraged the opposition, and ultimately secured the Bill's demise; but Saunderson was ecstatic, vigorously proclaiming the unity of Ulster loyalism in favour of the measure.[60]

Yet his support expressed more than a limited pleasure at Balfour's caution, and it transcended the narrow demands of party loyalty. It was, rather, a token of a new confidence for the future of Ireland and for his cause—a confidence which contrasted with his state of mind in 1887–8, and which was related to the comparative strength of Irish Unionism in the aftermath of the Parnellite schism:

> I support this Bill because I do not despair at all of the future of Ireland. I believe that without Home Rule, which I believe in our time we shall never see, there are all the elements of future prosperity in Ireland. I think the most sanguine Unionist six years ago never could have imagined in his wildest dreams that Ireland would be as peaceful as prosperous and as contented as she is now . . .[61]

Even though such comments were rooted in Nationalist division, Saunderson had evinced a new faith in his fellow Irish people. Balfour's Local Government Bill was jettisoned in the last weeks of the Salisbury government, but Saunderson's new, and almost patriarchal, tone remained and developed. It was a strange, but none the less attractive, transition within the grim sectarian warrior of 1883–4.

Saunderson's new confidence in the future of Ireland was complemented by a growing faith in his own merits and abilities. These were years of unprecedented public exposure: his frequent parliamentary statements and relentless campaigning meant that the English public was becoming better acquainted with both Saunderson and his convictions. His name was on many lips, and he gleefully reported back to Helena whenever he found himself being discussed within his own earshot. One benign Catholic priest rather generously—given Saunderson's coruscating assaults on the Catholic hierarchy—deemed him to be 'a very good man'; an English companion on a train journey inadvertently provided a less flattering

[60] Ibid. iv. 1613 (23 May 1892): 'I do speak in the name of the most powerful section of the Irish people.'

[61] Ibid. iv. 1614 (23 May 1892).

assessment of Saunderson's physical attributes.[62] Saunderson was enchanted by fame: he was vain, and even relatively insignificant aspects of his celebrity were judged worthy of comment. When his portrait was painted by Edwin Long in 1889, he wrote back to Helena; when Pellegrini ('Ape') of *Vanity Fair* drew his caricature, he made several references to the accolade;[63] even the fact that a northern entrepreneur was reproducing his photograph for mass circulation was deemed worthy of report.[64]

He needed applause. And yet the success of his humour jeopardized his political standing. For while it would be over-simplistic to suggest that he wholly lost credibility, it seems that Saunderson often spoke in a jocular vein when a greater gravity would have been more appropriate. He was intensely proud of the success of his humour; and Helena was provided with the details of his various comic triumphs. Perhaps because of this combination of vanity and susceptibility—the unrelenting need to play to the gallery—Saunderson increasingly accepted the role of stage Irishman. It was an unsubtle ploy, but—to judge by the interpolation 'laughter' sprinkled through the reports of Saunderson's speeches in *Hansard*—his audience was responsive. It was a sad comment on British interest that in many Irish debates only the promise of Saunderson's slapstick belligerence attracted a substantial parliamentary audience. It was ironic that Saunderson's chief value as a Unionist proselytizer may have sprung from his ritual Irishness; and that his most effective ploy lay neither in rational argument nor in appeals to sentiment, but in a knockabout comedy.

His popularity in Ulster had long been established, and increased as the perception of external threat became clearer. R. D. Blumenfeld of the *Daily Express* was astonished by the veneration which Carson attracted in 1913, but in fact this had been foreshadowed in Saunderson's career: just as, at the height of the third Home Rule Bill drama, Blumenfeld witnessed a woman bending over to kiss Carson's hand, so Saunderson found himself similarly reverenced in July 1888.[65] But, while Carson remained acutely conscious of the vagaries of public opinion, Saunderson blithely accepted adoration, and looked for no more substantial token of popular esteem than

[62] ESP, T.2996/2B/381: Saunderson to Helena, 31 Mar. 1888; ESP, T.2996/1/106: Saunderson to Helena, 15 Sept. 1886.

[63] ESP, T.2996/2B/428: Saunderson to Helena, 17 Aug. 1889; ESP, T.2996/2B/432: Saunderson to Helena, 24 Aug. 1889; ESP, T.2996/1/125: Saunderson to Helena, 5 Feb. 1887.

[64] ESP, T.2996/1/133: Saunderson to Helena, 17 Feb. 1887.

[65] R. D. Blumenfeld, *R.D.B.'s Procession* (London, 1934); ESP, T.2996/2B/389: Saunderson to Helena, 15 July 1888.

the applause given at a meeting. When the Unionist government was defeated in July 1892, and Home Rule re-entered public debate, Saunderson's reputation seemed unassailable. A Titan within Protestant politics, he assumed that his foibles of class and creed would be accepted unflinchingly; and this assumption was justified—until the constitutional threat faded from among Unionist concerns.

IV

It would be quite wrong to judge the forms of Unionist opposition in 1892–3 as essentially or even symbolically middle-class: landed elements, represented most obviously by Saunderson, contributed as much as ever.[66] The input of Belfast mercantile Toryism into political displays and organizational structures was not significantly greater at the time of the second Home Rule Bill than at the time of the first. The earliest symptoms of middle-class ascendancy within Ulster Unionism only came much later (as indeed Nicholas Mansergh recognized as long ago as 1936[67]).

Thus the Ulster Unionist Convention of June 1892, once hailed as symbolic of middle-class triumphalism, in reality only illustrates the class consensus within Unionism.[68] Plans for such a monster meeting had been laid in 1886, when the landed element remained undeniably crucial for Unionism, and even in 1892 much of the development of the convention scheme lay with decidedly gentrified elements.[69] The idea for a convention was revived early in that year by six 'representative' Liberal Unionists and Conservatives, meeting in the Ulster Reform Club. A fuller debate took place on 31 March, at Downshire House in Belgrave Square, London, where seventeen senior Irish Unionists gathered under the presidency of Lord Arthur Hill. Of this group eight were landed gentlemen, and two were lawyers with strong family ties to the land: Arthur Hill was an uncle of the sixth marquess of Downshire, one of the greatest landed proprietors in Ireland.[70] Saunderson was one of three Irish Unionist MPs appointed to

[66] *Pace* Peter Gibbon, *The Origins of Ulster Unionism: The Formation of Popular Protestant Politics and Ideology in Nineteenth-Century Ireland* (Manchester, 1975).

[67] Nicholas Mansergh, *The Government of Northern Ireland: A Study in Devolution* (London, 1936), 244. Mansergh's source is J. W. Good, *Irish Unionism* (Dublin, 1920), 226: Good distinguishes between landlords and 'men, who having made money in business, aspired to crown their achievement by entering the ranks of the county families'.

[68] Gibbon, *Origins of Ulster Unionism*, 130–1.

[69] *BNL*, 22 Apr. 1886, p. 5.

[70] Ibid., 1 Apr. 1892, p. 5.

a parliamentary standing committee which was designed to liaise with the activists in Ulster.[71] Furthermore, despite his unblushing landlordism, Saunderson was one of the principal speakers at an important meeting held in Belfast on 8 April to further plans for the convention.[72] And on 9 May he chaired a meeting of Irish Unionist members in London in which 'matters connected with the forthcoming Convention in Belfast were discussed in detail and certain preliminary arrangements were made'.[73] On the day of the convention, 17 June 1892, Saunderson played an important, but not pre-eminent, role in the proceedings: this reticence was of a piece with his earlier behaviour, when he had been influential in organizing key demonstrations only to shrink from public participation.[74]

Still, other landlords (Hugh de Fellenberg Montgomery, for example) were more consistently involved with the details of local organization; and there was a certain amount of apologetic in Saunderson's public statements when, at the end of June 1892, he made a rare visit to North Armagh in order to be re-elected as MP. Indeed, his election address referred prominently to the 'great forbearance' of his supporters in the constituency 'which has enabled me to devote myself principally to Unionist work on the other side of the water'.[75] Similarly, in a letter of 7 June 1892 to his constituents, he explained in a rather peeved tone that 'I am doing better work over here than I could be doing in Ireland. I should much rather be with you but I could not throw over the meetings on this side without very bad results.'[76] He was proclaiming a priority which he had long felt, and expressing, too, a confidence in the loyalist solidarity which he had helped to construct.

Yet while he campaigned in Britain, partly through preference, and partly through a calculation of political advantage, he felt no unequivocal sense of Britishness. His loyalism, whether in 1886 or in 1892, was of the contractual form defined and dissected by David Miller.[77] He did not accept that a British government could legitimately force a Home Rule Bill on to the statute books: on 8 April, speaking in Belfast, he explicitly denied that Westminster 'had the right to hand us over to another law-making

[71] *BNL*, 1 Apr. 1892, p. 5. See also Thomas Macknight, *Ulster as It Is*, 2 vols. (London, 1896), ii. 291–3.

[72] *BNL*, 9 Apr. 1892, p. 7.

[73] Ibid., 10 May 1892, p. 5.

[74] Ibid., 18 June 1892, p. 5.

[75] Ibid., 30 June 1892, p. 4.

[76] Ibid., 7 June 1892, p. 5.

[77] David W. Miller, *Queen's Rebels: Ulster Loyalism in Historical Perspective* (Dublin, 1978), *passim*.

power to which we have never given our allegiance and never shall'.[78] And in his election address (which was ecstatically endorsed by the *Belfast News Letter*) he questioned the legitimacy of a Home Rule policy by resorting to an imputation of conspiracy: Gladstone was attempting to thrust Irish loyalism under Romish tyranny in return for a sordid parliamentary majority.[79] Ultimately—in 1912–14—this denial of British authority would be used to justify preparations for rebellion. But from Saunderson's English and parliamentary perspective, such arguments chiefly served a rhetorical function—one of the many methods of scaring Englishmen, and of discrediting Home Rule and its architect, Gladstone. Saunderson was therefore a negative Unionist, an anti-Home Ruler, and he was not as yet interested in any more intricate creed.

Not quite British, and yet often exiled from Ireland, Saunderson turned to a sentimental conception of national identity. His cloying Irishness before the House of Commons has already been noted: it should also be emphasized that many Irish Unionists (and Nationalists) with a firmer Irish base than Saunderson rarely stated their identity with his bluntness. It was sometimes a self-mocking caricature, and it was linked to his slow retreat from the more demanding complexities of the Irish political scene. Donning his nationality before English audiences, he appealed to their prejudices, making few claims on their (or indeed his own) political imagination. Campaigning in England released Saunderson from a more demanding local audience: he was free from the need to flex class and denominational conviction, free from having to sustain an unhappy rhetorical balance between incitement and moderation.

Saunderson was bitterly shaken by the Unionist defeat at the general election of 1892, and for a time it seemed that he had come to believe that local organization in Ireland, and specifically in Ulster, represented a more effective Unionist resource than support within Britain. Writing to the Grand Master of the Belfast Orangemen on 11 July 1892, he complained about the perfidy of the British electorate; and he effectively confessed that his seven years of political evangelism in Britain had been wasted:

> the course of events in England and Scotland should teach Ulster loyalists that, in the long run, they must trust to their own strength and unflinching determination . . . if a just cause could win the support of the British voter we should now be in an overwhelming majority.[80]

[78] *BNL*, 9 Apr. 1892, p. 7.
[79] Ibid., 30 June 1892, p. 4.
[80] Ibid., 13 July 1892, p. 6.

Yet, despite this revelation, Saunderson still distanced himself from certain crucial developments within Ulster. He signed the manifesto which launched the Ulster Defence Union, but there is no evidence of any more substantial input to this organization. He played little or no role in the formation of the Ulster Convention League, and the Templetown Unionist Clubs.[81] For all his despair, he clung rigidly to the political arena which he had claimed as his own: the British House of Commons, and the British campaign trail. Illness and weakness had erased some of the desperate vitality which he had once displayed, but in the winter recess he could still deliver speeches at Bath (where Helena and he had gone for a cure), Glasgow, at the Non-Conformist Council in London, and, on 20 December, at Lurgan—his sole visit to the constituency between the general election and the introduction of the Home Rule Bill.[82] On 16 March 1893, in the midst of his parliamentary commitments, he travelled to Liverpool in order to address a noisily appreciative demonstration of Orangemen.[83]

But he remained parliamentary leader of the Irish Unionist movement, and it was in the House of Commons, during the debates on the second Home Rule Bill, that Saunderson focused his energies. In aggregate it was a sombre and revealing performance, with Saunderson oscillating between defiance and despair. Like many Irish Unionist MPs, he seemed convinced that the government's indelicate handling of local susceptibilities might provoke violence; but he was an old enough parliamentary hand to know that the House would not tolerate anything like blackmail. Thus he often offered only allusions—and even these provoked a certain mockery.[84] Yet there were occasions when it seemed that his single-minded Unionist truculence would give way to an icier pragmatism. At the very beginning of the Bill's progress—the debate on the Introduction—Saunderson had blustered his opposition ('I do not care and my people do not care a farthing about the details of the Bill').[85] By the committee stage, in May 1893, Saunderson's statements were beginning to lend credence to the old rumour that he tacitly accepted the inevitability of Home Rule ('their stand was that if there was to be Home Rule in Ireland, then it ought to be the

[81] *BNL*, 17 Mar. 1893, p. 5 (the publication of the Ulster Defence Union manifesto); ibid., 9 Jan. 1893, p. 7 (the formation of the Unionist Clubs movement).

[82] Ibid., 3 Nov. 1892, p. 5 (Bath); ibid., 5 Nov. 1892, p. 4 (Glasgow); ibid., 20 Dec. 1892, p. 6 (Lurgan); ibid., 11 Nov. 1892, p. 4 (London).

[83] Ibid., 16 Mar. 1893, p. 5.

[84] *Hansard*, ser. 4, viii. 1328 (13 Feb. 1893): 'I have no intention at the present moment—and there is no need that I should utter any threats ...'; ibid. xi. 856 (20 Apr. 1893).

[85] Ibid. viii. 1328 (13 Feb. 1893).

least noxious kind of Home Rule that the House could devise').[86] He would later explain these odd lapses from orthodoxy by arguing that he had been attempting to wreck the Bill—but he might have furthered this end in a more destructive and less ambiguous fashion. It may well be that Saunderson, for all his posturing, had quietly accepted that on the constitutional, as on the land question, he was merely fighting a doomed rearguard action.

This is further suggested by the bitterness of his attitude towards Britain. Having once flirted with the notion of a contractual bond between loyalism and the British government, he now regarded the Home Rule debate as a breach of its terms. This, in Saunderson's reasoning, justified active resistance in Ulster; but a sense of betrayal also underlay the dyspeptic tone of his contribution. He loudly proclaimed his indifference to British interests, and indeed to the British connection itself—in the event of Home Rule. His anger did not alter his convictions about who should control the Royal Irish Constabulary and the judiciary: whatever its demerits, British control offered marginally greater security than any Home Rule executive.[87] But his faith extended little further. Thus he argued for the removal of the British army from Home Rule Ireland—so that loyalists should be preserved from any deadly collusion between the Irish and British parliaments, and British military force.[88] Similarly, all Irish members (he included himself, evidently) should be withdrawn from Westminster—again in order to prevent Home Rulers putting pressure on a British government, and possibly infringing loyalist rights.[89] When Edward Grey, one of the few Liberal ministers who was publicly prepared to take seriously Saunderson's disquiet, promised that the British government would guarantee the rights of the Irish minority, Saunderson reacted scathingly: 'I ask him [Grey] what suffering minority has this country ever protected?'[90] And when the financial clauses of the Bill were under consideration (on 25 July 1893), Saunderson was equally tetchy on the issue of Ireland's contribution to the Imperial Exchequer: 'if they snapped the connection between this country and Ireland, so far as the collection of British tribute was concerned, he for one did not care a farthing'.[91]

The Home Rule Bill was given a third reading on 3 September—and,

[86] Ibid. xii. 486 (9 May 1893).
[87] Ibid. xiii. 284 (5 June 1893); ibid. xv. 150 (20 July 1893).
[88] Ibid. xii. 486 (9 May 1893).
[89] Ibid. xiv. 1227 (10 July 1893).
[90] Ibid. xvi. 1775 (1 Sept. 1893). John Atkinson, a former Unionist MP for North Derry and Lord of Appeal, uttered similar sentiments in 1908: Jackson, *Ulster Party*, 122.
[91] *Hansard*, ser. 4, xv. 498 (25 July 1893).

shortly afterwards, on 8 September, was rejected by the House of Lords. This outcome had of course been widely forecast, though the likelihood of the Bill's demise had done nothing to reassure Saunderson and his colleagues. Gladstone had made several ominous allusions to the reform of the Upper House in the event of sustained Unionist obduracy, and Saunderson had thought these threats worth rebutting before the Home Rule Bill passed through the House of Commons.[92] Even with a Tory majority, there was still the possibility that the Lords might be coerced; and even when they defiantly rejected the Bill, Gladstone's threat remained.

Thus constitutional uncertainty in 1893 extended beyond the question of the Union, and while the fate of the Home Rule Bill might have been predictable, the fate of the Lords—and therefore of a key Unionist bulwark—was more problematic. Given this political atmosphere, Saunderson's acute and enduring anxiety becomes comprehensible.[93] Equally, this dual uncertainty at the heart of government explains and vindicates Saunderson's neglect of his constituency and of Belfast in favour of parliament. In the long term this choice of priorities would damage his local credibility, but in 1893 he had emerged triumphant from what had been, in essence, a parliamentary contest.

[92] *Hansard*, ser. 4, xvi. 1775 (1 Sept. 1893).

[93] This concern was not confined to Saunderson, of course. The leading Tory QC and Belfast-born Unionist, Sir William T. Charley, was moved to write *The Crusade Against the Constitution: An Historical Vindication of the House of Lords* (London, 1895): pp. 354–63 deal with the relevance of the Lords' veto to the Home Rule debate.

9

The Implications of Victory, 1893–1900

I

Home Rule moved further from the realms of practical politics with the retirement of Gladstone in March 1894 and the defeat of the Liberal Government at the general election of June 1895. Saunderson, therefore, found himself one of the victors in a constitutional struggle which had lasted virtually a decade. And, within the span of his life, the victory became definitive: as Reginald Lucas commented in 1908, 'Saunderson's labours in one sense were at an end. He was not to live to see another serious attempt to establish Home Rule.'[1] Within the Commons, in the short term, this political realignment was only dimly perceived: the constitutional uncertainty of the Home Rule years was maintained by Rosebery's continued and threatening references to the future of the House of Lords. But, in the rural constituencies of Ulster, the defeat of Home Rule was immediately interpreted as an irrevocable achievement which cleared the political agenda, and which permitted reform agitation. From one perspective, therefore, the victory of 1893 was of equivocal value, for it exposed the profound inadequacy of the Unionist alliance just as surely as it demoralized the Liberals.

In certain respects the national debate had been undemanding for Unionists like Saunderson—once, that is, the outline of their response to Parnell had been formulated (as it was between 1883 and 1887). The constituent parties and sections within Unionism might compete for terms—but they were ultimately committed to the survival of their alliance. After 1893 this commitment was no longer so evident, at any rate at a local level; and Saunderson, as the parliamentary leader of Unionism, was faced with an uniquely complicated task of party diplomacy. That he rejected this challenge only proved that he had been no less affected by the liberation of 1893 than the Ulster tenants. Instead of promoting a new form of Unionist consensus, Saunderson slowly sacrificed his popularity and his

[1] Reginald Lucas, *Colonel Saunderson MP: A Memoir* (London 1908), 206.

leadership by meeting the class politics of the farmers with a sectional case of his own.

The last twelve years of his life were dominated by a recrudescence of the land debate. The period was a sad appendage to earlier years of immense celebrity and considerable achievement, in Ireland and especially in the House of Commons. Saunderson had become a prisoner of his own reputation; the heroic and articulate warrior of the Home Rule struggle would not shed his defiance in the light of new political conditions. The consequence was that Saunderson became a secondary figure within virtually all his earlier fields of action. By the turn of the century, he had become almost a cipher: a venerable, if occasionally embarrassing, relic, decidedly more useful as part of the mythology of 1886 than as a real and active figure.

Yet it would be wrong to suggest that Saunderson was a wholly immobile political force through the mid- to late 1890s, for, within the limitations of his political stand, he displayed ingenuity and resourcefulness. The problem was that his stand was limited; and, while other Tories swayed and trimmed according to local rural opinion, Saunderson remained an unrepentant advocate of landlord rights. He retained a reputation for principle, and for violent rhetoric; but it soon became clear that unpopular principles expressed in acerbic language would not promote either the continued success of his own leadership, or the health of Irish Unionism.

His defence of landlordism had developed from his tentative beginnings as a Gladstonian Liberal, and as a progenitor of the loyalist alliance in the early 1880s. Freed from the shackles of party loyalty in 1893, Saunderson articulated his class prejudices with greater vigour—and with disastrous consequences for his reputation among some of the most important elements of Irish Unionism. For when, after late 1893, Unionist farmers began to agitate, Saunderson responded not with effective compromise, but by conjuring up the prospect of an anti-bourgeois alliance. If the larger, and more radical farmers were going to threaten an essentially conservative coalition, then Saunderson was prepared to consider other forms of electoral combination. If the loyalist class alliance of 1886 was failing, then he would project a new—and more constrained—alliance for a new political environment.

II

Saunderson's relations with middle-class and urban Unionists had always been cool.[2] This was partly because the reform demands of comparatively prosperous northern farmers had clashed with his own, landed interests. But the difficulty extended beyond a brutal conflict of class. Saunderson had several times fallen foul of the industrial and mercantile élite within Belfast Toryism.[3] Moreover, he held prejudices against specific elements of the middle-class establishment, and in particular against the legal profession (an important vehicle for upward social mobility in late-nineteeth-century Ireland). While this sentiment was shared by radical tenant representatives like T. W. Russell, Saunderson believed that it was the landlords who were the principal victims of legal parasitism.[4]

Against this dark vision of middle-class avarice, Saunderson erected a much more favourable image of rural labourers and textile workers, and (to a lesser degree) the urban working classes; and it was to the plight of these groups that he turned in order to place farmer demands in a comparative perspective. He took a paternalist interest in limited reforms: he was, for example, a consistent advocate of better conditions of employment for handloom weavers (who constituted an important element of his electorate). On a number of occasions he attempted to push through an ameliorative Bill—but without success, either in the private members' ballot, or in terms of enlisting the interest and backing of parliamentary colleagues (he once confessed to a constituency meeting that only Henry Labouchere had offered his firm support).[5] Certainly Irish linen barons, such as W. R. Young of Galgorm, County Antrim, were uniformly offended by this strategy.[6] Saunderson was equally persistent in pursuing the rights of rural labourers (particularly with regard to the allocation of adequate housing and land). For, as with the handloom weavers, he viewed the labouring

[2] See above, p. 68.

[3] See above, pp. 91–4.

[4] Saunderson's opinion of lawyers had changed little over the years. In this context see *Hansard*, ser. 4, xxxi. 359 (4 Mar. 1895): 'the lawyers were the only people that had fattened on the land in Ireland'; also ibid. xxxii. 962 (4 Apr. 1895): 'they [lawyers] would reap a crop every 10 years instead of every 15. The expenses would come mainly out of the pockets of the landlords.'

[5] *BNL*, 20 Dec. 1892, p. 6 (speaking at Lurgan). Saunderson described the weavers as 'an industrious and law-abiding class', identifying them as his electoral mainstay.

[6] PRONI, W. R. Young Papers, D.3027/7/8–11: MS of 'Recollections of 75 Years in Ulster' (Nov. 1931), fo. 146: 'In 1888 I was unfortunately brought into collision with Col. Saunderson over a Linen Hand-loom Bill which the gallant Member had introduced into the House of Commons.'

class as a useful buttress to loyalism—indeed more useful because less demanding and less provocative than the farmers.

These class commitments translated into a virtually uniform rejection of the Liberal government's successive land initiatives between 1892 and 1895. Saunderson was still careful to retain some semblance of sympathy towards Unionist farmers, but more characteristic were his savage denunciations of those measures which were intended to benefit them. Thus, when in April 1894 John Morley introduced a Bill to reinstate evicted tenants, Saunderson characterized it as an effort 'to whitewash the Plan of Campaign and its authors': it was a 'direct attack upon the landowning class'.[7] Although T. W. Russell pleaded for greater caution, Saunderson (acting with the blessing of the opposition front bench) moved the rejection of the Bill on 20 July.[8] A humiliated Russell looked for compensating Tory flexibility during the sittings of Morley's Select Committee on the Irish Land Laws; and, finding none, he turned to organized farmer agitation in Ulster during the winter of 1894–5.[9]

Although Russell's initiative aligned an impressive section of northern farming opinion behind Morley, Saunderson was angrily dismissive. Part of the purpose of the agitation had been to coerce Ulster Unionist MPs into supporting Morley's forthcoming Land Bill; and even setting aside the farmers' specific demands (such as compulsory purchase), Saunderson had been irritated by the fact of this presumptuous interference. Compulsory purchase was of course anathema—but the milder Land Bill, introduced in March 1895, proved little more attractive. There were certainly some aspects which he was able to commend. But he was particularly aggrieved by a clause which would have guaranteed to farmers both the value of their improvements *and* the amount by which the whole farm had increased in value.[10] This smacked of dual ownership—vesting the tenant with 'a distinct ownership in the soil', and Saunderson had always treated this pusillanimous Gladstonian concept as being tantamount to expropriation.[11] It seemed as if he wanted all improvements on the land carried out before 1850 to be deemed the landlords' property (Morley had apparently suggested that all improvements made before 1850 might be judged the

[7] *Hansard*, ser. 4, xxiii. 925 (19 Apr. 1894).

[8] Ibid. xxvii. 435 (20 July 1894); Alvin Jackson, 'Irish Unionism and the Russellite Threat, 1894–1906', *IHS* 25/100 (Nov. 1987), 385.

[9] Jackson, 'Russellite Threat', 385.

[10] *Hansard*, ser. 4, xxxi. 358 (4 Mar. 1895): 'there were many things in the Bill with which he was inclined entirely to agree.'

[11] Ibid. xxxi. 357–8 (4 Mar. 1895).

property of the tenants); but he was evidently confused on this score, and the Chief Secretary had to offer correction.[12]

Russell's agitation had privately convinced Saunderson that some concessions would have to be made in order to dampen unrest—but the Colonel was equally certain that Morley's Bill was an inappropriate emollient.[13] Thus, he deprecated a decision, taken by the Unionist leaders, to permit the Bill an unopposed second reading—and, having been overruled, he advertised his qualified disapproval in the House of Commons.[14] He questioned Morley's sincerity in promoting the measure, imputing devious Home Rule ambitions to the Chief Secretary: the latter was seeking 'to sweep the landlords away, and to try, if possible, to throw down a bone of contention in Ulster, over which the Unionist Party could fight'.[15]

Whatever the reality of Morley's intentions, his Land Bill had certainly inflamed the latent class divisions within Ulster Unionism; and Saunderson's rhetoric and attitude had done nothing to reconcile the demands of farmers with landlord interests. There were no overtures to farmer representatives, no private negotiations with Russell, and there were few appropriately temporizing statements of opinion. In the event, the Bill died along with the Rosebery government in June 1895. But, while Saunderson may have rejoiced privately that his opposition had prevented any precipitate settlement, the reality was that Morley had bequeathed both a difficulty and the outlines of a settlement to his Unionist successor, Gerald Balfour. It would rapidly become obvious that, given the fissile state of Ulster Unionism, Morley had represented a not unfriendly arbiter (or, at any rate, a useful scapegoat for the grievances of Unionist farmer and landowner). That it was a Unionist government which had to devise a Land Bill meant that it was a Unionist Chief Secretary who had to act as arbiter and scapegoat: and this bleak equation suggested a whole new range of schism within the loyalist alliance.

Yet any argument that the policies of Gerald Balfour and of his successor as Chief Secretary, George Wyndham, actually caused loyalist division would be unrealistically glib.[16] Indeed, it would probably be more accurate to assume that many Unionist reforms for Ireland were conceived

[12] Ibid.

[13] HH, Salisbury Papers, E/Saunderson/19: Saunderson to Salisbury, 19 Mar. 1895 ('That some Bill was needed is not denied . . .').

[14] Ibid. The letter, *inter alia*, strongly argues against a second reading of the Bill.

[15] *Hansard*, ser. 4, xxxii. 965 (4 Apr. 1895).

[16] *Pace* Andrew Gailey's argument in his important *Ireland and the Death of Kindness: The Experience of Constructive Unionism, 1890–1905* (Cork, 1987), 136–7, 210–11.

at least partly as an exercise in damage limitation—as an effort to minimize pre-existing tensions among Irish Unionists by appeasing the electorally influential and disenchanted farmers at the expense of the socially influential and disenchanted landlords.[17] The fact was that, while their solidarity was generally exaggerated, the threat of division and disaster for Irish Unionists could be much greater under a Liberal regime. The flirtation between northern farmers and the Land League in the early 1880s, or the co-operation between T. W. Russell and John Morley over land reform in 1894–5, raised more problems for Irish Unionism than any Conservative measure of reform. In the context of Dublin or Ulster—in Unionist terms the only areas of political strength—there were comparatively few loyalists who really cared about the expropriation of the landlords or the democratization of local government. These few recusants certainly had a high political profile; but, against a background of mass disapproval, or at best apathy, they could register their opinions with only an ephemeral success. The really crucial divisions in Ulster Unionism—the constituency tensions of the turn of the century—had more to do with older structural weaknesses in the movement than with British legislation. Popular disquiet at loyalist unrepresentativeness, for example, had little direct connection with Dublin Castle and the Irish Office. It has been said that 'killing Home Rule by kindness' came close to dispatching Irish Unionism; but the truth was that Irish Unionism was more than capable of killing itself.[18]

The evidence for this argument lies not merely in the popular political initiatives created by T. W. Russell, but also with the élite politics of a fellow Liberal Unionist, Horace Plunkett.[19] Plunkett was a son of the sixteenth Baron Dunsany, and was prominent as a pioneer of agricultural co-operation in Ireland: after 1892 he sat as the Liberal Unionist MP for South County Dublin. He was an astonishingly maladroit politician, but his broadly based experience of agricultural issues and his creative approach to the constitutional question provided him with an influence far beyond the official structures of Irish Unionism. As a nobleman, and as an Etonian and Oxonian—he was an exact school contemporary of Gerald Balfour—he had political resources denied to Saunderson. He swiftly

[17] Jackson, *The Ulster Party: Irish Unionists in the House of Commons, 1884–1911* (Oxford, 1989) 168–9.

[18] Gailey, *Death of Kindness*, 137.

[19] For Plunkett's career see: Trevor West, *Horace Plunkett, Co-operation and Politics: An Irish Biography* (Gerrards Cross, 1986); Margaret Digby, *Horace Plunkett: An Anglo-American Irishman* (Oxford, 1949). See also Carla Keating (ed.), *Plunkett and Co-operatives: Past, Present and Future* (Cork, 1983).

emerged as one of the ideologues influencing the central thrust of British Conservative strategy in Ireland between 1895 and 1900; and as such, he frequently and casually offended his Irish Unionist colleagues.

In August 1895, shortly after the return of the Unionists to power, Plunkett wrote to the press, recommending the creation of an all-party conference to discuss state assistance for Irish agriculture.[20] He hoped that this appeal would transcend Irish party divisions; and indeed he, as a Unionist MP, constructed the committee with the assistance of a veteran of the Plan of Campaign, T. P. Gill. John Redmond joined Plunkett's convention (which, sitting outside the parliamentary session, was soon labelled the 'Recess Committee'); Justin McCarthy, the anti-Parnellite leader, demurred. Saunderson, whose suspicions were aroused by Gill and Redmond's involvement, also condemned the proposal, and claimed that the underlying motivation was Nationalist.[21] But he was to some extent wrong-footed. Although the two principal northern Unionist newspapers at first echoed his qualms, Ulster Liberal Unionists endorsed the scheme, and decisively influenced mainstream loyalist opinion.[22] Saunderson was therefore isolated by his stand, and this, combined with his opposition to T. W. Russell, meant that he appeared to be out of touch with the most thoughtful and enlightened elements of his own community.

The Recess Committee episode confirmed Saunderson in his landed convictions, but it also permanently soured his political relationship with Plunkett. Plunkett had an extensive influence with a political constituency—Unionist intellectuals, the Balfour brothers, Liberal Unionism in Ireland—which was often beyond Saunderson's grasp, and this worked against his loyalty to the Irish Unionist parliamentary party, and against his loyalty to Saunderson. Plunkett flagrantly defied his party in February 1896, by speaking in favour of an amnesty for Fenian prisoners: unsurprisingly this contribution outraged his Irish Unionist colleagues—and many of his suburban constituents—and Saunderson reluctantly wrote 'a stiff letter' by way of rebuke.[23] The financial relations controversy of 1896–7 brought Plunkett and Saunderson back into an alliance, but this proved to be purely pragmatic, and short-lived. Although in February 1900 Plunkett still claimed to be on good personal terms with his leader, the appointment of T. P. Gill as the Secretary of the new Irish Department

[20] West, *Plunkett*, 41 ff.

[21] Ibid. 45; Lucas, *Saunderson*, 240–3.

[22] West, *Plunkett*, 45.

[23] Lucas, *Saunderson*, 247; Jackson, *Ulster Party*, 107. See also Alvin Jackson, 'The Failure of Unionism in Dublin, 1900', *IHS*, 26/104 (Nov. 1989), 377–95.

of Agriculture angered Saunderson and those Unionists who had hoped that the office would be awarded to a Catholic loyalist.[24] By 1900, therefore, Saunderson had clashed with Irish Liberal Unionism in the forms represented by both Russell and Plunkett; by 1900 it was becoming clear that Saunderson was merely the captain of a conservative fragment of Unionism.

III

The tensions between Saunderson and radical Irish Unionists were not, therefore, an external Tory creation or an English imposition: they were integral to Irish Unionism in the years after the defeat of the second Home Rule Bill. The land reforms of Gerald Balfour's reign as Chief Secretary for Ireland from 1895 to 1900 helped to create a small but extremely noisy coterie of landed malcontents; but they also mitigated potentially more disastrous unrest, expressed in the rural constituencies of Ulster between late 1893 and mid-1896. That Saunderson identified himself prominently with the landlord revolt undoubtedly contributed to the parliamentary and press exposure which it received. But this could not obscure the fact that, from the popular perspective, Saunderson had bound himself to a marginal and damaging cause.

Gerald Balfour outlined his Land Bill to parliament on 12 April 1896, offering reform in three vital areas of debate: the law of tenure, the procedure of the Land Commission, and purchase arrangements.[25] Many Unionist members, especially those sitting for Ulster constituencies, registered warm approval, and the *Belfast News Letter*, reflecting the tactical perceptions of urban Toryism, provided similar endorsement.[26] But Saunderson was among a small number of Irish landowners who, while not unequivocally discouraging, were much more restrained than their loyalist colleagues. Saunderson was at first cautiously supportive, emphasizing the need for amendment; but his speeches, never particularly rigorous or detailed, now suggested more theatrical than business capacity—and while effectively approving much of the Bill, he also lapsed into familiar,

[24] HH, Salisbury Papers, E/Saunderson/26: Saunderson to Salisbury, 30 June 1900.

[25] *Hansard*, ser. 4, xxxix. 781 (12 Apr. 1896).

[26] *BNL*, 14 Apr. 1896, pp. 4, 5 (editorial and London letter); ibid., 18 Apr. 1896, p. 4 (editorial); ibid., 19 June 1896, p. 5 (editorial). *Hansard*, ser. 4, xli. 640 (8 June 1896, D. P. Barton); ibid. xli. 1005 (12 June 1896, James Rentoul).

lugubrious rhetoric.[27] It was emotion—despair, anger—which would characterize his future contributions. Partnered by Edward Carson and Arthur Smith-Barry, Saunderson provided a belligerent underpinning to their more reasoned assault on the Bill.

Landlord hopes centred on the Committee Stage, and on the government's willingness to excise some of the Bill's more objectionable features. And, indeed, for a time a reconciliation seemed possible on the basis of an amended measure: Saunderson had several meetings with ministers, culminating on 26 June 1896 when he joined Gerald Balfour and Edward Carson in conclave.[28] Balfour at any rate felt confident that a compromise might be struck: 'on some of the points on which they lay most stress', he reported to Salisbury, 'I think that it would be possible to arrive at something like an agreement.'[29] This optimism seemed to be vindicated when the landlords' anger faltered and when several of their amendments were incorporated into the Bill. As late as 20 July Saunderson was claiming that 'he had no desire to injure the Bill, but he wanted it to be a success'; on the following day, however, a rather bleaker perception had gained currency.[30]

The government's responsiveness to the landlords was determined partly by Salisbury's prejudices, but also very largely by parliamentary experience—by an incomplete, but still vivid perception of the landlords' nuisance value.[31] Their willingness to accept landlord amendments was thus in part a limited operation to deflate what was perceived as simply an irritating and temporary opposition. When even these gestures threatened the tentative support of tractable Nationalists (like T. M. Healy) for the Bill, and also threatened to precipitate T. W. Russell into a new agitation in Ulster, Gerald Balfour abandoned all palliatives; and the landlords, humiliated by this new revelation of government priorities, marched defiantly out of the Commons on 21 July.[32] At the end of the month, on 29 July, Saunderson and Smith-Barry returned to move the rejection of the

[27] *Hansard*, ser. 4. xli, 651 (8 June 1896): Saunderson's major speech on the second reading of the Bill.

[28] HH, Salisbury Papers, E/Gerald Balfour/20: Gerald Balfour to Salisbury, 25 June 1896; ibid., E/Londonderry/170: Londonderry to Salisbury, 14 May 1896.

[29] Ibid., E/Gerald Balfour/20: Gerald Balfour to Salisbury, 25 June 1896.

[30] *Hansard*, ser. 4, xliii. 227 (20 July 1896).

[31] For Salisbury's landlordism see Peter Marsh, *The Discipline of Popular Government: Lord Salisbury's Domestic Statecraft, 1881–1902* (Hassocks, 1978), 155–65.

[32] *BNL*, 11 July 1896, p. 5 (London letter), and 13 July 1896, p. 5. In the 13 July edn. the prospect of Russell's resignation was debated: by 14 July it was clear that Russell had been squared by his ministerial colleagues.

Bill.[33] From Saunderson's point of view it was the logical culmination of years of disquiet at the actions of the Tory front bench, and of the Ulster farmers. He had now wholly shed the mantle of class compromise, and had resigned himself to the isolation of last-ditch politics. Abandoning all hope of a truly consensual approach, whether in Britain or in Ireland, Saunderson embarked upon a career of independent dissent.

This dissent took various forms—but its inspiration generally emanated from the London committee of the Irish Landowners' Convention. The convention was the representative body of Irish landlordism, and its London committee existed to lobby politicians and opinion-formers of all kinds. Four Ulster Unionist members, out of a complement of perhaps twenty-five, sat on this committee, but it was Saunderson who generally carried the responsibility for presenting convention opinion to the House of Commons.[34] Their grievances at first concerned unacceptable rent reductions and the questionable professionalism of the temporary officials of the Irish Land Commission; and their bitterness deepened when, in 1898, the report of Sir Edward Fry's Royal Commission on Irish land vindicated many of these complaints.[35] Thereafter Saunderson's parliamentary agitation focused on the enactment of the Fry recommendations.

While the landlord campaign had a limited legislative impact (in the Tithe Rent Charge Act of 1900, for example), Saunderson's flight from Tory discipline took him to less fertile issues. In 1896, in the aftermath of the Childers Report on Irish finance, he became a proponent of a revision in the fiscal relationship between England and Ireland. He chaired a joint protest meeting with the Nationalists on 9 March 1897, and intermittently raised the subject in the Commons until July 1898, when a full debate was held.[36] But the subject generated little interest and less enthusiasm. Only the Nationalists were wholly in favour of a reduction in Irish taxation, and even then they clashed with Saunderson in explaining their joint stand.[37]

This dissent was essentially a display of class pique—and the price of self-indulgence was heavy. As parliamentary leader of the Irish Unionist party, Saunderson had a responsibility to loyalist consensus; but, pres-

[33] *Hansard*, ser. 4, xliii. 940 (29 July 1896).

[34] Jackson, *Ulster Party*, 162.

[35] Agnes Fry, *A Memoir of the Rt. Hon. Sir Edward Fry, GCB* (Oxford, 1921), 109–11; *Hansard*, ser. 4, lxi. 1279 (15 July 1898); ibid. lxvii. 59 (21 Feb. 1899).

[36] Thomas Kennedy, *A History of the Irish Protest Against Over-Taxation from 1853 to 1897* (Dublin, 1897), 131; *Hansard*, ser. 4, lx. 1122 (5 Jul. 1898).

[37] *Hansard*, ser. 4, lx. 1123–4 (5 July 1898).

sured and inflamed by Unionist farmers, he endangered the concept of an independent loyalist party in the interests of a greater commitment to his class. Saunderson, and indeed Russell, had been comparatively flexible on land-related issues in the 1880s. Though class-based tension had developed within Unionism, and at a personal level between Saunderson and Russell, as early as 1887 over Arthur Balfour's first Land Bill, the political implications of this only became fully apparent in 1894, when Russell broke with landlord Unionists over the Morley reform programme, and when his attitude was endorsed by an agitation in rural Ulster.

Saunderson's leadership had been on trial over the tenants' claims—and his dismissive response revealed both an ignorance of local conditions, and a hopelessly static conception of Unionism. He may have come to believe that the Irish Unionist parliamentary party had outlived its usefulness (as a means of regulating and articulating a conservative alliance): at any rate after 1896 he did little to encourage its survival. Saunderson remained parliamentary leader—but of a landed rump, consisting of perhaps six MPs, only one of whom sat for an Ulster constituency. This was Colonel Thomas Waring, member for North Down between 1885 and his death in 1898, and one of Saunderson's closest parliamentary colleagues; the other four supporters were the two members from Trinity and two Irish Unionists representing British constituencies—all of whom could articulate their landlordism with electoral impunity.[38] The Trinity representatives endorsed Saunderson's stand on the financial relations question. But the great majority of Irish Unionist members followed constituency opinion, dissociating themselves from this maverick landlord campaign—so that the divisions within Unionism, viewed from a broad constituency perspective, were in fact limited in scope. Gerald Balfour was widely regarded as a vaguely beneficent figure: at any rate there was no scope for a successful agitation against his administration. If popular Unionism was in search of a bogy, it was not Balfour but Saunderson himself who was threatened with the role.

Nevertheless, outside the land debate Saunderson showed a greater sensitivity to popular opinion. Irish Unionists varied in their response to the prospect of democratic county government, opinion cleaving along north/south lines; but within Ulster there was probably a consensus in favour of this reform. Saunderson at any rate had indicated his support as

[38] These six were the only members present at a meeting of the Irish Unionist parliamentary party held on 11 June 1896: this agreed to oppose a move by the government to suspend the 12 o'clock rule. *BNL*, 12 June 1896, p. 5.

early as 1889, and, sweetened by concessions on the Agricultural Rating Grant, he revived his approval in 1898, when Gerald Balfour's Local Government Bill passed through the Commons.[39] He fought hard to incorporate better guarantees for minority representation and protection (two-member constituencies for the new councils, the removal of autocratic powers to dismiss their employees, the exclusion of all ministers of religion); and privately he may have sympathized with those southern Unionists who were disturbed by the Bill.[40] Certainly, among his approving platitudes traces of an older bitterness and suspicion re-emerged: he ranted against Catholic clericalism, and committed an odd lapse on 14 July which implied that his support was of a somewhat qualified character: 'I acknowledge freely in the House that if the Bill had been unaccompanied by a [agricultural rating] grant such as had been given to the rest of the country, I should have opposed it.'[41] Yet these doubts were swathed in Balfourian rhetoric about the purpose and responsibilities of Unionism, and the opportunities for conciliation created in the new county councils. Saunderson clung to a grudging integrationism, viewing the Bill as 'the inevitable sequitur to the policy of the Unionist party. I do not believe that the government could avoid ... bringing in a Bill of this kind.'[42]

But these were the politics of submission; for the fact was that, whatever his private opinions, Saunderson had little alternative but to support the Bill. Given the government's flexibility on the rating question—a crucial grievance—some landlord anger had been defused. In any case it would have been hard, and particularly so now, in the wake of concession, for Saunderson to have remained a supporter of the government while consistently opposing its Irish policy.[43] Saunderson's stand on local government therefore broke a long period of truculence: local government provided him with the opportunity to come in from the cold periphery of landed extremism.

This was also true at the level of local politics. From a variety of perspectives, county government constituted a vital lifeline between Saun-

[39] Andrew Gailey, 'Unionist Rhetoric and Irish Local Government Reform, 1895–99', *IHS*, 24/93 (May 1984), 62. *Hansard*, ser. 4, xlix. 1049 (21 May 1897); ibid. liii. 1261 (21 Feb. 1898); ibid. lxii. 161 (18 July 1898).

[40] *Hansard*, ser. 4, lvi. 1287 (27 Apr. 1898): doubling of representation; ibid. lvi. 1329 (27 Apr. 1898): raising of membership qualifications; ibid. lvii. 229 (3 May 1898): no powers of dismissal for councils; ibid. lvii. 249 (3 May 1898): state control of asylums; ibid. lviii. 484 (23 May 1898): exclusion of ministers of religion.

[41] *Hansard*, ser. 4, lvi. 981 (14 July 1898).

[42] Ibid. lv. 497 (21 Mar. 1898).

[43] Gailey, 'Unionist Rhetoric', 62.

derson and political reality. In symbolic terms his support meant that he was temporarily saved from being deemed a political relic—hopelessly addled with class prejudice, and clinging on to an unattractively negative Unionism. In practical terms it meant that he could align himself with the consensus of approval within the Ulster party, and begin to make good the damage done by his stand on the Land Bill of 1896. Local government was not just a question of trusting the Irish people (Saunderson reserved judgement on this score); it was also a question of trusting the loyalist democracy of the north. Given the rumblings of disquiet about the unrepresentativeness of the loyalist leadership, neither Saunderson nor the Ulster Party could afford to resist local government. Thus, while he might refer to the self-sacrifice which his stand involved, the truth was that he was merely fabricating a parliamentary virtue out of a local necessity.[44]

And there were other congruities between Saunderson's politics in the late 1890s and popular Ulster Unionist opinion. His Protestant orthodoxy was (as yet) unimpeachable. He violently rejected the Nationalist demand for a Catholic university when the subject was debated in February 1898.[45] He opposed the principle of denominational education; though his opposition to the Irish application of this principle was more likely to have been founded on an intense suspicion of the Catholic hierarchy than on theoretical niceties. While to all intents and purposes a vigorous anti-papist, it was also true that his convictions were free-ranging and included an indiscriminate anticlericalism: his disquisitions on the iniquity of the Catholic hierarchy stemmed from an almost paranoid fear of priestly ascendancy, wherever it might be found. Thus, clerical pretension within the Church of England and the Church of Ireland was also a profound source of worry; and Saunderson was an outspoken anti-ritualist, prepared to contrast the greatness of Protestant Britain—great *because* sceptically Protestant and anticlerical—with those feebler 'nations that have bowed down to the sacerdotal yoke'.[46]

44 *Hansard*, ser. 4, lv. 493–5 (21 Mar. 1898).

45 Ibid. liii. 796 (16 Feb. 1898): John Dillon's motion.

46 Ibid. lxvi. 399 (9 Feb. 1899): Samuel Smith's anti-ritualist motion. Saunderson opposed the Church Discipline Bill of 1899: Lucas, *Saunderson*, 302. See also ibid. 310–11, for Saunderson's connection with Lady Wimborne's League for the Defence of the Reformed Faith of the Church of England. The young F. E. Smith was also connected with the Wimborne League: John Campbell, *F. E. Smith, First Earl of Birkenhead* (London, 1983), 91–3.

IV

Whatever Saunderson's private convictions this Protestant rhetoric was calculated to win the commendation of Orange Ulster. But an equally important point of contact—especially with the lower middle classes of Belfast—lay in jingoism.[47] Saunderson had always cast his Unionism in an imperial mould, but it was only in the 1890s, and particularly in the context of Britain's position in southern Africa, that he contributed to imperial debate without an Irish pretext. By the mid-1890s he had dimly perceived that the rhetoric of empire might promote him from an Irish celebrity of declining importance to a broader renown (his contribution to the battle over the Union had already provided fame in England, and to a lesser extent, in North America and the colonies). When, in 1895, he was offered an Irish Privy Counsellorship, he politely refused—on the grounds that his work had been 'acknowledged all over the British Empire as being of an imperial, not local character'.[48] Yet there is very little evidence to suggest that, in the early years of the Home Rule debate, Saunderson himself was particularly upset by the imperial implications of Irish Home Rule. Moreover, the fact was that he only really excelled in parliament when he presented local detail; abstract foreign and imperial parallels were not his forte at this time, and indeed he once derided an attempt by Gladstone to broaden discussion of the Home Rule question, arguing that Ireland was *sui generis* ('there was but one Ireland on the face of this planet').[49] It was also true—and this was the crux—that an Irish Privy Counsellorship was a rather paltry reward for ten years of Unionist endeavour; and the Irish Viceroy had in fact originally recommended that Saunderson be given a baronetcy (Salisbury apparently objected).[50] As it was, Saunderson's pious stand on imperial principles meant that he received (in 1898) the rather grander distinction of a British Privy Counsellorship.[51]

[47] For an illuminating insight into lower-middle-class jingoism see Richard Price, 'Society, Status and Jingoism: The Social Roots of Lower Middle Class Patriotism, 1870–1900', in Geoffrey Crossick (ed.), *The Lower Middle Class in Britain, 1870–1914* (London, 1977), 89–112.

[48] House of Lords Record Office, Cadogan Papers, CAD.797: Saunderson to Cadogan, 30 Dec. 1895. See also Lucas, *Saunderson*, 246.

[49] *Hansard*, ser. 4, xii. 597 (10 May 1893).

[50] House of Lords Record Office, Cadogan Papers, CAD.780: Cadogan Memorandum, 19 Dec. 1895; ibid., CAD.790: S. K. MacDonnell to Cadogan, 28 Dec. 1895.

[51] Lucas, *Saunderson*, 282; HH, Salisbury Papers, E/Saunderson/24: Saunderson to Salisbury, 29 Dec. 1898.

Yet empire was not just a matter of personal vanity; for Saunderson increasingly perceived and articulated a parallel between the plight of the Irish minority apparently threatened by majority aggression, and the plight of an English minority in the Boer republics, apparently threatened by an Afrikaner majority. Viewed from this perspective, the Jameson Raid of 1895, while nominally 'unjustifiable', in fact took on a dashing and heroic aspect: 'the British public would believe', Saunderson suggested in February 1896, 'that he [Jameson] and his followers were actuated by brave and chivalrous motives'.[52] When the report of the British South Africa Committee was debated in the House of Commons in July 1897, and criticism was directed at Cecil Rhodes, Saunderson presented the same combination of token condemnation and persuasive apologetic.[53] This stand, allied with the useful circumstance that the loyalist Duke of Abercorn was chairman of the board, ensured that Saunderson and a group of friendly MPs were invited to spend much of the winter of 1897–8 as guests of the British South Africa Company.[54] While in Cape Colony he expanded on the Irish parallel, likening the Afrikaner Bond to the Irish National League, and the Uitlanders of the Transvaal to the Unionists of Ulster. Chamberlain as an expansionist Secretary of State for the Colonies earned even greater veneration than he had in his earlier capacity as as recruit to Unionism.[55] Given this Hibernocentric rationalization of South African politics, it was perhaps inevitable that Saunderson should view the war of 1899 almost as a holy crusade; and his defence of the British cause was all the more passionate because Irish Nationalists had begun to articulate the plight of the Boers.

On the other hand his unwavering faith in an imperial destiny did not deter Saunderson from cultivating one of Britain's greatest rivals in the struggle for colonial expansion. Kaiser Wilhelm II's well-publicized interest in Ulster Unionism did not date from his controversial, though apparently inconsequential, interview with Carson at Bad Homburg in August 1913: rather he had established a close connection with Carson's predecessor twenty years earlier.[56] The basis of their contact, as with so

52 *Hansard*, ser. 4, xxxvii. 188 (12 Feb. 1896).

53 Ibid. li. 1152 (26 July 1897).

54 Lucas, *Saunderson*, 265–78; ESP, T.2996/1/197–203: Saunderson to Helena, letters written in Nov. 1897; ESP, T.2996/3/2: Saunderson to the second duke of Abercorn, n.d.

55 Lucas, *Saunderson*, 272–3.

56 Edward Marjoribanks and Ian Colvin, *The Life of Lord Carson*, 3 vols. (London, 1932–6), ii. pp.193–4; H. Montgomery Hyde, *Carson: The Life of Sir Edward Carson, Lord Carson of Duncairn* (London, 1953), 337–8; A. T. Q. Stewart, *Edward Carson* (Dublin, 1981), 85.

much of Saunderson's social and political network, was yachting; and it was in August 1894 at the Royal Yacht Club at Cowes that they first met, the Kaiser gently chaffing Saunderson about 'having another go at my enemies in the House'.[57] Conversation was initially confined to 'boats and centre boards', but they seem to have discussed Ireland a few days later, on 12 August, when Saunderson was summoned to a dinner-party hosted by Wilhelm.[58] At any rate, Saunderson subsequently and controversially claimed to his constituents that the German emperor had expressed his sympathy for the Irish loyalist cause: 'The most powerful man living at the present moment was perhaps the Emperor of Germany', Saunderson informed a Portadown audience in November 1894, 'and he [the Emperor] told him ... that he and the great majority of his people undoubtedly sympathised with the plucky stand taken by the Orangemen of Ulster.'[59]

Their next recorded encounter was in June 1899, again evidently a casual meeting, brought about by Saunderson's presence at Kiel during a yachting competition. As in 1894, social pleasantries gave way to a more serious discussion, and Saunderson was able to inform Helena that he and the Kaiser had had:

> half an hour's talk on politics. He is much incensed against England about Samoa. Lord Salisbury has evidently succeeded in roughing him up to an extraordinary extent. He evidently means me to repeat what he has said. I think Lord Salisbury ought to smooth him down ...[60]

The dual outcome of this exchange—conducted initially over tennis—was an invitation to dinner at the imperial court, and a letter from Saunderson to Salisbury arranging a debriefing session with an official of the Foreign Office.[61] The last recorded meetings between the German emperor and the Ulster leader occurred in April and May 1902, under similar circumstances to those of the later interview between Wilhelm and Carson. In April 1902, as in 1913, a German spa town provided the venue; though Carson's greater caution allied with the gloomier circumstances of 1913 meant that he availed himself of the Kaiser's hospitality with less gusto

[57] ESP, T.2996/2B/478: Saunderson to Helena, 8 Aug. 1894.

[58] Ibid.

[59] ESP, T.2996/2B/480: Saunderson to Helena, 12 Aug. 1894; ESP, T.2996/2B/481: Saunderson to Helena, 13 Aug. 1894; BNL, 6 Nov. 1894, p. 7 (the opening of an Orange Hall at Knocknamuckley, Portadown).

[60] ESP, T.2996/1/207: Saunderson to Helena, 26 June 1899; ESP, T.1996/1/206: Saunderson to Helena, 23 June 1899; ESP, T.2996/2B/549: Saunderson to Helena, 25 June 1899.

[61] HH, Salisbury Papers, E/Saunderson/25: Saunderson to Salisbury, 7 July 1899.

than Saunderson (the latter 'dined with the Emperor, and went with him to the opera, and sat in state in uniform on his right hand').[62] Junketing at Wiesbaden led subsequently to a more intimate conversation within the imperial palace at Berlin: 'a long talk' in private was only interrupted by the appearence of the empress (who had also befriended Saunderson) and the little princess Victoria Louise.[63]

It is difficult to assess the broader significance of these meetings. From Saunderson's perspective contact with an emperor may simply have been a flattering experience at a time when he was being cut off from sources of power in Britain. Such contact was also part of a lifelong loyalist evangelism, and the Kaiser was undoubtedly targeted as a potentially useful sympathizer. But the development of this relationship also occurred as Saunderson was beginning to develop his career along much broader imperial and European lines. The peculiar circumstances of his childhood had given Saunderson an experience of the wider world which was unique among contemporary loyalist leaders; and when, after 1893, his career (and indeed Irish Unionism in general) was thrown into flux, it was perhaps unsurprising that he should have revived a European perspective. Wilhelm II was thus only part of a much broader experiment in personal political alignment.

Much about the relationship smacked of fantasy, and of a withdrawal from the monochrome politics of Lurgan and Portadown. The meetings between the Kaiser and Saunderson generally took place at yachting clubs or spa towns where the Ulster Unionist leader was relaxing: and this last circumstance in itself hinted at a sharp decline in Saunderson's political commitment and his willingness (and indeed his physical ability) to campaign incessantly, as he had done under the second Salisbury government. By 1902 he was 65, and ill; but even in the mid-1890s, when his health was better, he was spending little time in the constituency. In earlier years he compensated for this neglect by his English campaigning and by a sustained presence at Westminster, but this gradually ceased to be true. By 1900, when Saunderson stood for re-election, he found angry voters in Armagh, and the prospect of a contest for the first time since 1886.

[62] Lucas, *Saunderson*, 326–7.
[63] Ibid. 327–8; ESP, T.2996/1/214: Saunderson to Helena, 23 Apr. 1902.

V

Far removed from the rarified politicking of Cowes and Wiesbaden, the North Armagh election campaign of 1900 exposed the ambiguities of Saunderson's position since the defeat of the second Home Rule Bill.[64] Dissatisfaction had developed within the agricultural districts of the constituency, and not only because of Saunderson's unrepentant landlordism. Allegations of neglect and the fact that he lived outside the constituency (and thus, by implication, was ignorant of local conditions) also emerged to threaten Saunderson's majority. Speaking on 3 October 1900, he was obliged to concede: 'that there were several people he had rubbed the wrong way, who perhaps thought he was casual and indifferent, and had lost the confidence and affections of the people.'[65] Thus, though the ostensible bone of contention between Saunderson and his opponents was a land-related issue—the Colonel's refusal to support compulsory sale—what was really under debate was Saunderson's fifteen-year record as member for North Armagh.

The contest was the first significant test of Saunderson's response to a political landscape from which the national question had been largely excised—and the evasions and apologies of his stand since 1893 were assembled together for the first time. His experiment in anti-bourgeois rhetoric was revived: condemned by his opponent, James Orr, as the 'landlord of landlords', Saunderson appealed again to an anti-farmer combination of urban worker and rural handloom weaver.[66] While he claimed that 'the farmers of the constituency had stuck by him' he was forced to confess that a majority of the class was probably unsympathetic.[67] And as Orr pressed home Saunderson's record on the Land Bill of 1896, the Colonel reverted to jejune appeals to the weavers and to the 'working men': 'an immense amount had been done for the farmers', he commented to an audience at Portadown on 3 October, '[and] he did not grudge it to them, but very little had been done for the working men.'[68] Adhering to the particular class bias of this approach, he claimed that his own Weavers' Bill had been defeated by one of the representatives of industrial Belfast,

[64] See Duke of Manchester, *My Candid Recollections* (London, 1932), 41–5, for a vivid—if occasionally inaccurate—memory of the contest.

[65] *BNL*, 4 Oct. 1900, p. 7 (Portadown).

[66] Ibid., 5 Oct. 1900, p. 9 (Orr at Derryadd).

[67] Ibid., 29 Sept. 1900, p. 9 (Lurgan).

[68] Ibid., 4 Oct. 1900, p. 7.

Sir Edward Harland.[69] Bourgeois Toryism, whether embodied in the prosperous farming class or in industrial capitalism, had, in Saunderson's calculation, combined to suppress more worthy elements of society.

He presented the contest in an imperial and European context, in keeping with a broadened perspective on his own achievements. Against a background of the South African War and European Anglophobia, Britain, he argued, needed sturdy, battle-hardened patriots like himself. James Orr was 'a respectable gentleman'—but utterly lacking in experience of public affairs.[70] With the renewed threat of Home Rule, or at least of devolution, now that Henry Campbell-Bannerman was Liberal leader, Orr's amiable incapacity emerged as an ever more frightening political liability.

Broaching Home Rule was part of a broader appeal to loyalist fundamentalism. Having identified himself as a proponent of the landlord class, Saunderson needed every available handle on public opinion, and this meant parading his Protestant credentials before the Orange democracy in the constituency. Such an appeal involved little trimming or flexing of principle so far as ritualism or Home Rule were concerned: Saunderson roundly condemned each, both in private and in the course of his campaign.[71] He may conceivably have been more flexible on the issue of a Catholic university, but the pressure of organized Orangeism ensured that his equivocation was never publicly revealed.[72]

Compulsory sale of course had no part in Saunderson's conservative and paternalistic conception of loyalism—and it was compulsory sale which, following T. W. Russell's conversion to the principle in September 1900, was beginning to enthuse the rural north. In a sense this was to Saunderson's advantage, since it enabled him both to side-step the specific inadequacies of his personal record in the constituency, and to deal with a more general issue of class and principle. Unrest in North Armagh had diverse roots, and compulsion, though a prominent issue, merely focused a variety of complaints stemming from Saunderson's neglect of the constituency. This was true, too, for South Antrim where William Ellison-Macartney found himself opposed by an independent Unionist—and where compulsory sale masked widespread disappointment (expressed

[69] Ibid., 29 Sept. 1900, p. 9 (Lurgan).
[70] Ibid., 1 Oct. 1900, p. 10 (Clantilew).
[71] Ibid., 4 Oct. 1900, pp. 6–7 (Loughgall and Portadown).
[72] Gailey, *Death of Kindness*, 143.

even by the *Belfast News Letter*) that Macartney had not used his ministerial office for local advantage.[73]

Forced to deal with his stand on compulsory sale, Saunderson could lament the circumstances of birth which had left him a landowner.[74] But he could also argue that he was not unsympathetic to the rights of farmers (his support for the 1870 Land Act re-emerged), and that Unionism had had a splendid fifteen-year record of reform. Moreover, farmers were only one constituent of the electorate; and Saunderson was undoubtedly articulating more than a landlord prejudice when he claimed that the farming class had nudged other groups out of the government's reform priorities.[75] By contrast, whenever he dwelt on his own political record, Saunderson was less convincing: there were many references to 1886 and to 1893, while little was said about his stand on the Land Act of 1896.[76] His record of defending local interests collapsed into embarrassed generalities. It was not surprising, therefore, that Saunderson continually urged that personal allusions should be kept out of the contest; unsurprising that he emphasized that the only distinction between Orr and himself lay in compulsory purchase.[77] Orr battled to present a broader indictment of Saunderson's record; but, faced with a grimly effective combination of rhetorical moderation and (occasionally) physical violence from Saunderson's supporters, his was a forlorn campaign.[78] And, in the event, Saunderson topped the poll, gaining a majority of 1,111. Just over 6,000 votes had been cast, and around 1,000 Unionist farmers had defected to the independent candidature.[79]

Yet behind this result and the apparent self-confidence of Saunderson's public pose lay a more remarkable electoral realignment. After years of sullen loyalty to orthodox Unionism, many farmers in North Armagh had joined with Nationalist voters in supporting Orr. Saunderson's appeal to them had never been more than half-hearted, and they had answered his ambivalence in kind. His electoral base had been gradually whittled down

[73] *BNL*, 27 Sept. 1900, p. 4.

[74] Ibid., 29 Sept. 1900, p. 9 (Lurgan): 'The only crime of which he was guilty ... was that he was a landlord.'

[75] Ibid., 4 Oct. 1900, p. 7 (Portadown).

[76] Ibid., 29 Sept. 1900, p. 9 (Lurgan). Saunderson opened the speech with a lengthy summary of his achievements for loyalism.

[77] Ibid., 4 Oct. 1900, p. 7 (Portadown): 'that was not a contest between a man called Orr and a man called Saunderson.'

[78] Ibid., 11 Oct. 1900, p. 6 (Lurgan). This is probably the meeting so cynically described by the Duke of Manchester, *Candid Recollections*, 42–3.

[79] Walker, *Parliamentary Election Results in Ireland, 1801–1922* (Dublin, 1978), 327; *BNL*, 15 Oct. 1900, p. 6.

to an urban core, embracing the towns of Lurgan and Portadown; and, more shocking, this retreat hinted at a general diffusion of the elements within northern loyalism.

While there was a provincial context to this result, it was a personal setback, for it was the logical outcome of at least seven years of political rigidity: seven years of trading off past glories, and working from a redundant political consensus; seven years of disdain for constituency pressure. The result underlined that Saunderson had never really developed from the conditions of the mid-1880s; it underlined his conviction that the parliamentary veterans of the Home Rule struggle had been elevated beyond all responsibility to sectional pressure. Indeed, he always tended to portray such pressure as an isolated and ephemeral nuisance, without serious electoral implications. When farmer and Presbyterian grumbling graduated into open revolt in 1900, Saunderson was shocked. Yet this blunt awakening to local unrest was mixed with considerable incomprehension. Writing to William Ellison-Macartney, under threat in the South Antrim constituency, Saunderson indicated that his conception of political debate had been jolted, but left substantially intact:

> What distresses me is that all your past services are to be forgotten by the Unionists and Protestants and Orangemen of your constituency, and that it is proposed to reject you, not because you have failed in the past, but because you are tarred with the landlord brush.[80]

Incomprehension gave rise to despair (both states of mind are evident in a letter which he wrote to Lord Dufferin and Ava in October 1900): three days before the poll in North Armagh he could still privately envisage defeat.[81] This despair was merely symptomatic, however, of his inflexibility—for his anxiety was not converted into any new political agility. When failure seemed possible, Saunderson offered nothing beyond condemnation of 'rotten' Protestants and ingrates; when victory was secured, he offered little more, perceiving only the blunt facts of success and the defeat of his opponents.[82] Learning nothing from the outcome of the contest, and forgetting none of the sores, Saunderson stood poised on the edge of supersession in the very aftermath of victory.

As a champion of landed recusancy, Saunderson was peculiarly ill equipped to deal with the internal crises experienced by Ulster Unionism

[80] PRONI, Ellison-Macartney Papers, D.3649/20/51: Saunderson to Macartney, 1 Oct. 1900.

[81] PRONI, Dufferin and Ava Papers, D.1701/H/B/F: Saunderson to Dufferin, 9 Oct. 1900.

[82] *BNL*, 15 Oct. 1900, p. 6 (Saunderson's victory oration).

at the beginning of the twentieth century—crises which, indeed, he had helped to exacerbate. He responded sullenly to what was, in effect, the collapse of his tactical and institutional vision; and his religious and social militancy melted into resignation as the indications of failure became inescapable. Plagued by illness, and distressed by the evidence of his own political fallibility, Saunderson retreated—as he had done after 1874—into a world of yachts and golf and structured idleness. There was a brief period—eighteen months—of heightened parliamentary activity at the end of his life, but the years between 1901 and his death in October 1906 otherwise saw him reduced to comparative insignificance within the Unionist movement.

The chief obstacle denying Saunderson access to popular opinion was his utter refusal to accept the principle of compulsory sale as advocated by Russell and his supporters. At a time when all other Ulster Unionist members, whatever their class origins, had given way to the pressure of farmer opinion, Saunderson rejected the possibility of pragmatic concession in favour of his perception of propertied right. His stubbornness alternately angered and impressed radical middle-class leaders like Russell; but it was a stand which led even those who had been sympathetic to regard Saunderson as a political fossil.

His association with an antique and enervated style of parliamentary opposition was confirmed by an almost studied lack of business capacity. Saunderson's enthusiasms and abilities were well suited to crusade politics: but crusade politics went out of fashion after 1893—and charismatic leadership was similarly at a discount. Unionist electors were now primarily interested in an MP's responsiveness to local opinion, and in his efficiency in fulfilling the humdrum duties of constituency administration. Saunderson performed badly on both counts. He rarely visited North Armagh, and he had a poor record in forwarding local grievances to the House of Commons. He was an uncommitted patron of supplicating constituents, even though he shamelessly pressed the interests of his own family: he pursued Lord Wolseley and Lord Cadogan in order to further the military career of his eldest son, Somerset, and he lobbied Gerald Balfour on behalf of a younger son, Edward Aremberg.[83] His general record in processing business, however, was lamentable. He once wrote to Helena confessing that he had stood before a confused pile of correspond-

[83] East Sussex Record Office, Wolseley Papers: Saunderson to Wolseley, 24 Dec. 1896. House of Lords Record Office, Cadogan Papers, CAD.977: Cadogan to Saunderson, 25 Dec. 1896 (copy); ibid., CAD.1009/1: Wolseley to Cadogan, 8 Jan. 1897. ESP, unclassified: Gerald Balfour to Saunderson, 16 June 1899.

ence feeling 'like an idiot'; and it seems that this was more broadly indicative of his failings as a workaday representative of local feeling.[84] Many important letters dispatched by Saunderson, as chairman of the Irish Unionist parliamentary party, to leading British Unionists were drafted carelessly.[85] Often he did not trouble to reply to correspondents, thereby generating an intense hostility among certain influential local elements.[86] This grievance weighed heavily with those Unionists who ran James Orr: waiting on Orr in September 1900 his supporters claimed that 'everyone had the same story—that no matter how important the business about which he had to be written, the letters of his constituents were thrown by Colonel Saunderson in the waste basket unanswered'. Joshua Peel, the Unionist agent for the neighbouring constituency of mid-Armagh, had evidently encountered Saunderson's nonchalance, and refused to make any further supplication: 'I will not ask Colonel Saunderson for any favour.'[87] Within North Armagh Saunderson offered even greater evidence of his disdain: when the town clerk and, later, the town surveyor of Portadown wrote to him on the subject of the Local Government Bill, neither man received even an acknowledgement in reply. It was an ironic testimony to their plight that these two officers of Orange Portadown should have had to approach P. G. H. Carvill, the Nationalist member for Newry, in order to obtain satisfaction. Thereafter, 'it was not the Colonel who was asked for any guidance that might be required'.[88] The town commissioners of Lurgan, having requested assistance from Saunderson, suffered a similar slight; more tenacious, they adopted the expedient of journeying to London in order to beard their elusive MP. But they, too, ultimately had to approach another member for assistance.[89]

Saunderson's amateurism was scarcely tailored for an age of popular politics, and in this, as in much else by 1900, he evinced an utter disregard for electoral reality. He had helped to teach political flexibility to the landed élite of the 1880s; but, while they now swayed with every expression of popular opinion, Saunderson himself had lost faith in the advantages of a Protestant class alliance, and in the advantages of strategic

[84] ESP, T.2996/1/125: Saunderson to Helena, 5 Feb. 1887 ('I get into a horrible mess over my letters. I sit in front of the growing pile and feel like an idiot . . .'). See also Lucas, *Saunderson*, 227–8.

[85] It is also noticeable that Saunderson—unlike many of his contemporaries—often did not trouble to revise the proofs of his *Hansard* contributions before they went to press.

[86] In 1885, during his contest with John Monroe, Saunderson had been accused of rudely delaying his replies to correspondence: *BNL*, 3 Sept. 1885, p. 8.

[87] PRONI, Joshua Peel Papers, D.889/4C/1/805: Peel to Barton, 25 Oct. 1895.

[88] *BNL*, 11 Oct. 1900, p. 6.

[89] Ibid.

concession. While sectional pressure racked Ulster Unionism, while many Protestant voters were dismayed by an inefficient and clique-ridden party organization, Saunderson remained stolid and immovable. An isolated beacon of intransigence, he came to epitomize not only the glories of antique Unionism, but also its failings of tone and structure. In the last years of his life he was increasingly perceived as a liability by his own party, and especially by the professional and industrial representatives who had always been distrustful. Venerating Saunderson and his achievements, they grew impatient of his failings; and in the end both he and his perception of Unionism were relegated to the sidelines of Unionist politics while a more rigorously middle-class movement took form.

10

Middle-class Ascendancy, 1900–1906

I

Between 1901 and 1905 Saunderson suffered setbacks in almost every sphere of his political activity. His tenacious landlordism embarrassed his allies and delighted his opponents; his rigid paternalism irritated those more acutely aware of the need for reform within Unionism. But, most startling of all, Saunderson's Orange fundamentalism was impugned—first by the fiery politicians of the Belfast Protestant Association, and later by a broader cross-section of Unionist opinion.

The Belfast Protestant Association was founded in 1894 as an evangelical and loyalist antidote to the Independent Labour party which had recently been established in the city.[1] The sectarian demagogue, Arthur Trew, raised this Association, and was its captain for eight years; but, in July 1901, Trew and his principal lieutenant, Richard Braithwaite, were imprisoned for disturbing the peace, and the command of the body fell into other hands. During Trew's sojourn in the Belfast gaol-house, Thomas H. Sloan, 'a semi-skilled shipyard worker with a talent for public speaking' captured the leadership. Through several audacious assaults on official Unionism, Sloan gained valuable publicity, and strengthened the political authority of the organization far beyond the point achieved by Trew.[2] Sloan redefined the BPA manifesto, sharpening its critique of the Irish Unionist parliamentary party and condemning the party's stand on the 1902 Education Act and on factory inspection; he ably confronted the party's most prominent members. He was more articulate than Trew, and much more strategically aware; he was proportionately more dangerous. And yet, like Trew, he was initially—and fatally—dismissed by the Unionist elders as a sectarian gadfly.

On 12 July 1902 Sloan disrupted an Orange meeting at Castlereagh, near

[1] J. W. Boyle, 'The Belfast Protestant Association and the Independent Orange Order, 1901–10', *IHS* 13/50 (Sept. 1962), 118.

[2] Ibid. 119. For Sloan, see Austen Morgan, *Labour and Partition: The Belfast Working Class, 1905–23* (London, 1991), 44–5.

Belfast, heckling the patriarchs of the Order, and finally clambering on to the platform in order to interrogate the speakers more efficiently.[3] Saunderson, as Grand Master of the Belfast Orangemen, was present and, as chairman of the Irish Unionist parliamentary party, he was the target of Sloan's invective. Sloan's grievance was that the Unionist government had pursued a Romanizing policy in almost every sphere: in education, with regard to the royal oath question, over the factory question, and over Ireland. More specifically, he accused Saunderson of having opposed the inspection of convent laundries during a debate on the Factory and Workshop Amendment Bill of 1901. Saunderson was in fact free from any such lapse into broadmindedness; but the BPA charge was merely a symptom of a wider disquiet at the quality and effectiveness of Unionist representation.[4]

The assault on Saunderson was a brilliant *coup de théâtre*, gaining Sloan massive—and often sympathetic—publicity. Building on the success of this confrontation, Sloan carried the BPA gospel to Lurgan and Portadown, the heartland of Saunderson's constituency. The satirical periodical, *Nomad's Weekly*, expressed its doubts about the wisdom of this strategy, observing in a mock Belfast patois that there was:

> not good news from Portadown. The Kurnel is well thought of there, an' if the new BPA company go up to make animal versions [animadversions?] about him there, they'll get a dig in the gob, so they will, an' serve them right, too. It's a mane thing to fill [foul?] yor own nest, and ends in defate, I hear.[5]

But, far from incurring 'defate', the BPA managers swiftly built up a substantial and loyal following in North Armagh, audaciously highlighting the failings of the Irish Unionist party in the home territory of its leader. Emotional occasions—pre-eminently Trew's release from prison in July 1902—were exploited through monster demonstrations; and Sloan's sensitive voicing of popular loyalist anxiety at these meetings and elsewhere won the approval even of hardened supporters of the Colonel (such as the *Portadown News*).[6] Sloan eloquently represented what Austen Morgan has called 'dispossessed Protestants'—those vulnerable urban workers and

[3] Henry Patterson, 'Independent Orangeism and Class Conflict in Edwardian Belfast', *PRIA*, 80c/4 (May1980), 9–11.

[4] Reginald Lucas, *Colonel Saunderson MP: A Memoir* (London, 1908), 321–2; *Hansard*, ser. 4, lxxxxix. 718 (13 Aug. 1901); Morgan, *Labour and Partition*, 45: 'Sloan's obsession was with state control of Catholic nuns—Protestant evangelicals had long been fascinated by their imagined sexual exploitation by priests and bishops.'

[5] *Nomad's Weekly*, 174 (22 Nov. 1902).

[6] See e.g. *Portadown News*, 16 Aug. 1902 and 27 Sept. 1902; Morgan, *Labour and Partition*, 59.

lower middle classes who had been engaged only fitfully and exploitatively by the Unionist leadership. Saunderson treated this onslaught contemptuously, as a localized and ephemeral irritation; but it soon became evident that the BPA's rabble-rousing was merely a side-show, and that Sloan was looking beyond North Armagh to a greater prize.

On 17 July 1902 William Johnston of Ballykilbeg, one of Saunderson's closer parliamentary supporters, died, leaving a vacancy in the representation of South Belfast. The timing of Johnston's demise could not have been more advantageous for the opponents of official Unionism, since they had recently found a charismatic leader in Sloan, and were in the midst of engineering a successful agitation. The South Belfast by-election contest offered the BPA both a splendid opportunity for publicity, and—with Sloan as an independent candidate—a fair chance of returning an able spokesman to the House of Commons. Moreover, abundant financial support for Sloan came from his former employer, the shipping magnate W. J. Pirrie. Sloan's vicious indictment of the trimming and lacklustre Irish Unionist leadership was sustained throughout his campaign in August 1902, and it attained a broader significance through being echoed and developed in the columns of the Belfast press. As leader of the Irish Unionist party, Saunderson had been the original victim of Sloan's abuse, and, with his party on trial through the campaign, he remained a prominent target. A final, painful, rebuff came when, on 18 August, the polls closed. For Sloan captured South Belfast by a margin of 826 votes, trounced the official candidate, C. W. Dunbar-Buller, and overturned William Johnston's majority of almost 4,000.[7]

Humiliated by this result, his leadership maligned by the popular Protestant press, and by sections of working-class loyalist opinion, Saunderson retired from Belfast Orangeism in January 1903.[8] It was an act of pique, which was opposed by colleagues like William Moore, and by the County Grand Lodge of Belfast.[9] But Saunderson was unused to abject failure within the hitherto reassuringly static arena of Protestant politics—especially when such failure implied a devastating condemnation of his own parliamentary career and political values. Given that, in Moore's verdict, Saunderson 'never had any taste à la Kitchener for fighting inch by

[7] Patterson, 'Independent Orangeism', 13–14; id., *Class Conflict and Sectarianism: The Protestant Working Class and the Belfast Labour Movement, 1868–1920* (Belfast, 1980), 45; Brian M. Walker, *Parliamentary Election Results in Ireland, 1801–1922* (Dublin, 1978), 320; Morgan, *Labour and Partition*, 46–7.

[8] Lucas, *Saunderson*, 321–3; PRONI, Ellison-Macartney Papers, D.3649/20/67: Saunderson to Macartney, 11 Jan. 1903.

[9] Lucas, *Saunderson*, 322; ESP, T.2996/6/3: William Moore to Lucas, 25 Nov. [1907].

inch', he could offer no response to this popular censure beyond a peevish retreat.[10]

II

The long-term electoral significance of the BPA, and of its offshoot, the Independent Orange Order, should not be exaggerated, but its condemnation of official Unionism reflected a much wider movement of Protestant dissent. T. W. Russell's successful appeal to Presbyterian farmers between 1900 and 1905 was also founded, at least in part, on a caricature of the inadequacies within official Unionist representation. Before the passage of George Wyndham's Land Act this indictment, combined with the call for compulsory purchase, achieved an astonishing popular currency, and by the end of 1903 three former bastions of county Unionism had been won for Russell.[11] The threat was awesome: yet, here again, as with Sloanite sectarianism, Saunderson offered no new initiative, or indeed any worthwhile response, to undercut this opposition. And it was left to Saunderson's younger, middle-class colleagues, and—indirectly—to George Wyndham, to rescue Ulster Unionism from electoral annihilation. Saunderson, preoccupied with golf, and with his failing health, merely offered his approval for a series of counter-measures devised by others. Reduced to insignificance, he blithely endorsed the repudiation of his own most fundamental tactical convictions.

Saunderson's political isolation had been nowhere clearer than in the land debates of the 1890s. Viewed with suspicion by both farmers and urban Tories, his support had been narrowed down to the Irish Landowners' Convention. But even here, in the light of the agitations of T. W. Russell and the United Irish League, Saunderson's qualities of leadership were perceived by some as inadequate; and, just as his defence of Orangeism had engendered schism within the Belfast Order, so too his defence of proprietorship helped to induce division within the Landowners' Convention. Thus, even though he had abandoned the ambigu-

[10] ESP, T.2996/6/3: William Moore to Lucas, 25 Nov. [1907].

[11] Alvin Jackson, *The Ulster Party: Irish Unionists in the House of Commons, 1884–1911* (Oxford, 1989), 266–73.

ities of class diplomacy ten years earlier, Saunderson found that he still lacked a clearly defined political base. If he had conceived of his retreat to landed fundamentalism as a viable political strategy, then this calculation seemed to be flawed. Having staked his career on Orangeism and landlordism, Saunderson's gamble appeared increasingly reckless, for the core of Unionist fundamentalism was disintegrating, and Unionism itself was being refined and redeployed.

The Irish Landowners' Convention had been a bulwark of fundamentalism in the 1890s, and yet by the early Edwardian period even these most trenchant defenders of property grasped the need for a more consensual approach to the land question. When, in August 1902, a proposal was floated for a negotiation with hardline tenant opinion—a land conference—this was taken up by a significant element within the convention, and endorsed in a referendum by over 1,100 Irish landlords. The leaders of these moderates were the earls of Dunraven and Mayo; and it was Dunraven who chaired the conference of landlord and tenant when it came to be held in December 1902. The conference report, published on 3 January 1903, was widely acknowledged as the basis for Wyndham's subsequent Land Purchase Act.[12]

The negotiating landowners had mostly been southerners, impressed by the mounting rural agitation of the United Irish League, and anxious for a lasting settlement within an anomalous land system. Northern landowners like Saunderson contributed little towards this *détente* save a gloomy repetition of their class interests. However, they did ultimately endorse the land conference report: Wyndham found, while staying at Mountstewart in January 1903, that the Duke of Abercorn and Lord Londonderry were pleasantly surprised by its contents.[13] Saunderson later admitted in parliament that he had been wrong to dismiss out of hand an invitation to participate in the conference.[14] Yet, while Orange landowners accepted the settlement, they lacked the sense of urgency and commitment which motivated many southern moderates. And here, too, they were isolated from northern middle-class Unionists: bourgeois representatives like C. C. Craig and J. B. Lonsdale viewed the landlord case dispassionately, and were much more acutely aware of the electoral dangers associated with defiance—especially with the glaring evidence of T. W. Russell's success.

[12] Lord Dunraven, *Past Times and Pastimes*, 2 vols. (London, n.d. [1922]), ii. 3–11; Andrew Gailey, *Ireland and the Death of Kindness: The Experience of Constructive Unionism, 1890–1905* (Cork, 1987), 189–91.

[13] J. W. Mackail and Guy Wyndham (eds.), *The Life and Letters of George Wyndham*, 2 vols. (London, n.d. [1925]), ii. 453.

[14] *Hansard*, ser. 4, cxviii. 831 (25 Feb. 1903).

Thus, while Saunderson and many northern landlords were essentially uninterested in change, their class confederates in the south and party allies in the north had constructed a much more radical strategy for political survival.

Saunderson's support for the land conference report extended naturally to George Wyndham's Land Bill, introduced into the House of Commons in March 1903. He was consistently sympathetic, though as usual he eschewed any technical debate: 'I have no intention whatever of wandering through these financial mazes in which my right hon. Friend trod with such an easy and fairy step.'[15] He was careful, too, to articulate his old interest in the living conditions of the Ulster labouring class, and to juxtapose the more conspicuous landlord–tenant conflict with that prevailing between farmer and labourer:

> if a labourer, living in a hovel not fit for a pig, petitioned to have a house built, he would be instantly turned off the farm; consequently, however much the Irish tenants disliked the Irish landlords, the labourers disliked the tenants more...[16]

But this was only a momentary lapse into his former rhetoric. When the Bill was read for a third time in July 1903, Saunderson offered a gushing paean on the abilities of Wyndham and on the merits of his measure; and, echoing the old Tory orthodoxy on conciliation, he looked forward to the spread of 'peace and loyalty' under the 'beneficent shadow of the Bill'.[17]

Saunderson and northern landlords had every reason to be gratified—since the Bill, embodying an extension of British-funded voluntary purchase, fell short of the most extreme farmer demands, and, in particular, of compulsion. But the Bill did not merely offer landowners a satisfactory financial settlement; it also threatened to undercut the unrest in rural Ulster which had been mobilized so efficiently by T. W. Russell. Russell had subscribed both to the land conference report and to the Bill, thereby effectively abandoning his call for compulsory purchase; but, in achieving further concessions based on the voluntary principle, part of the purpose of his assault on Ulster Unionism had apparently been nullified. Saunderson had grasped this point, and had candidly informed the House of Commons that he believed the Bill would 'take out of the hands of the Irish political agitators a great lever which enabled them to hold out to the Irish people the not far distant prospect of getting their land for nothing'.[18]

While Saunderson may have looked forward to the death of Russel-

[15] *Hansard*, ser. 4, cxx, 216 (25 Mar. 1903).

[16] Ibid. cxxv. 39 (8 July 1903).

[17] Ibid. cxxv. 1332 (21 July 1903).

[18] Ibid.

lism, the fact was that the Russellite movement had exploited a much broader lack of confidence in the official leadership than his prophecy implied. Landlordism, for Russell, had not only bred economic inequality, it had also produced a disproportionate political influence for a propertied minority; and he had frequently drawn attention to the clique-dominated, undemocratic procedures of local Unionism. Indeed, while the Act of 1903 spelt the demise of a landed political ascendancy, it also threatened the Unionist political structures around which this ascendancy had been tailored. In an obvious sense the local political relationships which sprang from land ownership were threatened by the spread of purchase; but northern landowners had also shown themselves to be dangerously limited and obdurate when confronted with popular pressure from within Unionism. And this inadequacy—their willingness to threaten the solidarity of Unionism in the interests of the 'classes' as opposed to the 'masses'—was in itself a strong argument for the restructuring of Unionism along new, and more popular, lines. Reorganization, when it came in 1904–5, was thus not only conceived as an effort to save Unionism from any external threat; it was also intended to save Unionism from a now vulnerable, but still potent and damaging, landed élite.

III

If individual landlords like Saunderson were proving themselves to be a political liability, then the policies and structures with which they were associated were also being discredited. This had been obvious since at least 1896: Saunderson's die-hard bravura over the Land Act of that year had not been calculated to be popular—and it has already been argued that his defiant renewal of this stand had brought a serious measure of political isolation by 1900.[19] But the landed character of Unionist politics extended far beyond the obduracy of individual leaders like Saunderson. For the very structures of the movement had been laid down in an age of landed ascendancy, and they were now proving largely inadequate as a means of channelling popular opinion—and especially the grievances of farmers, Presbyterians, and of urban working-class elements. Unionist organization, outside of the years 1886 and 1893, meant a parliamentary party resting on a generally narrow and inadequate constituency base. There was

[19] See above, pp. 136–42.

also a plethora of loyalist pressure groups, but few beyond the Orange Order could claim a mass membership, and virtually none had long survived the defeat of the second Home Rule Bill. Unionism, therefore, was for all practical purposes a parliamentary movement; and it was to the MP and to the House of Commons that northern Protestants looked for political redress or for personal advancement.[20]

This popular dependence on a parliamentary party worked quite well—so long as Saunderson and his Irish Unionist MPs could demonstrate that they enjoyed access to government, and influence over its actions. Also, members of parliament had to be extremely attentive to local opinion, registering grievances, processing patronage requests, and mollifying dissidents. In short, Irish Unionist MPs had to command a balance between retaining local popular credibility and exercising parliamentary influence; and, since these two were by no means easily compatible, the appropriate balance was extremely difficult to achieve. Yet, despite the inefficiency or relative unpopularity of certain Irish Unionist members, this system of representation survived unscathed for almost twenty years. It was only when, under Arthur Balfour's premiership, central government became wholly inaccessible to Irish Unionist parliamentary pressure that the structure became clearly inadequate.

Saunderson and the Ulster party had had an ambivalent relationship with British ministers, and especially after 1896. On the whole, though, the government remained receptive to loyalist pressure until the last years of George Wyndham's Chief Secretaryship. The appointment in 1902 of an Irish Catholic, Sir Antony MacDonnell, to the post of Under-Secretary for Ireland had enlivened loyalist suspicion—and particularly because MacDonnell was the brother of the Nationalist member for Queen's County.[21] By 1904 leading Irish Unionists believed that a policy of official discrimination was being pursued, masterminded by MacDonnell, and endorsed by a miserably pliant Chief Secretary. In general terms it was thought that this 'policy' was directed against Protestants, who, whether corporately or individually, had occasion to lobby central government. In specific, parliamentary, terms loyalist spleen focused on what were alleged to be four cases of malpractice: the refusal of the government to carry out a comprehensive scheme of drainage along the River Bann, two cases of apparently unfair clerical influence over Dublin Castle (in the Constable

[20] For an expansion of this argument see Jackson, *Ulster Party*, 322–6.

[21] Sir Antony's brother was Dr M. A. MacDonnell, anti-Parnellite MP for Queen's County between 1892 and 1906. Sir Antony's Home Rule sympathies worried Arthur Balfour: Mackail and Wyndham, *George Wyndham*, ii. 752.

Anderson case and at Roundstone, County Galway), and an instance of discrimination at Ballinasloe, County Galway.[22] But, while these cases engaged the anger of several leading Irish Unionist members, they only palely foreshadowed the much more significant fissure which opened over the devolution question.[23]

The paradox at the heart of this developing confrontation was that while, on the Irish Unionist side, it was a largely middle-class movement, its immediate tactical precedent lay in the landlord revolt of 1896. Parliament was a useful vehicle for landlord political achievement, and men like Saunderson had been able to exercise an immense influence through a network of family and social contacts. Viewed from this perspective, the action of Saunderson and other Irish landowners in rejecting Gerald Balfour's Land Act of 1896 reflected a serious miscalculation of class interest. This lay rather in continually demonstrating that the House of Commons worked for all Irish Unionists—of whatever class. For so long as the Commons lay at the heart of the Unionist world-view, then the inadequacies of Unionist organization—its unrepresentativeness, its landlord bias—were irrelevant. So long as the political objectives were attained, then the machinery of success was relatively unimportant.

In 1896, therefore, Saunderson had not only threatened his own political position, he had also impaired the parliamentary strategy which was the chief prop of his class. In seeking a precedent for revolt between 1903 and 1905, bourgeois loyalists did not have to look further than this, the record of their own landed leadership. But, where the landlords had defied Tory discipline, they had not exploited any alternative organizational resource (beyond the Irish Landowners' Convention); indeed, short of representative reforms within loyalism, there *was* no alternative resource. Middle-class defiance went much further than this. While the suicidal nature of the landlords' action had been proclaimed by their inability to provide any other, constructive initiative, middle-class loyalists were able to exploit their own parliamentary revolt through a comprehensive local reorganization of their movement—that is, through the consolidation of their own position within the Party.

Thus, leading middle-class Unionists like the two Craig brothers, James and Charles, J. B. Lonsdale, and William Moore, were confronted with a

[22] *Hansard*, ser. 4, cxxxi. 1291 (16 Mar. 1904); ibid. cxxxii. 468 (22 Mar. 1904): Bann drainage; ibid. cxxxvii. 1030 (7 July 1904): Ballinasloe; ibid. cxxxvi. 706 (21 June 1904) and cxxxix. 736 (3 Aug. 1904): Constable Anderson case.

[23] There are several accounts of the 1904–5 devolution episode: F. S. L. Lyons, 'The Irish Unionist Party and the Devolution Crisis of 1904–5', *IHS* 6/21 (Mar. 1948), 1–22; Andrew Gailey, *Death of Kindness*, esp. 210–31; Jackson, *Ulster Party*, 260–6.

difficult legacy from the years of Saunderson's ascendancy. In the county constituencies the limited and landed character of Unionism had spawned Russellism and Presbyterian dissent; and, while the popular revolt in Belfast was still restrained by a sectarian leash, it was no less threatening and potentially damaging.[24] If the landlords had helped to provoke constituency schism, then they had by no means enhanced the pliability of the government. Thus, by 1903–4 it seemed that the delicate balance implied by parliamentary Unionism—between mollifying the constituency, and squeezing the government—had wholly collapsed, with the result that Unionist politicians were sandwiched unhappily between a rebellious electorate and an unresponsive administration. Thrashing around for a solution, Moore and the Craigs deployed several tactical initiatives; but in the end it was George Wyndham who, through the devolution issue, unwittingly released them from their plight.

Saunderson wholly failed to perceive either the weaknesses of his own leadership, or the enormity of the threat building up against his movement. It was the Craigs, William Moore, and J. B. Lonsdale—not Saunderson—who worked most fervently to defeat Russell, breathlessly campaigning in Ulster and in the House of Commons. Saunderson languidly sympathized with their general goal, while distancing himself from their vehemence—and offering little material help.[25] When the Craigs and Moore sought to develop their campaign, through an assault on the government, Saunderson remained overtly sympathetic, while emerging as much milder and more emollient than his lieutenants. While the middle-class leaders saw the tactical advantages of leading an initiative against the government, Saunderson had now too much faith in the advantages of parliamentary dialogue to risk a breach in the Commons in the interests of local gain. This was partly because he remained curiously unimpressed by popular dissent; but it was also true of course that he had a class interest in binding himself to parliament.[26]

This chasm dividing Saunderson and his younger lieutenants first opened with the Bann drainage question. The River Bann flowed from Lough Neagh through Saunderson's constituency, and regularly flooded large tracts of low-lying land. There was clearly a need for an extensive drainage scheme, but it was calculated that this might well cost £150,000; equally, it was judged that the ratepayers of Armagh could not afford this

24 Patterson, *Class Conflict*, 42–61; Jackson, *Ulster Party*, 222–9.
25 Jackson, *Ulster Party*, 273–5.
26 See above, p. 149.

sum.[27] Local leaders therefore turned to the government, arguing for a subvention, and citing the great generosity displayed towards apparently less worthy Nationalist projects in the south and west of Ireland. Saunderson took up the cause in a half-hearted and ineffective fashion, winning polite words but little action from Wyndham: as the *Portadown News* commented abrasively in November 1901 after one deputation had waited fruitlessly on Wyndham, 'soft words butter no parsnips, neither will they drain the Bann valley'.[28] But the issue had a much broader resonance, and it was soon taken out of Saunderson's hands: in July 1903 the Irish Unionist parliamentary party, interpreting the Chief Secretary's attitude as evidence of his general disregard for loyalist interests, agreed to press the Bann drainage dispute in the House of Commons.[29] By late 1903, and early 1904, Bann drainage was being seen by a broad section of Irish Unionism as symptomatic of the failings of Balfourism in general; and Saunderson's persistent failure to secure any subvention was increasingly seen as symptomatic of the failure of his parliamentary strategy.

On 16 March 1904 the question of Bann drainage was raised in a debate on the Civil Service estimates, but, though Saunderson pleaded for action, he remained comparatively polite about the government: he voiced his conviction that Wyndham 'really desired to further the progress and prosperity of Ireland'.[30] The issue was revived on 22 March, with Saunderson and Craig each speaking on behalf of the Ulster Party: Saunderson preserved an impression of mild annoyance while his younger colleagues fumed and raged, delivering a caustic indictment of the government's neglect of Irish loyalism.[31] This charge, albeit in different guises, would be repeatedly directed against Wyndham until early 1905, and on virtually every occasion, Saunderson would be outpaced in extremism by William Moore or C. C. Craig.[32] Although outshone, he did enough to prevent any serious constituency revolt. But local Unionists had few illusions concerning the effectiveness of his efforts: Henry Richardson, one of the chief agitators on the Bann issue, damningly observed that 'he thought Colonel

[27] Lucas, *Saunderson*, 352; *Portadown News*, 13 Aug. 1904.

[28] *Portadown News*, 9 Nov. 1901.

[29] Ibid., 4 July 1903.

[30] *Hansard*, ser. 4, cxxxi. 1291 (16 Mar. 1904).

[31] Ibid. cxxxii. 468 (22 Mar. 1904); Saunderson was followed by the more vituperative C. C. Craig.

[32] Aside from the main Irish Unionist grievances see *Hansard*, ser. 4, cxxxiv. 467 (4 May 1904): Boland's motion condemning the Criminal Law and Procedure Act. Saunderson's address was mild in comparison to that of William Moore.

Saunderson had been doing his best in a quiet way', and made clear that 'his best' had brought little consolation.[33]

Saunderson increasingly gave the impression of being caught up in a political game which was being directed by others. In the debates on the Irish Labourers Bill (24 June 1904) and on the Ballinasloe and Anderson cases (7 July and 3 August) he consistently failed to set the standards of loyalist intransigence; and in the earlier debate he was only a secondary speaker, following the major presentations of younger colleagues.[34] There is no evidence that he had any discreet tactical role: indeed it is fairly clear that the strategic command of parliamentary loyalism had fallen into the hands of J. B. Lonsdale, the party secretary and an ally of Moore and Craig.[35] On the other hand, there is some evidence to suggest that Saunderson retained faith in Wyndham, and saw himself as an intermediary between the Chief Secretary and his own, more extreme, lieutenants in the Irish Unionist parliamentary party.[36] If this interpretation is correct, then Saunderson had clearly miscalculated the balance of Wyndham's sympathies, and soon realized that he done so: by January 1906 he was openly admitting that 'the worst man he ever had to deal with was Mr. Wyndham'.[37]

Thus, the Ulster Unionist right wing had found more able and subtle exponents than the Colonel; and, while these new leaders attempted to reconstruct support around a call to fundamentalism, Saunderson pursued a more eccentric path. Deprived of his monopoly on intransigence, and weakening in health, Saunderson quietly slipped into the role of loyalist elder statesman, judicious and mildly disinterested. He was the medium of communication between a haughty government and an obdurate Ulster party; he was the Orange Tory who could yet lavish praise on Horace Plunkett's 'most excellent work for Ireland'.[38] His speeches were still occasionally rancorous (else he would have lost all contact with younger colleagues); but there was a new, sad, and almost valedictory element.[39]

[33] *Portadown News*, 16 Apr. 1904.

[34] *Hansard*, ser. 4, cxxxvi. 1149 (24 June 1904); see also n. 22 above.

[35] For J. B. Lonsdale, see Vicary Gibbs and H. A. Doubleday, *The Complete Peerage*, 13 vols. (London, 1912–59), xiii. 272. The best collection of Lonsdale's correspondence is in PRONI, H. B. Armstrong Papers, D.3727/E/46.

[36] See e.g. Jackson, *Ulster Party*, 250–1.

[37] *Portadown News*, 13 Jan. 1906.

[38] *Hansard*, ser. 4, cxxxvi. 1038–43 (23 June 1904).

[39] e.g. *Hansard*, ser. 4, cxxxii. 1051 (29 Mar. 1904): Swift MacNeill's motion of local control of the Royal Irish Constabulary.

It was the devolution affair which most thoroughly exposed the limitations of a parliamentary policy—and it was through the devolution affair that Saunderson lost all organizational initiative within his party. He had tended to protect Wyndham's reputation by blaming all the iniquities of the administration on Antony MacDonnell, but when Wyndham became associated with a programme of devolved government in Ireland this equivocation was no longer tenable. The accusations and venom of Moore and Craig had apparently been vindicated—and it was they, not Saunderson, who seized both the popular credit and the campaign advantage.

On 26 September 1904 the Irish Reform Association (a derivative of Lord Dunraven's land conference) published a proposal for an Irish Financial Council which would have limited control over the Irish economy and possess certain powers of legislative initiative.[40] This was of course roundly condemned by almost every representative or organ of Ulster Unionism; and, as the brainchild of a comparatively insignificant organization, the scheme might well have enjoyed no further exposure or debate.[41] What transformed this minor political event into a major controversy was the rumour, subsequently corroborated by the Attorney-General for Ireland, that Dublin Castle lay behind the proposal, and that it was the price paid by George Wyndham for the co-operation of the Nationalist leaders over the Land Bill of 1903.[42]

The anxiety which infected prominent Irish members of the Unionist establishment (Carson, John Atkinson, James Campbell) was felt more widely in Ulster; and this in turn provided the guardians of loyalist fundamentalism with a following and a credibility which they had hitherto lacked. Moore and Craig's earlier appeals to sectarian feeling had been of only limited value in the campaign against Unionist dissent, but the devolution affair provided a much more fertile opportunity. The alleged treachery of Wyndham, against the background of a longer legacy of iniquity, had proved that loyalist organization was both misconceived, in terms of its parliamentary focus, and inadequate, in terms of its local weakness. And in the days following the appearance of the Reform Association programme, Moore and Craig published their own, more limited vision of the future—a vision of loyalism propped up by local repre-

[40] Dunraven, *Past Times*, ii. 27; see n. 23 above.

[41] See e.g. the condemnation offered by *BNL*, 27 Sept. 1904, p. 4 (editorial), p. 5 (report on the Irish Unionist Alliance reaction).

[42] Dunraven, *Past Times*, ii. 29. See also *BNL*, 13 Oct. 1904, p. 7, for an important address given by John Atkinson, Attorney-General for Ireland, at Portadown.

sentative institutions, and co-ordinated in Belfast.[43] Here was the response of the loyalist middle classes to the outmoded structures of their movement; here was their response to the electoral threat posed by Unionist dissent.

Saunderson's own contribution, both to the subsequent development of the devolution controversy, and to the redefinition of loyalism, was slight—but whether this reflected merely indifference or a more active political judgement will never be known. For in October 1904 he contracted pneumonia and subsequently underwent an operation for an abscess on one of his lungs.[44] Thus, during one of the most critical phases of the party's evolution, Saunderson was absent, recovering from his ordeal at the home of his daughter and son-in-law at Strangford, County Down. He played no part in a preliminary meeting, held on 3 December 1904, to discuss the creation of a central co-ordinating body for Ulster Unionism; and he was absent, too, from parliament in February 1905, when the devolution affair entered its climax.[45] He would certainly have been well enough to attend the first meeting of the new Ulster Unionist Council, held on 3 March 1905 in Belfast—and indeed the preliminary publicity informed the public that he would take the chair; but instead he journeyed to Bordeaux in order to continue his recuperation.[46] He sent a letter, lauding the new council, but his real commitment can only have been slight.[47] For the new association, even if only in principle, represented a check on the freedom of Irish Unionist members of parliament; moreover, it was the creation of men who were pushing him to the sidelines of Ulster Unionist politics. It confirmed a tendency towards a new and localized form of political activity which had little to do with Saunderson's English and parliamentary achievement. It was the triumph of middle-class narrowness over Saunderson's own, more splendid and autocratic, conception of loyalist leadership.

The Ulster Unionist Council did not immediately revolutionize loyalist politics, and its progenitors had no desire for a public and radical overhaul of the party machinery.[48] Thus, at the first session, on 3 March 1905, there

[43] *BNL*, 27 Sept. 1904, p. 5 (Moore and Craig, letter no. 1); ibid., 29 Sept. 1904, p. 5 (Moore and Craig, letter no. 2).

[44] Lucas, *Saunderson*, 356.

[45] *BNL*, 3 Dec. 1904, p. 10; Jackson, *Ulster Party*, 264–5.

[46] *BNL*, 4 Mar. 1905, p. 9. Lucas, *Saunderson*, 359.

[47] *BNL*, 4 Mar. 1905, p. 9; Saunderson sent a polite message from Rostrevor, County Down, to William Moore, 'wishing the proceedings every success'.

[48] Patrick Buckland, *Irish Unionism 2: Ulster Unionism and the Origins of Northern Ireland, 1885–1922* (Dublin, 1973), 21; Jackson, *Ulster Party*, 235–40.

were fulsome tributes to the conduct of the Irish Unionist parliamentary party over the devolution affair; and the chairman of the meeting, Colonel J. M. McCalmont, opened his contribution with a lugubrious reference to their stricken leader, Saunderson.[49] In more practical terms, Saunderson was given significant powers of nomination to the vital Standing Committee of the Ulster Unionist Council: the constitution of the UUC provided for a Standing Committee of fifty members, ten of whom were to be appointed by the chairman of the parliamentary party. But at least one leading county Unionist, Joshua Peel of mid-Armagh, was horrified at the prospect of Saunderson wielding so much influence over the new committee.[50] And the creeping and qualified nature of the reform could not obscure the fact that the new UUC represented an indictment of the parliamentary leadership. This was quite evident in the powers which it claimed, and in the complementary restrictions which were erected around the parliamentary party. The settlement of parliamentary policy was no longer to be the sole responsibility of Saunderson's body: responsibility was now to be shared with the UUC.[51] Moreover, the UUC, and not the parliamentary party, was to be 'the medium of expressing Ulster Unionist opinion';[52] it was evasively described as 'a further connecting link between Ulster Unionists and their parliamentary representatives'—a necessary bond, that is, between the parliamentary party and local reality.[53] For all the self-congratulation prevalent among Unionist MPs, a new and uncomplimentary definition of the parliamentary party was promulgated in March 1905: gone was the freebooting irresponsibility of the Saunderson era. Little wonder, then, that the parliamentary chairman should have reacted so ambivalently to a new and usurping loyalist institution. The surprise is rather that his ambivalence did not graduate into open repudiation.

[49] *BNL*, 4 Mar. 1905, p. 9: 'he had so far recovered that his absence that day was due to his being engaged in completing by a visit to the continent the establishment of his health.'

[50] Ulster Unionist Council, Constitution for 1905 (Belfast, 1905); John F. Harbinson, *The Ulster Unionist Party, 1882–1973: Its Origins and Development* (Belfast, 1973), 35–6; PRONI, Joshua Peel Papers, D.889/4C/3: Peel to Lonsdale, 24 Nov. 1904: 'I think it wholly wrong to put the absolute power of nominating 10 members of the Standing Committee in the hands of Col. Saunderson.'

[51] Harbinson, *Unionist Party*, 35.

[52] Ibid.

[53] Ibid.

IV

Saunderson returned to the House of Commons on 31 May 1905, and was warmly greeted—even by opponents like T. P. O'Connor.[54] But the old violence of speech and manner had gone, to be replaced by mildness and not a little self-indulgence. He had been made aware of his age; and, more than ever, he alluded to ancient parliamentary triumphs, and to his own, extended career: 'He himself had now almost reached the allotted span of life', he told the Commons on first returning, 'he had been in the House for many years and he believed hon. Gentlemen opposite, although they disagreed with him, would believe him when he said he also loved his country.'[55] He was sad and weary, and—never the most loyal of parliamentarians—his attendance grew increasingly fitful.[56] Yet he had not quite outlived his political usefulness, for while he had failed to respond to developments in Ulster, he retained a network of parliamentary contacts and a reputation for influence. Cowed and emollient, he was the subject of sympathetic Tory reappraisal at the end of his life. Indeed one of the recurrent ironies of Anglo-Irish relations has been that Unionist leaders have only become attractive to the Tory command after losing their bond with the loyalist democracy: they are only deemed approachable, that is, when their effective influence has long gone.[57]

Saunderson mediated between the extremism of Moore and Craig and the Tory administration in Dublin. George Wyndham had resigned in March 1905 from the Chief Secretaryship, hounded from office by a suspicious and rebellious Irish Unionist party. He was replaced by Walter Long, the President of the Local Government Board, and a choice calculated to assuage loyalist anger. But, despite unimpeachable orthodoxy, Long continued to endure the protracted and difficult aftermath to the devolution affair. Irish loyalists remained angry; and, while they grudgingly accepted the rule of a confessedly devolutionist Lord Lieutenant, a campaign was mounted to expel Antony MacDonnell from the Under-Secretaryship. On 1 April 1905, while Saunderson was still in France, the

[54] *Hansard*, ser. 4, cxlvii. 385 (31 May 1905). Lucas, *Saunderson*, 361–2. This mutual good will did not, however, last long: L. W. Brady, *T. P. O'Connor and the Liverpool Irish* (London, 1983), 178, 211.

[55] *Hansard*, ser. 4, cxlvii. 385 (31 May 1905).

[56] Lucas, *Saunderson*, 362–6.

[57] Carson's career bears this out. Carson was a more attractive and accessible figure for British politicians after the outbreak of the Great War had liberated him from the immediate demands of Ulster loyalist politics. Brian Faulkner also comes to mind in this respect.

Irish Unionist members of parliament withdrew their support from the Castle administration, pending the removal of MacDonnell; and, backed by the loyalist press in Belfast, the leaders of the revolt against Wyndham—Lonsdale, Moore, and Craig—constructed a campaign against Walter Long.[58]

It was thus to an obtusely assertive and rancorous party that Saunderson returned, but he paid little heed to their aggression. On 1 June 1905 he defied his party colleagues by voting with the government during a division on a crimes motion; and, given his stature, and the fact that he had only recently recovered from a dangerous operation, there was very little that the rebels could do to punish this breach of discipline.[59] Yet his action had discredited the Ulster revolt, and his old acquaintance, Walter Long, recognizing the crucial nature of his intervention, was appropriately grateful.[60] Long retained MacDonnell, but his policies were otherwise well calculated to mollify loyalist opinion. For his part, Saunderson remained supportive, and was gradually drawn into the confidence of the Chief Secretary, being consulted on matters of policy and—the perennial Irish grievance—of patronage. Long was prepared to drive from Dublin to Castle Saunderson in order to solicit the old loyalist's opinion; and he valued Saunderson's views highly enough to lay them before the Prime Minister, Balfour.[61]

Thus, in the summer and autumn of 1905 Saunderson did much to prevent Ulster Unionism slipping out of contact with British Toryism. He publicly lauded Walter Long ('[Ulster Unionists] have not had a Chief Secretary for years past in whom they have had more implicit confidence'); and he further chivvied the disgraced Wyndham in order to highlight the virtues of his ministerial successor.[62] He and Long often worked as partners, discussing important appointments like that of the Irish Solicitor-General, or the vexed question of John Atkinson's promotion. When Long wanted to mollify the extremists by appointing William Moore to an Irish law office, he first sounded out Saunderson; and he also recruited the Colonel's support in his campaign to defer the general election to the

58 *BNL*, 1 Apr. 1905, p. 7.

59 Ibid., 2 June 1905, p. 7.

60 Walter Long, *Memories* (London, 1923), 145, 172–4.

61 Henry Robinson, *Memories: Wise and Otherwise* (London, 1924), p. 172.

62 *Hansard*, ser. 4, cl. 98 (24 July 1905); private possession, George Wyndham Papers, T.3221/1/364, 365: Wyndham to Sibell Grosvenor, 4 and 5 Dec. 1905. BL, Arthur Balfour Papers, Add. MS 49805, fo. 106: Wyndham to Balfour, 1 Dec. 1905; ibid., fo. 108: Wyndham to Balfour, 4 Dec. 1905; ibid., fo. 110: Wyndham to Balfour, 4 Dec. 1905.

spring of 1906.[63] In this last, as in his battle to win a Lordship of Appeal for John Atkinson, Long transmitted Saunderson's opinion to the cabinet.[64]

The months between the devolution revelations and the fall of the Unionist government were crucial to the development of the relationship between Toryism and loyalism. Loyalist suspicions had apparently been vindicated during the debates of February 1905; but, while there was considerable sympathy for the Ulster Unionist case, the tenacity with which loyalists had sustained their vendetta eventually came to alarm and repel influential elements within the English party. Arthur Balfour in particular had been always disdainful of loyalist aggression and sentimentality, but he regarded their single-minded pursuit of Wyndham and MacDonnell as peculiarly repulsive.[65] For their part, Ulster Unionists like William Moore flagrantly defied Tory party discipline, denouncing the survival of MacDonnell as Irish Under-Secretary, and harrassing Walter Long's administration. While they reiterated their loyalty to the broader objectives of the Balfour government, they demonstrated a rather greater commitment to loyalist independence and self-reliance. Thus, the relationship between British and Ulster Unionism remained under threat, condemned by British disgust and loyalist paranoia. The general election of 1906, and the return of a Liberal government, allowed a tentative *rapprochement* on the basis of the Union; but, given the earlier tendency towards drift, this was by no means a predictable outcome. The survival of the bond owed much to the rigorous partiality of Walter Long, though Saunderson contributed usefully, disrupting the solidarity of the Ulster Unionist rebellion, and liaising with the English minister. Ulster Unionism emerged from the general election replete with the structures of independence, yet still a component of the British party. The full implications of the Ulster Unionist Council would only be worked out over the next twenty years: in the short term Saunderson and Long had constructed a cosmetic, but a none the less vital, party unity.

Saunderson was unopposed in North Armagh; and he returned to the House of Commons to find that his significance had developed in propor-

[63] BL, Walter Long Papers, Add. MS 62409: Long to Saunderson, 10 Nov. 1905 (copy); ibid., Saunderson to Long, 11 Nov. 1905; ibid., Saunderson to Long, 24 Nov. 1905 (correspondence on the subject of Moore's promotion and the date of the general election).

[64] BL, Arthur Balfour Papers, Add. MS 46776, fo. 127: extracts from a telegram sent by Saunderson to Long, 26 Nov. 1905; ibid., Add. MS 49776, fo. 141: Arbuthnot to Sandars, n.d. (misplaced covering letter for fo. 127). See also ibid., Add. MS 49858, fo. 40: Saunderson to Balfour, 18 Nov. 1905 (on the date of the general election).

[65] See e.g. Blanche E. C. Dugdale, *Arthur James Balfour, First Earl of Balfour KG, OM, FRS & c*, 2 vols (London, 1936), i. 421–2.

tion to the devastation wrought within Unionism in the 1906 general election. He had long venerated Joseph Chamberlain, and had publicly embraced tariff reform during his brief re-election campaign in Lurgan and Portadown: he now found that the Chamberlains reciprocated his interest and sympathy.[66] He corresponded with Austen Chamberlain in early 1906, and was courted by the Birmingham camp as a potentially useful ally in the struggle to coerce Balfour. Austen wrote to Saunderson on 7 February 1906, suggesting that he should call for a more determined style of Unionist leadership; and the loyalist undertook this task at the famous party convocation held on 14 February.[67] Like his rival, Walter Long (and like earlier Unionists on the make), Austen Chamberlain was alive to Saunderson's usefulness as a lever on loyalist militancy. In fact both Long and Chamberlain may have been conscious that the wild Ulster MPs now represented a disproportionately significant element of the Unionist parliamentary party—and a potentially vital source of personal support.[68]

Saunderson's briefly restored pre-eminence was reflected not only in letters of political courtship from the contender for leadership, but also in debate, and in the attentions of the new, Liberal, Chief Secretary. He was chosen to move the first Unionist amendment to the motion for an Address, and on 21 February he fulfilled this commission, registering a protest against the government's commitment to Irish devolution. In a sense, Saunderson was an easy and obvious choice for this accolade since, given the fissile condition of British Unionism, it was appropriate for the leadership to exploit the party's guardians of fundamentalism and orthodoxy. Blunt Unionism was a common tactical resort whenever crisis afflicted the party; but, while Saunderson's narrow politics singled him out on this occasion, his usefulness was enhanced because he had distanced himself from the worst excesses of loyalist anger over devolution.[69]

On the opening day of the parliamentary session, 19 February, Saunderson and James Bryce, the new Chief Secretary and a fellow Ulsterman,

[66] Saunderson's appreciation of Chamberlain dates back at least to Jan. 1902, when he provided a remarkable tribute to the Colonial Secretary in a constituency speech: *BNL*, 11 Jan. 1902, p. 7. See also Lucas, *Saunderson*, 348–9.

[67] ESP, T.2996/3/3: Austen Chamberlain to Saunderson, 7 Feb. 1906. Note Lucas's discreet gloss on this in *Saunderson*, 369. See also David Dutton, *'His Majesty's Loyal Opposition': The Unionist Party in Opposition, 1905–15* (Liverpool, 1992), 19–32.

[68] Birmingham University Library, Austen Chamberlain Papers, AC/4/1/11: Austen to Mary Chamberlain, 27 Oct. 1906: 'He [Saunderson] is a real loss, especially at this time, as he exercised some influence over that wild body of men, the Irish Unionist M.P.s'.

[69] *Hansard*, ser. 4, clii. 372 (21 Feb. 1906).

exchanged notes regarding amendments to the Loyal Address.[70] A meeting was arranged to discuss the likely course of Irish business, and it is probable that Saunderson broached a number of long-standing grievances, including Bann drainage, and the condition of the rural labouring class.[71] Their relationship was amicable, and Saunderson was prepared to support certain of Bryce's ameliorative measures: on 13 June 1906 he offered heartfelt support for the Labourers (Ireland) Bill.[72] When the Colonel died, one of the most touching letters of condolence came from the Chief Secretary.[73]

But these tokens of recognition within the House did not reflect any restoration of confidence at a lower level of the political hierarchy. The Orangemen, labourers, and weavers of North Armagh remained sentimentally tolerant of their distant and ailing MP, yet in the last years of his life he had been no more committed to the constituency than at any earlier time. At the general election of 1906 he had been absent from his nomination as candidate, and his campaigning had been effectively limited to two speeches, delivered at Lurgan on 28 November 1905 and at Portadown town hall on 9 January 1906.[74] Even the eulogists at the time of his death were worried by this record.[75] His illness discouraged potential critics within the division; and it was almost certainly embarrassment and sympathy which held together his constituency, rather than any more fundamental loyalty.

This sentimentality did not, however, extend to Belfast where Saunderson had never been fully accepted, either by the Tory fathers of the city, or by the Sloanite democrats. For his part, Saunderson had always felt that 'the Belfast lot did not suit me', and while in January 1906 he was prepared to reconsider this judgement, his tolerance was short-lived.[76] On 3 January he was invited by William Moore to address a Unionist demonstration in the Ulster Hall—but the event proved a fiasco, with supporters of Tom Sloan strongly represented in the audience, and noisily making their presence evident. Moore defied the anger of the mob, delivering his speech to the reporters' table. Saunderson, weak and dispirited, was shouted down: 'If you want to hear me, I will go on; but, if not, I will stop', he

70 Lucas, *Saunderson*, 369.

71 Ibid.

72 *Hansard*, ser. 4, clviii. 981 (13 June 1906).

73 ESP, T.2996/9/3: Bryce to Helena, 23 Oct. 1906.

74 *BNL*, 22 Oct. 1906, p. 8 (obituary, col. 3).

75 Ibid.

76 PRONI, Ellison-Macartney Papers, D.3649/20/67: Saunderson to Macartney, 11 Jan. 1903.

proclaimed—but the crowd did not want to hear.[77] On 16 January he was asked to attend a rather more carefully vetted meeting of Orangemen, again in the Ulster Hall. But he had done with Belfast politics, and he sent his apologies.[78] The Orangemen of the city had planned on this occasion to present him with a blackthorn stick, inscribed in silver with the words:

> We have great pleasure in presenting you with this Irish blackthorn with which to thrash Home Rulers, Russellites, and Lundyites out of the House of Commons, and may you be long spared to wield it in defence of the Union.[79]

It was clear, given his frightening experience of Belfast politics, that both the nature of the gift, and its bellicose inscription, were only too apt.

V

The ill health which helped to drive Saunderson from the debilitating round of local politics eventually compelled him to withdraw from the Commons. He had not the strength to build on his comparatively favourable position, achieved in the first weeks of the 1906 parliamentary session, and he retired with Helena to Archacon.[80] He had a heart attack, but recovered sufficiently to be able to travel to Paris and Biarritz, where he met and befriended a former adversary, the devolutionist Viceroy Lord Dudley.[81] In June and July he was again in London, and felt strong enough to address the Commons on a number of occasions. But these were to be his last appearances, and on 26 July he delivered what would be his valedictory address.[82] His bitter opponent of ten years, T. W. Russell, touchingly 'congratulated the right hon. and gallant Gentleman on his restored health', and suggested that he had 'seldom spoken with more vigour'. But if the text of Saunderson's speech only hints at his frailty, more intimate and acute observers noted that he had aged dramatically and pathetically.[83]

He spent much of August 1906 idling on Lough Erne, but in September

[77] *BNL*, 3 Jan. 1906, p. 7; ibid., 17 Jan. 1906, p. 8: speaking at Lurgan, Saunderson referred to the disruption of the Ulster Hall meeting and suggested that an Orange police force should be formed in order to silence such critics. Morgan, *Labour and Partition*, p. 51.

[78] *BNL*, 22 Oct. 1906, p. 6 (obituary, col. 5).

[79] Ibid.

[80] Lucas, *Saunderson*, 370.

[81] Ibid. 371.

[82] *Hansard*, ser. 4, clxi. 1525 (26 July 1906).

[83] Ibid. and Lucas, *Saunderson*, 366; see also Lucas, *Saunderson*, 370 n. 1.

he returned briefly to the political arena by means of a well-publicized letter to the London *Times*.[84] Walter Long had resurrected an aspect of the devolution controversy which had driven George Wyndham from office in March 1905; and Saunderson, true to his old friend, endorsed Long's demand that all letters relating to the appointment of Sir Antony MacDonnell should be published.[85] The conflict between Long and MacDonnell briefly fired the English and Irish press at a season when copy was scarce; and Saunderson's letter, as the contribution of a leading Irish Unionist, attracted proportionate notice. As ever, he found the publicity flattering, and on 18 October he attempted to capture more column space by means of a second letter to *The Times*, dealing on this occasion with Irish local government.[86] The letter was published on the day before his death.

Despite his periodic relapses, the end came suddenly. Obituarists lugubriously remembered that Saunderson had welcomed a younger son, Armar, with his American bride, at Castle Saunderson only a few weeks earlier.[87] On Sunday 7 October he went to the little chapel at the castle; on Wednesday 17 October he wrote his last letter to the press.[88] On Thursday he went yachting on the Lough, when a last photograph was taken.[89] That evening he suffered a sudden nosebleed; alarmed, he fled to Helena.[90] On Friday he wired apologies for his absence to a Belfast Orange Lodge (a characteristic, though now understandable, act).[91] Later that day he was taken with a violent fit of coughing, and admitted that he had long experienced pain, while fearing that he should be kept from his yacht.[92] On Saturday, according to the macabre chronology subsequently established by the press, he showed signs of failing circulation; and early on the morning of Sunday 21 October, he died.[93]

The cause of death was pneumonia, contracted on the Lough.[94] It was a grimly ironic but fitting circumstance that he should have been at last a martyr to his beloved yacht, rather than to any political activity.

[84] Lucas, *Saunderson*, 372; *Irish Times*, 26 Sept. 1906, p. 7.
[85] The best account of the episode is Ronan Fanning, 'The Unionist Party and Ireland, 1906–10', *IHS* 15/58 (Sept. 1966), 151–60.
[86] Lucas, *Saunderson*, 372.
[87] *BNL*, 22 Oct. 1906, p. 8 (obituary, col. 1).
[88] Ibid., 25 Oct. 1906, p. 5 (funeral, col. 3); Lucas, *Saunderson*, 373.
[89] Lucas, *Saunderson*, 373, and illustration opposite.
[90] Ibid. 373.
[91] *Irish Times*, 22 Oct. 1906, p. 5 (obituary, col. 2).
[92] Lucas, *Saunderson*, 373.
[93] *BNL*, 22 Oct. 1906, p. 8 (obituary, col. 1).
[94] *Irish Times*, 22 Oct. 1906, p. 5 (obituary, col. 2).

III

THE SAUNDERSON ESTATES

11

The Estate

I

Throughout his life, Edward Saunderson's politics had been rooted in the land. He had run for the House of Commons in 1865 because his family had a longstanding parliamentary interest in County Cavan, and because he instinctively associated proprietorship with political participation.[1] He re-entered politics in 1882–3 because other landlords in the Erne basin were becoming politically active, and because the gentry were coming under a new and systematic challenge from the farming community. Saunderson's Unionism, and therefore the Unionist movement as a whole, should be judged as a symptom of the Irish agrarian crisis of the late 1870s and early 1880s; indeed Saunderson's Unionism may reflect a wider crisis within the European rural order. The 1880s were, as David Cannadine has remarked, 'the most troubled decade . . . for the titled and territorial classes of Europe since the 1840s or 1790s';[2] and throughout Europe these classes, faced by ruin, turned to a pro-active conservatism.

However, the Irish strain of this crisis had a different pathology to its continental European parent. Through much of Europe the rural crisis of the 1880s had two points of origin: European agriculture suffered from external competition—American or antipodean; and it also suffered political and economic relegation in the face of accelerating industrialization. But in Ireland there was no significant industrial growth outside of Belfast; and although other primarily rural nations (such as Spain) had distinctive industrial regions (Catalonia), nowhere in Europe was the regional industrial base so tightly confined and so external in orientation as in Ireland. Moreover, the peculiarly close constitutional and economic relationship

[1] *Anglo-Celt*, 22 July 1865. Saunderson and his supporters referred frequently to the political services of the Saunderson family, and to his status as a prosperous landlord, 'living and spending locally'.

[2] David Cannadine, *The Decline and Fall of the British Aristocracy* (New Haven, Conn. 1990), 25.

between England and Ireland after 1801 simultaneously impeded Irish industry and enhanced Irish agriculture. Paradoxically, therefore, the development of British and European industrialization served to confirm the centrality of agriculture in Ireland.

The Irish rural crisis, like its European parent, was partly the product of external competition, and partly the result of poor harvests. Unlike its European parent, however, it arose precisely because agriculture remained vitally important to Irish society. Land disputes were worth fighting in Ireland, because land remained the principal foundation for wealth, for social station, and for the exercise of political power. The Irish land crisis arose not because of the marginalization of agriculture, but because of an internal struggle in Irish rural society to determine the control of agricultural profits.[3]

The bitterness of this crisis reflected the relative, though shifting, strength of the combatants: the Irish gentry class and the major farming interests. The mid-eighteenth century had been the golden age of the Irish landed gentleman, an age characterized by lavish building programmes, and by a political confidence which found its fullest expression in an assertive Irish patriotism.[4] Thereafter the economic ascendancy of the gentry became more vulnerable: after the 1798 rising their political confidence withered, and with it their patriotism. Increasing economic vulnerability and political challenge gave birth to a more uniform political conservatism. The Famine of 1845 brought reductions in rental income, collateral increases in the burden of the poor rate, and enormous difficulties in sustaining a humane and viable estate administration.[5] Smaller landlords fell victim to these pressures, either selling up and disappearing into impoverished retirement in England, or struggling onwards with a crippling mortgage burden. But the owners of the middling and great estates, though frequently frightened by the prospect of bankruptcy (pen-

[3] This is effectively James S. Donnelly's argument in *The Land and the People of Nineteenth Century Cork: The Rural Economy and the Land Question* (London, 1975), summarized on pp. 6–7. For correctives see W. E. Vaughan, *Landlords and Tenants in Ireland, 1848–1904* (Dundalk, 1984), 31–2, and id., 'Landlord and Tenant Relations in Ireland between the Famine and the Land War, 1850–70', in L. M. Cullen and T. C. Smout (eds.), *Comparative Aspects of Scottish and Irish Economic and Social History, 1600–1900* (Edinburgh, 1977), 212–26. See also W. E. Vaughan, *Landlords and Tenants in Mid-Victorian Ireland* (Oxford, 1994), 208–16, and esp. 212–13.

[4] David Dickson, *New Foundations: Ireland, 1660–1800* (Dublin, 1987), 104.

[5] Donnelly, *Land and People*, 100–7.

ury and disgrace weighed heavily with Alexander Saunderson), survived to benefit from the agricultural upturn of the 1850s.[6]

As in the late eighteenth century, so between 1850 and 1880 landlords did not effectively harness agricultural wealth, and in these years rents lagged behind prices.[7] Nevertheless, the condition of the landlord class, and in particular of comparatively wealthy landlords like the Saundersons, was more healthy than such comparisons, or the rhetoric of their critics, might have implied. Only the smallest landlords bore unmanageable burdens of mortgage debt (what Cannadine has defined as 'ruinous' debt).[8] Middling and major landowners frequently had their income constrained by marriage entail and other family charges; but, until the rent reductions of the 1880s, the mortgage burden of these classes was, on the whole, tolerable.[9] And there were other crumbs of comfort for Irish landlords after 1850. The operation of the Encumbered Estates Court eased the lot of heavily indebted landowners by facilitating the disposal of their lands. The salutary effects of this measure should not be overstated; but it is clear that the level of landlord investment and improvement rose after 1850, and possibly as an indirect result of the Act.[10] Landlords certainly benefited from the final disappearence of the middleman class in the famine period, for this permitted a more direct control of the estate, and a more direct exploitation of its resources. The ending of middleman leases occasionally meant that landed income could grow on the (otherwise unlikely) basis of a declining estate rental.[11]

But it would be quite wrong to disguise the fundamental drift within the landlord–tenant relationship. From the mid-eighteenth century on, the distribution of economic power in rural Ireland was shifting in favour of the farmer interest. Long leases, issued through much of the century, benefited the farmers at the expense of the landlord because farmers could thereby more directly exploit agricultural growth; rising prices and modest

[6] NLI, Vernon Papers, MS 18953/2: Alexander Saunderson to John E. Vernon, 26 Mar. 1847 ('I feel as part of a crew of a sinking ship'); ibid., 1 Apr. 1847 ('I may have my furniture sold by the accumulation of rates from the nonpayment of those who cannot pay'); ibid., 26 June 1847 ('so you see that unless I allow my whole income to be spent at Castle Saunderson, I let Mrs Saunderson and my children starve').

[7] Dickson, *New Foundations*, 107; Donnelly, *Land and People*, 194. This is the dominant view in the literature. For a recent, tentative revision see B. J. Graham and L. J. Proudfoot, *An Historical Geography of Ireland* (London, 1993), 328–9. See also Vaughan, *Landlords and Tenants in Mid-Victorian Ireland*, 226.

[8] Quoted in L. P. Curtis, 'Incumbered Wealth: Landed Indebtedness in Post-Famine Ireland', *American Historical Review*, 85/2 (Apr. 1980), 365.

[9] Ibid. 363–5, 367.

[10] Donnelly, *Land and People*, 164.

[11] Ibid. 52–3, 116.

rental increases between 1850 and 1880 had a similar effect on the balance between landlord and tenant interests. Political structures gradually reflected this shift in economic relationships: the movement towards emancipation benefited from the increasing strength and confidence of the Catholic farming classes; general franchise extensions in 1850, 1868, and 1884 diminished landlord electoral control. The Ballot Act of 1872 similarly impaired the landlord's capacity to direct the votes of his tenantry. The rising farmer class produced party structures directly antagonistic to the landlord interest: the Independent Irish party of the 1850s, and ultimately the National Land League. The rising farmer class fed men and money into the Catholic Church, aiding its institutional growth, and helping thereby to create an alternative focus for local political and spiritual loyalty.

In 1880 landlords still dominated the established structures of Irish politics and of rural society. Their wealth was still formidable. But their political dominance was increasingly formal and increasingly nominal, and their wealth was either encumbered, or of a type (rambling buildings, old-fashioned plate, and jewellery) which defied easy liquidation. The wealthiest and most debt-free landlords—such as Edward Saunderson—had sufficient parliamentary power to flout tenant agitation, and sufficient capital to withstand rent strikes; they also tended to be northern.[12] Viewing the wounded and disoriented gentry class from a relatively cushioned perspective, northern landlords like Saunderson had the economic resources and the political confidence to act creatively in their defence. And the strategy which Saunderson and the other landlords of the Erne basin chose in the early 1880s was to unite the interests of the waning gentry class to the popular and burgeoning Unionist movement. It was an alliance which very nearly destroyed both partners; but in the event they each survived, and landlordism temporarily found a new purpose and a new vigour within the protective structures of Unionism.

II

What, then, were the lands which determined the politics of Edward Saunderson, and which thereby influenced the fate of the gentry class as a

[12] Curtis, 'Incumbered Wealth', 366–7.

whole? At the time of its sale, between 1911 and 1925, the Saunderson estate comprised approximately 9,690 acres, which were divided into (roughly) three groupings, and spread across the rich lowlands of the barony of Loughtee in north and central County Cavan; in addition there were some 103 acres in the neighbouring county, Fermanagh.[13] In the seventeenth century there had been Saunderson land in both County Tyrone and County Monaghan, but this was later bequeathed and sold beyond the main line of family descent. Nevertheless, by 1900 the Saunderson estate still fell only a little short of its greatest acreage, despite the political and economic pressure on the gentry throughout the preceding century. Modest expenditure, sensible marriages, an immunity to gambling, actresses, and chorus girls, had helped to preserve the estate in a form which the seventeenth-century family would have recognized.

The main portion of what was a highly fragmented estate amounted to 8,035 acres, and was spread over twenty-nine townlands near Cavan town.[14] In the late nineteenth and early twentieth centuries there were some 400 tenants on this land: the average size of holding was therefore around twenty acres, and this in turn approximated to the overall Irish average. The holdings closest to the county town were regarded as being best in quality, and were used as meadowland, and for grazing. Further away from the town the land grew more hilly and more dense and rocky in texture. Here rents were lower, and the burden of cultivation greater: potatoes could only be planted by spade, because the steep gradients and stiff textures defeated the horse-drawn seed-planter. There was little timber on any part of the estate, but a memory of earlier woodland was preserved in the numerous bogs and plentiful turf. Roads through the estate were adequate in number, and in good condition. The inspector of the Land Commission, Lafferty, who visited Cavan in 1911 felt that, regardless of the quality of some of the land, the estate required no particular improvement, and indeed was characterized by industrious tenants and well-managed holdings. Lafferty found that there were few evicted tenants, and few landless labourers on the estate—a remarkable

[13] National Archive, Dublin, Irish Land Commission Records, EC.6412, 7938: Saunderson estate records; consulted in the Department of Agriculture, Dublin, Dec. 1990. P. J. Duffy, 'The Evolution of Estate Properties in South Ulster, 1600–1900', in William J. Smyth and Kevin Whelan (eds.), *Common Ground: Essays in the Historical Geography of Ireland Presented to T. Jones Hughes* (Cork, 1988), 85. Eileen McCourt, 'The Management of the Farnham Estates during the Nineteenth Century', *Breifne*, 4/16 (1975), 533.

[14] Duffy, 'Estate Properties', 89.

absence, given Edward Saunderson's concern for, and strictures on, these classes.[15]

The other substantial portion of the Saunderson estate lay in the centre of County Cavan, close to the town of Virginia. This amounted to some 1,600 acres, divided into two separate but contiguous sections, and with an annual rental of around £765. The rent per acre (£2.10), and the average size of holding (22 acres) were little different from the main component of the estate at Cavan town and Belturbet (£2.30 and 21 acres). As a smaller area, this part of the estate had fewer variations in the quality of land. In general the soil was of a gravelly type, which offered good drainage and provided the basis for successful mixed farming enterprises. The land inspector John A. Smith, who visited the area in July 1911, found that the farms, though small, were in 'fair' condition, and were 'well cultivated'. Farm buildings were soundly roofed in thatch or in slate, and were deemed to be in 'good repair'. As with the main estate, the political mood was tranquil here, undisturbed by restless and impoverished labourers, or by aggrieved evicted tenants.[16]

By the end of the nineteenth century this land was generally held by farmers on leasehold tenure. As with most Irish estates, the landlord's leasing policy at Castle Saunderson had changed markedly since the seventeenth-century land settlements. Throughout Ireland there was a drift from leases of between seven and twenty-one years' duration in the late seventeenth century to longer, thirty-one-year, or three-life, leases by the early eighteenth century. Leasing policy was broadly determined by market conditions, and the difficult years at the beginning of the eighteenth century had encouraged more flexibility on the part of landlords and thus more generous rental terms. By contrast, the economic upturn of the later eighteenth century persuaded landlords that shorter and more constrictive leases offered a better opportunity to harness agricultural profits. Although the eighteenth-century boom had broken by 1815, a still-spiralling population enabled landlords to pare away at leases, so that, by 1845, annual tenancies had become the predominant feature of Irish landholding.[17] English tenancy practice in Ireland had thus reverted to its

[15] National Archive, Dublin, Irish Land Commission Records, EC.6412: estate of Captain S. F. Saunderson (General Report of the Inspector, 27 June 1911).

[16] Ibid., EC.7938: estate of Captain S. F. Saunderson (General Report of the Inspector, 13 July 1911).

[17] Donnelly, *Land and People*, 11, 200–1; Graham and Proudfoot, *Historical Geography*, 230. See also W. H. Crawford, 'Economy and Society in South Ulster in the Eighteenth Century', *Clogher Record*, 8/3 (1975), 244.

mid-seventeenth-century origins. In the years immediately after the Famine some of the more painful features of the early-eighteenth-century Irish economy were replicated, and leases grew accordingly in length and generosity (although the duration and generosity of the early-eighteenth-century lease were never fully matched).

The leasing policy at Castle Saunderson corresponded, broadly, to this general Irish pattern. Leases were long at the very end of the seventeenth century, became appreciably shorter after 1750, and remained truncated until the 1820s. But there were some features of the Castle Saunderson policy which slightly bucked the general Irish trend. First, long leases, in particular three-life leases, appear to have been favoured at Castle Saunderson a little earlier than was generally true elsewhere in Ireland. Secondly, one-life or thirty-one-year leases appear to have remained customary on the estate even in the early nineteenth century. And, thirdly, the national trend notwithstanding, three-life leases, and the virtually automatic renewal of three-life leases, remained a consistent feature of estate management at Castle Saunderson between 1695 and 1850.[18]

How may these apparent anomalies be explained? In general Castle Saunderson leases were longer than those prevailing in the rest of Ireland. This generosity reflected the wealth of the estate, and the comparatively great and unencumbered nature of the Saunderson rental. Three-life or perpetuity leases were introduced into the Saunderson estate in the mid-1690s, a little ahead of their popularity elsewhere.[19] The lease was, as has been observed, a by-product of the agricultural recession of the early eighteenth century; but its hasty introduction at Castle Saunderson may reflect the particular, if temporary, difficulties experienced by Robert Sanderson and other Cavan landlords. The Saunderson patrimony suffered extensive damage between 1689 and 1691, and required considerable investment thereafter. A ransacked estate, combined with the naturally indifferent quality of land in Cavan, may have forced Robert Sanderson to offer leasehold concessions ahead of some of his landed contemporaries.

The three-life lease survived at Castle Saunderson into the nineteenth century: Alexander Saunderson, Edward's father, created a three-life

[18] Information based on the surviving lease record for the estate: PRONI, Saunderson Estate Papers, D.3480/13/1–2. There appear to be similarities with the Farnham leasing policy: McCourt, 'Farnham Estates', 535. Charles Coote observed that the original term of leases was three lives, but that one life or twenty-one-year leases had become more common: Coote, *A Statistical Survey of the County of Cavan* (Dublin, 1802), 37.

[19] See e.g. PRONI, Saunderson Estate Papers, D.3840/13/2: lease in perpetuity from Robert Sanderson of Castle Sanderson to Josiah Kellett, 16 July 1695.

renewable lease on ninety acres as late as May 1838.[20] Three-life leases, originating in the 1690s, were commonly renewed in the early nineteenth century, with the approval of either Francis Saunderson or Alexander Saunderson. Many of these antique leases were issued to, or renewed by, the Sandersons of Cloverhill, who were distant relations of the main Saunderson line. The Castle Saunderson family enjoyed close ties with this cadet branch, and may well have issued preferential leases out of a sense of loyalty or obligation. If so, then these antique leases may be seen as a reflection not just of the relative prosperity of the Saundersons, but also of the unusually good relationship which was sustained on the estate between landlord and head tenant.

This excellence of relations was a particular feature of Alexander Saunderson's management in the years between 1827, when he inherited Castle Saunderson, and his death, in 1857.[21] Alexander was a sensitive and paternalistic landlord, who knew and was on good terms with most of his tenants. Yet, during the last years of his life he was an absentee, fleeing from Castle Saunderson first to Mullagh in south-east Cavan, and from there, in 1847, to northern France. Between 1847 and his death Alexander, his family, and their small entourage shuttled between fashionable French resorts on the Channel coast and, in winter, Nice, at that time still a part of the Kingdom of Sardinia.

Crudely interpreted, Alexander Saunderson was an absentee, living comfortably in France while the Famine was racking his Cavan tenantry, and scything through the cottiers of Ireland. In reality, however, Alexander's career illustrates the force of Anthony Malcomson's strictures on the definition and nature of absenteeism.[22] Alexander's personality and circumstances bore little relation to nineteenth-century Nationalist characterizations of the leech-like proprietor, bloated on the life-blood of the farming classes. True, Alexander was an absentee through most of the Famine, but he was not cynically rejecting Ireland, or arbitrarily dismissing the responsibilities of property ownership. Nor was he a latterday Lord Donegall 'draining a manufacturing county of £36,000 a year ... to build palaces in another land where he is unknown or disregarded'.[23] It was not

[20] PRONI, D.3480/13/2: lease from Alexander Saunderson to James Sanderson, Cloverhill, Cavan, 15 May 1838; McCourt, 'Farnham Estates', 536.

[21] A comprehensive record of Alexander Saunderson's managerial record may be found in NLI, Vernon Papers, MS 18953.

[22] A. P. W. Malcomson, 'Absenteeism in Eighteenth-Century Ireland', *Irish Economic and Social History*, 1 (1974), 15–35.

[23] Quoted in Malcomson, 'Absenteeism', p.20.

cynicism, or hedonism, but rather a combination of ill health and a rapidly declining income which compelled Alexander to retreat from Castle Saunderson in 1846. In the eighteenth century impoverished Irish landlords had often bolted to England to lead a life of genteel beggary, and to escape from the costs of maintaining face and station in Ireland. The impecunious Alexander chose first to withdraw to a quiet corner of his own estate, where he could live more cheaply than at the castle; but, when he lost a leg in a riding accident, and suffered unremitting pain as an after-effect, he broke altogether with Cavan and Ireland in order to find a gentler climate and physical relief.

Neglect, however, was not a consequence of this retreat. Taut with pain, Alexander maintained a close and apprehensive supervision of the estate from his bed or couch at Le Havre and Nice. The rapid improvement in transportation and in the postal service achieved in the 1840s meant that an absentee landlord could, if he were sufficiently motivated, monitor the condition of his property. The efficiency of this procedure depended on the reliability of the landlord's agent, and in the mid-nineteenth century (as J. S. Donnelly's work makes clear) disastrously inefficient agents were by no means uncommon.[24] Alexander's agent in the 1840s, a Mr Bell, was not in the same destructive league as Thomas Poole, the frighteningly reckless agent of the Viscounts Midleton; but it seems probable that Bell's mismanagement was mitigated only because he enjoyed less independence and a weaker status at Castle Saunderson than would have been the case elsewhere in Ireland.[25] Alexander operated an informal and cumbersome system of management wherein the agent was responsible for the daily administration of the estate, but was supervised both by a local squire, John Vernon, and indirectly—through the mail—by Alexander himself.[26] Bell seems to have reported by post to Alexander, but Vernon, a family friend and a relative of the Saundersons, maintained a more regular, frank, and—for Alexander—a more decisive correspondence. Through Vernon's weekly letters to France, Alexander had a grip on his affairs which many resident landlords might well have envied.

Managing his managers was Alexander's greatest, but by no means his

[24] Donnelly, *Land and People*, 173–87. See also Vaughan, *Landlords and Tenants in Mid-Victorian Ireland*, 108–13.

[25] Donnelly, *Land and People*, 173–4.

[26] For Alexander's complaints concerning Bell see NLI, Vernon Papers, MS 18953/2: Saunderson to Vernon, 26 June 1847, 27 June 1847.

only administrative problem. The Famine and agricultural crisis of the late 1840s had a weaker impact in Cavan than in much of the rest of the island, but the results were still tragic and distressing. The potato failure of 1846 meant that only 10 per cent of the Saunderson estate was planted in 1847.[27] This ensured a second disastrous harvest, a collapse of the farmers' profits, and the shrinking of Alexander's rental income. A declining income, coupled with widespread rural poverty, dramatically increased the burden of the poor rate: as J. S. Donnelly has written of Cork during the Famine, 'collecting rent and meeting increased charges for both poor rates and employment were undoubtedly the two most important problems' for the Irish gentry.[28]

Alexander Saunderson's reaction to this avalanche of problems and anxieties can be monitored through his extensive surviving correspondence with John Vernon. His fundamental fear was, of course, that the estate should be lost and his family reduced to penury.[29] Alexander was a sensitive man, lingering in pain, and prone to depression; these cancerous anxieties tortured him, and frequently broke through the tremulous restraint of his letters to Vernon. Yet it would be quite wrong to imply that he was essentially neurotic or selfish in his reactions. A pervasive concern of the letters is with his tenantry, whose circumstances he clearly knew. Alexander felt keenly the responsibilities of Christian proprietorship, and had a paternal and emotional interest in the condition of these tenants. Those who had been loyal to the family he rewarded with rent abatements as early as April 1847 (two years before such abatements became common); there was also a general reduction, or waiving, of rents on the estate, as elsewhere in Ireland, in the summer of 1849.[30] Those tenants who betrayed his trust or affections were treated as unloving and embarrassing children—with rebukes and assisted passages to the United States. Those persistent defaulters on rent for whom Alexander felt no strong personal responsibility were evicted and employed as labourers on the estate. He thought that work could be created through land improvement, and he was intensely irritated by what he saw as the 'wasteful' roadwork schemes of 1845. Like other Irish landlords, Alexander was keen to unite the smaller

[27] NLI, Vernon Papers, MS 18953/2: Saunderson to Vernon, 26 Mar. 1847; Terence P. Cunningham, 'The Great Famine in County Cavan', *Breifne*, 2/8 (1965), 413–37.

[28] Donnelly, *Land and People*, 100; Graham and Proudfoot, *Historical Geography*, 232.

[29] See n. 6 above.

[30] NLI, Vernon Papers, MS 18953/2: Saunderson to Vernon, 1 Apr. 1847.

and more inefficient holdings, and pursued this strategy of eviction and re-employment as the most humane way of attaining this end.[31]

Without unduly compromising his Christian paternalism, or incurring crippling debt, Alexander kept his lands. The cost to him and to his family was trivial compared to the experiences of many Irish farmers and cottiers, but withal painful. Alexander's income had collapsed in 1846–7, with receipts of £1,100 out of a theoretical rental of perhaps £7,000.[32] But, through humiliating penny-pinching—living in rented accommodation removed from the most expensive areas of the Channel and Mediterranean coasts—Alexander preserved the Castle Saunderson estate. Small acreages were sold to raise cash; the demesne was rented out in 1849.[33] But, in general, extreme measures of this kind were rare, and the estate was bequeathed by Alexander to his sons in much the same condition as he had inherited it from his own father in 1827.

III

Edward, the third surviving son of Alexander and Sarah Saunderson, was the principal beneficiary under his father's will. The normal method of bequest among the Irish gentry was male primogeniture, with the eldest inheriting the bulk of the family estates. Frequently, however, these lands might be encumbered by family settlement—in particular by marriage settlements: in the 1840s 40 per cent of the rental on the Downshire estate was tied up through earlier family bequests and provisions.[34] In several respects the Saunderson family departed from these norms; and these deviations shed light on the range of non-economic influences which helped to condition gentry inheritance patterns in the nineteenth century.

[31] Ibid.: Saunderson to Vernon, 26 Mar. 1847. A few Catholic clergy condemned certain Cavan landlords for 'wanting in common humanity' and for orchestrating 'a terrible persecution carried on against the poor'—but Saunderson was evidently not among those so described: Cunningham, 'Great Famine', 414–15, 419.

[32] NLI, Vernon Papers, MS 18953/3: Saunderson to Vernon, 29 July 1847. For the desperate condition of some of the Cavan tenantry see Brian O Mordha, 'The Greville Papers: A Cavan Estate on the Eve of the Great Famine', *Breifne*, 1/3 (1960), 272–4. There is no precise record of Alexander Saunderson's rental capacity in the 1840s: John Bateman, *Great Landowners of Great Britain and Ireland*, 4th edn. (London, 1883), 396, recorded the rental of Edward Saunderson's 12,362 acres as £7,370 p.a.. Bateman uses figures culled from *The Modern Domesday Book* (1876).

[33] NLI, Vernon Papers, MS 18953/3: Saunderson to Vernon, 25 Jan. 1849; ibid. MS 18953/4: Saunderson to Vernon, 16 Aug. 1849.

[34] Curtis, 'Incumbered Wealth', 339.

Edward inherited Castle Saunderson although he was only a third son. It was Edward's mother, Sarah, who determined this succession, for she seems to have had an absolute influence over her ailing and suggestible husband. Several of Alexander's letters to John Vernon have messages from Sarah superimposed: her strong hand practically obliterates the cramped and silken scrawl of her husband, serving as a metaphor for their relationship.[35] These messages and Sarah's other letters suggest not merely a benevolent domination of Alexander, but firm—even insensitive—attitudes towards her children. Somerset and Alexander, Edward's older brothers, receive no mention in Sarah's surviving correspondence, even though it is very largely devoted to family matters. Her eldest daughter, Julia, won only glancing comments, mostly savage criticisms of her marriage ('this distasteful subject') to an impoverished clergyman ('this designing man [who] crossed her path in a luckless hour').[36] Sarah's unmarried daughter, Rose, features only as a foil to Edward.[37]

Edward inherited the estate because his elder brother, Somerset, had defied Sarah's ascendancy within the family, and because the eldest brother, Alexander, was disabled (and Sarah decreed, with characteristic brutality, that 'she would never allow the place to go to a cripple').[38] Little provision was made for Julia because of her injudicious marriage; and little provision was made for Rose because of her injudicious celibacy—because she had not married into a suitably noble family, and borne suitably noble children. Llewellyn, the youngest son, was regarded by Sarah with a mixture of affection and contempt, and is portrayed in her letters as an irremediable scallywag.[39] He inherited a small estate at Dromkeen, in northern Cavan, although after 1886 he chose to retreat to Protestant suburbia, and to Kingstown, County Dublin.

Aside from Dromkeen the Saunderson lands went in their entirety to Edward. Sarah's affections were focused on him virtually to the exclusion of her other children. Of all the siblings, Edward responded most completely both to his mother's evangelical faith, and to her authority within the family: 'he has indeed a most amenable and upright nature', Sarah opined in 1858, 'and is worthy of all my love'.[40] It was Edward—his minor ailments, his flirtations, his petty attainments, his suitable marriage—who dominated Sarah's apprehensions; and it is Edward who dominates

[35] See e.g. NLI, Vernon Papers, MS 18953/5–6.

[36] Ibid., MS 18953/6: Sarah Saunderson to Vernon, n.d. [1860].

[37] Ibid.: Sarah Saunderson to Vernon, n.d.

[38] Henry Saunderson, *The Saundersons of Castle Saunderson* (London, 1936), 58.

[39] NLI, Vernon Papers, MS 18953/6: Sarah Saunderson to Vernon, n.d.

[40] Ibid.: Sarah Saunderson to Vernon, n.d.

Sarah's surviving correspondence. Edward was his father's principal legatee because he spoke the same emotional and evangelical language as his mother. Love and religion won Castle Saunderson; love and religion bucked the usual inheritance patterns of the Irish gentry.

Edward's style of estate management was paternalist and mild, determined by his evangelical sensibilities, and facilitated by the comparative wealth of the Saunderson estate. The model of his father also weighed heavily with him, and in his early constituency speeches he referred piously to Alexander's legacy, and to the pervasive influence of his actions: the model supplied by the Lords Farnham may also have been important.[41] Like his father he kept a tight rein on the expenses and outgoings of the family. Even in the later 1890s, when his income was healthy, and when the political confidence of the landed classes was reasonably sure, Saunderson's dowdy appearance seemed to express poverty. He habitually travelled second-class on the underground railway; in 1898, having been appointed a Privy Counsellor, he complained half-humorously about the expense of court dress.[42] This anxiety over money may well have been inculcated by his father during the famine years, when Edward was an impressionable and sensitive child. It was certainly an anxiety which he carried into manhood, and which was nourished in the periodic troughs of the Irish agrarian economy. In 1879, when the outlook was peculiarly bleak, Saunderson baulked at the most trivial expenditure, refusing to acquire a pony on the grounds that 'we must refrain from buying any unnecessary article, as the prospects are very bad in the country'.[43] Saunderson's complaint was to his wife, but the command, and its lugubrious tone, might well have been borrowed from Alexander Saunderson's letters to John Vernon in the famine years.

Saunderson's financial state depended on the integrity of his rents, and on his own expenditure. At the end of the 1870s his rental income shrank from its normal level of over £7,000, and the family outgoings retreated in line with this shrinkage. The combination of a falling rental and reduced expenditure is thoroughly characteristic of most Irish landlords at this time: the most significant exception is the urban, especially the suburban, proprietor. For those Irish landowners whose incomes were harnessed by mortgage debt or by family settlement, the agricultural crisis of the late

[41] *Anglo-Celt*, 22 July 1865: 'my father and grandfather represented you. I do hope fervently that the spirit which animated them may exist and continue in me.' McCourt, 'Farnham Estates', 546–51, 553–5.

[42] CC, William Bull Papers, 3/12: extract from a diary, Sept. 1905; Almeric Fitzroy, *Memoirs*, 2 vols. (London, n.d. [1925]), i. 9.

[43] ESP, T.2996/2B/153: Saunderson to Helena, 2 July 1879.

1870s and early 1880s proved to be calamitous. Larger estates, and the estates of Ulster, tended to be more solvent than the smaller properties of the south and west of Ireland.[44] And the Saunderson estate conforms to this generalization, being simultaneously large and northern and solvent. Edward seems to have inherited no mortgage debt from his father; and, since the provision made by Alexander and Sarah for their other children was embarrassingly slight, his income was not overburdened by family settlements. Nor did he squander these advantages: he was addicted to none of the vices of the Irish gentry, having no interest in building or gambling or drink: except for his yachts (which were built locally and on the cheap), his recreations were Pooteresque in their modesty and simplicity. He married sensibly: Helena de Moleyns was so perfect a partner, as the daughter of a (comparatively) solvent peer, that one might suspect Edward of cynical social ambition, or suspect that Sarah had arranged the match. But, as we have seen, the marriage was founded in love, a mutual sensitivity, and a shared evangelical passion.

Thanks to Sarah's mercurial affections, and to Edward's sensible management, the Saunderson estates survived the troubled 1880s. The family was not rich by the standards of industrial Belfast, but its lifestyle was reasonably modest, and its overheads were correspondingly low. Until the era of land purchase its wealth lay in fixed assets: its disposable income could be slight, and generally was so in years of recession. Costly purchases were kept to a minimum, and debt was regarded as pernicious. Only once, apparently—in 1875—did Edward overcome this inherited aversion to mortgage debt in raising £2,000, and the circumstances of the loan were quite exceptional.[45] Edward's neighbours included farmers who rented glebe land at Drummully, Coole, and Annaghmore in County Fermanagh. Under the purchase clauses of the Irish Church Act of 1869 these men and women, in common with other tenants of the Church of Ireland, were entitled to buy the freehold of their property; equally, they were permitted to convey their holding to another party. It seems that nine farmers were willing to sell their land on to 'another party'; and between August 1874 and August 1875 Edward Saunderson seized this opportunity, acquiring 103 acres for a little under £1,800. This was clearly an exceptionally large outlay for the family, and in 1875 Edward took out the £2,000 mortgage at

[44] Curtis, 'Incumbered Wealth', 363–7. See also the discussion of landlord indebtedness in Vaughan, *Landlords and Tenants in Mid-Victorian Ireland*, 130–7.

[45] The details of the mortgage may be found in PRONI, Land Registry Papers, Box 2134: mortgage deed, 3 Nov. 1875. See also *House of Commons, Report of the Commissioners of Church Temporalities in Ireland, 1869–1880*, 167–8.

5 per cent interest to cover the cost. The lenders were the trustees of his marriage settlement (John Vernon and his brother-in-law, Edward de Moleyns); and, though they can scarcely have been the most carnivorous of creditors, they offered few concessions in their interest charges. In the 1870s only a heavily encumbered proprietor, which Saunderson was not, generally paid 5 to 5½ per cent interest, while peers and bankable commoners enjoyed interest rates of around 4 per cent.[46] Presumably the slight expense of the mortgage was offset by the indulgent nature of the lenders, who were scarcely likely to foreclose on the debt, or otherwise abuse the debtor. And in fact the mortgage was redeemed as late as 1912, and only then by Somerset Saunderson, acting under the direction of his father's will.[47]

Solvency permitted Edward Saunderson to inherit, and in some ways to sustain, the paternalist regime constructed by his father. But he tampered with this legacy; and, in any case, the changing political and economic condition of rural Ireland forced an independent redefinition of the paternalist relationship. As in the factories of later Victorian England, so on Irish estates like Castle Saunderson, paternalism had both an economic and moral basis. Christian, and especially evangelical, conviction bound the employer to his employee and helped to create a moral community out of a disparate workforce, or a disparate tenantry. Christian conviction saddled both employer and employee with a sense of mutual obligation, and responsibility. Paternalism was also, as Patrick Joyce has remarked, 'a paying proposition'.[48] It satisfied the spiritual and material needs of workers, consolidated their institutional loyalty, and made for a more efficient industrial or agricultural enterprise. *Laissez-faire* dogma was the chief brake on mid-Victorian paternalism; and it played a key role in defining economic relations, whether in the industrial Lancashire of Patrick Joyce, or in the rural Cavan of Alexander Saunderson.[49] Saunderson's otherwise generous concern for his tenants in the famine years was fatally tinctured by the tenets of self-help.

Before the Land War Edward Saunderson was a conventional paternalist, emphasizing the community of interests on his estate, and acting as a model of responsible Christian proprietorship. Like his father, Edward was a benefactor of both the Catholic and Protestant churches on

[46] Curtis, 'Incumbered Wealth', 339–40.

[47] PRONI, Land Registry Papers, Box 2134: mortgage deed, 3 Nov. 1875.

[48] Patrick Joyce, *Work, Society and Politics: The Culture of the Factory in Victorian England* (London, 1982), 146.

[49] Ibid. 152–3.

his estate, supplying land for building and cash for maintenance. Like the industrial magnates of Victorian Lancashire and West Yorkshire, he was a patron of local education; like his neighbour and kinsman, Lord Farnham, he sponsored day schools and Sunday schools;[50] like Alexander Saunderson, he was slow to evict, although his *laissez-faire* convictions and economic pragmatism meant that persistent rent defaulters on the estate were regarded as fair targets. Like the Victorian industrial magnates, Edward Saunderson threw open his demesne to his tenants, to local teachers, and local church excursionists.[51] He was, as the *Anglo-Celt* purred, 'a kindly and indulgent landlord'.[52]

After the 1870s the quality of Edward's paternalism changed. His rhetorical emphasis on the integrity of the rural community, on the unifying bond of Irishness, and on the rights of farmers gave way to a more explicit defence of the landlord caste. In the House of Commons, as has been observed, he graduated from a halting support of the farmers to a passionate assertion of the landlord case. There is some evidence to suggest a parallel chilling of relations on the estate. Castle Saunderson escaped the worst of the Land War; and it was not among those properties targeted by the organizers of the Plan of Campaign. There were few evicted tenants, and few problems arising from eviction. Yet Saunderson's emergence as a proponent of landlord right undoubtedly angered his tenantry, and helped (for example) to scupper the voluntary sale of his estate during his lifetime. In 1905 Saunderson issued a circular to his tenants suggesting terms of sale: these were hotly debated, condemned as inadequate, and were trumped by a radical counter-proposal. There was, of course, a glaring discrepancy between Saunderson's original demands and his tenants' reply, and the outcome was some ill-natured posturing and a lasting stalemate. Only in 1911 was the estate sold—on terms not far short of what Saunderson had proposed, but which the Cavan farmers had not been prepared to accept from their wayward and provocative landlord.[53]

If the principal brake on mid-nineteenth-century landed paternalism was *laissez-faire* dogma, then the principal constraint on late Victorian paternalism lay in the doctrines of tenant right. Saunderson's paternalism, as defined by his father, was a code of behaviour for both landlord and tenant: it was a contractual bond which tied the landlord to sensitive

50 Lucas, *Saunderson*, 43; McCourt, 'Farnham Estates', 553–5.

51 *Anglo-Celt*, 6 Feb. 1869; D. M. McFarlan, *Lift Thy Banner: Church of Ireland Scenes, 1870–1900* (Dundalk, 1990), 44.

52 *Anglo-Celt*, 1 July 1865.

53 Laurence Geary, *The Plan of Campaign, 1886–1891* (Cork, 1986), 153–78; *Portadown News*, 16 Apr. 1904; *Lurgan Mail*, 9 Dec. 1905.

management and bound the tenant to a deferential response. The premisses governing this paternalism were the unassailable legitimacy of landed authority and the legitimacy of landed proprietorship. But in Ireland these premisses had never won uniform acceptance, since the pattern of land ownership was of a peculiarly contentious and recent manufacture. And in both Britain and Ireland agricultural recession and rural politicization in the late nineteenth century made for a more assertive tenantry, and for a breakdown in the traditional patterns of landed control. The extension of the county franchise in 1850 and again in 1885, and the abolition of the secret ballot in 1872, brought liberation and strength to the tenant cause, and helped to focus the farmer unrest which swept through Britain and Ireland in the 1880s. Paternalism was mortally wounded by the political emancipation of British and Irish tenants; and the collapse of paternalism presaged the collapse of landlordism itself.

Given this context, Edward Saunderson's metamorphosis becomes more comprehensible. Alexander Saunderson's paternalist regime was constructed upon the presumption of tenant deference and pliability. On the few recorded occasions when Alexander's authority was defied by a tenant, he responded in a confused and wounded manner; but his reactions were aggressive, and not pacific—retaliatory, and not emollient.[54] Paternalism only worked where there was an unquestioning acceptance of the landlord's legitimacy; it only worked for so long as the landlord was solvent and free from threat. Alexander's sensitivity and responsiveness in the famine years were directly related to his economic security.

Edward Saunderson's paternalism was a style of management inherited from his father along with the responsibilities of the Castle Saunderson estate. It was a style of management which became irrelevant, with the development of new focuses for authority and legitimacy in the Irish countryside. The consolidation of the Catholic Church had reinforced the moral authority of the priest at the expense of the landlord; and after 1850 new parliamentary and political organizations annexed the secular authority once exercised by landlord-dominated parties. Given this class and sectarian polarization, the paternalism of Protestant landlords was both difficult to sustain, and—in terms of tangible benefit—not worth the effort. The obsolescence of Saunderson's paternalism was first demon-

[54] NLI, Vernon Papers, MS 18953/2: Saunderson to Vernon, 26 June 1847. Saunderson complains, *inter alia*, of 'Donelly of Knacreery' 'to whom I had been very kind and who I made out of a poor, bare-legged, ragged boy into the sturdy fellow he now is . . .'. McCourt, 'Farnham Estates', 558: 'he [the 5th Lord Farnham] laid out certain codes and rules for them [his tenants]; if they obeyed them, he treated them well. If they failed, he treated them with displeasure, and sometimes even with contempt.'

strated in 1874, when (despite his liberal rhetoric, and a good record as a landlord) he was rejected at the polls by the farmers of Cavan. The Land War and the prospect of expropriation in the early 1880s drove Saunderson into the Orange counter-attack, and further damaged the legitimacy of his authority as landlord. His emergence as a Protestant and Unionist leader in the mid-1880s destroyed the semblance of lofty impartiality and ecumenism which had been a necessary feature of paternalist administration at Castle Saunderson. Saunderson's career as a landlord activist after 1895, and his dismal relations with his tenantry in the early Edwardian era, merely reflected a shift of attitudes which had occurred much earlier.

Other Unionist representatives, like J. B. Lonsdale, were sensitive to the economic strains within the loyalist alliance; some, like Horace Plunkett, advocated a neo-paternalism, the re-engagement by Irish landlords in Irish affairs.[55] But Edward Saunderson had learned in 1874 the limits of concession, and had discovered in 1886, with the success of Unionism, the power of stridency. Alexander Saunderson, broken by pain and by the demands of conscience, had fretted about the condition even of his most wayward tenant. Edward practised a much less tortured style of management than his father; he also practised a more overtly self-interested form of politics.

In the short term Edward's confrontational strategy undoubtedly helped to arrest landlord decline. Yet by 1911 the only tangible remnant of the Saunderson patrimony was Castle Saunderson itself. And—partly as a consequence of Edward's stridency and rejection of his father's moderation—even Castle Saunderson was now vulnerable to attack.[56]

[55] The fullest statement of Plunkett's convictions on this score may be found in Horace Plunkett, *Noblesse Oblige: An Irish Rendering* (Dublin, 1908). For Lonsdale's careful handling of economic resentments within his mid-Armagh constituency see Alvin Jackson, 'Unionist Politics and Protestant Society in Edwardian Ireland', *Historical Journal*, 33/4 (1990).

[56] Saunderson, *The Saundersons*, 72–3.

12

The House and Demesne

Like the Majestic Hotel at J. G. Farrell's Kilnalough, Castle Saunderson was a stolid, neo-Gothic pile, built on a peninsula, and pretending to a greater antiquity than it in fact possessed.[1] As with the Majestic Hotel, the history of Castle Saunderson is a diminished version of the history of the Irish gentry. The castle had its origins in the seventeenth century as a fortified dwelling-house, but this early building was twice burnt—once in the 1641 rising and, again, in 1689: it was then abandoned, and ultimately demolished. The Castle Saunderson which survives as a shell today is largely an eighteenth-century inspiration, begun after the social and economic turmoil of the Williamite wars, and extensively remodelled at the end of the eighteenth century and in the first years of the nineteenth century.[2] This was, as David Dickson has argued, the era of the middling gentry, and in Cavan, as elsewhere in Ireland (and indeed in England), extensive building programmes testified to the enhanced authority and grandeur of the class.[3] Castle Saunderson was a tangible expression of the consolidation of these middling gentlemen. But the expensive mock fortifications of the remodelled house, and its strategic location, betrayed its defensive origins, and hinted at the continued insecurity of its owners.

In 1827 the castle was inherited by Alexander Saunderson. Mindful, perhaps, that he bore the name of the Edinburgh undertaker of 1619, and mindful of the embattled history of his home, Alexander reclothed it in the Scottish baronial style, with looming towers and intricate castellation.[4] As we have seen, Alexander was invalided in later life, and spent his last years migrating between Le Havre and Nice; but his many letters home suggest the unremitting pain of his enforced exile, and the strong sense of place which Elizabeth Bowen identifies as the hallmark of the Irish gentry.[5]

[1] J. G. Farrell, *Troubles*, pbk. edn. (Harmondsworth, 1975), 7–8. See the lyrical description of Castle Saunderson provided by Charles Coote, *A Statistical Survey of the County of Cavan* (Dublin, 1802), 103–4.

[2] Henry Saunderson, *The Saundersons of Castle Saunderson* (London, 1936), 50.

[3] David Dickson, *New Foundations: Ireland, 1660–1800* (Dublin, 1987), 104.

[4] Saunderson, *The Saundersons*, 59.

[5] The best—indeed the only surviving—collection of Alexander's letters is in NLI, Vernon Papers, MS 18953/1–2; see above, pp. 174–7.

Lame and prone, he fretted about the maintenance of his Cavan home and the management of his estates: his recurrent fear, expressed in the correspondence, was that he should be compelled to sell up, and that his connection with Cavan should be brutally disturbed. A lingering fear of this pained and sensitive gentleman was that his convalescence would develop into a permanent rootlessness.[6]

The pretty location of the castle and of its demesne did not simply reflect Alexander's romanticism, but rather the more practical concerns of his forefathers. Castle Saunderson stood on the River Erne, between Lough Erne itself and Lough Oughter, in a strategically and economically significant site. It guarded an important stretch of the river, controlled access to two loughs, and played, therefore, a crucial role in the development of trade within the area. In this part of northern Cavan, in the baronies of lower Loughtee and Tullygarvey, lay the economic focus of the county, created partly by the presence of the county town, and partly by the meeting of two main trade routes: the 'Clones corridor', linking Cavan to Belfast, and the turnpike road linking Cavan to Dublin.[7] Northern Cavan was therefore a gauze of intersecting roads and rivers; and, as with similar areas elsewhere in Ireland, it was here that the demesnes of many of the great estates were located (Farnham Castle, Cootehill, and Castle Saunderson itself).[8]

The families who dwelt in these Big Houses of Tullygarvey in northern Cavan grew up together, mixed socially, intermarried, and united in politics. But, though an identifiable community, they also fitted into a wider and more complex social structure. From the lakes of Fermanagh to the drumlins of south-east Down there stretched an arc of interlocking estates and interconnecting gentry families of whom the Saundersons were among the wealthiest and the politically most prominent. The aristocratic clans and mansions of Cavan formed part of what has been described as 'Ireland's most complicated web of great landed properties'; and this dense web constituted a formidable social and political resource for those who found themselves wrapped in its cocoon.[9]

At the heart of this web loomed Castle Saunderson and its family. The social horizons of the Saundersons were broad, and marriage partners were found as far away as south Connacht, Munster, and, indeed, the south of

6 NLI, Vernon Papers, MS 18953/2: Alexander Saunderson to Vernon, 27 June 1847.

7 T. Jones Hughes, 'Landholding and Settlement in the Counties of Meath and Cavan in the Nineteenth Century', in Patrick O'Flanaghan, Paul Ferguson, and Kevin Whelan (eds.), *Rural Ireland: Modernisation and Change, 1600–1900* (Cork, 1987), 114.

8 Ibid. 105.

9 Ibid.

England. In the size of their marital catchment area, and in their social aspirations, the Saundersons differed little from the Anglo-Irish gentry as a whole. Edward Saunderson's uncle, Hardress, married Lady Maria Olmius, a daughter of the earl of Carhampton; his cousin, Hardress Junior, married a daughter of the earl of Portarlington, and Edward himself married a daughter of Lord Ventry. But, while matrimonial opportunities were diverse, it should be noted that the men and women of the Saunderson family more regularly found partners from the aristocratic and gentry clans of the Fermanagh–Down nexus. Edward's mother was a Maxwell, a daughter of the fourth Baron Farnham; Edward's brother, Somerset, married Lady Emily Cole, a daughter of the fourth earl of Enniskillen; and Edward's son, John, married into a newly established gentry dynasty, the Mulhollands, barons Dunleath, whose estate was at the north-eastern end of the Fermanagh–Down arc, on the Ards peninsula. Through such connections the young Saundersons helped to reinforce a social and political alliance which would prove to be of lasting significance for Irish landlordism.

These closely knit families of southern Ulster, northern Leinster, and northern Connacht represented a tidal barrier protecting the Irish gentry against the surge of tenant influence in the mid- and late nineteenth century. They constituted a formidable political lobby which operated creatively and aggressively in the Conservative interest when that interest was buckling under the pressure of the Liberal and Home Rule assault. Edward Saunderson's neighbours and relatives by marriage, the Coles, Crichtons, and Maxwells, fought together for the Church of Ireland in 1869–70, for property right in the 1880s and 1890s, and for the Orange Order and the Union throughout the later nineteenth century. They helped to incorporate the economic concerns of the gentry into a more popular, loyalist platform, and thereby helped to prolong the effective political life of northern landlordism far beyond its normal course elsewhere in Ireland. It was this group which supplied many leaders, pre-eminently Edward Saunderson, to the early Unionist movement; it was this group which supplied the tone and emphases of early Unionism. These families, and this area, supplied Edward Saunderson with political allies and with a constitutional creed; they constituted, quite simply, the nursery of modern Unionism.[10]

Marriage, geographical proximity, and economic interest were the three elements which bound the gentry of southern Ulster. Yet this simple

[10] See Christopher McGimpsey, '"To raise the banner in the remote North": Politics in County Monaghan, 1868–83', Ph.D. thesis (Edinburgh, 1983).

equation conceals as much as it reveals, for each of these three features was dependent, in turn, upon a remarkable range of local conditions. First, the economic and political interest and identity of the south Ulster landowners was heightened, as nowhere else in the province, by the early success there of both the land agitation and the Home Rule movements: for example, only in south Ulster did the Plan of Campaign achieve any success.[11] Second, the peculiar clustering of estates in south Down, north Cavan, and around the lakes in south Fermanagh created a particular sense of community among the local nobility and gentry. Third, and as with other branches of the Irish landowning class, marital opportunities in south Ulster depended very largely upon the recreational culture of the area. But in Fermanagh, and in north and west Cavan, the chief recreation of the gentry was yachting, a sport which—as practised on Lough Erne—involved both men and women, and all ages. Arguably, the recreation and leisure culture of the south Ulster gentry was more social and less individualistic than that of their fox-hunting counterparts elsewhere in Ireland. Certainly yachting helped to consolidate the links binding the gentry families of the area, and to provide an entrée into the more rarified society of the English aristocracy and *haute bourgeoisie*, whether at Cowes or other fashionable south-coast resorts. Yachting was a first-rate social and political asset for the young Edward Saunderson.[12]

Just as, in Somerville and Ross, lavish and chaotic hospitality complemented the chase, so at Castle Saunderson it complemented the contests on water. The Big House and its demesne acted as a community centre for the local landed classes—a 'socially exclusive entertainment venue', in J. V. Beckett's phrase—providing opportunities for social exchange, for informal politicking, and for sporting activity.[13] In addition, the Big Houses served as focuses for the Church of Ireland and for its activities. More particularly, in Cavan, families like the Maxwells and Saundersons were early converts to evangelicalism, and helped to foster a more emotional and assertive Protestantism among the landed classes than was to be found elsewhere: the Big Houses and gentry families of Cavan were important in nurturing evangelical religion throughout southern Ulster;[14]

[11] See the map of targeted estates in Laurence Geary, *The Plan of Campaign, 1886–1891* (Cork, 1986), 151.

[12] See above, pp. 42–3.

[13] J. V. Beckett, *The Aristocracy in England, 1660–1914* (Oxford, 1986), 341.

[14] For the Maxwells and evangelicalism see David Hempton and Myrtle Hill, *Evangelical Protestantism in Ulster Society, 1740–1890* (London, 1992), 86–91; for English parallels see Beckett, *The Aristocracy in England*, 351–3.

in doing so, they were helping to consolidate both a local Protestant identity, and the cohesion of the Protestant community.

Parties, politics, and yachts are recurrent themes in the surviving accounts of Castle Saunderson in the era of Colonel Edward. Evangelical piety is scarcely less significant as a feature of these narratives. Touring Unionist luminaries—party elders, military leaders, journalists—were invariably invited to Castle Saunderson for informal discussion and recreation amidst the chaos of the Saunderson family. Michael J. F. McCarthy, the prominent anti-Catholic polemicist, visited the castle in February 1903, and was impressed by the dual role of Christianity and yachting in the family home. McCarthy noted the church in the demesne, where Edward Saunderson preached; he recorded the unconscious intermingling of politics and piety which was the distinguishing feature of the Colonel's outlook. When the second Home Rule Bill had been rejected, the Colonel was—appropriately—in the Holy Land, and McCarthy was regaled throughout his two-day visit with happy reminiscences of the spiritual and political aspects of the tour.[15]

But both McCarthy and a later visitor, Walter Long, were especially amused by the Colonel's relentless passion for boats: 'he was', as McCarthy observed, 'greatly addicted to yachting'.[16] The walls of the billiard room at Castle Saunderson were lined with models of the Colonel's yachts; guests' bedrooms were adorned with water-colours of yachts.[17] Walter Long, as Chief Secretary for Ireland, visited Castle Saunderson in September 1905, having motored up from Dublin in the company of the redoubtable Sir Henry Robinson. Despite their importance, and despite their arduous journey, Long and Robinson were kept waiting because the Colonel was occupied 'with a most complicated and intricate calculation in connection with a boat he was engaged in building'.[18] Social convention and hierarchy stood little chance of survival in the face of the Irish gentry, and of its quirks and whims.

English tourists reading Lever or Trollope or, in the 1890s, Somerville and Ross, expected the Irish gentry to be quaintly deviant. However, visitors like William Bull, the MP for Hammersmith and Walter Long's Parliamentary Private Secretary, were rarely prepared for the peculiarly subtle blurring of the conventional and unconventional, of the English and

[15] Michael J. F. McCarthy, *Rome in Ireland* (London, 1904), 189.

[16] Ibid. 187.

[17] Ibid. CC, William Bull Papers, 3/12: extract from a diary, Sept. 1905.

[18] Walter Long, *Memories* (London, 1923), 172; Henry Robinson, *Memories: Wise and Otherwise* (London, 1924), 172.

un-English, which characterized Castle Saunderson. Visiting Cavan in 1905, Bull was captivated by the castle and by its owner, entranced by the intermingling of what he perceived as English and Irish characteristics.[19] The purpose of Bull's visit was to consult Saunderson privately and informally on behalf of the Chief Secretary: like any English country house, therefore, Castle Saunderson was functioning as an antechamber to the House of Commons. Bull's preconception of the Irish Big House was governed by his limited knowledge of its English counterpart, and by literature (he was an enthusiastic theatre-goer). Castle Saunderson startled Bull because it looked and functioned like an English home, while lacking its formality; it startled him because it looked much more costly than the penny-pinching economies of Edward Saunderson had led him to imagine.[20] Social relations were unexpectedly relaxed; social hierarchy had a much less overt significance than Bull, a middle-class lawyer, evidently expected. Certain aspects of the household were recognizable: Saunderson's English groom; the society painter in attendance on Saunderson and his wife; dressing for dinner; confidential, gentlemanly conversation over a whiskey and soda in the library. But the familiar swiftly degenerated into the surreal: after dinner the men of the Saunderson family played tricks with their expensive wineglasses, flicking them so that they performed somersaults, and causing several breakages.[21] These tricks were resumed on the following day, during a river outing and picnic. Here the features of conventional society regressed further into Wonderland, with a scruffy old man, who looked like a gillie, and who was woolgathering by a jetty, emerging as the earl of Erne, KP.[22] An encounter with another yacht revealed Viscount Crichton and the Viceroy of Ireland, the earl of Dudley, in alarmingly jovial form. The contagious anarchy of Castle Saunderson and the lakelands had evidently afflicted Dudley, who, 'acting like a boy', used the boat's signalling cannon to pepper an old hat box.[23]

Bull's account is a sensitive personal record, amused but appreciative, and certainly free from any taint of condescension or burlesque. Bull and other visitors, including Michael McCarthy, were impressed by the good humour and informality of the castle community, by its relaxed and accessible Christianity, and by the piercing natural beauty of its location. They were intrigued by Helena Saunderson, and by the bond between her

[19] CC, Bull Papers, 3/12: Extract from a diary, Sept. 1905.
[20] Ibid. [21] Ibid.
[22] Ibid. [23] Ibid.

('this veritable *grande dame* with aristocratic features and a languid, soft voice') and the apparently more affable and approachable Colonel.[24] In reality Helena was apprehensive and shy, crushed perhaps by the heavy convictions of her partner: certainly her *hauteur* stiffened in the presence of visiting dignitaries such as Bull, and relaxed with more modest or less intimidating visitors such as McCarthy. Bull thought her a '*grande dame*'; but McCarthy found a different Helena, 'a considerate and charming hostess whom only a shy and awkward man can adequately appreciate'.[25]

Helena Saunderson's creativity found its fullest expression in the gardens around the castle, and in particular the bog garden. This last was laid out by Helena in around 1900, the land having been reclaimed from several acres of peat bog, and then drained and landscaped according to her instructions. Several small lakes were excavated, and the soil used to create headlands and hills on the shores of Lough Erne. Shrubs and trees—in particular rhododendra—were planted, iron railings and gateways erected, and gravel paths constructed. In the centre of the bog, on an artificial rise, a rest-house was built.[26]

Helena's bog garden may be placed within a variety of Irish landed traditions. The creation of gardens or, on a larger scale, parks, was a favoured form of landlord improvement, and a characteristic expression of landlord paternalism.[27] Gardens were also the recognized territory of gentry women—one of the few areas of the estate or demesne where, commonly, their authority and creativity might be exercised without challenge. Edith, Lady Londonderry laid out formal gardens at Mount-stewart, County Down, in the 1920s, when her husband, the seventh marquess of Londonderry, was Minister of Education in James Craig's government. Like Helena Saunderson, Edith possessed a ramshackle and gloomy home—'the dampest, darkest and saddest place'—which she

[24] Ibid.: 'a stately lady who greeted me I thought a little haughtily—a veritable *grande dame* with aristocratic features and a languid soft voice—she must have been a very beautiful girl.'

[25] McCarthy, *Rome in Ireland*, 187–8. It is possible that Helena did not altogether share her husband's political opinions: T. M. Healy, *Letters and Leaders of My Day*, 2 vols. (London n.d. [1928]), ii. 414.

[26] Reginald Lucas, *Colonel Saunderson MP: A Memoir* (London, 1908), 337–8; Saunderson, *The Saundersons*, 66–7; McCarthy, *Rome in Ireland*, 188–9. The impact of the garden on William Bull was profound: 'regardless of the heavy dew I lay down at full length for a minute to enjoy the exquisite beauty of this miniature scene' (CC, Bull Papers, 3/12: Extract from a diary, Sept. 1905).

[27] B. J. Graham and Lindsay Proudfoot, *An Historical Geography of Ireland* (London, 1993), 246–8. See also W. E. Vaughan, *Landlords and Tenants in Mid-Victorian Ireland* (Oxford, 1994), 121.

struggled to beautify.[28] Like Helena, Edith was an underemployed politician's wife who, neglected by her husband, engaged some of her creative energy in the Mountstewart gardens.

Gardens required intensive labour, both in creation and maintenance; at the same time they were of little direct economic benefit to the household. Thus, the construction of intricate gardens tended to reflect landed confidence; it also tended to reflect a glut in the supply of agricultural labour. Helena Saunderson destroyed an economic resource—the bog—and created an economic liability in the shape of an attractive but expensive garden. This seemingly illogical course of action is to be explained partly by Helena's particular enthusiasms, and partly by the Saunderson family's commitment to the impoverished and declining labouring class. Moreover, Helena's garden was built around 1900, in an interlude characterized by depressed agricultural wages, and by relative landed confidence. Just as the construction and maintenance of the Mountstewart gardens was made possible by the cheap labour supplied by demobilized soldiers in the early 1920s, so Helena's garden depended upon the broader condition of the Irish economy.[29] Even in this detail, therefore, the precariousness of the Irish gentry, and of their lifestyle, is painfully apparent.

The bog garden and the surrounding demesne land were much more than a recreational resource for the family, and for its peer group: it was home to the many servants of the Saunderson family, and served as a social focus for a wider section of the people of Cavan.[30] As with English country houses, the Irish Big House acted as a focus for the local community; but, as the nineteenth century developed, and the chasm between the gentry and tenantry broadened and deepened, so the parallel with England grew less exact. The social and political structures which sustained rural deference survived more hardily in England than in Ireland, and the community of interest between English landlord and English tenant was perceived therefore as being closer and more lasting. By the early twentieth century, as will be made clear in the next chapter, the Big House and its family were much more isolated than formerly, and of much slighter significance for the wider rural community.

The bond between the family and its servants, especially the higher servants, was close. Religion was a potential source of domestic tension, for Saunderson was an ardent evangelical within the Church of Ireland; but

[28] H. M. Hyde, *The Londonderrys: A Family Portrait* (London, 1979), 242; Anne de Courcy, *Circe: The Life of Edith, Marchioness of Londonderry* (London, 1992), 159–61.

[29] Hyde, *The Londonderrys*, 242; de Courcy, *Circe*, 159–61.

[30] See below, p. 206.

his Protestant convictions seemingly did not distort his employment practice. Catholics were well represented among the estate staff, and their religious sensitivities were respected. By contrast, Edward's neighbours, the Maxwell family, were much less sympathetic in their dealings with the Catholic community, even though they and the Saundersons shared the same evangelical enthusiasms: the Maxwells were in fact associated with some of the most brazen proselytizing of the Second Reformation.[31] Edward's brother, Llewellyn, who also owned a Cavan property, had an equally undistinguished record: Llewellyn dismissed six Catholic workmen in 1872 because they had taken, without consultation, a holiday on the Feast of the Circumcision. The *Anglo-Celt*, a determined opponent of 'the religious Babylon called the Established Church', and a shrewish observer of Edward Saunderson's religious career, took the opportunity to compare the attitudes of the brothers, Edward and Llewellyn, towards their respective Catholic employees:

> By way of contrast [with Llewellyn] we may mention that Mr Edward Saunderson has never permitted the slightest interference with the religious convictions of his workmen. They are afforded without interruption or movement the fullest opportunity of observing the holidays of their Church.[32]

Sensitive to the developing liturgical demands of nineteenth-century Catholicism, Saunderson was also responsive to the demands of its expansion. A determined patron of the Church of Ireland, he also facilitated the growth of Catholicism by freely providing land for church-building projects. In this way, and despite his fiery Protestantism, he indirectly contributed to the spiritual needs of his Catholic servants and tenants.

As with landlord patronage in the Church of England, so Saunderson's patronage of Catholicism in north Cavan need not be seen as wholly disinterested. The Church hierarchs were scarcely well disposed to the gentry, and younger priests were frequently associated with advanced political causes. Yet, on balance, the Church was a socially conservative and politically influential force; and, on balance, an electorally exposed landlord like Saunderson was wise to cultivate all available sources of support, however lukewarm.

But any crudely cynical interpretation of Saunderson's attitudes would be quite inaccurate. Saunderson was not a calculating and pragmatic strategist, and he failed repeatedly to flex deep-seated principles in the

[31] Hempton and Hill, *Evangelical Protestantism*, 86–91. See also Desmond Bowen, *The Protestant Crusade in Ireland, 1800–1870* (Dublin, 1978), 94–5.

[32] *Anglo-Celt*, 20 Jan. 1872.

interests of political gain. He was not naïve, and he was certainly ambitious. Yet he was also paternalistic and generous in most of his personal dealings, and genuinely interested in the spiritual and material welfare of his servants and tenants. Among his soulmates were Catholic servants such as his boat-builder: it has already been noted that on one occasion, in September 1905, the Chief Secretary for Ireland was kept waiting while Saunderson talked boats with this old man.[33] Among the dearest friends of Saunderson's heir, Somerset, was his Catholic steward, Michael John Macauley. Macauley paid bloodily for his loyalty to the Saundersons and to the gentry order, for he lost two sons in the First World War, and was himself held at gunpoint during an IRA raid on Castle Saunderson in 1920. With the final collapse of the gentry Macauley's vision of 'old Ireland' was shattered. When Somerset left for Newbury, Berkshire, in 1922, Macauley and his wife followed, and when Somerset died in 1927 the only bequest outside of the Saunderson family went to his devoted steward.[34]

At the end Somerset and Macauley were Quixote and Sancho Panza, entrapped by an anachronistic, paternalist, and romantic vision of social relations. Their lives had centred on the castle. They had become aware of radical forces beyond Belturbet—but as long as these did not directly impinge on their daily routine and on their immediate environment they seemed intangible and unthreatening. Their Ireland was defined by the walls of the demesne, and when, in 1920, these were breached by the IRA, reality intruded. The self-deception of earlier years meant that the end appeared to be all the more brutal and disorienting; this self-deception meant that Ireland lost in an instant all sense and familiarity. England proved in some ways to be just as exotic and just as threatening. But at least in Newbury master and servant could witness an appropriately genteel end to the social order which each had recognized and understood.

[33] See n. 18 above.

[34] Saunderson, *The Saundersons*, 72–3. PRONI, Land Registry Papers, Box 2134: Probate of the Will of Major Somerset Saunderson, Deceased (5 Nov. 1927).

13
Land Purchase

Between 1910 and 1922 England experienced a transformation in property ownership as thorough, it is said, as after the Norman Conquest or the dissolution of the monasteries.[1] Between 1903 and 1925 Ireland experienced a parallel transformation as thorough as those of the Cromwellian plantations, or the Williamite confiscations. Between 1903 and 1925 the Saundersons were caught up in a whirlwind legislative process which destroyed the seventeenth-century land settlements, fractured the family estate, and reshaped the family's prosperity. By 1925 the Saunderson patrimony had been dispersed, and the wealth of the family had been transferred out of Ireland. By 1925 the Saundersons had retreated to the Home Counties, living like genteel carpet-baggers, and roaming far from the land which had defined their power and purpose for three hundred years. On 25 July 1927 the last resident owner of the estate, Somerset Saunderson, died in a nursing home at Marylebone, broken by his exile and his losses. At his funeral in Newbury, the 'Londonderry Air' was played before a congregation of Anglo-Irish refugees, as nostalgic as White Russians, and just as thoroughly divorced from their homes and their past.[2]

But Ireland's revolution was no 1917, and Ireland's revolutionaries were no Bolsheviks.[3] They were socially frustrated and ambitious *petits bourgeois* from the provinces, whose politics had been defined by Catholic doctrine and by English Liberalism.[4] The transformation of Irish rural society had been accomplished, not by these men and women, but by the British, and particularly by British Conservatives, in responding to farmer protest between 1885 and 1906. The Conservatives' land legislation owed as much to well-established precedent as to experiment and novelty; it owed as much to parliamentary pressures and short-term tactics as to a

[1] David Cannadine, *The Decline and Fall of the British Aristocracy* (New Haven, Conn., 1990), 89.

[2] Henry Saunderson, *The Saundersons of Castle Saunderson* (London, 1936), 73.

[3] Kevin O'Higgins's famous remark that he and his colleagues in Cosgrave's government were 'the most conservative revolutionaries who had ever lived' may be recalled: K. T. Hoppen, *Ireland Since 1800: Conflict and Conformity* (London, 1989), 256. For other remarks on this score see R. F. Foster, *Modern Ireland, 1600–1972* (London, 1988), 533.

[4] See Tom Garvin's excellent *Nationalist Revolutionaries in Ireland, 1858–1928* (Oxford, 1987), *passim*.

coherent Unionist philosophy.[5] But there were consistent, if shaky, principles binding the different measures, and the work of different Conservative governments. Successive leaders of the party—Salisbury, Balfour, Bonar Law—were intellectually and emotionally committed to the Union, and sensitive to the claims of Irish landlords as propertied and influential loyalists.[6] These leaders, and especially Salisbury, were sympathetic to the plight of Irish landlords because they saw the interrelationship between British and Irish land legislation, and the threat to British property represented by the victory of the agitators.[7] But the Conservative party could not treat Ireland consistently as the toy of the gentry, and it could not govern in ruthless defiance of tenant protest. The essence of the party's dilemma was that emotion and blood-ties bound it to the landlord caste, while political pragmatism bound it to seek a settlement with the tenantry.

The Conservatives sought to satisfy these mutually antagonistic claims through land purchase, but this proved to be less a reconciliation of opposites than an evasion of responsibility. Predictably, given these ambiguities, the principle of purchase was a Gladstonian inspiration. The idea originated with the Liberals' Irish Church Act of 1869, by which Church of Ireland tenants could buy out their holdings, raising three-quarters of the purchase price on a 4 per cent mortgage.[8] Purchase was one of the very few features of Gladstone's ruminations on Ireland and on Irish land which could be reconciled to Conservative principles and to party interest. Accordingly, successive Tory Chief Secretaries set aside ever greater amounts of government stock to fund tenant mortgages, and to buy out ever greater numbers of landlords.

The goals of the policy were also essentially Gladstonian in origin. Purchase was designed to remove landlords from the cauldron of political controversy, and to free them for a socially more constructive role; it was designed to address the historical grievances of Irish tenants, to direct them from agitation towards social conservatism and political passivity. It was a bipartisan policy, sanctioned by both Conservatives and Liberals; and it was a policy which in almost every respect—in its principles and mechanisms—defied the expectations of its promoters.

[5] This is Andrew Gailey's hypothesis, argued persuasively in *Ireland and the Death of Kindness: The Experience of Constructive Unionism, 1890–1905* (Cork, 1987).

[6] See Alvin Jackson, *The Ulster Party: Irish Unionists in the House of Commons, 1884–1911* (Oxford, 1989), 154–8 for the relationship between Salisbury and the Irish landlords.

[7] F. M. L. Thompson, 'Presidential Address: English Landed Society in the Twentieth Century: I, Property: Collapse and Survival', *TRHS*, 5th ser., 40 (London, 1990), 16.

[8] See above, p. 180. Ernest F. Leet and R. R. McCutcheon, *A Sketch of the Law of Property in Ireland* (Dublin, 1937), 29–30.

The apogee of the Tory commitment to purchase was the Irish Land Act of 1903 fathered by George Wyndham. This differed from earlier measures in its political origins, in its shape, and in its inducements—and naturally it proved to be much more sweeping in its impact than its precursors: more than any other single measure, the Act reversed a 300-year-old land settlement and, like a twist of the kaleidoscope, fundamentally altered the pattern of rural proprietorship. As has been observed, the measure exploited a predetermined political consensus in the shape of Captain Shawe-Taylor's landlord and tenant conference of December 1902. So the Act was satisfactory to landlords in so far as landlords had helped to shape its origins and content; but it was also satisfactory to tenants in so far as it offered—effectively for the first time—a realistic opportunity to purchase their holding. Earlier tenant ambitions on this score had stumbled on two craggy obstacles: the voluntary principle, and restraints on government credit. With all the Conservative purchase measures landlords had to be induced to sell voluntarily: they could not be compelled. And they could only sell if there was available state credit. Poor inducements and limited credit had defused the first purchase measures, and had rendered purchase a teasing uncertainty rather than a legislative right. The enhanced inducements and lavish credit supplied by the Act of 1903 made purchase a realistic goal for all Irish farmers.

For landlords like Edward Saunderson the Act had a number of advantages beyond the earlier, and more dilatory, purchase measures: it offered payment in cash of the entire purchase sum, where under previous Acts, and under the later Land Act devised by Augustine Birrell, payment was through guaranteed land stock. Land stock was liable to depreciate, and did so through most of the period to 1914—so it scarcely constituted an attractive form of compensation. Cash was clearly preferable, and all the more so since the Act guaranteed payment in full on the completion of the sale. In addition to the lure of cash, the government offered a bonus payment of 12 per cent of the total purchase money. This was intended to make good any expenses which the landlord might have to bear in moving from rents to an investment income. But it was also designed to encourage voluntary sale, and indeed was seen by critics of the Act as a crude sweetener.[9]

[9] J. R. O'Connell, *The Landlords' and Tenants' Handy Guide to Land Purchase* (Dublin n.d. [1904]), pp. viii–ix, xv–xvii. For an excellent summary of the shifting attitude of the Irish parliamentary party to the Act see R. G. Mullan, 'The Origins and Passing of the Irish Land Act of 1909', MA thesis (Queen's University, Belfast, 1978), fo. 56 ff.

The Act also contained safeguards against unrealistically cheap sales. The government offered tenants a 68½-year mortgage which was to be serviced by a purchase annuity. The annuity of course varied according to the agreed purchase price; but it was calculated as a fraction of the tenant's former rent, and it could not embody any reduction of less than 10 per cent or more than 30 per cent of those rents which had been fixed after 1896. Purchasing tenants were thus given a legal guarantee that their annuity would be appreciably less than their old rent; vulnerable selling landlords were also given legal protection against any ruthless bargain-hunters amongst their tenantry.[10]

Cash payment, the bonus, and the legal constraints on the purchase price all weighed heavily with the Saundersons. Indigent or embattled landlords seized upon other clauses of the Act—those, for example, which facilitated both the sale of demesne land and the sale of an estate directly to the Land Commission. But the Saundersons were not so badly off that they had to mortgage or sell the Castle Saunderson demesne. And there was sufficient enthusiasm for purchase and a sufficient spirit of co-operation among the Saundersons' tenants to permit direct sales without the mediation of the Commission. Different aspects of the Act, therefore, tempted different types of landlord. For large, solvent proprietors such as the Saundersons the cash benefits, memories of recent insecurity, and the prediction of future penalties all combined to break any last, sentimental bond with their patrimony.

By 1903 Edward Saunderson had emerged as the principal spokesman for Irish landlordism. Yet, in comparison with his violent opposition to the Land Bill of 1896, and other measures in the later 1890s, his reaction to the Wyndham Act was constructive and mild-mannered.[11] He was a member of a cabal of MPs, representing the Irish Landowners' Convention, which had met daily while the Bill was under debate in the House of Commons. Yet he offered his blessing to Wyndham, and to the measure inside the House. He was, as we have seen, the only Irish Unionist MP who would not commit himself to compulsory land purchase. Yet, outside of the House of Commons, he praised a measure which had been hailed by T. W. Russell as 'compulsion by inducement'.[12] Saunderson supported the Bill, not because he was enthusiastic about purchase, but because it offered a good deal to landlords after an era of legislative torture. In any event, opposition would have been meaningless, and possibly counter-produc-

[10] O'Connell, *Landlords' and Tenants' Handy Guide*, pp. xx–xxiv.

[11] See above, p. 148.

[12] Jackson, *Ulster Party*, 163.

tive. Irish landlords were now too weak in and out of the House of Commons to sustain any credible assault on the government. And Saunderson, aware of the weakness of his class, and increasingly conscious of his own mortality, had no longer any stomach for lonely and futile campaigning. Age and weakness brought pragmatism to the Colonel, and this is nowhere more apparent than in his attitude to the Land Act of 1903.

This pragmatism was evident both at Westminster and at Castle Saunderson. One of the central purposes of Alexander Saunderson's political and managerial career had been the preservation of the family estate; and this driving force had been transmitted to Edward. Yet, despite his father's principles and the gentry's obsession with the soil, Edward was quite prepared to sell his patrimony—on the right terms. Early in the winter of 1905–6 he issued a circular to all his tenants in Fermanagh and Cavan, offering to initiate sales under the terms of the 1903 Act.[13] The terms he proposed were severe, but not unrealistic: he suggested that first-term tenants—tenants whose rent had been fixed before 1896—pay 22¼ years' purchase, and, further, that second-term tenants—whose rents were lower, having been fixed after 1896—pay 25¼ years' purchase. These prices guaranteed purchasing first-term tenants a reduction of 27½ per cent on their existing rent, and guaranteed second-term tenants a reduction of 17½ per cent: both these percentages were well within the scale (or 'zones') sanctioned by Wyndham's Act and regulated by the Land Commission.

Rather more brutal—though still legally defensible—were some of the sub-clauses of Saunderson's offer. Saunderson reserved to himself all sporting rights on the estate, and all turbary, mineral, and timber rights. By any standards—the demands of other landlords, the terms of the Land Act, the views of the Land Commission—this was harsh. The Land Act had reflected the enthusiasms of the Irish gentry to the extent that it had provided for the reservation of sporting rights. So at least, in this one respect, Saunderson was acting in accordance with the expectations both of the drafters of the Act, and of the Land Commission. But in going further and demanding turbary and mineral rights Saunderson was consciously defying administrative expectations, and testing legal ambiguities. The Land Act did not clearly proscribe such demands, but it did embody the assumption that turbary rights would be awarded to the purchasing

[13] *Lurgan Mail*, 9 Dec. 1905; *Portadown News*, 16 Apr. 1904. Saunderson appears to have first aired his offer in 1904, and later—in 1905—to have issued a more formal proposal.

tenant, and that mineral rights would rest with the Land Commission. In its legal definition, therefore, land purchase was a rather more radical proposition than Saunderson affected to believe.[14]

Given that Saunderson's offer was much more harsh than was superficially apparent, it might well be argued that he was merely posturing and procrastinating—that he was fundamentally uninterested in a sale. This is a possibility which deserves serious consideration in view of the strategies of other landlords. Miss Chaine, an Antrim proprietor, demanded 27 years' purchase from her second-term tenants—a price which represented the slightest rent reduction permitted by the Land Act. Her explanation for this provocative strategy was disarmingly simple: she didn't want to sell her family property, and would only do so at the highest legally permitted price.[15] Other Ulster landlords were more cynical, claiming large sums, partly because they had no enthusiasm for purchase, but largely because they wanted to exploit the prosperity and passivity of their tenants.[16] Outside Ulster different economic circumstances sometimes produced a similar attitude towards purchase: comparatively low prices and substantial rent reductions outweighed the distress caused by tenant agitation, and encouraged landlords to resist sale. In County Clare those landlords whose personal circumstances had compelled them to sell up often did so for trifling sums: before 1914 the average rent reduction embodied in Clare sales amounted to 34 per cent—fully 6 per cent more than the average for the whole of Ireland. A peculiarly intense Protestant pride and poor prices combined to entrench the landlords, and to prolong the mechanisms of purchase. Solvent landlords did not want to sell, and were prepared to haggle and to dither and to fight legal wars of attrition.[17]

But there is little in Edward Saunderson's career to suggest any skill at gamesmanship of this kind, or any sharp business sense. Saunderson's offer might perhaps have been a preliminary negotiating position; yet, given his political style, it is more likely to have been a blunt statement of his requirements, embodying little scope for subsequent movement. The context and timing of the offer suggest that it was genuine, and that Saunderson had at last reconciled himself to sale. The terms were severe, but not out of line with the demands of some other Ulster landlords: E. M. Archdale, whose Fermanagh estate lay close to Castle Saunderson,

[14] O'Connell, *Landlords' and Tenants' Handy Guide*, pp. xii, 21.

[15] Mullan, 'Land Act of 1909', fo. 17.

[16] Ibid.

[17] David Fitzpatrick, *Politics and Irish Life, 1913–21: The Provincial Experience of War and Revolution* (Dublin, 1977), 48.

demanded 26 years' purchase from his second-term tenants, as compared with the 25¼ years' purchase required by Saunderson.[18] Saunderson devised the offer in November 1905, over two years after the passage of the Wyndham Act, and one year after the passage of the amending Irish Land Act of 1904. There had therefore been time in which to judge the operation of purchase; and there had been evidence of the good prices wrested by Ulster landlords from their tenants. The offer was made when Saunderson knew that there would be a general election, and that there might well be a Liberal victory. A Liberal victory meant, in turn, the likely revision of land purchase along lines more favourable to the tenant and to the Treasury. By late 1905 it could clearly be seen that Wyndham's Land Act represented the high tide of landlord influence over purchase; by late 1905 it was clear that landlords would sell on no more generous terms, and might well be compelled to sell less advantageously. Saunderson's offer was therefore a rational and pragmatic response to market conditions, and reflected his fears for the political future.

Predictably and decisively, Saunderson's tenants rejected his terms, and submitted a counter-proposal.[19] In this they offered 20 years' purchase on first-term rents and 23 years' purchase on second-term rents (representing reductions of 35 per cent and 25 per cent respectively). Saunderson had offered reductions of 27½ per cent and 17½ per cent, so at the outset there was a serious disagreement between the parties over the basic purchase price. But even more glaring discrepancies occurred within the details of the two offers: the tenants unanimously claimed all sporting, mineral, and turbary rights, where Saunderson had wanted these for himself. Saunderson died within ten months of these negotiations, so it cannot be known whether he and his tenants could have reconciled their differences. It is clear, however, that Saunderson himself might well have proved truculent; it is also probable that, while the tenants' proposal may simply have been an opening bid, they were firm on the issue of turbary rights. It may be inferred, therefore, that Edward Saunderson's death, and the succession of Somerset Saunderson, rescued the negotiations, and improved the chances of a mutually satisfactory settlement.

Somerset was a bachelor until late in life, and he had been a professional soldier: he therefore lacked his father's commitment to the estate, and to the landed cause. Yet his circumstances were similar to those of his father in so far as outside pressures compelled them both towards an agreement

[18] Mullan, 'Land Act of 1909', fo. 17.
[19] *Lurgan Mail*, 9 Dec. 1905.

with their tenants. It was clear to Somerset, as it had been to Edward, that the favourable terms of the Wyndham Act would not last for ever, and that the Liberal government would pursue a policy more completely in agreement with the Irish parliamentary party and with the farmer interest. In 1907 and early 1908 evidence for this prognosis mounted. In April 1907 Horace Plunkett, the constructive Unionist and rural conciliationist, was replaced as vice-president of the Irish Department of Agriculture by T. W. Russell, the rural agitator and architect of compulsory purchase. The Evicted Tenants Bill of August 1907 wielded Russell's principle of compulsion by forcibly reinstating 2,000 veterans of the Land War.[20]

From the perspective of Castle Saunderson and other Big Houses it looked as if John Redmond appeared to be both the designer and the intended beneficiary of these measures. For the Irish parliamentary party's criticisms of the Wyndham Act had become ever more coruscating, and had been channelled into a radical amending measure within a year of the Liberal victory: this was the Hogan Bill, introduced in February 1907. Though this Bill failed, it was approved in principle by Augustine Birrell, and it appeared to condition subsequent Liberal thinking; moreover the Irish party's critique of the Wyndham Act continued to win ministerial sanction, and not least in the King's Speech of January 1908.[21] By November 1908 Birrell could introduce his own reform measure—a measure which addressed the inadequacies of the Wyndham Act by supplying the remedies of the Hogan Bill. Birrell's proposal was lost in December, but, reintroduced in the new year, and slightly modified, it became the Irish Land Act of 1909. Under this cash sales were abandoned, the landlord bonus was placed on a sliding scale, and compulsory purchase was introduced in congested districts and other impoverished areas. The Irish parliamentary party reacted with gratitude and self-satisfaction; Irish landlords reacted by rushing to lodge their purchase agreements before the Bill became law.[22]

Somerset Saunderson had struck a bargain with his tenants, and had initiated the formal purchase procedure in April 1908.[23] Like other Irish

[20] Mullan, 'Land Act of 1909', fo. 93.

[21] Ibid., fos. 83–4.

[22] Ibid., fo. 103. The rush to lodge purchase agreements was further encouraged because the Treasury was empowered to recalculate the landlord bonus in Nov. 1908. It was of course expected that a less generous revised bonus would be offered.

[23] National Archive, Dublin, Irish Land Commission Papers, EC.6412: Schedule of Tenancies on the Saunderson Estate. The date of the originating application to the Commission is recorded as 29 Apr. 1908.

landlords he recognized that the auguries were doom-laden, and he was anxious to clinch an agreement while Wyndham's Act remained in force, and unamended. But he avoided the panic rush to sell which gripped many of the Irish gentry in late 1908 and the first months of 1909: perhaps, given his father's contacts, his political intelligence-gathering was better than that of other proprietors—or perhaps his negotiations with the tenants, which had of course originated with his father as early as November 1905, had naturally run their full course. In any event, because his sale had been formally initiated before 24 November 1908, Saunderson benefited from the bonus arrangements of the Wyndham Act; in addition, because it had been initiated before 1 March 1909 Saunderson enjoyed the more favourable terms offered by Wyndham. Forty-two acres of the Saunderson estate in Cavan were sold under the terms of the Irish Land Act of 1909; 110 acres in Fermanagh were compulsorily sold under the terms of the Northern Ireland Land Acts of 1925 and 1929. But, thanks to his own and his father's political sensitivity, the bulk of the Saunderson lands, amounting to almost 10,000 acres, was sold under the preferential terms of the great Act of 1903. And this meant that, however devastating the impact of land purchase, it did not ruin the Saunderson family.[24]

The legal vehicle for purchase—the Act of 1903—suited the family; and the components of the bargain were equally attractive. Edward Saunderson had tried to retain mineral and turbary rights on his former estates, but this claim was speedily dismissed—both by the tenants and by the officers of the Land Commission. On the other hand, the tenants moved very considerably from their original purchase offer of December 1905. In the agreement lodged in 1908, first-term tenants on the largest portion of the Saunderson estate pledged 21·8 years' purchase, as compared to their initial bid of 20 years; and second-term tenants pledged 24·8 years' purchase as compared to their first bid of 23 years. From the Saundersons' point of view, these figures compared well both with their original demand, and with the high prices sought by Ulster landlords immediately after the passage of the Act. From the tenants' point of view the deal embodied substantial reductions on their existing rent; and it embodied concessions in the contentious area of turbary. The tenants might have made marginal gains if they had held out until the passage of the Land Bill of 1909; but,

[24] Ibid., EC.6412, EC.7938: Record of Sales on the Estate of Captain Somerset Saunderson. PRONI, Land Registry Papers, Box 2134: Land Purchase Commission, Northern Ireland, Northern Ireland Land Purchases Acts, 1925 and 1929 (record no. NI 1968). See also Thompson, 'Property: Collapse and Survival', 10.

since the provisions for compulsion within this Bill did not apply to comparatively prosperous and uncongested estates, it is probable that Somerset Saunderson would have vetoed any sale. Had the estates been sold under Birrell's Land Act, the chief casualty of the transaction would have been Somerset Saunderson, and the chief beneficiary would have been the British Treasury. The tenants' gain on an estate such as Castle Saunderson would undoubtedly have been slighter than that of the Chancellor of the Exchequer: Birrell's Land Act was, after all, in the verdict of its critics, 'a Treasury relief bill'.[25]

By 16 November 1911 9,400 acres of the Saunderson estate had passed from the hands of the family to their former tenants and the Irish Land Commission had advanced to Somerset Saunderson almost £98,000 in cash and guaranteed land stock. It appeared, therefore, that land purchase had merely toyed with social organization, and economic inequality in Ireland. Even allowing for the depreciation of their stock, the Saundersons remained a very wealthy clan; their tenants, though richer by the difference between the old rents and their new mortgages, continued to exist in humble circumstances.[26] The Saundersons still dwelt in the Big House, and remained masters of a substantial demesne. Their former tenants were proprietors in name only, paying smaller rents than formerly to a less paternalistic and more officious landlord. Land purchase could have little immediate effect on the fundamental patterns of the rural economy in Cavan and elsewhere in Ireland; land purchase could not in itself create agricultural innovation or efficiency.

It would be wrong, therefore, to hang too great a burden of interpretation on a flimsy chain of land purchase legislation. Land purchase contributed to social and economic change, but as a catalytic rather than as an originating force. It helped to weaken the financial status of some landlords, especially those selling under the Land Act of 1909. But the debt burden of Irish landlords in general had been developing since the Famine, and had reached disastrous proportions—especially for smaller proprietors—with the agricultural depression of the later 1870s.[27] Land purchase helped to weaken the social and political status of the Irish gentry. But, once again, this was a process whose genesis was much older.

[25] Mullan, 'Irish Land Act of 1909', fo. 55.

[26] Cf. Thompson, 'Property: Collapse and Survival', 10: 'a loss of wealth in so far as it resulted from taxation policies *has followed* a prior loss of social and political position' (emphasis added).

[27] L. P. Curtis, 'Incumbered Wealth: Landed Indebtedness in Post-Famine Ireland', *American Historical Review*, 85/2 (Apr. 1980), 365–7.

The social ascendancy of the gentry had arguably begun to be undermined in the mid-eighteenth century, when their disastrous leasing policies had cut them off from the main benefits of the agricultural upturn. Certainly since Daniel O'Connell's campaigns and victories of the 1820s there had been a swift collapse in popular deference, and a more gradual official intrusion into landed authority. The clearest institutional reflections of these trends were the retreat of the Irish gentry from the House of Commons after 1880, and their disappearence from local government after 1898–9. For Edward Saunderson pellucid evidence of the demise of his class was provided in 1874, when his Catholic tenants, breaking the bonds of paternalism, rejected him as their parliamentary representative.[28]

Yet the symbolic and tangible impact of purchase on the gentry demands investigation. Land purchase symbolized the formal ending of the seventeenth-century land settlements—the 'wiping out of the last traces of the foreign domination of Cromwell', as the rebarbative Arthur Lynch commented.[29] Land purchase emancipated Irish tenants from economic servitude to an alien gentry. For the numerous O'Reilly tenants on the Saunderson estate, land purchase returned to the family land which had been seized by a foreign soldier almost three hundred years before.

Land purchase helped to weaken the ties between a proprietor and his tenants. Purchase finally broke the economic relationship between landlord and tenant—a relationship which had already been redefined and weakened with the growth of government regulation. The extension of official interference and the emergence of a strong priesthood and a popular Nationalism meant that the social role of the landlord had gradually been usurped. A more vigorous Catholicism had highlighted the anomalous Protestantism of the gentry; a class-conscious Nationalism had highlighted their parasitical and Anglocentric qualities. By the early twentieth century there had been an almost total erosion of deference: the doffing of hats to the gentry, and obsequious modes of address, had been almost totally abandoned by tenants, and were in any event viewed sceptically.[30] Stripped of any broader social significance, the bond between landlord and tenant seemed by 1900 to be crudely exploitative: it was

[28] See above, pp. 40–2.

[29] Fitzpatrick, *Politics and Irish Life*, 51.

[30] Ibid. 51–2, 79, 84. W. E. Vaughan has warned, however, that 'there is no evidence about hat-lifting: the constabulary supplied no statistics of its incidence' (*Landlords and Tenants in Mid-Victorian Ireland* (Oxford, 1994), 226).

entirely encompassed by the payment of rent. And the Land Acts of 1903 and 1909 severed even this vestigial connection.

Land purchase highlighted the divergent economic interests of landlord and tenant, and brought them into conflict. Throughout Ireland the landlord entered into what were often bad-tempered and protracted negotiations with his tenant over the details of the purchase transaction. At Castle Saunderson ill feeling was created by the length—two and a half years—of the arbitration process, and by the glaring difference between the prices demanded by the proprietor and offered by the tenants. But elsewhere in Ireland—in County Clare, for example—animosity was rooted in the landlords' refusal to sell.[31] It is probable that such delays in the context of other, more ancient resentments, heightened the isolation and vulnerability of landlords during the revolutionary era. And it is equally probable that the anger focused by even successful transactions prepared the way for the raids and arson attacks of the Anglo-Irish War.[32]

Divested of any communal function, and isolated by anger, Big Houses such as Castle Saunderson became offensive symbols and foreign territory. The passage of the age of paternalism meant that demesnes and gardens were more rarely opened, more rarely the playground of local daytrippers. The end of paternalism and increasingly constrained gentry incomes meant that smaller numbers were employed as domestic servants or on the demesne. Big Houses such as Castle Saunderson became physically more remote for most Irish people. Few had access, and few saw the House as even marginal to their concerns and aspirations. Hubert Butler has argued eloquently that the Irishmen who burnt the Big Houses of Tipperary 'were sawing away the branch on which they were sitting'.[33] Yet it is clear that for most Irish people the Big Houses had become a cancerous limb, whose destruction brought, not self-mutilation, but the promise of future growth.

For Somerset Saunderson land purchase brought both social isolation and a waning economic commitment to Ireland. For all Irish landlords, but especially for those selling under the Wyndham Act, land purchase meant an economic disengagement from Ireland and reinvestment elsewhere. Wyndham's Act, offering vendors at least part payment in cash, permitted greater flexibility than the more austere Birrell Act, which offered only land stock. And many of those who sold under the Wyndham Act—like Somerset Saunderson—transferred their newly liquidated wealth to England or to the empire.

31 Fitzpatrick, *Politics and Irish Life*, 49–50, 72.
32 Mullan, 'Irish Land Act of 1909', fo. 149; Fitzpatrick, *Politics and Irish Life*, 72.
33 Hubert Butler, *Escape from the Anthill* (Mullingar, 1985), 102.

This type of liquidation and reinvestment was not unique to Ireland, and was indeed an international phenomenon. A central feature of the economic relocation of the British aristocracy at the beginning of the twentieth century was a dual shift from rental income to share income, and from fixed British assets (chiefly land) to liquid, imperial wealth.[34] A central feature of the decline of the Irish gentry was, similarly, a heightened enthusiasm for empire, and the pursuit of a social dignity in the colonies which was no longer attainable in Ireland: in both economic and political terms the empire acted as a kind of booby prize for the Irish gentry. It provided proconsular grandeur, or proconsular ambitions, for failed loyalist politicians (Arthur Hill, William Johnston, William Ellison-Macartney), and it provided more modest employment for the otherwise unemployable sons and daughters of the Protestant gentry. J. G. Farrell's vignette of 'Miss Olive Kennedy-Walsh, B. A. (Pass Arts), H. Dip. Ed. (T. C. D.)', the human cannon-ball in a Singapore fun-park, describes the pathetic—but by no means implausible—fate of one Anglo-Irish exile.[35] None of Edward Saunderson's four sons were reduced to seeking such bizarre careers in the colonies, though two pursued an alternative survival strategy by marrying wealthy American wives.[36]

The empire provided professional opportunities for those Anglo-Irish who could not, or would not, stay in Ireland; and it provided investment opportunities for Anglo-Irish wealth which could not, or would not, be retained in Ireland. Edward Saunderson had an active political interest in the empire, and tended in his later years to reinterpret his career as an imperial, rather than a narrowly Irish, quest. He was, as has been noted, a close friend of the second duke of Abercorn, the chairman of the British South Africa Company, and he travelled extensively in South Africa as the guest of the Chartered Company.[37] Yet he does not seem to have been a shareholder. Saunderson's wealth was almost exclusively bound up in his estate: there is little evidence to indicate that he had a significant shareholding of any kind, and there is no evidence to suggest that before 1905 he was willing to diversify his wealth by selling land. In his narrow and tenacious faith in land, Saunderson was thoroughly typical of the Irish

34 Cannadine, *Decline and Fall*, 443–4.

35 J. G. Farrell, *The Singapore Grip* (London, 1978), 162–3.

36 Cf. F. M. L. Thompson, 'Presidential Address: English Landed Society in the Twentieth Century: II, New Poor and New Rich', *TRHS*, 6th ser. 1 (London, 1991), 13. See also id., 'Presidential Address: English Landed Society in the Twentieth Century: III, Self-Help and Outdoor Relief', *TRHS*, 6th ser. 2 (London, 1992), 8–9, where he plays down the significance of American wives for the survival of gentry fortunes.

37 Reginald Lucas, *Colonel Saunderson, MP: A Memoir* (London, 1908), 265–78.

gentry in the nineteenth century. Land ownership remained—until an unrealistically late hour—'the chief determinant of the social as well as the economic status of Protestants'.[38]

In County Clare this rigid commitment to an antique order lasted longer than in areas such as Cavan, where the distance between landlord and tenant was less marked. Within two years of inheriting his father's estate, Somerset Saunderson had concluded a preliminary agreement with his tenants; within five years he was preparing a programme of reinvestment. By the time of his death, in 1927, Somerset retained from his Irish patrimony only the crumbling Castle Saunderson demesne: 10,000 acres of Irish land had been converted into an extensive colonial share portfolio.[39] He owned shares in a South African mine and citrus farm, in the Hudson's Bay Company, and in 'Russo-Asiatic Consolidated'. He had invested in Malayan rubber, and in Australian copper. The Saunderson holding extended beyond the empire: Somerset invested in South American railways, owning shares in two separate companies. It was a cleverly diverse portfolio, and it spanned the globe. Only in Ireland did Somerset resist investment. There were doubtless sound reasons for avoiding any large-scale financial commitment in the ailing industries of inter-war Belfast or in Cosgrave's austere Irish Free State. But it is a telling symptom of Saunderson's bitterness that he should so completely disengage from his homeland. What remained for him in Ireland in 1927 was merely a derelict mansion, and pathetic, sunny memories of a confident Unionism, and a flourishing estate.

Land purchase contributed to the physical isolation of gentry families such as the Saundersons, but it also brought a political and psychological desolation. The pragmatic or constructive Unionism of 1895 to 1905, of which the land purchase programme formed an element, profoundly injured the connection between the Irish gentry and the British party system. Liberalism had been a heresy since 1886. Landlord representatives such as Edward Saunderson now responded equally aggressively to the unsatisfactory legislation proferred by the Conservatives. The Land Act of 1903 was formally approved by many landlords, including Saunderson, but its details and operation provoked a much greater rancour. And superficial, public reactions often only hinted at a more complex sense of resentment and a more profound malaise amongst the gentry. 'Landlords',

[38] Fitzpatrick, *Politics and Irish Life*, 50.

[39] Some of the details of Somerset's share portfolio may be gained from his will. PRONI, Land Registry Papers, Box 2134: Probate of the Will of Major Somerset Saunderson, Deceased (5 Nov. 1927).

recalled Elizabeth Bowen, 'were, or felt themselves to be, sacrificed to the hopes of the successful continuance of that very Union to which they had looked to maintain their authority.'[40] Unionism, which landlords like Saunderson had hoped would develop as a champion for social conservatism, had outgrown its origins. It had been adopted and degraded by knowing Englishmen who had given it a more vulgar accent, and a more cheaply fashionable garb.

Aubrey de Vere commented with a cold-blooded tranquillity uncharacteristic of his class that Irish landlords had received 'from many of their English friends in both houses of parliament a treatment different from that which they had expected'.[41] This was the nub of the matter. Land purchase did not break the Irish gentry, but it did not correspond to their definition of Unionism. Unionist land purchase in itself brought no bankruptcies, but it represented a profound betrayal of expectations: 'one felt injured in spirit, if not in purse', Bowen lamented.[42]

Land purchase widened the distance between the gentry and their ex-tenants; it also widened the distance between the gentry and their English allies. For landlords like Somerset Saunderson, living on the fringes of Ulster, the threat of partition made this sense of isolation quite complete. The six-county partition scheme which looked viable in 1916 threatened to confine the bulk of the Unionist gentry as the solitary inmates of a Nationalist gaol-house. Somerset Saunderson's despair in 1916 and after screams out from his surviving letters.[43] An IRA arms raid in September 1920, conducted without damage or injury, and in the absence of Somerset and his wife, merely provided the family with a pretext to withdraw from Castle Saunderson.[44] In reality Somerset's emotional, political, and economic retreat had taken place much earlier.

His last years were divided between what was nominally his home, at Newbury, and convalescence on the Côte d'Azure. Like his father and grandfather he sought good health in the south of France; unlike these forebears he felt a rootlessness which his travels helped a little to soothe. Unlike Edward and Alexander, who complained rhetorically about the government and their tenants, Somerset could provide tangible evidence

[40] Elizabeth Bowen, *Bowen's Court* (London, 1942), 293.

[41] Ibid. 294.

[42] Ibid. 293.

[43] PRONI, Edward Carson Papers, D.1507/A/17/17: Somerset Saunderson to Carson, 15 June 1916; ibid., D.1507/A/17/21: Somerset to Carson, 17 June 1916; ibid., D.1507/A/18/22: Somerset to Carson, 15 July 1916.

[44] Saunderson, *The Saundersons*, 72–4.

of maltreatment. He was wounded by a sense of universal betrayal and of comprehensive defeat.

In Ireland he had lost everything beyond a derelict mansion. The popular political authority of the family had died with his father in 1906; the high political influence of the family ended with his brother, Edward Aremberg's, resignation from Dublin Castle in July 1920. Land purchase had obliterated the estate; land purchase had finally broken the social ascendancy of the family. When, during the Anglo-Irish War, Castle Saunderson and other houses were ransacked, they and their owners lost even a residual mystique. The mortality and fallibility of the Saundersons was at last exposed, as looters stacked their books and furniture on to farm wagons in that bitter spring of 1921.[45]

[45] Ibid. See the elegant conclusion to P. J. Duffy's valuable essay, 'The Evolution of Estate Properties in South Ulster, 1600–1900', in William Smyth and Kevin Whelan, *Common Ground: Essays on the Historical Geography of Ireland Presented to T. Jones Hughes* (Cork, 1988), 106–7.

IV

THE LEGACY

14

The Unmaking of a Martyr, 1906–1910

For all the evidence of his fallibility, it seemed for a brief period that the dead Edward Saunderson, his career and reputation conscientiously laundered, would prove to be a highly marketable political commodity. The living Saunderson had been—at the end—an embarrassment, and had been shunted politely but irrevocably to the sidelines of the loyalist command; but, in death, his misdemeanours would be quietly shed, and a pristine figure would briefly join the Orange pantheon. For several years after 1906 Saunderson would be accepted by Unionist Ulster as a latterday George Walker, venerated in literature and in stone.

When Saunderson died, the chief organ of Ulster Unionism, the *Belfast News Letter*, provided a piously exaggerated account of his abilities and political stature. For the London correspondent of the paper, Saunderson was 'this great man'—'the greatest Irish parliamentarian of his generation'; while the main editorial referred to him as 'leader of our Party throughout the whole of the Home Rule struggle up to his death'.[1] The Colonel had occasionally referred to himself as the leader of Ulster Unionism, but his contemporaries—and particularly the *Belfast News Letter*—had generally been more circumspect, describing him only as parliamentary leader. One day after his death he had achieved the nominal ascendancy which had so often been denied him in life.

Shock and grief were widespread. One journalist commented lugubriously that 'it is difficult, painfully difficult, to realise that Colonel Saunderson is dead'.[2] In the main Presbyterian church of Londonderry a clergyman interrupted evening service on 21 October with the news of the Colonel's death: in Armagh the sceptical Joshua Peel, personally suspicious of Saunderson, conceded that his death had been 'a great shock'.[3] Austen Chamberlain, writing to his stepmother, was similarly moved—though Betty Balfour, wife of Gerald, reacted to the death in a manner which was probably more representative of the English Unionist hierarchy

[1] *BNL*, 22 Oct. 1906, p. 6 (editorial).
[2] Ibid., 22 Oct. 1906, p. 7 ('Our London Letter').
[3] PRONI, Joshua Peel Papers, D.889/4C/3, fo.599: Peel to J. B. Lonsdale, 22 Oct. 1906.

(or at any rate of the Cecil clan): 'so Saunderson is dead. He is a prominent figure gone, and tho' I did not like him he was not the worst of the Irish Unionists ...'.[4]

Saunderson's funeral was held on 24 October, and he was buried at a place chosen by himself only weeks before his death: beneath an oak tree, close to the chapel at Castle Saunderson which he had regularly attended, and where he had occasionally preached. Like so many Irish funerals, it was a splendid set-piece, a demonstration of loyalist solidarity and strength. Walter Long represented the English party, and was among the chief mourners, while the Orange and loyalist establishment turned out in force to mourn their most recent martyr. Those sections of Unionism which had regarded Saunderson disdainfully while he was alive now demonstrated the profundity of their grief: Belfast Toryism was well represented in Sir Daniel Dixon, the Lord Mayor, while Tom Sloan, unavoidably absent in London, sent a magnificant wreath of carnations and dahlias. Again the *News Letter* was only too alert to the political dimension, conscientiously proclaiming the importance of the occasion, and providing details with an, at times, grisly enthusiasm. The description of the funeral, bordered in black, covered almost an entire page of the newspaper; while the accompanying sandwich of headlines again suggested both Saunderson's ascendancy and the political importance of the event: 'Funeral of the Irish Unionist Leader'—no quibbling here about the title of parliamentary leader; 'A Representative Assemblage'; and—the final descent into bathos—'Remarkable Manifestations of Sorrow'.[5]

The attitude of the *News Letter* was all the more telling because of the timing of Saunderson's demise—for, coming when it did, his death possessed a significance which it could not have had even a year earlier. Saunderson died having been restored to the political arena after a long convalescence; he died with a Liberal government in power, with the need for a united Ulster opposition, and with his own simple leadership priorities possessed of a new credibility. Confronted by an unfriendly British administration in 1906, Irish loyalists found little to comfort them in the attitude of their own English leaders—Saunderson's death came at a focal point in the long struggle between loyalists and the Balfour regime over the MacDonnell affair. Temporarily isolated, the loyalist press found solace in

[4] Birmingham University Library, Austen Chamberlain Papers, AC.4/1/11: Austen to Mary Chamberlain, 27 Oct. 1906. Whittingehame, North Berwick, Gerald Balfour Papers (consulted in the National Register of Archives, Scotland), NRA.10026/273: Lady Betty Balfour to Gerald Balfour, n.d.

[5] *BNL*, 25 Oct. 1906, p. 5.

reciting and embellishing Saunderson's parliamentary triumphs. The political circumstances of 1906 recalled those of 1886 and 1892, and Saunderson's witty and emphatic intransigence in the earlier years seemed once again appropriate and yet tragically unobtainable. Reviled and redundant in 1904 and 1905, Saunderson died just when he had again become relevant—and the popular sense of loss was accordingly enhanced. 'We have need to cherish the memory now he is gone', declared the *News Letter*, 'for he has been called away at a critical time'.[6]

'Cherishing the memory'—establishing a cult of the dead leader—took various forms. Newspaper panegyrists exhausted the range of appropriate superlatives. A leading Belfast printing firm produced a postcard portrait of Saunderson, designed for mass circulation, and priced accordingly (at 6*s*. the gross). A volume of the Colonel's sermons was edited by the Church of Ireland Bishop of Ossory, and published in 1907: a full biography and a memorial statue were commissioned.[7]

Amateur poets and apologists risked profanity in characterizing the sanctity of their martyr. Edward Coyle subconsciously evoked an Easter dirge in his 'Ode on the Death of Colonel Saunderson':

> The King is dead
> The Royal Edward sleeps.
> No crown adorned his kingly head
> Except of thorns.[8]

Coyle warmed to his theme, enumerating Saunderson's political and personal virtues and glancing at the fate of Parnell ('no wicked woman dared to taint his fate | by misalliance . . .'); and he alluded to the Nationalist leaders using bestial imagery which Saunderson would have happily condoned ('He heard the Home Rule howl | As when the night wolves growl').[9] The archbishop of Armagh provided *The Times* with a slightly less florid, but no less Gothic tribute ('The Right Honourable Colonel Edward Saunderson, MP: In Memoriam'); but here, too, the Deity was invoked, now as the source of the Colonel's political dexterity:

> Thine was the rhetoric of books unsent,
> God's finger laid upon the tongue and brow,
> One touch whereof is immortality![10]

[6] Ibid., 22 Oct. 1906, p. 5.

[7] These sermons were printed as Colonel E. J. Saunderson, *Present and Everlasting Salvation: Three Addresses with a Preface by the Bishop of Ossory* (Dublin, 1907). A copy may be inspected in the NLI.

[8] *BNL*, 25 Oct. 1906, p. 5. [9] Ibid.

[10] Reginald Lucas, *Colonel Saunderson MP: A Memoir* (London, 1908), 375–6.

No secular figure within late-nineteenth-century Irish Unionism—not even William Johnston of Ballykilbeg—had inspired such an intense and diverse veneration.

At a time of political anxiety, loyalism had elevated its dead leader into a symbol of the party's triumphs over old adversity—a symbol of heroic inflexibility. Saunderson the man was also remodelled according to popular priorities. He had led an unremarkably pious life, enjoying his yachts, cigars, and good company. But loyalism needed more than respectability and restraint; and Saunderson, more Cromwellian in looks than in inclination, emerged in popular myth as a puritan saint, the epitome of Protestant asceticism.

Thus the Saunderson legacy was potentially useful—and it was certainly worth monopolizing. Ulster Unionists had an obvious claim on the Colonel's career, and they desperately sought to iron out his idiosyncracies in order to provide their movement with a meaningful historical paradigm. But their claim was by no means undisputed, for the value of the Saunderson myth was open to exploitation even by his former Liberal opponents. Visiting Belfast in February 1907, David Lloyd George accepted the image of an heroic Saunderson in order to highlight the apparent inadequacies of his successors in the Ulster Unionist command: 'there was Colonel Saunderson—a fine old warrior of the north, whose swordsmanship was always the delight of friend and foe in the House . . . in those days Ulster Unionism had something to be proud of . . .'.[11] T. W. Russell, however, showed a more thorough and sentimental commitment to the Colonel's legacy, coming close to depicting himself as the direct heir to Saunderson's talents—and even to some of his principles; indeed, Unionist leaders like William Moore felt it necessary to decry the Liberal's attempt to claim Saunderson as his own. Russell was a temperance advocate, and he had found Saunderson highly sympathetic even to extreme proposals for reform. He was able to exploit this memory of co-operation, referring to Saunderson has having been 'one of the safest temperance votes in the House'.[12] He could recall on a public platform a discussion with the Colonel in which Saunderson had offered a sweeping pledge of support: 'you may take me as against the liquor traffic through and through.'[13] If Russell and the loyalist hero had been united in their temperance, then the new Irish Unionist parliamentary party fell far short of the Colonel's virtue—and Russell lamented 'the decline in moral

[11] *BNL*, 9 Feb. 1907, p. 8.
[12] Ibid., 4 Oct. 1911, p. 4.
[13] Ibid.

sentiment on this question which had taken place in the Ulster representation during the past few years'. But Russell discovered other congruities, immodestly presenting himself and Saunderson as the only two Unionist MPs 'who could make a speech in the House. All the rest were the most stupid lot of creatures that ever represented a free people.'[14]

By the time that Russell delivered these comments—in October 1911—his long battle with Ulster Unionism had been lost, and the fight for the legacy of Edward Saunderson had therefore become irrelevant. The prospect of a Home Rule Bill, and the reality of the Parliament Act, had promoted more contentious issues, and more demanding personalities than Saunderson and his memory. For Unionism the Colonel had become part of a sterile past, the domain of septuagenarian veterans like the Ulster Liberal leader. And even Russell's references were taking on the quality of reminiscence rather than any more purposeful political character.

The first major blow to the developing cult of the dead leader came with the publication, in May 1908, of Reginald Lucas's biography, *Colonel Saunderson MP: A Memoir*. Until then the popular attitude towards Saunderson's memory had been founded on hazy recollections of 1886 and 1893, and hyperbole was all the more plausible because there was no alternative and authoritative assessment of the Colonel's career and achievements. Lucas's volume provided an, on the whole, accurate if pedestrian orthodoxy; and this swiftly and surely deflated the more outrageous characterizations of Saunderson's political stature. From the point of view of party propaganda, Unionism needed a short and fiery panegyric on its dead leader cheaply produced for mass circulation. What the movement got was an affectionate, but—significantly—a not uncritical assessment which ran to 379 pages of text, and which was handsomely produced by the house of John Murray. Unlike R. Barry O'Brien's biographies of Parnell and Lord Russell of Killowen, there was no subsequent cheap edition. Lucas's *Saunderson* went on sale at 12*s*.—and because of the publisher's dispute with *The Times* Book Club, it was not available at a discount and for wider distribution through this increasingly important outlet.[15] To judge by the present scarcity of the volume, the print-run was probably very small indeed.

If the details of its production meant that the biography could not be a popular memorial, then the discreet bias of its authorship was no less an obstacle. Reginald Lucas, the bachelor son of a millionaire builder, had been Unionist MP for Portsmouth during Saunderson's last years in the

[14] *BNL*, 4 Oct. 1911, p. 4.

[15] *Times Literary Supplement*, 21 May 1908.

House of Commons, and it had been noted that 'he was evidently Colonel Saunderson's intimate and devoted friend'.[16] This personal connection, allied with Lucas's modest reputation as a man of letters, singled him out when Helena Saunderson was preparing to authorize a record of her husband's career. It is possible that his claims were independently argued by another parliamentary intimate of the Saunderson family, W. L. A. Burdett-Coutts: Burdett-Coutts was certainly an important force behind the project, and may even have underwritten the costs of production.[17]

Three factors are of crucial importance in approaching Lucas's achievement. First, he had been one of the victims of the Unionist defeat in 1906, and when the biography appeared it was politely insinuated by reviewers that his career was far from being at an end.[18] Thus, Lucas had undertaken a work of contemporary political narrative, in itself a daunting labour; but his difficulties were compounded by the fact that he was writing the life of a man who had been frequently at odds with the Unionist front bench. And it was here, to the Unionist leadership, that Lucas, the thwarted member of parliament, still looked for political favour. The second and more obvious feature of his authorship is that the book is written as a personal memoir by an Englishman who had little direct experience of Irish politics. Thirdly, Lucas received his commission shortly after Saunderson's death, gathered his material throughout the latter half of 1907, completed the task of writing in early 1908, and achieved publication in May of that year. The pace of production was thus rapid, the biography appearing only eighteen months after the death of its subject. This fact tended to highlight Lucas's personal approach, mournful anecdotes and sombre tributes displacing all possibility of a more detached assessment of Saunderson's political achievement.

Yet, despite the speed of authorship, Lucas's biography was no mere graveside panegyric, although it had elements of the dirge: many reviewers noted sympathetically that it was permeated with a profound sense of loss. Rather, the fact that Lucas had no real political attachment to Saunderson argued for a measure of objectivity. In fact Lucas's loyalties lay with those Unionist leaders whom Saunderson regarded with, at best, a mild distrust: no British Unionist, with the sole exception of Randolph Churchill, is

[16] *Observer*, 24 May 1908.

[17] Lucas, *Saunderson*, p. vi. In addition to his historical work, Lucas wrote two novels: *Felix Dorrien* and *Hoist with her own Petard*.

[18] The *Observer*, 23 May 1908, referred to Lucas as 'one whose promising career has been but temporarily interrupted'.

referred to in any other than wholly positive terms.[19] This decidedly English loyalty and perspective affected the work in a number of ways. Lucas tended to provide too much background material on the state of parliamentary politics, occasionally using his own knowledge to supplement the existing accounts; and this provoked unease among many reviewers of the work in May and June 1908.[20] He was rather less confident in his treatment of Irish affairs, and the book offers very little insight into the development of local loyalism, or into the tactical priorities of the loyalist command. Indeed his commitment to Irish Unionism was in general highly circumscribed. The militant loyalism which he witnessed during the agonized last months of his life—he died of throat cancer in May 1914—was treated as a vulgar aberration, and seen as characteristic of a violent and backward political culture: Carson 'was a Mahdi and the [Ulster] Volunteers were Dervishes'.[21]

Lucas's English Unionist sympathies, while hardly rampant, manifested themselves beyond matters of balance. Liberal and Nationalist reviewers noted his reverence for Salisbury, and in particular stressed that he had made no reference to Salisbury's part in the meeting held between Parnell and Lord Carnarvon in August 1885.[22] Also the *Westminster Gazette*, while acquitting Lucas from any charge of consistent party bias, complained that his gloss on Balfour's role in the Mitchelstown riot concealed the minister's 'responsibility' for the deaths which occurred on that occasion.[23] Partisanship induced a certain timidity, therefore, and this is particularly evident in Lucas's description of the state of Unionism before the death of Saunderson. He refused to enter into the details of the tariff reform and devolution controversies, offering only an anodyne lament on the divisions which had arisen within the party.[24] He was reticent about any suggestion of Chamberlainite intrigue: when Saunderson was approached by Austen Chamberlain in January 1906, it was with a view to condemning the lackadaisical style of leadership associated with Arthur Balfour. Lucas made use of this letter, but only in a laundered and barely recognizable form: 'Saunderson was asked at the last moment to say something as an old and distinguished member of the Party.'[25]

[19] See e.g. Lucas, *Saunderson*, 115–16.

[20] *Observer*, 23 May 1908.

[21] PRONI, Theresa, Marchioness of Londonderry, Papers, D.2846/1/6/12: Reginald Lucas to Lady Londonderry, 21 Apr. 1914. Lucas died on 9 May 1914.

[22] *Westminster Gazette*, 10 June 1908.

[23] Ibid.

[24] Lucas, *Saunderson*, 330–1, 345, 369.

[25] Ibid. 369.

Furthermore, Lucas's party loyalties meant that he tended both to emphasize Unionist unity, and to play down any loyalist dispute with the British leadership. The biography conveys little sense of the ways in which Irish Unionism was drifting further beyond British influence: it offers no assessment of the implications of Saunderson's call to independence in 1885–6, and it is equally coy in outlining the repercussions of the Irish landlord revolt of 1896. Lucas was unconcerned by, and did not discuss, the broader issues tied up with the Irish Unionist reaction to the devolution scheme of 1904. When he did detail a dispute, he tended to endorse the British case, while sustaining a friendly condescension towards loyalist pretensions.

This condescension extended, arguably, to Saunderson himself. Though one reviewer acquitted Lucas of patronizing his subject, almost all recognized that he had exposed, albeit affectionately, Saunderson's faults.[26] Very little of the hyperbole which infected many preliminary assessments of the Colonel's career was accepted by Lucas: he remained sympathetic, but tenaciously realistic, noting the limitations of Saunderson's oratory, his attitude towards the Catholic hierarchy, and his political vanity. *Colonel Saunderson, MP* was no work of political propaganda, therefore, and its personal perspective, its patience and apparent objectivity, were better suited, as one reviewer noted, to a small audience of the Colonel's intimates, than to a mass readership.[27]

Yet the biography had a decisive effect on the mythology surrounding Saunderson's career. It was perhaps inevitable that a more circumspect tone should prevail after a period of unrestrained eulogy. But *Colonel Saunderson, MP* was not merely a by-product of this reaction: based on Saunderson's papers and self-evidently reasonable and honest in its judgements, the book endorsed a more modest view of his achievements, and ensured that the 'warts and all' portrait would remain the single dominant image. Because its faults and limitations were not apparent, and because Saunderson never underwent any subsequent reappraisal, Lucas's biography has held sway as a lapidary judgement on its subject.

When Saunderson's memory was next publicly venerated—at the unveiling of his statue on 29 March 1910—the attitudes and concerns of loyalist propagandists had shifted. Journalists on the *Belfast News Letter*, and the speakers at the ceremony, culled their judgements from the Lucas biography, highlighting the Colonel's sterling personal qualities rather

[26] *Saturday Review*, 30 May 1908; *pace* James Loughlin, *Gladstone, Home Rule and the Ulster Question, 1882–1893* (Dublin, 1986), 231.

[27] *Observer*, 24 May 1910.

than his political acumen. Walter Long quoted approvingly Reginald Lucas's dictum that 'panegyric and excess of eulogy serve no man's memory'; and he offered an appropriately understated testimony in suggesting that the Colonel would have been no more than 'a help to us in these difficult times'.[28] William Moore, while avowing his friendship with Saunderson, was also reluctant to assign any unique status to the dead leader: Saunderson was merely 'typical of the highest form of Ulster leader of men', rather than himself a paramount commander.[29] Only Lord Londonderry recalled earlier assessments of the Colonel's life by referring to his role in combating the second Home Rule Bill:

> I say deliberately that the great triumph which was gained by the rejection of the Home Rule Bill in 1893 was due in a large measure to the skill displayed by Colonel Saunderson in organising his forces and in letting the people of England and Scotland know the horrors of Home Rule.[30]

Even this accolade was somewhat qualified by the prefatory observation that 'I was not a member of the House of Commons during the critical years between 1892 and 1895'.[31] And, having paid obeisance to the nominal subject of the day's celebrations, Londonderry rapidly proceeded to deliver a conventional party address.

In fact, by disposing of Saunderson so summarily, Londonderry was merely underlining that the purpose of the event was less a memorial than a party gathering. The general election of January 1910 had restored Home Rule to the political agenda, and it was this new threat, combined with the government's designs on the House of Lords, which conditioned most of the speeches at the unveiling ceremony. The most appropriate earlier parallel to this state of play was the parliament of 1892–5—hence Londonderry's reference to Saunderson and to the second Home Rule Bill. But there were aspects of the situation which were new—the row over the Budget, the attitude of the Tory-dominated House of Lords, and the now explicit attitude of the Liberal government towards the Lords. And Saunderson's career and achievements were relevant to very little of this—and irrelevant, therefore, to a new range of loyalist and Unionist priorities. Unity between British and Irish Unionism was now actively sought and apparently close to being realized. For most of Saunderson's career, on the other hand, he and his movement had casually defied their nominal British leaders. He had been one of the chief forces behind the

[28] *BNL*, 30 Mar. 1910, p. 8. [29] Ibid.
[30] Ibid. [31] Ibid.

drive for loyalist independence in 1884–5; he had negotiated with the front bench as leader of a distinct parliamentary group during the formative years of the Unionist alliance. Furthermore, unity within Ulster Unionism was now, in 1910, scarcely less of a priority than in the 1880s; and while Saunderson had once helped to forge the class and sectarian alliance within Unionism, an abiding memory of his career was the campaign for landlordism conducted over the last decade of his life. Unionism within Britain and Ireland was now seeking a democratic and reforming image, and Saunderson, on the evidence of Lucas, was hardly a useful asset in the fulfilment of this quest. Confronted by a career which combined spasms of orthodoxy with prolonged rebellion, the loyalist leaders tacitly concluded that, except in his essential Unionism, Saunderson was an inappropriate figure-head for the party of 1910. Much of his thought and actions belonged to an overtly seigneurial and now unacceptable Toryism; and it was only as a caricature, stripped of embarrassing complexities, that he survived in loyalist rhetoric.

It was J. B. Lonsdale, the MP for mid-Armagh, who—with characteristic acuteness—voiced the new and secondary importance of the Saunderson myth. For Lonsdale, as for preceding speakers on 29 March 1910, Saunderson's achievement lay solely in his belligerent and obdurate Unionism. But Lonsdale took this process of rationalization and generalization a stage further, arguing that the 'keynote' of the ceremony should be the continuity of the Unionist faith, and not any more direct reference to Saunderson's personal achievement. Saunderson was rather one outstanding link in an apostolic succession of loyalist fidelity: 'it was characteristic of a great national movement that while the banner was handed on from one leader to another, the principles on which the movement was founded remained unchanged'.[32] Viewed from this perspective, the statue was not so much a celebration of an individual as a monument to a community and to a tradition—a reminder of ancient loyalties, and a guide to contemporary action:

> The statue was something more than a memorial to a great man; it was a visible embodiment of the great principles for which their forefathers had fought and bled, and which Irishmen of the present generation were determined to uphold and maintain . . .[33]

It was this simple perception of Saunderson as the temporary guardian of loyalist piety which would gain currency. Contemporary political expedi-

[32] *BNL*, 30 Mar. 1910, p. 9. [33] Ibid.

ency, and to some extent the evidence of the Lucas biography, suggested no more significant reading of his career. And, with the development of the struggle over the third Home Rule Bill, this pedestrian reputation was swiftly overtaken by the more vital and more carefully propagated public image of Edward Carson.[34]

But the unchallenged ascendancy of Carson was not the only blight on his political forebears. Saunderson was a wholly parliamentary politician, and his greatest achievements were within the British House of Commons and on the British campaign trail. He played with the idea of military resistance, but his allusions seem to have been no more than rhetoric. There is no clear evidence to suggest that he was connected with any loyalist army in Ireland.[35] Lucas noted ominously that there were price-lists for weapons among the Saunderson papers, and this naturally provoked the Liberal press.[36] But it is not clear whether these lists were actively solicited by Saunderson, nor is it clear what use he made of them. Some Liberal and Nationalist reviewers of the Lucas biography were also worried by an exchange of correspondence between Saunderson and a Colonel Lewis Dawney, in which the latter solicited and obtained encouragement for the creation of a loyalist militia in Yorkshire.[37] But there is nothing to suggest that, from Saunderson's perspective, this was anything other than bluster, designed as a means of impressing Englishmen with the strength of Ulster loyalist conviction. Indeed, the Liberal *Westminster Gazette* sensibly declared that it found these apparent revelations of militancy 'unconvincing'.[38]

The lacklustre constitutionalism of Saunderson's career meant that it was of little interest to the armed and angry loyalist democracy of 1912–14. The drama and menace of an Ulster Volunteer Force, a provisional government, and of the gunrunning episodes threw up new heroes and inflated the currency of loyalist extremism beyond the limits established during Saunderson's lifetime. Contemporary opinion, endorsed by subsequent Unionist self-analysis, came to regard Saunderson as a quixotic but insubstantial precursor to Carson: Saunderson's Unionism was merely what came before 1912. Thus the classic texts of Unionist historiography—Ronald McNeill's *Ulster's Stand for Union* (1922), Marjoribanks and Colvin's *Life of Lord Carson* (1932–6), St John Ervine's *Craigavon:*

[34] Alvin Jackson, 'Unionist Myths, 1912–85', *Past & Present*, 136 (Aug. 1992), 171–3.
[35] See above, pp. 88–9.
[36] Lucas, *Saunderson*, 101.
[37] Ibid. 195–6.
[38] *Westminster Gazette*, 10 June 1908.

Ulsterman (1949)—all focus on the third Home Rule Bill and subsequent events, treating Saunderson's career as a fiery and comic prologue.[39] Other, lesser works in the Unionist canon are equally dismissive (where they mention Saunderson at all): H. D. Morrison's *Modern Ulster* (*c.*1920), Lord Midleton's *Records and Reactions* (1939), Hugh Shearman's *Not an Inch* (1942), F. H. Crawford's *Guns for Ulster* (1947). With the exception of Midleton's autobiography, most of these important revelations of the Unionist historical perception were, if only indirectly, by-products of the debate on partition. Most had a narrow concern with those loyalist politicians who struggled to make the Government of Ireland Act work in the North; and in a sense they constituted a historiographical prop to the state of Northern Ireland. Shearman's *Not an Inch*, for example, was designedly a 'popular' biography of James Craig, written and priced (at 6*s.*) for wide circulation.[40]

So, if a historiographical boom has been one of the inadvertent by-products of partition, then little further light has been cast on the career of Edward Saunderson. Living outside what would become the borders of Northern Ireland, happier in Dublin than among the Tories of Belfast, Saunderson could, by no stretch of the imagination, be conceived as a prophet of partition. Escaping the debate on the merits of Northern Ireland, and of its creators, Saunderson escaped, too, any rigorous scholarly or partisan reappraisal.

[39] D. W. Miller, *Queen's Rebels: Ulster Loyalism in Historical Perspective* (Dublin, 1978), 108–21. See also Alvin Jackson, 'Unionist History (1)', *The Irish Review* (autumn 1989), and 'Unionist History (2)', *The Irish Review* (spring 1990).

[40] Hugh Shearman, *Not an Inch: A Study of Northern Ireland and Lord Craigavon* (London, 1942), 5.

15

The Family Legacy, 1906–1921

I

Through his children Saunderson's reputation and ideas might well have been renovated and preserved; through his children his Unionism might well have been presented in an attractive and accessible form to later generations of Irish loyalists. The political dynasticism of the Irish gentry had been interrupted by the growth of Nationalism in the nineteenth century. But, even allowing for the electoral mutilation of landlords after the 1880s, there is nothing inherently unreasonable in the proposition that solvent northern proprietors such as the Saundersons might have maintained their political traditions throughout the twentieth century. Dynasticism has been a significant feature of the political élites in both parts of modern Ireland, with a residue of the gentry in Northern Ireland exercising an influence similar to that of a republican aristocracy in Dublin. Saunderson's political achievement scarcely qualified his children to compete with the Cosgrave, de Valera, FitzGerald, and MacBride clans; but the more gentrified northern tradition offered greater possibilities. Northern landed families such as the Abercorns, Brookes, Londonderrys, and O'Neills survived the democratization of Unionism, and sustained a position in the first rank of Stormont politics. The Saunderson family's near neighbours, the Archdales of Fermanagh, upheld a 300-year-old parliamentary tradition by supplying the Minister of Agriculture in James Craig's first parliament. But the representative traditions of the Saundersons, which originated in the Irish parliament of 1692, did not survive the death of Edward in 1906. And, with the abrupt termination of this tradition, an important vehicle for the transmission of Edward's glory was irremediably derailed.

After Edward no Saunderson sat in a parliament, whether in London, Dublin, or Belfast. Yet this is very far from saying that the family was now bereft of influence. On the contrary, Edward and Helena's children had both political ambition and the opportunity to shine. But, though the children had inherited Edward's self-confidence and vanity, they had also inherited his convictions and amateurism—and these would prove to be a rather more limiting and troublesome legacy. Edward's fundamentalist philosophy and mercurial style had become serious disabilities within his own lifetime, and would prove to be equally disastrous for his children. That his sons should emulate him so loyally would be both a measure of their love, and—ultimately—of their political fallibility.

Of the five children, two—Somerset and Edward Aremberg—had strong political interests, or exercised political authority.[1] Each benefited from their father's patronage; neither departed radically from his convictions. Each was fatally constrained by opinions and approaches which had characterized their father's politics, and which had been accepted as norms at Castle Saunderson.

II

Somerset inherited the estate in 1906, and with it a merely titular social position. In common with other Cavan gentlemen and businessmen, he held a Commission of the Peace—'the only influential public office in which provincial Protestants retained something of their old ascendancy'.[2] He was a Deputy Lieutenant for the county and held the High Shrievalty in 1907—a post which was defined in grandiloquent terms, but whose real duties could not be pinpointed even by the Dublin Castle authorities.[3] These were the baubles for which the Irish gentry was still competing between 1900 and 1920, and which dignified and soothed their decline into obsolescence. At a time when national office and honours were slipping beyond their grasp, Irish proprietors like Somerset settled for these tokens of local dignity. Indeed, with popular politics and parliament closed to Irish landlords, local office and local honours—the small change of the old order—assumed a much greater significance: by 1920 the Castle might not be able to supply an effective police force or a judicial system, but it could

[1] Another of Edward's sons, Armar, stood as an unsuccessful Unionist candidate in the marginal constituency of East Tyrone in Jan. 1910. This, otherwise insignificant, contest may be followed in PRONI, Ulster Unionist Council Papers, D.1327/23/1A: East Tyrone Constituency Papers; and also PRONI, R. T. G. Lowry Papers, D.1132/5/2. See also Tom Kettle, *The Ways of War* (London, 1917), 21.

[2] David Fitzpatrick, *Politics and Irish Life, 1913–21: Provincial Experience of War and Revolution* (Dublin, 1977), 55; *Burke's Genealogical and Heraldic History of the Landed Gentry of Ireland*, 4th. edn. (London, 1958), 630.

[3] Ibid.

still offer pseudo-medieval rhetoric on warrants of appointment to forgotten offices. The physical retreat of landlords to their demesnes is echoed in the limiting of their ambition to offices which supplied no power but offered a comfortingly elevated title. The impotence and irrelevance of landowners like Somerset can thus be measured by the nature of their aspirations. Like the artisans of the Primrose League, they were mollified by titles; like these artisans and clerks, they were thoroughly excluded from effective power.

Unionist opposition to the third Home Rule Bill was dominated by the commercial classes of Belfast; but the structures and institutions founded there harboured a number of landlords, and permitted them to exercise local political leadership, even though their estates had already been sold. Institutions such as the UVF helped to sustain a popular deference to landed authority in Irish Protestant society. In Cavan gentlemen such as Colonel Oliver Nugent or Lord Farnham were active Volunteer commanders, while Somerset Saunderson maintained a benign though intermittent interest in the movement: Somerset concealed weapons for the UVF in July 1913.[4] Like his father, Somerset was suspicious of Belfast Unionism, and resentful of initiatives originating with its leaders. Unionist organization in 1912–14 was focused in Belfast, and the campaigning tended to reinforce the political ascendancy of the city over a wider hinterland than had hitherto been the case. The Ulster Volunteers of Cavan, including Somerset, appear to have been resentful of this authority, and their campaign against Home Rule tended to reinforce a local identity rather than to acknowledge any external supremacy. Oliver Nugent, in command of 3,000 Ulster Volunteers, proclaimed that his was a *Cavan* Volunteer Force, which emphatically had no men to spare for work outside the county, and which—by the same token—did not expect 'except as a last necessity' any outside assistance.[5]

This localism was related to the suspicion that Ulster Unionism, as defined in Belfast, might not suit, or indeed include, Cavan. Cavan had not been one of the four counties nominated for exclusion from Home Rule by Thomas Agar-Robartes in June 1912; nor had it been one of the six

[4] For Arthur Kenlis Maxwell, 11th Baron Farnham, see Patrick Buckland, *Irish Unionism 1: The Anglo Irish and the New Ireland, 1885–1922* (Dublin, 1972), 180. For Sir Oliver Nugent, see PRONI, Nugent Papers, D.3835/E/7/1: political papers, 1912–14. See also Public Record Office, Kew, Colonial Office Papers, CO.904/40: RIC Report for Cavan, July 1913 (consulted on microfilm).

[5] PRONI, Nugent Papers, D.3835/E/7/1: defence scheme of the Cavan Volunteer Force (*c*.1914). There is a valuable account of the UVF in County Monaghan: Anne Carville, 'The Impact of the Partition Proposals in County Monaghan', *Clogher Record*, 14/1 (1991), 44–8.

counties around which Carson's strategies and affections had focused between 1914 and 1916. Cavan Unionists like Somerset Saunderson held to the paradoxical conviction that they could neither depend upon, nor yet break, the bond with Belfast; and until 1916 this belief promoted a sullen, but passive form of politics. But in June and July 1916, with Lloyd George pressing for an Irish settlement, Somerset came out at last in open defiance of Carson and the increasingly constrained vision of Unionism which Carson was urging on the Ulster Unionist Council. Somerset, as Edward Saunderson's son, may well have coveted a post of significance in the Unionist command; he was certainly a fundamentalist Unionist whose political vision did not stretch far beyond the frontiers of his own county. But, if he had his father's ambition, he was also capable of appalling tactical blunders. And so it proved with his challenge to Carson. Just as his father had sustained an embarrassing and futile defiance of the Conservative leadership over North Belfast in 1886, so Somerset pursued the wrong opponent, with the wrong issue, at the wrong time.[6] Carson's prestige in Ulster, while unquestionably less than in 1914, was still very great: he was an able and a well connected opponent, where Somerset was an untested Cavan squire, known only to the public through his father. The speedy collapse of Lloyd George's initiative in combination with the disastrous offensive on the Somme meant that Somerset's challenge exploded as noisily and ineffectually as a punctured balloon.

Yet the episode deserves some attention, for it had important consequences both for Somerset, and for the reputation of his father. As is well known, Lloyd George, acting on a general commission from the cabinet, secured the agreement of both Carson and Redmond for a six-county partition settlement.[7] On 6 June 1916 Carson outlined the merits of this proposal to a private meeting of the UUC, arguing that an ill-considered rejection would sacrifice all future British sympathy for the Unionist cause. He was received with an icy courtesy, which—after intense discussion—broke down into a tearful recognition of defeat. On 12 June the Council unanimously authorized Carson to negotiate further on the basis of the proposal which he had laid before them.

Though Carson and the UUC accepted the proposals three ministers—Walter Long, Lord Lansdowne, and Lord Selborne—proved to be much

[6] See above, pp. 91–4.

[7] For the Lloyd George proposals see: D. G. Boyce, 'How to Settle the Irish Question: Lloyd George and Ireland, 1916–21', in A. J. P. Taylor (ed.), *Lloyd George: Twelve Essays* (London, 1971), 137–66; John Grigg, *Lloyd George: From Peace to War, 1912–16* (London, 1985), 342–55; John Stubbs, 'The Unionists and Ireland, 1914–18', *Historical Journal*, 33/4 (1990), 879–84.

more truculent. These three, in particular Walter Long, were influenced by southern Unionist clamours, and by a surge of anxiety-ridden correspondence. Long, Lansdowne, and Selborne also helped to stimulate further apprehensions in loyalist Ireland, and not least at Castle Saunderson. Long, of course, had been one of Edward Saunderson's closest English allies, and he remained a friend to Edward's family. In June 1916 he talked extensively of betrayal to Somerset, explaining that Lloyd George's proposals had not had the sanction of the cabinet, let alone the approval of the Unionist ministers. Furthermore, Long could 'not see any reason connected with the conduct of the war for experimenting with a Home Rule parliament in the present condition of Ireland'.[8] To Somerset, who had listened sceptically to Carson on 12 June, this was a staggering but useful revelation. Carson's suggestion that to defy Lloyd George would be to invite isolation was revealed as utterly fallacious. Carson had apparently advocated a desertion of the Unionists of Cavan, Monaghan, and Donegal; he had therefore rocked the Unionism which Edward Saunderson had crafted and guarded. Carson had claimed to represent a higher logic, and a more subtle Unionist philosophy. Yet his logic was now exposed as a specious pragmatism; and his stern-faced convictions now scarcely masked treachery and buffoonery.

By recruiting Somerset to his cause, Long may have sought to bring pressure on Carson through the Unionists of the excluded counties. Somerset had influence there, and, acting with this power-base, and with a suitable brief, it was possible that he might persuade the UUC to rescind its motion of 12 June. Carson would thereby lose the sanction of the Council for his negotiations, and his career as a trimmer would be brought to a convenient close. Between 15 June and 19 June Somerset and Walter Long bombarded Carson with what Lady Spender dubbed 'reams of fury'.[9] Somerset also alerted his cousin, Lord Farnham—a luminary of the Irish Unionist Alliance, who was serving with the 36th Ulster Division on the Western Front—to the perfidy of the Unionist leadership. Farnham's letter to Carson, coming from a respected politician and a decorated officer, indicated the potential breadth and vigour of Somerset's challenge. More than the squalls of Long's temper, or Somerset's bombast, Farnham's gentle and querulous rebuke unnerved Carson: this was, in Ruby Carson's verdict, 'worst of all'.[10]

[8] PRONI, Edward Carson Papers, D.1507/A/17/17: Somerset Saunderson to Carson, 15 June 1916 (quoting Walter Long).

[9] PRONI, Spender Papers, D.1295/17/2: Lady Spender Diary, 19 June 1916.

[10] PRONI, Carson Papers, D.1507/A/17/22: Lord Farnham to Carson, 18 June 1916.

On 29 June Somerset bearded Carson in his London home. It was an angry and futile confrontation, which had little effect on the issues under debate, but which was charged with a broader significance and symbolism. Somerset 'abused' Carson 'up hill and down dale', and warned that he was leaving for Belfast in order to convene the UUC, and to depose its leader: Ruby Carson, who was briefed by her husband, was clear that Somerset believed that he could usurp Sir Edward's position in Ulster.[11] Somerset, like his father, may well have had an exaggerated faith in his own significance; like his father, he was certainly guilty of pomposity and boastfulness. But he also had Edward Saunderson's evangelical spirit and sense of mission; and he saw himself as one of the few who had not been ensnared by Carson's jesuitical logic, and who was therefore free to preserve the integrity of the loyalist faith.

The quarrel in Eaton Square on 29 June was a clash of the Unionist traditions, and not simply the angry outpourings of a frustrated fundamentalist and a wounded leader. For Somerset, Carson represented the revised Unionism of the Edwardian era—the more parochial, bourgeois, and demotic creed of eastern Ulster; despite his popular reputation, his Unionism was pragmatic and mendacious, strong on rhetoric, but cankered by a worldly cynicism. Carson had been Edward Saunderson's lieutenant in 1896—the young rebel who had helped Saunderson to defy the government, and who had yet been bought by office in 1900. He was the Dublin Unionist who in 1910 had sold his principles to Belfast; he was the leader who talked tactics, but who practised treachery. Carson had rejected the simplicity and candour of Edward Saunderson's Unionism and, imprisoned by his own flawed logic, had threatened to divide and betray it in the interests of his Belfast masters.

Somerset chose to fight the last battle of the old Unionism, not in Belfast, but on the more familiar and more appropriate territory of Monaghan. On 11 July he presented a lengthy statement of his case to the Unionist delegates of the county, arguing that they and their colleagues in Cavan and Donegal should reject Carson's strategy and the UUC resolution of 12 June.[12] The UUC, in mandating Carson to pursue his partitionist course, had been unaware that Lloyd George had both circumvented the cabinet, and had aroused serious opposition from several ministers of the coalition. Carson, Saunderson reported, had refused to be influenced by the evidence of double-dealing; indeed he was prepared to

[11] PRONI, Spender Papers, D.1295/17/2: Lady Spender Diary, 29 June 1916.

[12] PRONI, Carson Papers, D.1507/A/18/13: Somerset Saunderson to the Unionist Delegates of County Monaghan (*c.*11 July 1916).

court disaster by contributing further to Lloyd George's treacherous and unnecessary diplomacy. On the other hand, he might be released from his servitude to the Minister of Munitions, and be led back to the old faith, by means of a suitably worded resolution. What Somerset was seeking, in effect, was a motion of condemnation. On 13 July the Unionists of Monaghan met to consider Somerset's submission, and on that same day they unequivocally resolved to support the Ulster leader, Sir Edward Carson.[13]

Somerset had attempted to resurrect the uncomplicated Unionism of his father. The case which he chose had some merit, and he had powerful ministerial support. Indeed, in some ways, he was a victim of the strength of his cause. The opposition to Lloyd George's proposals evident at a Conservative party meeting in London on 7 July, combined with Lord Lansdowne's piercing criticisms in the House of Lords, meant that, regardless of what happened in Monaghan, progress towards a settlement was unlikely. By the time of the convocation at Monaghan, this was already clear, and the delegates would have grasped that Somerset's motion served little practical purpose. On the contrary, in rebuking Carson, and pressing a personal quarrel, Somerset risked a premature fragmentation of Ulster Unionism, and the isolation of its leader. It would have been a costly display of loyalist principle and personal honour which his father would have understood and blessed.

The Monaghan vote was a defeat on home territory, and crushed Somerset's bid to emerge as a die-hard saviour. Carson, recognizing that he had survived the first serious assault on his leadership, wrote in gratitude to Monaghan, and challenged Somerset to take his cause to Belfast and to the Ulster Unionist Council: 'if he can persuade them', Carson suggested, 'of the allegations contained in his letter, I shall most willingly, if I am so requested, make way for him or for any other leader.'[14] But the tone was ironic, and the challenge was no more than a humiliating jibe. For Somerset's credibility, and the democratic pretensions of his family, had died in Monaghan town on 13 July 1916. Thereafter Somerset retreated to his library. Surrounded by relics of the Colonel, he observed Ireland through the editorials of the *Irish Times* and the *Morning Post*.

[13] Ibid., D.1507/A/18/23: Carson to W. Martin, Monaghan Unionists, 17 July 1916; PRONI, Spender Papers, D.1295/17/2: Lady Spender Diary, 16 July 1916.

[14] PRONI, Carson Papers, D.1507/A/18/23: Carson to W. Martin, Monaghan Unionists, 17 July 1916.

III

Walter Long had sought to influence Irish politics through Colonel Saunderson, and, in 1916, through Somerset. With Somerset he had singularly failed—but the political usefulness of the family did not rest with the eldest son alone. Somerset was proud and emotional and, lacking any worthwhile political experience, over-ambitious. His younger brother, Edward Aremberg (known to friends and colleagues as 'Eddie'), was a rather more formidable man of affairs. Eddie shared some of Somerset's failings, being highly strung and inclined to exaggerate his own importance. Like Somerset, and like his father, he had a bluntness which might have been, and often was, interpreted as conceit; like Somerset he had a touching but purblind commitment to his father's political convictions. But Eddie had a training in party administration and in the Civil Service which Somerset utterly lacked. And Eddie had no family and little property to distract him from the pleasures of the great game: along with Reginald Lucas, he was a tireless foot-soldier in an army of bachelors who tramped around the verges of Edwardian high politics. Like Lucas, he had a talent for intimacy which served him well at the dinner tables of the influential.[15]

Before joining the Local Government Board in Ireland, Eddie was trained as a Conservative party agent in East Anglia. It is unclear whether he owed his party political apprenticeship to Walter Long or to another Conservative leader: Colonel Saunderson knew most of the Conservative elders, and they all of them—from Lord Salisbury down—would have been quite willing to consolidate Unionist relationships in this cheap and harmless manner. It is clear, however, that Long quickly saw that Eddie might prove to be a useful contact within the first rank of the party organization. The opportunity to press their mutual interests came with the electoral disaster of 1906.

This disaster was interpreted in a variety of ways, depending on the prejudices and principles of the commentator. The issues were highly confused, though there was some agreement that party organization had proved to be defective. Even here, however, critics and reformers addressed different aspects of the problem, and with very different motives. Joseph Chamberlain vigorously argued the need for a comprehensive

[15] Both men (along with others in similar circumstances) were taken up by Theresa Lady Londonderry. PRONI, Londonderry Papers, D.2846/2/14: letters from Lucas to Theresa Londonderry, 1910–14; ibid., D.2846/1/7/46–49: Eddie Saunderson to Theresa Londonderry, 1912–19.

rationalization and democratization of the Liberal Unionist and Conservative machinery. Chamberlain's plea chimed with the demands of the National Union of Conservative Associations for greater control over Conservative Central Office and thus over the administration of the party as a whole. Tariff reformers sought to consolidate their sectional hold on all aspects of the Conservative and Liberal Unionist machines. And ambitious individuals—Northcliffe, Walter Long—sought personal advantage from the turmoil and recrimination attendant upon the several reform proposals.[16]

The Chief Agency, held by the hapless Lionel Wells since the retirement of Captain Middleton, was the particular interest of the scheming Jeremiahs in 1906. This office, occupying the marchland between local and parliamentary Toryism, was of enormous strategic significance. Alfred Harmsworth, recently ennobled as Lord Northcliffe, sought to develop his role as a mentor to the party leadership by running William Bull, the MP for Hammersmith, as a replacement for Wells. Bull had a successful legal practice, and was hesitant: but Northcliffe talked airily of a baronetcy, an annual salary of £5,000, and a pension of £2,500.[17] Bull, naturally, seems to have accepted these astonishing terms: Conservative Central Office, naturally, dithered, thanked Bull and Northcliffe for their altruism, and looked elsewhere for a suitable candidate. Balfour, jealous of his prerogatives as leader, was not prepared to give ground either to the democrats of the National Union of Conservative Associations, or to the autocrats of the Harmsworth empire. And his attitude probably copper-fastened the decision to reject Northcliffe's overture.

At the end of June 1906 Bull lamented that 'Central Office have still dallied about the appointment of Chief Agent'.[18] But on 30 June Central Office, represented by Acland Hood and J. S. Sandars, had offered the post to Eddie Saunderson.[19] This gesture was, on the face of it, odd, and it deserves some attention. Saunderson was an Irishman and a fundamentalist Unionist whose militancy would have been neither understood nor accepted by many English Conservatives. Moreover, he was the son of the

[16] David Dutton, 'Unionist Politics and the Aftermath of the General Election of 1906: A Reassessment', *Historical Journal*, 22/4 (1979), 863; id., *'His Majesty's Loyal Opposition': The Unionist Party in Opposition, 1905–15* (Liverpool, 1992), 18ff; John Ramsden, *The Age of Balfour and Baldwin, 1902–40* (London, 1978), 23–7; Robert Blake, *The Conservative Party from Peel to Thatcher* (London, 1985), 188–9.

[17] CC, William Bull Papers, 3/13: Diary, 16 Feb. 1906.

[18] Ibid.: Diary, 'Retrospect for the First Half of 1906'.

[19] BL, Walter Long Papers, Add. MS 62410. Eddie Saunderson to Long, 30 June 1906; ibid., Add. MS 62410: John Gretton to Long, 27 Aug. 1906.

Irish Unionist leader, a politician whose devotion to the Conservative leadership had been, at best, questionable. Eddie was also by this time undoubtedly the protégé of one senior minister, Walter Long: Long sponsored his candidature for the post, and Long would have been the principal beneficiary from his appointment.

Yet the offer was made, and, given the importance of the post, there was naturally a persuasive case for appointing Eddie Saunderson. It was true that Saunderson was the nominee of Walter Long—yet in June 1906, the month before Joseph Chamberlain's stroke—Long was the slightest of Central Office's problems. Saunderson's family connections, and his links with Ireland, supplied a counterweight to the influence of Long, and were potentially of tremendous value (especially after the British election defeat). The Irish Unionist parliamentary party, commanded by Eddie's father, held a unique significance for the managers at Central Office: Eddie's appointment would undoubtedly have helped to unite troublesome loyalists within the Unionist family as a whole. Saunderson had thus a representative significance—but, even shorn of his broad networks and his Irish value, he was an attractive appointee. He was engaging and witty; and he was an experienced activist and agent, whose abilities were widely hailed. He was also young (only 34), and had no obvious English political interests to pursue. He was therefore a fresh face who would none the less be wholly under the control of the existing party leadership.

On this score Hood and Sandars were not prepared to take risks. In offering the post of Chief Agent, they made clear that Saunderson was to implement a scheme of party reform, the details of which were outlined to him at the interview. This was, as Saunderson commented, a 'mock democratic move' designed to disarm the reformers, while only slightly limiting the power of the chief whip: 'all I ask', Saunderson pleaded, 'is that a bona fides move shall be made in the direction on which we are all agreed as the only one likely to lead to successful results.'[20] More specifically, Saunderson sought to award the National Union control of its own executive, and to create a consultative or appellate committee in Central Office staffed by five MPs. But even a tentative 'bona fides' move held no interest for Hood or Sandars, who saw democratization of this kind as political apostasy. Saunderson had demanded a freedom of action which they were not prepared to tolerate; and he returned to his inspectorship at the Local Government Board in Ireland, and to the margins of public life. Percival Hughes, a creature of the leadership, was appointed as Principal

[20] BL, Walter Long Papers, Add. MS 62410: Eddie Saunderson to Long, 30 June 1906.

Agent, and survived to lead an unreformed organization through two election failures in 1910. Condemned by the Unionist Organization Committee—the comprehensive investigation which was needed and wanted in 1906—Hughes was dismissed in 1912.[21]

For twelve years after 1906 Eddie Saunderson led the cushioned life described so lovingly by Maurice Headlam in his *Irish Reminiscences*.[22] The rules governing his appointment prohibited any formal party activity, and he therefore took no active role in opposing the third Home Rule Bill. However, other fiery Unionists in government employment (like Wilfrid Spender) had been prepared to resign from office, and to take their chances in Ulster.[23] Saunderson, significantly, was not prepared to commit himself to a Unionism so different from that defined by his father. Like his boss at the Local Government Board, Sir Henry Robinson, Saunderson maintained an informal correspondence with a number of Conservative politicians, and exchanged low-grade gossip and confidences at Tory dinner parties and at weekend retreats. But between 1906 and 1918 he could not be anything other than an able but ill-informed observer of the political scene. Cut off from Ulster, and labouring in the junior ranks of the Civil Service, he was merely of antiquarian interest to Tory hostesses, as the son of the great Colonel.

In June 1918 Eddie was jolted back to political prominence by his old mentor, Walter Long. The occasion for this reversal of fortune was the installation of a new Irish executive in Dublin Castle. On 2 May the Chief Secretary for Ireland, H. E. Duke, racked by the pressures of office, resigned. Like many intelligent and sensitive administrators—like Saunderson himself—Duke had been reduced by the bureaucratic miasma of the Castle to a worn and vacillating wreck: 'he had quite broken down', in the assessment of Christopher Addison.[24] Against his advice, conscription had been nominally extended to Ireland, provoking a successful popular defiance based on the Sinn Fein movement: 'this', as A. J. P. Taylor has breezily remarked, 'was the decisive moment at which Ireland seceded from the Union.'[25] With Duke went the vain and posturing Lord Lieuten-

[21] Ramsden, *Age of Balfour and Baldwin*, 60, 68.

[22] Maurice Headlam, *Irish Reminiscences* (London, 1947). Headlam was the Treasury Remembrancer in Ireland. A copy of his autobiography, with a revealing letter of presentation, is preserved in the library of Corpus Christi College, Oxford.

[23] The details of Spender's resignation are intricately reconstructed in A. T. Q. Stewart, *The Ulster Crisis: Resistance to Home Rule, 1912–14* (London, 1967), 83–5.

[24] Quoted in Eunan O'Halpin, *The Decline of the Union: British Government in Ireland, 1892–1920* (Dublin, 1987), 155.

[25] A. J. P. Taylor, *English History, 1914–45* (Oxford, 1965), 104.

ant, Lord Wimborne, the Attorney-General, James O'Connor, and—a little later—the military commander, General Bryan Mahon. The conscription crisis of April 1918 and the resignation of Duke had thus provoked an alteration in the executive as complete as if there had been a change of government in London.[26]

The new Viceroy was Viscount French, ageing and scarred by failure on the Western Front. Under his command the political importance of the Chief Secretaryship receded, although the post remained dangerous and demanding, and the turnover of occupants remained correspondingly high. But French presided over a reshaping of Irish government which extended beyond the senior members of the Irish executive. More than earlier Lord Lieutenants, French was prepared to upset the Castle hierarchy by courteously ignoring senior officials and seeking guidance from their juniors. After January 1919 the pivot of the administration was Sir John James Taylor, who owed his office (the Assistant Secretaryship) to Walter Long. More than earlier Lord Lieutenants, French devolved power on to his private secretary. And after June 1918 this key official was Edward Aremberg Saunderson, who also owed his preferment to Long.[27]

Until July 1920 Eddie Saunderson was an important, occasionally the most important, individual influence on the government of Ireland. Inheriting a post of comparatively limited constitutional and actual significance, he expanded its powers, and at times effectively deputized for French. Liked and trusted by his viceregal master, Saunderson, in combination with Sir John Taylor, helped to destroy the Liberal influences on French, and to sustain the cause of die-hard loyalism. He was strongly swayed by the memory of his father and by the old Colonel's principles. And he helped to build into the Irish government of 1919–20 much of the Colonel's uncompromising Protestantism.[28]

Saunderson was able to expand the responsibilities of his position partly because the structures of government were in flux, and partly because—willingly or unwillingly—French delegated authority. French had arrived in Ireland convinced, through his military experiences, of the value of coherent and efficient administration. What he found in the Castle—'an extraordinary lack of any method of co-ordination in thought and in

[26] O'Halpin, *Decline of the Union*, 157–8, 163–4.

[27] Wiltshire Record Office, Walter Long Papers, 947/229: Long to French (copy), 29 May 1918; French to Long, 31 May 1918; Long to French (copy), 3 June 1918; French to Long, 6 June 1918.

[28] O'Halpin, *Decline of the Union*, 164.

act'—fell far short of this military ideal.[29] In an effort to centralize and regulate decision-making French created an interlocking array of councils: this initiative was also a hesitant gesture towards a more consensual form of government, and therefore towards Home Rule.[30] The Executive Council, created in May 1918, was designed as a viceregal cabinet, incorporating the Chief Secretary, Commander-in-Chief, and Lord Chancellor, and with a general responsibility for the government of Ireland. French served as chairman, with Saunderson, the secretary, having responsibility for the agenda and minutes. Complementing this was a Military Council created to provide French and the executive with a more complete supervision of the army hierarchy. Here again French chaired the committee, while Saunderson acted as his assistant and secretary. The third element of French's conciliar system was a think-tank, the Viceroy's Advisory Council, which was intended to keep the administration in touch with public opinion: 'in the absence of any representative assembly', French noted in a characteristic understatement, 'it is impossible to keep in sufficiently intimate touch with the state of feeling in distant parts of the country'.[31] Castle government had a tendency to balloon into fantasy, and the Council was to serve as an anchor on the Irish turf. Saunderson was of course directly involved with the experiment.

French proved to be 'an inconsistent and capricious chief' with each of these committees, and increasingly he relied upon Saunderson for direction and for ideas.[32] By the end of 1918, when the Viceroy and his Liberal Chief Secretary, Edward Shortt, were locked in competition, Saunderson's fortunes were rising. This new-found dignity was reflected both in an increasingly peremptory or patronizing tone—applied even to the unimpressed Long—and in increasingly ambitious reform initiatives. French's interest lay in defeating the challenge posed by Shortt; Saunderson's interests lay in the aggrandizement of the office of Lord Lieutenant. In December 1918 French chose to take a stand on the issue of post-war reconstruction, and a comprehensive plan of action—almost certainly inspired by Saunderson—was forwarded to the coalition cabinet.[33] This was designed to force French's views on to a reluctant Chief

[29] Imperial War Museum, London, Sir John French Papers, 75/46/12: text of speech, 10 Oct. 1918.

[30] Ibid.

[31] Ibid.

[32] O'Halpin, *Decline of the Union*, 166; see also O'Halpin's concluding assessment on pp. 206–7.

[33] WRO, Long Papers, 947/347: Eddie Saunderson to Long, 4 Dec. 1918; O'Halpin, *Decline of the Union*, 174–6.

Secretary, and to strengthen French's financial control within the administration. Given that French was ailing and mercurial, and given his trust in Saunderson, any expansion of his office indirectly benefited his private secretary. And it is clear that, independent of the reconstruction issue, Saunderson was planning a comprehensive reform of the Irish administration which would have resolved tensions within the executive by converting the Chief Secretaryship into a Civil Service appointment.

Shortt fell from office in January 1919, complaining that 'French is now entering under the influence of Saunderson': it is scarcely an exaggeration to suggest that he was a victim of 'a subterranean conspiracy' hatched by Saunderson at Viceregal Lodge.[34] He was replaced by the more conservative and pliable Ian Macpherson, whose ambitions were slighter, and whose competitive instinct less well-developed. Macpherson's accession coincided with French contracting pneumonia, and with the further consolidation of Saunderson's influence. In Dublin Castle Saunderson's ally, Sir John Taylor, was successfully challenging his Catholic superior, Macmahon, for control of the Irish Civil Service. Given Saunderson's personal ascendancy, and the enhanced influence of his loyalist and Protestant convictions, his administrative proposals of late 1918 no longer had any meaning, and were accordingly dropped. By 1919 an ultra-loyalist, Taylor, controlled the Castle bureaucracy and an ultra-loyalist, Headlam, controlled Treasury expenditure in Ireland; a lieutenant of Carson, J. H. M. Campbell, was, as Lord Chancellor, the head of the Irish judiciary. The son of the first Unionist leader deputized, in effect, as Viceroy. French, preoccupied by illness and by his mistress, Mrs Bennett, played Tiberius to Eddie Saunderson's Sejanus.

This loyalist ascendancy within the Irish executive and Castle administration lasted until the early summer of 1920. The period was characterized by an acceleration of IRA activity, with small-scale raids and isolated murders through 1918 and 1919 giving way to more spectacular sieges and ambushes by the winter of 1919–20. The attempted assassination of French at Ashtown in December 1919 marked the opening of this second, more ambitious, phase of the IRA campaign. By the summer of 1920 the

[34] O'Halpin, *Decline of the Union*, 179. For Saunderson's animus against Shortt see Wiltshire Record Office, Long Papers, 947/347: Eddie Saunderson to Long, 28 Aug. 1918: 'this fiery-blooded radical [Shortt] must be at once given to understand that these frolics of his with his elephantine feet ... must forever cease.'

IRA had forced the Royal Irish Constabulary into retreat, and had paralysed the British judicial system.[35]

Like his father, Saunderson judged violence of this kind purely as a criminal conspiracy, and, like his father, he believed that the only appropriate response lay in heightened security. His correspondence of 1919–20 was dominated by a concern for the deteriorating condition of the country, and by a sequence of policing proposals. In June 1919 Saunderson was preoccupied with the lamentably weak and understaffed political branch of the Dublin Metropolitan Police.[36] By late 1919 poor detection rates and the generally decrepit state of the DMP command were causing him acute anxiety: a committee of enquiry was constituted, and further resources demanded from the Treasury.[37] In early 1920 Saunderson's concerns shifted to what he saw as the over-centralized British military campaign, and he became an enthusiastic advocate of 'quiet mixed patrols through the disturbed areas'.[38] The security initiatives of Arthur Balfour's Chief Secretaryship were reactivated in a proposal for District Commissioners to co-ordinate police and army efforts in five designated areas of unrest. But even in April 1920, three months before his final departure from Ireland, Saunderson was forced to concede that his father's ideals, and the lessons of the recent past, were untrustworthy guides. He was facing an enemy different to that defeated by his father; one whose condition challenged the preconceptions which he had inherited from his father. For Eddie Saunderson, the most frightening and bewildering aspect of this violence was that 'well-educated and in the ordinary sense clean living young men of the country regard murder as a duty'.[39]

Political creativity had not been a part of Colonel Saunderson's legacy ('there was practically nothing of the constructive statesman in Colonel Saunderson', the *Northern Whig* once noted); and Eddie Saunderson did not think to disarm these 'clean living young men' by diplomacy.[40] Eddie's political response to the crisis was confined to the Castle hierarchy, where he saw trimming and treachery. The reform initiatives of 1918—the

[35] The best account of the Anglo-Irish War remains Charles Townshend, *The British Campaign in Ireland, 1919–21: The Development of Political and Military Policies* (Oxford, 1975). For a more succinct rendering see Townshend's excellent *Political Violence in Ireland: Government and Resistance since 1848* (Oxford, 1983), 322–64.

[36] Wiltshire Record Office, Long Papers, 947/347: Eddie Saunderson to Long, 1 June 1919.

[37] Ibid., 947/348: Eddie Saunderson to Long, 15 Dec. 1919.

[38] Ibid.: Eddie Saunderson to Long, 24 Jan. 1920.

[39] Ibid.: Eddie Saunderson to Long, 20 April 1920.

[40] *Northern Whig*, 6 June 1908.

Executive Council, the Military and Advisory Councils—were inappropriate to the pressures of 1919, and were accordingly dropped. Equally, Saunderson's constitutional initiative of December 1918 had no longer any relevance once his ascendancy over French had been secured. Beyond these highly calculated and strategic proposals, Saunderson had little interest in constitutional innovation; and he was certainly not prepared to betray the memory of his father by implementing Home Rule. In 1919–20 Saunderson saw the political demands of the crisis as requiring minor adjustments to the power and interrelationship of the senior officials. And, in particular, he sought the enhance the authority of Sir John Taylor over all areas of policing and crime.

The narrowness of this approach begs a discussion of Saunderson's political judgement. He had inherited the evangelical Protestantism, though not the piety, of his father, and the memory of the Colonel was an active influence at times of crisis: when, in April 1920, his relationship with French was deteriorating, he remarked to Long that 'in moments of uncertainty, I often thought back to the old Colonel'.[41] But this legacy was ambiguous, offering a sense of security which was, at times, utterly false. Eddie shared his father's anti-Catholicism and—even though his closest ally, Taylor, was a Catholic—this prejudice severely distorted his political sense. Like his father and other evangelical Unionists he had a conspiratorial vision of the Catholic Church. In January 1919 he saw the Church as fighting for control of the Castle bureaucracy, using the 'dangerous weapons' of 'soft solder and blather'.[42] In April 1920 he warned that the incoming Chief Secretary, Hamar Greenwood, 'will have to be very careful—or he will find the Church in control of the machine'.[43]

Like his father he saw political crime in terms of its criminality, and not its politics. He had some sense of the grubbier aspects of Nationalism, but no conception of the idealism which it could contain. He had only the most superficial understanding of Sinn Fein, and as late as February 1918 thought that it could be written off as inconsequential.[44] His old mentor at

[41] Wiltshire Record Office, Long Papers, 947/348: Eddie Saunderson to Long, 27 Apr. 1920.

[42] Ibid., 947/347: Eddie Saunderson to Long, 28 Jan. 1919.

[43] Ibid., 947/348: Eddie Saunderson to Long, n.d. ('Sunday'). By June Saunderson felt that his apprehensions had been justified: 'I am greatly afraid that Greenwood is being carried away by Papist blather and flattery' (Ibid., 947/348: Saunderson to Long, 19 June 1920).

[44] Wiltshire Record Office, Long Papers, 947/410: Eddie Saunderson to Long, 18 Feb. 1918. For Henry Robinson on Sinn Fein see e.g. Imperial War Museum, London, French Papers, 75/46/12: Robinson to Saunderson, 17 Dec. 1918.

the Local Government Board, Sir Henry Robinson, had, by contrast, a much surer grasp of the morphology of the movement.

These failings of perspective were linked to a sensitivity and morbidity which propelled him towards disaster. In 1919–20, writing to Long and other correspondents, he depicted Dublin Castle as a Renaissance court, and in the language of a revenge tragedy. Like John Webster, he deployed the imagery of disease and decay to evoke the condition of his workplace. In May 1919 the Irish body politic was 'a fever patient settling down after the crisis', but threatened by 'another inoculation with the germs of disease'; in March 1921 he compared Lord Derby, preparing to diplomatize in Dublin, to 'a doctor who is called in and finds his patient harassed by mischevious germs'.[45] His letters became casualty lists. Frequently he would describe the merits of a policeman or civil servant, and invest hopes in their capacity, only to have these hopes dashed in murder.[46]

His life imitated the art of his correspondence. Imprisoned in Viceregal Lodge, he was cut off from family and from society. He grew nervous and ill: in February 1920 he complained that he was 'laid up at present in this House [Viceregal Lodge] but as I rarely get time to go out, it does not make much difference'.[47] His letters grew more strained, and more peremptory, marred by an undercurrent of hysteria. He grew more irritable and intolerant. His contempt for French became more open and offensive.

The break came in the summer of 1920. On 30 July a close friend, Frank Brooke—a colleague on the Advisory Council, and a member of the lakeland gentry set—was assassinated by the IRA at Westland Row Station in Dublin. That evening French went to see Saunderson in his room at Viceregal Lodge: the Viceroy had been irritated and alarmed by Saunderson's recent demeanour, and tactfully sought, in the aftermath of the

[45] Randolph S. Churchill, *Lord Derby, 'King of Lancashire'* (London, 1959), 403; Wiltshire Record Office, Long Papers, 947/347: Eddie Saunderson to Long, 4 May 1919.

[46] See e.g. Wiltshire Record Office, Long Papers, 947/348: Eddie Saunderson to Long, 15 Dec. 1919. Saunderson invested much optimism in the reorganization of the DMP. He backed the appointment as Assistant Commissioner of 'a very able D[istrict] I[nspector] from the R.I.C., Redmond by name ... to take charge of political crime'. But Redmond was assassinated within a month of his promotion. See Townshend, *The British Campaign in Ireland*, 42.

[47] Wiltshire Record Office, Long Papers, 947/348: Eddie Saunderson to Long, 17 Feb. 1920.

murder, to advise rest and a temporary escape from Ireland.[48] But Saunderson interpreted the Viceroy's solicitude as condescension and a want of trust; and he was evidently not prepared to be patronized by a man whom he, by now, so thoroughly despised. He refused to take a holiday, explaining that he still had responsibilities—responsibilities so confidential that he could not yet reveal their nature to the Viceroy. French was insulted by this secretiveness, and, on 31 July, in a formal interview, he demanded an explanation. There was an angry exchange, and French summoned an aide-de-camp. The offer of leave was repeated, though now in a more hostile and peremptory tone. Saunderson curtly refused, and made a histrionic exit: 'I will go away for ever, as I do not mean to stay here to be insulted.'[49]

In the last days his obsession with secrecy verged on paranoia, and his arrogance became egomania. Like French, he had been unnerved by his responsibilities. But French had seen carnage in South Africa and at Loos, and could find comfort in the arms of Mrs Bennett. Saunderson had experienced only the verbal violence of a departmental memorandum, and the metaphorical bloodshed of an office *coup*: he had no partner to offer distraction and comfort.

He rested for the remaining summer months of 1920. Thereafter he played a minor and self-appointed role as an advisor on Irish politics. He corresponded with Lord Derby and with Walter Long; he was a guest at Whittingehame.[50] But his effective influence, and that of the Saunderson dynasty, had ended in a neurotic tantrum at Viceregal Lodge on 31 July 1920.

[48] Responsibility for the affair is difficult to apportion. Both men were under very considerable emotional strain, and each was disposed to question the mental balance of the other. Saunderson's correspondence indicates his state of nervous anxiety fairly clearly. French, on the other hand, had admitted to Lord Riddell that 'he had been a good deal rattled ... the life [in Ireland] was very fatiguing' (Lord Riddell, *Intimate Diary of the Peace Conference and After* (London, 1933), 202). For the context and development of this confrontation see: Imperial War Museum, London, French Papers, PP/MCR/C32, reel 4: Diary entries for 30, 31 July 1920; ibid., French Papers, 75/46/13: French to Long (copy), 1 Aug. 1920; Wiltshire Record Office, Long Papers, 947/348: Eddie Saunderson to Long, n.d. [2 Aug. 1920].

[49] Imperial War Museum, London, French Papers, 75/46/13: French to Long (copy), 1 Aug. 1920.

[50] 50. Churchill, *Lord Derby*, 403–4. Wiltshire Record Office, Long Papers, 947/350: Eddie Saunderson to Long, 3 Dec. 1922 (on the position of Castle civil servants under the Irish Free State government).

16

Conclusions

Colonel Edward Saunderson was the single most significant figure in the early development of organized Unionism in Ireland. He helped to inspire and to mould the institutions of the movement; he provided direction, and imbued it with his own economic and evangelical convictions. Within his own lifetime his political conception was shown to be inadequate—and subsequent generations of Unionists were therefore reluctant to dissect his career. But fallibility and influence are not necessarily incompatible, and Saunderson's failings had massive repercussions.

Irish Toryism had always been a maverick entity, straining at, and occasionally escaping from, the leash of British control. Saunderson, whose political descent can be traced from the Whigs of the Irish parliament, felt little instinctive loyalty for British party institutions; and he helped to encourage the freedom of Irish Tories, both through promoting a cross-party loyalism, and by developing the organizational structures of his alliance.[1] He directly challenged British Toryism in the aftermath of the Redistribution debate, and under the first Salisbury government; but he also confronted the Irish Tory establishment, both in North Armagh in 1885 and in North Belfast in June 1886. In theory a Tory himself, his flippant approach to party discipline was an essential catalyst in reconciling Tory to Liberal. Under his own party label, he acted as no staider partisan was prepared to do—urging an amalgamation of loyalist interests, and the rejection of an apparently treacherous British command.

He successfully promoted loyalism in the House of Commons: he founded the independent Unionist parliamentary party which still survives and which continues to wield an influence. Nominally a component of a wider parliamentary alliance, Saunderson's 'Ulster party' frequently followed its own line, blustering its defiance of Tory policy, and mobilizing its impressive resources to bring pressure on the party leadership. At times of crisis for the British party, Saunderson's group usefully articulated the fundamentals of Unionism; and Saunderson himself emerged as an

[1] Reginald Lucas, *Colonel Saunderson MP: A Memoir* (London, 1908), 80–1.

irascible but necessary patriarch, not universally respected, but unquestionably influential.

As a parliamentarian, Saunderson successfully and truculently represented the Ulster Unionist case, his humour and passion compensating for indolence and inflexibility. He had a gift for riling his Nationalist enemies, alternately provoking and bewildering them through irony and apposite quotation. The novelist F. Frankfort Moore, in *The Ulsterman*, has his Mr Alexander say:

'Ay, it's a long time since we had a man that could make a speech to sting them [the Nationalists] as Colonel Saunderson used. If Saunderson was alive now, and if poor Chamberlain was his old self again, we wouldn't hear much about a gang of Nationalists ruling the Empire.'[2]

There is plenty of evidence from contemporary Nationalist memoirs to confirm this allusion to the sharpness of Saunderson's 'sting'.[3]

Yet, however repugnant the content of his message, and however piercing its form, allies and opponents alike were prepared to listen to Saunderson, and to accept the sincerity with which he put forward his opinions. He can have made few converts on the opposition benches, but he was held in high regard by the backbench squirearchy within Toryism. He was certainly not admired by Arthur Balfour and his acolytes—but then few politicians, and even fewer Irishmen, were actively esteemed by the 'Souls' and their collateral networks. Saunderson, in any case, had alternative ministerial allies and patrons in Salisbury and Walter Long.

His personal qualities provided him with popularity; and he was thus an effective ambassador for his cause where cleverer and more bitter colleagues proved to be less tolerable. He moved effortlessly at the most rarified level of English society, charming either with his wit or with the many quick-fire caricatures which he sketched in ink and passed on to friends and acquaintances.[4] But, at least in the late 1880s, he was also prepared to leave the dinner-tables and salons of the influential in order to work as a stump orator for the Unionist cause. He was an invaluable popular spokesman at a time when the Unionist front bench was not over-endowed with accessible leaders. Indeed, in a limited sense, Saunderson took on the mantle of Tory democracy (or, at any rate, Tory

[2] F. Frankfort Moore, *The Ulsterman* (London, 1914), 74.

[3] See e.g. T. M. Healy, *Letters and Leaders of My Day*, 2 vols. (London, n.d. [1928]), i. 259.

[4] See Margot Asquith, *Autobiography* (London, 1920), 32, for an e.g. of Saunderson's art. See also PRONI, W. R. Young Papers, D.3027/5/6/6: scrapbook containing, *inter alia*, a sketch of Gladstone by Saunderson.

demagoguery) shed by Randolph Churchill. One London journalist, reviewing Saunderson's career, commented:

After the resignation of Lord Randolph Churchill, the Unionists were in want of a champion, for neither Lord Salisbury nor the Duke of Devonshire excited the enthusiasm of mass meetings . . . Into the vacant post stepped Colonel Saunderson, and no one was ever better fitted by nature and accident for the role . . .[5]

This was an acute, but perhaps over-generous judgement. Nevertheless, it reflected a widespread perception of Saunderson's popularity in England—a perception shared by his Irish Unionist colleagues, and by the Unionist managers. While he was scarcely the successor of Lord Randolph, Saunderson was indeed an immense asset both to his own movement, and to the British Unionist alliance, in the first agonized years of their existence.

He can be most accurately regarded as an Irish rather than Ulster Unionist; and his career saw little of the drift between the northern and southern movements which became conspicuous after 1905.[6] Though he sat for the strongly Orange seat of North Armagh, his home was in the 'frontier' county of Cavan. This fact, allied to his strong association with Dublin Toryism, meant that he had knowledge of those comparatively small Unionist communities who dwelt among a predominantly Nationalist population. A subsequent generation of loyalist leaders, on the other hand—the Craig brothers, William Moore, J. B. Lonsdale—were more firmly rooted in areas of Unionist strength, and cultivated a more rigorously northern, Ulster Unionist, identity. Saunderson certainly had official bonds with Belfast Orangeism, but—as has been shown—these were acrimoniously severed in 1903.[7] Moreover, he had never felt comfortable with Belfast Toryism, whereas there is no evidence to suggest that he found the Dublin party other than congenial.

He was a firm defender of southern Unionism—like many northern Unionists. Much more significant, however, were his political style and strategy—for both helped to preserve an all-Ireland movement. He thought primarily in terms of parliamentary and English activity rather than the mass local organization favoured by Craig—and which implied an Ulster-based movement. Moreover, he came to fame as a critic of Parnel-

[5] *Saturday Review*, 30 May 1908.

[6] Thomas Macknight, *Ulster as It Is*, 2 vols. (London, 1896), ii. 383; Healy, *Letters and Leaders*, ii. 437.

[7] See above, pp. 145–6. Also: James Loughlin, *Gladstone, Home Rule and the Ulster Question, 1882–1893* (Dublin, 1986), 234 for Saunderson's views on separation or partition; D. W. Miller, *Queen's Rebels: Ulster Loyalism in Historical Perspective* (Dublin, 1978), 110–11.

lism, rather than as a more constructive Unionist, or as a crypto-Ulster Nationalist.[8] If the title of his pamphlet was *Two Irelands*, then this was not so much a reference to Ulster and Ireland, as to the loyal and disloyal who existed all over the island. It was only a later generation of northern Unionists who placed this dichotomy within a geographical framework.

If Saunderson influenced the structural and electoral development of Irish Unionism, then he also moulded its strategic priorities and its public image. He was an ardent member of the Church of Ireland, and a 'convinced Protestant'; and though he often publicly endorsed the ideal of a non-sectarian loyalism, his bitter attitude towards the Irish hierarchy scarcely constituted an encouragement to Catholic Unionists. He pandered to Protestant feeling in the crucial months of the Nationalist 'invasion' of Ulster; though it may also have been true that this attitude was less an encouragement of intolerance than a recognition of political reality. Nevertheless, as a stridently Protestant figure, it is hard to escape the conclusion that Saunderson indirectly contributed to the evolution of an exclusivist Protestant political alliance. For, whatever the warmth of his personal relations with all Irish people, he did too little to make his movement more broadly acceptable.

This narrowness of vision also fatally impaired his perception of class. Michael Davitt accurately grasped that landlordism lay at the heart of Saunderson's political outlook; and Saunderson himself was never slow to acknowledge the influence of his landed identity.[9] An old-fashioned conception of the responsibilities of property lay heavily on the Colonel; and he believed that landlords had a vital political mission, even after the parliamentary reforms of 1884–5. Like his father, he was deeply paternalistic, willing to countenance many aspects of rural reform, while remaining suspicious of a politically ambitious and predatory farmer lobby. He made common cause with the poorest elements of rural and urban society, directing this alliance against middle-class pretensions: he was, however, deeply suspicious of organized labour, fobbing off approaches from the Irish Trade Union Congress.[10] He was only too aware of the threats to the survival of the landlord caste; and indeed he became reconciled to an equitable and gradual transfer of land to a peasant proprietorship. But even in an age of popular politics—in fact, especially in an age of popular politics—Saunderson believed that the most versatile

[8] Alvin Jackson, 'The Rivals of C. S. Parnell', in Donal McCartney (ed.), *Parnell: The Politics of Power* (Dublin, 1991), 73–89.

[9] *Irish Independent*, 22 May 1908.

[10] Emmet O'Connor, *A Labour History of Ireland, 1824–1960* (Dublin, 1992), 60.

landowners could still successfully place their abilities at the disposal of the community. Campaigning in 1885, he conceded that political responsibility was no longer an automatic by-product of land ownership; but, if landlords could not get elected by virtue of their estates, then their abilities would still ensure them a voice in the direction of public affairs:

> at the present moment the political power had entirely drifted away from the class to which he belonged, and had been conveyed into the hands of the farmers and working men of the county ... the industrial classes possessed the political power, but what they wanted was proper men to represent them ...[11]

He was one of the early advocates of class consensus within a loyalist alliance; and, while he subsequently emerged as a bitter advocate of landlord rights, his plausibility and flexibility did much to hold Irish Unionism together in 1886 and 1893. Like Parnell, he had devised a recipe for the survival of landlords within Irish popular politics; and his own success as a Unionist evangelist apparently vindicated the broader claims which he made for his class.[12] His career to 1895 suggested that landlords could be both successful, popular politicians on the constitutional question, and yet remain tolerant and accessible on other public questions.

It was of course a profoundly undemocratic political creed. Saunderson approached both potential Catholic supporters and the northern Orange democracy largely on his own, blinkered terms. He was intolerant of painstaking negotiation, baulked at responsibility to colleagues and to popular opinion, and was happiest as an unrestrained and swashbuckling advocate of his own principles. In the mid- and late 1890s, when popular pressure was building for the democratization of Ulster Unionism, Saunderson was uninterested, and offered no appropriate response: he was equally immobile in the face of Independent Orangeism and T. W. Russell's campaign for compulsory purchase. What did engage his sympathies in these years was a narrow landlordism; and he was drawn inexorably into a series of fratricidal class disputes. By 1900 he had emerged as an unrepentant sectional politician, more active within the Irish Landowners' Convention than any more broadly based movement. The devolution affair and Liberal victory of 1906 allowed him a finale in the role of loyalist partisan; but by that time—the months before his death—true leadership within the movement had fallen into other, more dextrous hands. After his death his sons, especially Somerset and Eddie, attempted to re-enact his

[11] *BNL*, 19 Aug. 1885, p. 8.
[12] Paul Bew, *C. S. Parnell* (Dublin, 1980), 137–8.

creed within their own careers. But, in the presence of new political forces both within and beyond Unionism, it was a forlorn hope, and brought only frustration and neurosis.

He was the first leader of the Irish Unionist party, and one of the key designers of Unionist institutions and ideology; nevertheless, the inheritors of his tradition have erased Edward Saunderson from their historical perception. One of the tragedies of Unionism, as indeed of Nationalism in Ireland, is that its partisans are unmoved by the pacific standard-bearers of their faith: Michael Collins, the bluff manufacturer of terror has always been a more accessible hero than Arthur Griffith; Edward Carson, the melancholy architect of civil war, has attracted greater veneration than Edward Saunderson.[13] Saunderson was the militia officer who never went to war—the colonel whose skirmishing and leadership were confined to the the Palace of Westminster. He was neither a ruthless commander, nor a reckless strategist and yet he, too, helped to fashion the political landscape of modern Ireland.

[13] See e.g. Richard Davis, *Arthur Griffith and Non-Violent Sinn Fein* (Dublin, 1974), p. xi.

Bibliography

PRIMARY SOURCES

1. Personal Papers

Birmingham University Library

Austen Chamberlain Papers
Joseph Chamberlain Papers

Bodleian Library, Oxford

Papers of Sir Antony MacDonnell, first Lord MacDonnell
J. S. Sandars Papers
Papers of William Waldegrave, second Earl of Selborne

British Library, London

H. O. Arnold-Forster Papers
Papers of Arthur Balfour, first Earl Balfour
Papers of Walter Long, first Viscount Long
Papers of Sir Stafford Northcote, first Earl of Iddesleigh

Chatsworth House, Derbyshire

Papers of Spencer Compton, eighth Duke of Devonshire

Churchill College, Cambridge

Sir William Bull Papers
Lord Randolph Churchill Papers

East Sussex Record Office, Hove Reference Library

Papers of Garnet, first Viscount Wolseley

Hatfield House, Hertfordshire

Papers of Robert Arthur Talbot, third Marquess of Salisbury

House of Lords Record Office, London

Papers of Edward Gibson, first Lord Ashbourne
Papers of George Henry, fifth Earl Cadogan

Imperial War Museum, London

Papers of Sir John French, first Earl of Ypres

Kent Record Office, Maidstone

Papers of Aretas Akers-Douglas, first Viscount Chilston

National Library of Ireland, Dublin

Papers of the Lords Farnham
T. P. Gill Papers
John Vernon Papers

Plunkett Foundation, Oxford

Sir Horace Plunkett Papers

Public Record Office of Northern Ireland, Belfast

Papers of James, second Duke of Abercorn
H. B. Armstrong Papers
Papers of Armar Lowry-Corry, first Earl of Belmore
Papers of Somerset Richard, fourth Earl of Belmore
Carleton, Atkinson, and Sloan Papers
Papers of Edward Carson, first Lord Carson
Papers of Henry Chaplin, first Viscount Chaplin
Papers of James Craig, first Viscount Craigavon
F. H. Crawford Papers
Papers of Frederick Hamilton-Temple-Blackwood, first Marquess of Dufferin and Ava
C. W. Dunbar-Buller Papers
Papers of Windham Thomas, fourth Earl of Dunraven
Sir William Ellison-Macartney Papers
Papers of John Henry, fourth Earl of Erne
Falls and Hanna Papers
Papers of Arthur Acheson, second Viscount Gosford
William Johnston Diaries
Papers of Theresa, Marchioness of Londonderry
R. T. G. Lowry Papers
Hugh de Fellenberg Montgomery Papers
Sir Oliver Nugent Papers
Joshua Peel Papers
Edward Saunderson Papers
Sir Wilfrid Spender Papers
Robert H. Wallace Papers

Young of Galgorm Papers

Trinity College, Dublin

H. O. Arnold-Forster Papers
W. E. H. Lecky Papers

Whittingehame, North Berwick

Papers of Arthur Balfour, first Earl Balfour
Papers of Gerald Balfour, second Earl Balfour

Wiltshire Record Office, Trowbridge

Papers of Walter Long, first Viscount Long

Private Possession

Sir William Moore Papers (in the possession of Sir William Moore, Kilrea, Londonderry, and Dr Amanda Shanks, The Queen's University of Belfast)

Nina Patrick Papers (in the possession of Dr Amanda Shanks, The Queen's University of Belfast)

Edward Saunderson Papers (in the possession of E. J. Saunderson Esq., Newbury, Berks.)

George Wyndham Papers (in the possession of the Duke of Westminster, Eaton, Chester)

2. Estate and Institutional Records

National Archive, Dublin

Land Commission Records

Public Record Office, Kew, London

Colonial Office Papers (consulted on microfilm)

Public Record Office of Northern Ireland, Belfast

Papers of the Irish Loyal and Patriotic Union
Papers of the Irish Unionist Alliance
Land Registry Papers
Papers of the North Armagh Unionist Association
Saunderson Estate Papers
Ulster Unionist Council Papers

Representative Church Body, Dublin

Finance Committee Mortgage Ledgers

3. Newspapers

Anglo-Celt
Belfast News Letter

Freeman's Journal
Irish Independent
Irish Times
Lurgan Mail
Nomad's Weekly
Northern Whig
Observer
Portadown News
Saturday Review
Times Literary Supplement
Vanity Fair
Westminster Gazette

4. Published Autobiographies, Letters, and Diaries

ASQUITH, MARGOT, *Autobiography* (London, 1920).

BALFOUR, ARTHUR JAMES, First Earl of, *Chapters of Autobiography* (London, 1930).

BERESFORD, WILLIAM, *Correspondence of the Rt. Hon. John Beresford*, 2 vols. (London, 1854).

BLUMENFELD, R. D., *R.D.B.'s Procession* (London, 1934).

CAMPBELL, T. J., *Fifty Years of Ulster* (Belfast, 1941).

CHAMBERLAIN, Sir AUSTEN, *Politics from Inside: An Epistolary Chronicle, 1906–1914* (London, 1936).

COOKE, A. B., 'A Conservative Party Leader in Ulster: Sir Stafford Northcote's Diary of a Visit to the Province, October 1883', *PRIA*, 75c/4 (Sept. 1975).

—— and MALCOMSON, A. P. W., *The Ashbourne Papers, 1869–1913: A Calendar of the Papers of Edward Gibson, First Lord Ashbourne* (Belfast, 1974).

—— and VINCENT, JOHN, 'Select Documents XXVII: Ireland and Party Politics, 1885–7: An Unpublished Conservative Memoir (1)', *IHS*, 16/62 (Sept. 1969).

—— —— *Lord Carlingford's Journal: Reflections of a Cabinet Minister, 1885* (Oxford, 1971)

CRANBROOK, GATHORNE HARDY, First Earl of, *A Memoir: With Extracts from his Diary and Correspondence*, 2 vols. (London, 1910).

CRAWFORD, F. H., *Guns for Ulster* (Belfast, 1947).

DUGDALE, BLANCHE, 'The Wyndham-MacDonnell Imbroglio, 1902–6', *Quarterly Review*, 158/511 (Jan. 1932).

DUNRAVEN Earl of, *Past Times and Pastimes*, 2 vols. (London, n.d. [1922]).

FITZROY, Sir ALMERIC, *Memoirs*, 2 vols. (London, n.d. [1925]).

FRY, AGNES, *A Memoir of the Rt. Hon. Sir Edward Fry, GCB* (Oxford, 1921).

GRIFFITH-BOSCAWEN, ARTHUR S. T., *Fourteen Years in Parliament* (London, 1907).

HAMILTON, LORD ERNEST, *Forty Years On* (London, n.d. [1922]).

HEADLAM, MAURICE, *Irish Reminiscences* (London, 1947).

HEALY, T. M., *Letters and Leaders of My Day*, 2 vols. (London, n.d. [1928]).

JOHNSTON, NANCY E. (ed.), *The Diary of Gathorne Hardy, later Lord Cranbrook, 1866–1892: Political Selections* (Oxford, 1981).

LANG, ANDREW, *The Life, Letters and Diaries of Sir Stafford Northcote, First Earl of Iddesleigh*, 2 vols. (Edinburgh and London, 1890).

LONDONDERRY, CHARLES VANE, Marquess of, *Memoirs and Correspondence of Viscount Castlereagh, Second Marquess of Londonderry*, 12 vols. (London, 1848–53).

LONG, WALTER, Viscount, *Memories* (London, 1923).

MCCARTHY, JUSTIN, *Reminiscences*, 2 vols. (London, 1899).

MACKAIL, J. W., AND WYNDHAM, GUY (eds.), *The Life and Letters of George Wyndham*, 2 vols. (London, n.d. [1925]).

MACKNIGHT, THOMAS, *Ulster as It Is*, 2 vols. (London, 1896).

MANCHESTER, Duke of, *My Candid Recollections* (London, 1934).

MIDLETON, Earl of, *Records and Reactions* (London, 1939).

MURRAY, ALICE E., *A History of the Commercial Relations between England and Ireland from the Period of the Restoration* (London, 1903).

O'BRIEN, GEORGINA (ed.), *The Reminiscences of the Rt. Hon. Lord O'Brien* (London, 1916).

PEASE, ALFRED E., *Elections and Recollections* (London, 1932).

RIDDELL, LORD, *An Intimate Diary of the Peace Conference and After* (London, 1933).

—— *More Pages from my Diary 1908–14* (London, 1934).

ROBINSON, Sir HENRY, *Memories: Wise and Otherwise* (London, 1924).

ROSS, CHARLES (ed.), *The Correspondence of Charles, First Marquis Cornwallis*, 3 vols. (London, 1859).

ROSS, Sir JOHN, *The Years of My Pilgrimage: Random Reminiscences* (London, 1924).

ROSSMORE, Lord, *Things I Can Tell* (London, 1912).

TEMPLE, Sir RICHARD (ed.), *Letters and Character Sketches from the House of Commons: Home Rule and other Matters in 1886–7* (London, 1912).

VINCENT, JOHN (ed.), *The Crawford Papers: The Journals of David Lindsay, 27th Earl of Crawford and 10th Earl of Balcarres during the Years 1892–1940* (Manchester, 1984).

WYNDHAM, GUY (ed.), *The Letters of George Wyndham, 1877–1913*, 2 vols. (Edinburgh, 1915).

5. Contemporary Pamphlets and Political Comment

ANON. [R. Lindsay Crawford], *Orangeism: Its History and Progress. A Plea for First Principles* (Belfast, 1904).

ANON. [Joseph R. Fisher], *The Ulster Liberal/ Unionist Association: A Sketch of its History, 1885–1914* (Belfast, 1914).

ANON. [Revd. R. McCollum], *Sketches of the Highlands of Cavan and of Shirley Castle, in Farney, Taken during the Irish Famine* (Belfast, 1856).

ANON. ['MP'], *The History of Orangeism: Its Origins, Its Rise, and Its Decline* (Dublin, 1882).

ARNOLD-FORSTER, H. O., *The Truth about the League, Its Leaders and Its Teaching* 3rd edn. (Dublin, 1883).

BONN, MORITZ J., *Modern Ireland and her Agrarian Problem*, trans. T. H. W. Rolleston (Dublin, 1906).

CHAMBERLAIN, JOSEPH, *Speeches on the Irish Question: A Collection of Speeches delivered between 1887* and *1890* (London, 1890).

CHARLEY, Sir WILLIAM T., *The Crusade against the Constitution: An Historical Vindication of the House of Lords* (London, 1895).

DOWDEN, EDWARD, 'Irish Unionists and the Present Administration', *National Review*, 44 (Oct. 1904).

DUNRAVEN, Earl of, *The Crisis in Ireland: An Account of the Present Condition of Ireland and Suggestions towards Reform* (Dublin and London, 1905).

—— *The Outlook in Ireland: The Case for Devolution and Conciliation* (Dublin, 1907).

ELLIS, Revd THOMAS, *The Actions of the Grand Orange Lodge of the County of Armagh (and the Reasons thereof) on the 6th of July 1885* (Armagh, 1885).

General Synod of the Church of Ireland: Revision Committee Report Presented to the General Synod of 1873 (Dublin, 1873).

HEALY, T. M., *Loyalty Plus Murder* (Dublin, 1883).

IWAN-MUELLER, E. B., *Ireland: Today and Tomorrow* (London, 1907).

KENNEDY, THOMAS, *A History of the Irish Protest against Over-Taxation from 1853 to 1897* (Dublin, 1897).

LOUGH, THOMAS, *England's Wealth: Ireland's Poverty* (London, 1897).

LUCY, Sir HENRY, *A Diary of the Salisbury Parliament* (London, 1892).

—— *A Diary of the Unionist Parliament* (Bristol, 1901).

—— *The Balfourian Parliament* (London, 1906).

MCCARTHY, MICHAEL J. F., *Priests and People in Ireland* (Dublin, 1902).

—— *Rome in Ireland* (London, 1904).

MCNEILL, RONALD, *Ulster's Stand for Union* (London, 1922).

MORRISON, H. D., *Modern Ulster: Its Character, Politics, Customs and Industries* (London, n.d.).

PEEL, GEORGE, *The Reign of Sir Edward Carson* (London, 1914).

PLUNKETT, Sir HORACE, *Ireland in the New Century* (London, 1904).

—— *Noblesse Oblige: An Irish Rendering* (Dublin, 1908).

A Report of the Debate in the House of Commons of Ireland on Wednesday and Thursday the 5th and 6th of February 1800 on the King's Message recommending a Legislative Union with Great Britain (Dublin, 1800).

Report of Debates in the House of Commons of Ireland, Session 1796–7 (Dublin, 1797).

RUSSELL, T. W., 'The Unionist Policy for Ireland', *New Review*, 1 (June 1889).

——'Irish Land and Irish Rents', *Westminster Review*, 129/2 (June 1889).

——'A Résumé of the Irish Land Problems', *Nineteenth Century*, 36 (Oct. 1889).

——'The Land Purchase Question', *Fortnightly Review*, 47 (Feb. 1890).

——'The Irish Land Bill', *Fortnightly Review*, 53 (May 1890).

——*Compulsory Purchase: Five Speeches made by Mr T. W. Russell* (London, 1901).

——*Ireland and the Empire: A Review* (London, 1901).

SAUNDERSON, EDWARD J., *Two Irelands: Loyalty versus Treason* (London, 1884).

——*Present and Everlasting Salvation: Three Addresses with a Preface by the Bishop of Ossory* (Dublin, 1907).

TAYLOR, J. WALLACE, *The Rossmore Incident: An Account of the Various Nationalist and Counter Nationalist Meetings held in Ulster in the Autumn of 1883* (Dublin, 1884).

6. Literary Essays and Fiction

BOWEN, ELIZABETH, *Bowen's Court* (London, 1942).

BUTLER, HUBERT, *Escape from the Anthill* (Mullingar, 1985).

CONRAD, JOSEPH, *A Set of Six* (London, 1908).

DOYLE, LYNN, *An Ulster Childhood* (Dublin, 1921).

FARRELL, J. G., *Troubles*, pbk. edn. (Harmondsworth, 1975).

—— *The Singapore Grip* (London, 1978).

KETTLE, TOM, *The Day's Burden: Studies, Literary and Political* (London, 1910).

—— *The Ways of War* (London, 1917).

MOORE, F. FRANKFORT, *The Ulsterman* (London, 1914).

TROLLOPE, ANTHONY, *Phineas Finn*, pbk. edn. (Oxford, 1982).

7. Reference Works

BATEMAN, JOHN, *The Great Landowners of Great Britain and Ireland*, 4th edn. (London, 1883).

BENCE-JONES, MARK, *Burke's Guide to the Country Houses of Ireland* (London, 1978).

Burke's Landed Gentry of Ireland, 5th edn. (London, 1958).

COOTE, SIR CHARLES, *A Statistical Survey of the County of Cavan* (Dublin, 1802).

GASKELL, E., *Ulster Leaders: Social and Political* (London, 1914).

GIBBS, V., AND DOUBLEDAY, H. A., *The Complete Peerage*, 13 vols. (London, 1912–59).

House of Commons, *Accounts and Papers, 1878*, vol. lxii, pt. II (Members of Parliament).

——*Hansard, Parliamentary Debates*, series 3 and 4.

——*Report of the Commissioners of Church Temporalities in Ireland, 1869–1880.*

The Journals of the House of Commons of the Kingdom of Ireland, 19 vols. (Dublin, 1782–1800).

LEWIS, SAMUEL, *A Topographical Dictionary of Ireland, Comprising the Several*

Counties, Cities, Boroughs, Corporate, Market and Post Towns, Parishes and Villages, 2 vols. (London, 1837).

MOODY, T. W., MARTIN, F. X., and BYRNE, F. J. (eds.), *A New History of Ireland*, iii. *Early Modern Ireland, 1534–1691* (Oxford, 1976).

O'CONNELL, J. R., *The Landlords' and Tenants' Handy Guide to Land Purchase* (Dublin, n.d. [1904]).

The Parliamentary Register; or, History of the Proceedings and Debates of the House of Commons of Ireland, 15 vols. (Dublin, 1781–95).

THORNE, R. G., *The History of Parliament*, v: *The House of Commons, 1790–1820* (London, 1986).

WALKER, BRIAN M. (ed.), *Parliamentary Election Results in Ireland, 1801–1922* (Dublin, 1978).

YOUNG, R. M., *Belfast and the Province of Ulster in the Twentieth Century* (Brighton, 1909).

SECONDARY SOURCES

8. Articles, Biographies, and Monographs

ADONIS, ANDREW, *Making Aristocracy Work: The Peerage and the Political System in Britain, 1884–1914* (Oxford, 1993).

ANDREW, CHRISTOPHER, *Her Majesty's Secret Service: The Making of the British Intelligence Community*, pbk. edn. (New York, 1987).

ANON. [British and Irish Communist Organization], *The Birth of Ulster Unionism*, 5th edn. (Belfast, 1984).

ANON. ['E. O'H.'], *The O'Reillys of Templemills, Celbridge* (Dublin, 1941).

ANON. [R. M. Sibbett], *Orangeism in Ireland and throughout the Empire*, 2 vols. (London n.d. [1938]).

ASKWITH, Lord, *Lord James of Hereford* (London, 1930).

ASPINALL, A., 'Francis Saunderson', in R. G. Thorne (ed.), *The History of Parliament*, v: *The House of Commons, 1790–1820* (London, 1986).

BECKETT, J. C., *The Anglo-Irish Tradition* (London, 1976).

—— (ed.), *Belfast: The Making of the City, 1800–1914* (Belfast, 1983).

BECKETT, J. V., *The Aristocracy in England, 1660–1914* (Oxford, 1986).

BENCE-JONES, MARK, *Twilight of the Ascendancy*, pbk. edn. (London, 1993).

BEW, PAUL, *Land and the National Question in Ireland, 1858–1882* (Dublin, 1978).

—— *C. S. Parnell* (Dublin, 1980).

—— *Conflict and Conciliation in Ireland, 1890–1910: Parnellites and Agrarian Radicals* (Oxford, 1987).

—— and WRIGHT, FRANK, 'The Agrarian Opposition in Ulster Politics, 1848–1887', in S. Clarke and J. S. Donnelly (eds.), *Irish Peasants: Violence and Political Disturbance in Ireland, 1790–1914* (Manchester, 1983).

BIGGS-DAVISON, JOHN, *George Wyndham: A Study in Toryism* (London, 1951).

BLAKE, ROBERT, *The Conservative Party from Peel to Thatcher* (London, 1985).

—— and CECIL, HUGH (eds.), *Salisbury: The Man and his Policies* (London, 1987).

BOLTON, G. C., *The Passing of the Irish Act of Union: A Study in Parliamentary Politics* (Oxford, 1966).

BOWEN, DESMOND, *The Protestant Crusade in Ireland, 1800–1870* (Dublin, 1978).

BOYLE, J. W., 'The Belfast Protestant Association and the Independent Orange Order, 1901–10', *IHS*, 13/50 (Sept. 1962).

—— 'A Fenian Protestant in Canada: Robert Lindsay Crawford', *Canadian Historical Review*, 52/2 (1971).

BRADY, CIARAN, 'The O'Reillys of East Breifne and the Problem of Surrender and Regrant', *Breifne*, 6/23 (1982).

BRADY, L. W., *T. P. O'Connor and the Liverpool Irish* (London, 1983).

BUCKLAND, PATRICK, *Irish Unionism 1: The Anglo-Irish and the New Ireland, 1885–1922* (Dublin, 1972).

—— *Irish Unionism 2: Ulster Unionism and the Origins of Northern Ireland, 1886–1922* (Dublin, 1973).

—— *Irish Unionism 1885–1923: A Documentary History* (Belfast, 1973).

CALLANAN, FRANK, *The Parnellite Split, 1890–1* (Cork, 1992).

CALWELL, C. E., *The Memoirs of Major-General Sir Hugh McCalmont, KCB, CVO* (London, 1924).

CAMPBELL, JOHN, *F. E. Smith: First Earl of Birkenhead* (London, 1983).

CANNADINE, DAVID, *The Decline and Fall of the British Aristocracy* (New Haven, Conn., 1990).

CARVILLE, ANNE, 'The Impact of the Partition Proposals on County Monaghan', *Clogher Record*, 14/1 (1991).

CECIL, Lady GWENDOLEN, *The Life of Robert, Third Marquess of Salisbury*, 4 vols. (London, 1921–32).

CHADWICK, M. E. J., 'The Role of Redistribution in the Making of the Third Reform Act', *Historical Journal*, 19/3 (1976).

CHILSTON, ERIC, Viscount, 'Lord Salisbury as Party Leader, 1881–1902', *Parliamentary Affairs*, 13/3 (1960).

—— *Chief Whip: The Political Life and Times of Aretas Akers-Douglas, First Viscount Chilston* (London, 1961).

—— *W. H. Smith* (London, 1965).

CHURCHILL, RANDOLPH S., *Lord Derby, 'King of Lancashire'* (London, 1959).

CLARKE, SAMUEL, and DONNELLY, JAMES S., *Irish Peasants: Violence and Political Disturbance in Ireland, 1790–1914* (Manchester, 1983).

COOKE, A. B., and VINCENT, JOHN, *The Governing Passion: Cabinet Government and Party Politics in Britain, 1885–6* (Brighton, 1974).

CRAWFORD, W. H., 'Economy and Society in South Ulster in the Eighteenth Century', *Clogher Record*, 8/3 (1975).

CROSSICK, GEOFFREY (ed.), *The Lower Middle Class in Britain, 1870–1914* (London, 1977).

CULLEN, L. M., and SMOUT, T. C. (eds.), *Comparative Aspects of Scottish and Irish Economic and Social History, 1600–1900* (Edinburgh, 1977).

CUNNINGHAM, TERENCE P., 'The Great Famine in County Cavan', *Breifne*, 2/8 (1965).

CURTIS, L. P., *Coercion and Conciliation in Ireland, 1880–1892: A Study in Constructive Unionism* (Princeton, NJ, 1963).

—— 'Incumbered Wealth: Landed Indebtedness in Post-Famine Ireland', *American Historical Review*, 85/2 (Apr. 1980).

D'ALTON, IAN, 'Southern Irish Unionism: A Study of Cork Unionists, 1884–1914', *TRHS*, 5th ser. 23 (London, 1973).

—— 'Cork Unionism: Its Role in Parliamentary and Local Elections, 1885–1914', *Studia Hibernica*, 15 (1975).

DAVIS, RICHARD, *Arthur Griffith and Non-Violent Sinn Fein* (Dublin, 1974).

DE COURCY, ANNE, *Circe: The Life of Edith, Marchioness of Londonderry* (London, 1992).

DICKSON, DAVID, *New Foundations: Ireland, 1660–1800* (Dublin, 1987).

DIGBY, MARGARET, *Horace Plunkett: An Anglo-American Irishman* (Oxford, 1949).

DOLLEY, MICHAEL, AND SEABY, W. A., 'Le Money del Orraylly (O'Reilly's Money)', *British Numismatic Journal*, 36 (1967).

DONNELLY, JAMES S., *The Land and the People of Nineteenth Century Cork: The Rural Economy and the Land Question* (London, 1975).

DUGDALE, BLANCHE E. C., *Arthur James Balfour, First Earl of Balfour, KG, OM, FRS &c*, 2 vols. (London, 1936).

DUTTON, DAVID, 'Unionist Politics and the Aftermath of the General Election of 1906: A Reassessment', *Historical Journal*, 22/4 (1979).

—— *'His Majesty's Loyal Opposition': The Unionist Party in Opposition, 1905–15* (Liverpool, 1992).

EGREMONT, MAX, *The Cousins: The Friendships, Opinions, and Activities of Wilfrid Scawen Blunt and George Wyndham* (London, 1977).

ERVINE, ST JOHN, *Craigavon: Ulsterman* (London, 1971).

FANNING, RONAN, 'The Unionist Party and Ireland, 1906–10', *IHS*, 15/58 (1966).

FITZPATRICK, DAVID, *Politics and Irish Life, 1913–21: Provincial Experience of War and Revolution* (Dublin, 1977).

—— 'The Disappearance of the Irish Agricultural Labourer 1841–1912', *Irish Economic and Social History*, 7 (1980).

FOSTER, R. F., *Charles Stewart Parnell: The Man and his Family* (Hassocks, 1979).

—— 'Parnell and his People: The Anglo-Irish Ascendancy and Home Rule', *Canadian Journal of Irish Studies* (June 1980).

—— *Lord Randolph Churchill: A Political Life* (Oxford, 1981).

—— *Modern Ireland, 1600–1972* (London, 1988).

—— *Paddy and Mr Punch: Connections in Irish and English History* (London, 1993).

FRASER, PETER, 'The Liberal Unionist Alliance: Chamberlain, Hartington and the Conservatives, 1886–1904', *English Historical Review*, 77/302 (Jan. 1962).
GAILEY, ANDREW, 'Unionist Rhetoric and Irish Local Government Reform, 1895–99', *IHS*, 24/93 (May 1984).
——*Ireland and the Death of Kindness: The Experience of Constructive Unionism, 1890–1905* (Cork, 1987).
GARVIN, J. L., and AMERY, JULIAN, *The Life of Joseph Chamberlain*, 6 vols. (London, 1932–69).
GARVIN, TOM, *Nationalist Revolutionaries in Ireland, 1858–1928* (Oxford, 1987).
GEARY, LAURENCE, *The Plan of Campaign, 1886–1891* (Cork, 1986).
GENET, JEAN, *The Big House: Reality and Representation* (Dingle, 1991).
GIBBON, PETER, *The Origins of Ulster Unionism: The Formation of Popular Protestant Politics and Ideology in Nineteenth-Century Ireland* (Manchester, 1975).
GLENDINNING, VICTORIA, *Trollope*, pbk. edn. (London, 1993).
GRAHAM, B. J., and PROUDFOOT, LINDSAY, *An Historical Geography of Ireland* (London, 1993).
GRIBBON, SYBIL, 'The Social Origins of Ulster Unionism', *Irish Economic and Social History*, 4 (1977).
——*Edwardian Belfast: A Social Profile* (Belfast, 1982).
GRIGG, JOHN, *Lloyd George: From Peace to War, 1912–16* (London, 1985).
HAMER, D. A., *Liberal Politics in the Age of Gladstone and Rosebery: A Study in Leadership and Policy* (Oxford, 1972).
HAMMOND, J. L., *Gladstone and the Irish Nation* (London, 1938).
HARBINSON, JOHN, *The Ulster Unionist Party, 1882–1973: Its Origins and Development* (Belfast, 1973).
HARDINGE, Sir A. E. H., *The Life of Henry Howard Molyneux, Fourth Earl of Carnarvon, 1831–1890*, 3 vols. (London, 1925).
HAYES-MCCOY, G. A., 'Sir John Davies in Cavan in 1606 and 1610', *Breifne*, 1/3 (1960).
HEMPTON, DAVID, and HILL, MYRTLE, *Evangelical Protestantism in Ulster Society, 1740–1890* (London, 1992).
HICKS-BEACH, Lady V., *The Life of Sir Michael Hicks-Beach, First Earl St. Aldwyn*, 2 vols. (London, 1932).
HINDE, WENDY, *Castlereagh* (London, 1981).
HOLLAND, BERNARD, *The Life of Spencer Compton, Eighth Duke of Devonshire*, 2 vols. (London, 1911).
HOLMES, RICHARD, *The Little Field Marshal: Sir John French* (London, 1981).
HOPPEN, K. T., *Elections, Politics, and Society in Ireland, 1832–1885* (Oxford, 1984).
——*Ireland Since 1800: Conflict and Conformity* (London, 1989).
HYDE, H. MONTGOMERY, *Carson: The Life of Sir Edward Carson, Lord Carson of Duncairn* (London, 1953).
——*The Londonderrys: A Family Portrait* (London, 1979).

INGRAM, T. DUNBAR, *A History of the Legislative Union of Great Britain and Ireland* (London, 1887).

JACKSON, ALVIN, 'Irish Unionism and the Russellite Threat, 1894–1906', *IHS*, 25/100 (Nov. 1987).

——'The Failure of Unionism in Dublin, 1900', *IHS*, 26/104 (Nov. 1989).

——*The Ulster Party: Irish Unionists in the House of Commons, 1884–1911* (Oxford, 1989).

——'Unionist History (1)', *The Irish Review* (autumn, 1989).

——'Unionist History (2)', *The Irish Review* (spring, 1990).

——'Unionist Politics and Protestant Society in Edwardian Ireland', *Historical Journal*, 33/4 (1990).

——'The Rivals of C. S. Parnell', in Donal McCartney (ed.), *Parnell: The Politics of Power* (Dublin, 1991).

——'Unionist Myths, 1912–85', *Past & Present*, 136 (Aug. 1992), 164–85.

——*Sir Edward Carson* (Dublin, 1993).

JAY, RICHARD, *Joseph Chamberlain: A Political Study* (Oxford, 1981).

JENKINS, T. A., *Gladstone, Whiggery, and the Liberal Party, 1874–86* (Oxford, 1988).

JOHNSTON, EDITH MARY, *Great Britain and Ireland, 1760–1800: A Study in Political Administration* (Edinburgh, 1963).

JONES, ANDREW, *The Politics of Reform, 1884* (Cambridge, 1972).

JOYCE, PATRICK, *Work, Society and Politics: The Culture of the Factory in Victorian England* (London, 1982).

JUPP, PETER, 'Irish Parliamentary Elections and the Influence of the Catholic Vote, 1800–1820', *Historical Journal*, 10/2 (1967).

——'County Cavan', in R. G. Thorne (ed.), *The History of Parliament*, v: *The House of Commons, 1790–1820* (London, 1986).

KEATING, CARLA (ed.), *Plunkett and Co-operatives: Past, Present and Future* (Cork, 1983).

KENDLE, JOHN, *Walter Long, Ireland and the Union, 1905–20* (Dublin, 1992).

KENNEDY, LIAM, and OLLERENSHAW, PHILIP, *An Economic History of Ulster, 1820–1939* (Manchester, 1985).

KIRKPATRICK, R. W., 'Landed Estates in Ulster and the Irish Land War, 1879–1885', *Irish Economic and Social History*, 5 (1978).

——'The Origins and Development of the Land War in Mid-Ulster', in F. S. L. Lyons and R. Hawkins (eds.), *Varieties of Tension: Ireland Under the Union: Essays in Honour of T. W. Moody* (Oxford, 1980).

LECKY, ELIZABETH, *A Memoir of the Rt. Hon. W. E. H. Lecky, OM* (London, 1910).

LEET, ERNEST, and MCCUTCHEON, R. R., *A Sketch of the Law of Property in Ireland* (Dublin, 1937).

LOUGHLIN, JAMES, *Gladstone, Home Rule and the Ulster Question 1882–1893* (Dublin, 1986).

LUBENOW, W. C., *Parliamentary Politics and the Home Rule Crisis: The British House of Commons in 1886* (Oxford, 1988).

LUCAS, REGINALD, *Colonel Saunderson MP: A Memoir* (London, 1908).

——*Lord Glenesk and the* Morning Post (London, 1910).

——*George II and his Ministers* (London, 1910).

——*Lord North, Second Earl of Guilford, KG, 1732–1792* (London, 1913).

LYONS, F. S. L., 'The Irish Unionist Party and the Devolution Crisis, 1904–5', *IHS*, 6/21 (Mar. 1948).

——*The Irish Parliamentary Party, 1890–1910* (London, 1951).

——*Charles Stewart Parnell* (London, 1977).

——and HAWKINS, R. A. J. (eds.), *Ireland under the Union: Varieties of Tension; essays in Honour of T. W. Moody* (Oxford, 1980).

MCCLELLAND, AIKEN, 'The Later Orange Order', in T. D. Williams (ed.), *Secret Societies in Ireland* (Dublin, 1973).

——'Orangeism in County Monaghan', *Clogher Record*, 9/3 (1978).

——*William Johnston of Ballykilbeg* (Lurgan, 1990).

MCCOURT, EILEEN, 'The Management of the Farnham Estates during the Nineteenth Century', *Breifne*, 4/16 (1975).

MCCUSKER, COLIN C., '"I made the House roar and the heathens rage": Saunderson and the Fight against Home Rule', BA diss. (University of Ulster at Coleraine, 1992).

MCDOWELL, R. B., *The Irish Convention, 1917–18* (London, 1970).

——*The Church of Ireland, 1869–1969* (London, 1975).

MCFARLAN, D. M., *Lift Thy Banner: Church of Ireland Scenes, 1870–1900* (Dundalk, 1990).

MCGIMPSEY, CHRISTOPHER, 'Border Ballads and Sectarian Affrays', *Clogher Record*, 11/1 (1982).

——'"To Raise the Banner in the Remote North": Politics in County Monaghan, 1868–83', Ph.D. thesis (Edinburgh University, 1983).

MCMINN, J. R. B., 'Presbyterianism and Politics in Ulster, 1871–1906', *Studia Hibernica*, 21 (1981).

——'The Myth of Route Liberalism in County Antrim, 1869–1900', *Eire-Ireland*, 17/1 (spring 1982).

——'Liberalism in North Antrim, 1900–1914', *IHS*, 23/89 (May 1982).

MAGEE, JOHN, 'The Monaghan Election of 1883 and the "Invasion of Ulster"', *Clogher Record*, 8/2 (1974).

MAGUIRE, W. A., *Belfast* (Keele, 1993).

MALCOMSON, A. P. W., 'Absenteeism in Eighteenth Century Ireland', *Irish Economic and Social History*, 1 (1974).

——*John Foster: The Politics of the Anglo-Irish Ascendancy* (Oxford, 1978).

——*The Pursuit of the Heiress: Aristocratic Marriage in Ireland, 1750–1820* (Belfast, 1982).

MANSERGH, NICHOLAS, *The Government of Northern Ireland: A Study in Devolution* (London, 1936).
—— *The Unresolved Question: The Anglo-Irish Settlement and its Undoing, 1912–72* (New Haven, Conn., 1991).
MARJORIBANKS, EDWARD, and COLVIN, IAN, *The Life of Lord Carson*, 3 vols. (London, 1932–6).
MARSH, PETER, *The Discipline of Popular Government: Lord Salisbury's Domestic Statecraft, 1881–1902* (Hassocks, 1978).
MAXWELL, Sir HENRY, *The Life and Times of the Rt. Hon. William Henry Smith, M.P.*, 2 vols. (London, 1893).
MILLER, DAVID W., *Queen's Rebels: Ulster Loyalism in Historical Perspective* (Dublin, 1978).
MORGAN, AUSTEN, *Labour and Partition: The Belfast Working Class, 1905–23* (London, 1991).
MULLAN, RAYMOND GERARD, 'The Origins and Passing of the Irish Land Act of 1909', MA thesis (Queen's University, Belfast, 1978).
MURPHY, RICHARD, 'Walter Long and the Conservative Party, 1905–21', Ph.D. thesis (Bristol University, 1984).
NEWTON, Lord, *Lord Lansdowne* (London, 1929).
O'BRIEN, CONOR CRUISE, *Parnell and his Party*, 2nd edn. (Oxford, 1964).
O'BRIEN, R. BARRY, *The Life of Charles Stewart Parnell*, 2 vols. (London, 1899).
O'CONNOR, EMMET, *A Labour History of Ireland: 1824–1960* (Dublin, 1992).
O'DAY, ALAN, *The English Face of Irish Nationalism: Parnellite Involvement in Irish Politics, 1880–1886* (Dublin, 1977).
—— *Parnell and the First Home Rule Episode, 1884–1887* (Dublin, 1986).
O'DONNELL, F. H., *A History of the Irish Parliamentary Party*, 2 vols. (London, 1910).
O'FERRALL, FERGUS, *Catholic Emancipation: Daniel O'Connell and the Birth of Irish Democracy* (Dublin, 1985).
O'FLANAGHAN, PATRICK, FERGUSON, PAUL, AND WHELAN, KEVIN (eds.), *Rural Ireland: Modernisation and Change, 1600–1900* (Cork, 1987).
O GRADA, CORMAC, *Ireland: A New Economic History, 1780–1939* (Oxford, 1994).
O'HALPIN, EUNAN, *The Decline of the Union: British Government in Ireland, 1892–1920* (Dublin, 1987).
O MORDHA, BRIAN, 'The Greville Papers: A Cavan Estate on the Eve of the Famine', *Breifne*, 1/3 (1960).
O MORDHA, SEAMAS, P., 'Hugh O'Reilly (1581?–1653): A Reforming Private', *Breifne*, 4/13 (1970).
—— 'Hugh O'Reilly (1581?–1653): A Reforming Private (II)', *Breifne*, 4/15 (1972).
—— 'Some Aspects of the Literary Tradition of the Breifne–Fermanagh Area', *Breifne*, 6/2 (1982).
O'REILLY, J. J., *The History of the Breifne O'Reilly* (New York, 1976).

O'REILLY, M. W., *The O'Reillys of Templebridge, Kildare* (Dublin, 1940).

O RIORDAN, MICHELLE, *The Gaelic Mind and the Collapse of the Gaelic World* (Cork, 1990).

O SNODAIGH, PADRAIG, 'Notes on the Volunteers, Militia, Yeomanry and Orangemen of County Monaghan', *Clogher Record*, 9/2 (1977).

PATTERSON, HENRY, 'Independent Orangeism and Class Conflict in Edwardian Belfast', *PRIA*, 80c/4 (May 1980).

—— *Class Conflict and Sectarianism: The Protestant Working Class and the Belfast Labour Movement, 1868–1920* (Belfast, 1980).

PATTON, HENRY, *Fifty Years of Disestablishment: A Sketch* (Dublin, 1922).

PROUDFOOT, LINDSAY, 'The Management of a Great Estate: Patronage, Income and Expenditure on the Duke of Devonshire's Irish Property, *c.*1816–1891', *Irish Economic and Social History*, 13 (1986).

—— 'Urban Patronage and Estate Management on the Duke of Devonshire's Irish Estates (1764–1891)', Ph.D. thesis (Queen's University, Belfast, 1989).

PUGH, MARTIN, *The Tories and the People, 1885–1935* (Oxford, 1985).

QUINAULT, R. E., 'Lord Randolph Churchill and Home Rule', *IHS*, 21/84 (Sept. 1979).

RAMSDEN, JOHN, *The Age of Balfour and Baldwin, 1902–40* (London, 1978).

RUSSELL, A. K., *Liberal Landslide: The General Election of 1906* (Newton Abbot, 1975).

SAUNDERSON, HENRY, *The Saundersons of Castle Saunderson* (London, 1936).

SAVAGE, D. C., 'The Origins of the Ulster Unionist Party, 1885–6', *IHS*, 12/47 (Mar. 1961).

SHANNON, CATHERINE, 'The Ulster Liberal Unionists and Local Government Reform, 1885–1898', *IHS*, 18/71 (Mar. 1973).

—— *Arthur J. Balfour and Ireland, 1874–1922* (Washington, DC, 1988).

SHEARMAN, HUGH, *Not an Inch: A Study of Northern Ireland and Lord Craigavon* (London, 1942).

SIMMS, KATHARINE, 'The O'Reillys and the Kingdom of East Breifne', *Briefne*, 5/19 (1977).

SMYTH, T. S., 'Freemen of the Borough of Cavan', *Breifne*, 1/2 (1959).

SMYTH, WILLIAM, and WHELAN, KEVIN, *Common Ground: Essays on the Historical Geography of Ireland Presented to T. Jones Hughes* (Cork, 1988).

SNODDY, OLIVER, 'Notes on the Volunteers, Militia, Yeomanry and Orangemen of County Cavan', *Breifne*, 3/2 (1968).

STEWART, A. T. Q., *The Ulster Crisis: Resistance to Home Rule, 1912–14* (London, 1967).

—— *Edward Carson* (Dublin, 1981).

—— *The Narrow Ground: The Roots of Conflict in Ulster*, 2nd edn. (London, 1989).

STUBBS, JOHN, 'The Unionists and Ireland, 1914–18', *Historical Journal*, 33/4 (1990).

TAYLOR, A. J. P., *English History, 1914–45* (Oxford, 1965).

TAYLOR, A. J. P. (ed.), *Lloyd George: Twelve Essays* (London, 1971).

TAYLOR, ROBERT, *Lord Salisbury* (London, 1975).

THOMPSON, F. M. L., *English Landed Society in the Nineteenth Century* (London, 1963).

—— 'Presidential Address: English Landed Society in the Twentieth Century: I, Property: Collapse and Survival', *TRHS*, 5th ser., 40 (London, 1990).

—— 'Presidential Address: English Landed Society in the Twentieth Century: II, New Poor and New Rich', *TRHS*, 6th ser., 1 (London, 1991).

—— 'Presidential Address: English Landed Society in the Twentieth Century: III, Self-Help and Outdoor Relief', *TRHS*, 6th ser. 2 (London, 1992).

THOMPSON, FRANK, 'The Armagh Elections of 1885–6', *Seanchas Ardmhacha: Journal of the Armagh Diocesan Historical Society*, vii (1977).

—— 'Land and Politics in Ulster, 1868–1886', Ph.D. thesis (Queen's University, Belfast, 1982).

—— 'Attitudes to Reform: Political Parties in Ulster and the Irish Land Bill of 1881', *IHS*, 24/95 (May 1985).

—— 'The Landed Classes, the Orange Order and the Anti-Land League Campaign in Ulster, 1880–1', *Eire-Ireland*, 22/1 (1987).

THOMPSON, J. A., and MEJIA, ARTHUR (eds.), *Edwardian Conservatism: Five Studies in Adaptation* (London, 1988).

THORNLEY, DAVID, *Isaac Butt and Home Rule* (London, 1964).

TOWNSHEND, CHARLES, *The British Campaign in Ireland, 1919–21: The Development of Political and Military Policies* (Oxford, 1975).

—— *Political Violence in Ireland: Government and Resistance since 1848* (Oxford, 1983).

VAUGHAN, W. E., *Landlords and Tenants in Ireland, 1848–1904* (Dundalk, 1984).

—— *Landlords and Tenants in Mid-Victorian Ireland* (Oxford, 1994).

WALKER, BRIAN, 'The Irish Electorate, 1868–1915', *IHS* 18/71 (Mar. 1973).

—— *Ulster Politics: The Formative Years, 1868–86* (Belfast, 1989).

WALLER, PHILIP, *Democracy and Sectarianism: A Political and Social History of Liverpool, 1868–1939* (Liverpool, 1981).

WEST, TREVOR, *Horace Plunkett, Co-operation and Politics: An Irish Biography* (Gerrards Cross, 1986).

WHYTE, JOHN HENRY, 'Landlord Influence at Elections in Ireland, 1832–1885', *English Historical Review*, 80/317 (Oct. 1965).

YOUNG, KENNETH, *Arthur James Balfour: The Happy Life of the Politician, Prime Minister, Statesman and Philosopher* (London, 1963).

INDEX